RADICAL POLITICS
IN
WEST BENGAL

Center for International Studies,
Massachusetts Institute of Technology

Studies in Communism, Revisionism, and Revolution
(formerly *Studies in International Communism*)
William E. Griffith, general editor

RADICAL POLITICS
IN
WEST BENGAL

Marcus F. Franda

The M.I.T. Press
Cambridge, Massachusetts, and London, England

To Samaren
and to Memories of *Adda*
and *Chingri Mach*
in Behala

CONTENTS

TABLES

FIGURES

ACKNOWLEDGMENTS

This study is the result of a personal involvement with Bengal that began eleven years ago. Since the time when I first became interested in Bengali at the University of Chicago in 1959, I have been fascinated, astounded, and confused by the twists and turns of radical movements in the region. Eventually, I suppose, anyone who has done extensive research on modern Bengal would be driven by curiosity to examine the nature of radical politics in some detail, since radicalism is so intricately related to the political and social life of the Bengali people.

Because this is a study that was done over an extensive period of time, it would be impossible to acknowledge fully the assistance I have received in collecting data. To acknowledge all the sources of what appears in the following pages would require another volume, perhaps larger than this one, and to acknowledge even the major sources of my eleven-year education in Bengal studies would occupy at least a fat chapter. I have tried to indicate in the footnotes the sources of information that would be most valuable for future scholars, and I will make one personal acknowledgment, to my wife Vonnie, who undisputably contributed more to the completion of the manuscript than anyone else. I must also acknowledge the help of the Colgate University Research Council, which contributed funds for portions of the study, and the permission of the editors of *Asian Survey*, *Pacific Affairs*, and the *Journal of Commonwealth Political Studies* to use materials that originally appeared in their periodicals.

Professors William E. Griffith and Myron Weiner of the Massachusetts Institute of Technology were especially important in encouraging publication, since they made it possible to secure funds and office space from the Center for International Studies at M.I.T. when the study was under way. Mina Parks and Robin Remington of M.I.T. were very helpful in providing typing and editorial assistance. In this connection I must also acknowledge an indirect debt to the late Max F. Millikan. I am deeply grateful for the opportunity to be associated with the center that was his creation.

Cambridge, Massachusetts   July 1970

ABBREVIATIONS

AICC	All-India Congress Committee
AICCCR	All-India Coordination Committee of Communist Revolutionaries
AIKS	All-India Kisan Sabha
AISF	All-India Student Federation
AITUC	All-India Trade Union Congress
CCP	Chinese Communist Party
CEC	Central Executive Committee
CIA	Central Intelligence Agency
CMPO	Calcutta Metropolitan Planning Organization
CPGB	Communist Party of Great Britain
CPI	Communist Party of India
CPM	Communist Party of India–Marxist
CPML	Communist Party of India–Marxist-Leninist
CPSU	Communist Party of the Soviet Union
CRP	Central Reserve Police
DMK	Dravida Munetra Kazagham
EPAL	East Pakistan Awami League
FB	Forward Bloc
FBM	Forward Bloc–Marxist
FBR	Forward Bloc–Ruikar
GL	Gurkha League
IAS	Indian Administrative Service
ICS	Indian Civil Service
INA	Indian National Army
INDF	Indian National Democratic Front
KMPP	Kisan Mazdoor Praja Party
LSS	Lok Sevak Sangh
MLA	Member of the Legislative Assembly
MP	Member of Parliament
NAP	National Awami Party
NEFA	Northeast Frontier Agency
PCC	Pradesh Congress Committee

PCP	Pakistan Communist Party
PCZ	Code initials used by the CPM faction in the united CPI in 1964–1965
PIFRC	Price Increase and Famine Resistance Committee
PML	Progressive Muslim League
POC	Provincial Organization Committee
PSP	Praja Socialist Party
PULF	People's United Left Front
PUSF	People's United Socialist Front
RCPI	Revolutionary Communist Party of India
RSP	Revolutionary Socialist Party
SSP	Samyukta Socialist Party
SUC	Socialist Unity Centre
SVD	Samyukta Vidhayak Dal
UF	United Front
ULDF	United Left Democratic Front
ULEC	United Left Election Committee
ULF	United Left Front
USOI	United Socialist Organization of India
WB	West Bengal
WBNGPEC	West Bengal Non-Gazetted Police Employees' Committee
WBPA	West Bengal Police Association
WPI	Worker's Party of India

1

INTRODUCTION

Political parties are often viewed as institutions or organizations designed to promote social and economic interests, or as mechanisms for the expression and management of conflict. Studies of American and British political parties usually take it for granted that the political systems in which parties operate are accepted as legitimate by the populations involved, that people are loyal to the nation-state, and that the actors within a given party system are in agreement on the nature of the relations that should exist among political participants. But such assumptions are not valid for all party systems: they were not valid at all times during the evolution of modern states, and they are not valid for much of Asia and Africa today. Political parties in Asia and Africa have frequently diverged more in their conceptions of legitimacy during the past few decades than parties that have participated in more established political systems. Since no set "rules of the game" have been established for party systems in independent Asia and Africa, political parties in these areas have had to formulate their own rules, and once a party has established itself in power, it has often come to regard its own formulations as binding on all other parties operating within the newly independent political environment. At the same time, there has been much experimentation, conscious and unconscious borrowing from Western modes of political organization, and great confusion and turmoil.

Among newly independent states, India enjoys one of the few political systems dominated by a highly institutionalized political party basing its claims to power on electoral democracy. The Congress party, which was formed in 1885 as a platform for Indian nationalists, has without question been the single most important institution in governing India since 1947, and both wings of the party are still attempting (since the split in 1969) to institutionalize channels of electoral participation and to get them accepted by more and more citizens in a highly diverse nation.[1] Essentially an aggregative movement, the Congress

[1] One of the most concise statements of Congress party attitudes toward political participation can be found in Myron Weiner, *Congress Party Elites* (Bloomington: Indiana University Department of Government, 1966); see especially pp. 1–2 and 17–19.

since Independence has stood against revolution, agitation, and insurgency, has attempted to smooth over conflicts that might lead to the collapse of the parliamentary system or to civil war, and has provided widespread opportunities for Indians to take part in the electoral process.

There are many political parties in India that do not share these conceptions of legitimate political party activity. Many Indians feel that the electoral system has been representative of too few interests; many feel that it has been representative of too many. Some argue that the system in particular states (or perhaps even at the national level) has been imposed by measures that have been exceedingly repressive; others argue that India's elected governments have been weak and vacillating, unwilling to use repressive measures when such measures are necessary. Almost everyone in India inveighs against the "corruption" of Congress regimes, very frequently meaning by "corruption" the operation of an elaborate system of political patronage. At the same time, almost everyone in India must necessarily engage in "corrupt" practices if he is to get anything done. Just as the Congress movement has increasingly sought to organize all the citizens who have an interest in maintaining the system that it has established, even attempting to attract the participation of opposition groups, many opposition parties have tried to organize large numbers of citizens who have an interest in doing away with the system itself. It is in this context that the Communist and Marxist Left parties in India have given expression to rather widespread feelings characteristic of the country's political life.

To label India's Communist and Marxist Left parties as political groups bent only on the destruction of electoral democracy would be highly misleading, however, since almost all of these parties have participated extensively in electoral politics at all levels of government. There is no question that they have derived some of their inspiration from indigenous and foreign political movements that have sought to weaken the Indian electoral system and parliamentary government, but at the same time many of these parties have gained supporters precisely because of their successful participation in electoral democracy. The resulting political situation is characterized by a dynamic and fluid struggle for power, in which both Congress and communist elites are constantly revising their strategies, tactics, and goals. While it is conceivable that large segments of the Congress movement could become disenchanted with the Congress "system" and join the revolutionaries of the Left (or of the Right), it is also conceivable that significant segments of the Communist and Marxist Left parties could be won over to electoral democracy and a parliamentary form of government.

The study of communism in this environment poses enormous problems for research, and particularly in states where Communist parties have come to power. One must be familiar not only with the complicated regional politics of a particular linguistic area within India but with the politics of the rest of the heterogeneous Indian Union since 1947, and with the polycentric tendencies of communism and socialism in this century. These problems become especially formidable when an area as large and as important as Bengal is involved. Considering the fact that Bengali is a language spoken by more than 100 million people (only six of the world's languages are spoken by more), it is not surprising that each of the four largest nation-states besides India (China, the United States, the Soviet Union, and Pakistan) has an abiding interest in the political affairs of this region. To the complex of research factors just mentioned, one must therefore add the additional factor of international politics, which have come to play a large part in modern Bengali political life.

This book represents an attempt to understand the various forces impinging on the communist movement in Bengal by focusing both on the actors and on the setting, on the Communists as political calculators and on the environment (regional, national, and international) in which they have their origins. While the scope of the study includes the Marxist Left, more attention must necessarily be paid to the Communists because of their central importance in organizing all the leftist parties in the Bengali-speaking region. Some attention is given to the organization of Communist and leftist parties in East Bengal (now in Pakistan), but the emphasis is on post-Independence communism in India. My principal concern throughout has been to try to determine the extent to which the Communist and Marxist Left parties in West Bengal have been able to modify the basic political alignments that came into being with Independence.

I do not claim to have written a history of the communist movement in West Bengal. Some of the principal sources for a historical analysis have been mentioned in the footnotes, but a comprehensive history would require a much closer look at textual materials and more authoritative data from inner-party documents. What this volume represents is an attempt to answer three broad and important sets of questions: (1) What are the sources of communism in West Bengal? Why have Bengalis been so active in the communist movement while other Indians have for the most part sought alternative outlets for political expression and participation? (2) What are Bengali Com-

munists attempting to accomplish and how do they go about it?
(3) What has been the impact of the Bengali communist movement
on state and national politics, and on the Communists themselves?

The next chapter seeks to describe the elite nature of the communist
movement in West Bengal and the major sources of leadership recruitment prior to Independence. Sources of elite recruitment, I argue, have
given rise to the major factional cleavages within the present Communist parties. Chapters 3 and 4 indicate ways in which the
experience of the Communists in electoral politics, when coupled
with their attachments to Moscow and Peking, have intensified the
factionalism that was inherent in the movement before Independence.
While Chapter 2 is a response to the first set of questions, Chapters 3
and 4 try to answer the second. The remainder of the book deals
with the third set of questions: Chapter 5 traces the impact of Communist factionalism on the electoral politics of the state; Chapters 6
through 8 seek to understand the major strategies that have resulted
from the decision of the Communists to enter the ministries. The final
chapter provides a summary and suggests some hypotheses for future
research.

2

PARTY LEADERSHIP:
SOURCES OF ELITE RECRUITMENT

West Bengal is one of two states in the Indian Union in which India's Communist parties have shared in the decision-making power of the ministries. From March 2, 1967, when the Congress party of West Bengal failed for the first time since Independence to gain a majority in the state Legislative Assembly, until November 21, 1967, when the governor of the state appointed a successor ministry, West Bengal was governed by a coalition of fourteen parties, including both the Communist party of India (CPI) and the Communist party of India–Marxist (CPM). After a period of President's Rule in 1968, the same coalition of parties was returned in the elections of February 1969, this time with a much larger number of seats in the Legislative Assembly and with a much larger role for the two Communist parties. Because the Communists dominated the United Front coalition in West Bengal in terms of votes, 8 of the 30 ministers in the West Bengal cabinet in 1969–1970 were members of the CPM, holding by far the most significant portfolios in the state government; 4 of the remaining ministers were members of the CPI, and many of the others were dependent on the two Communist parties for their electoral and ministerial positions.[1] The only significant foci of power in the state government that were not captured by the two Communist parties in 1969–1970 were the Chief Ministership and the state Finance Ministry, both of which were held by the Congress dissident leader, Ajoy Kumar Mukherjee. When the second United Front government was replaced by President's Rule in April 1970, the communist movement was considered by almost everyone concerned as the major political force in West Bengal.

---

[1] Members of the CPM held the following portfolios in 1969–1970: Police, Jails, and Press; Special and General Administration; and Constitution and Elections (all within the Home Ministry); plus the ministries of Land and Land Revenue, Education, Transport, Labour, Excise, Fisheries, and Refugee Relief and Rehabilitation. Members of the CPI held the portfolios of Local Self-Government, Planning, Development, and Housing; Irrigation and Waterways, Wells, Tubewells, and Pump Irrigation of Agriculture, and Small Irrigation; Cooperation and Social Welfare; and Relief.

When one considers the difficulties that have confronted the communist movement in West Bengal in recent years, it is rather surprising to find that its adherents could have moved into positions of power and influence so suddenly. As recently as late 1964 the Communists in West Bengal were in the midst of a series of party crises that had irrevocably split the movement, and the party was suffering severe losses in almost every single election it was contesting, even in former party strongholds. For a period of almost three years after the September 1962 Sino-Indian border incidents, the Communists were unable to stage a single successful demonstration in West Bengal, despite numerous attempts to do so; their members were being stoned at public meetings or burned in effigy as "traitors," and their previous political allies (the Marxist Left parties of West Bengal) were refusing to take part in any political activities in which Communist party members were involved. During this period party membership declined rapidly, while party subscriptions and activities virtually ceased for long intervals.

The Communist rise to power has therefore been accompanied by a very recent rebuilding of party units and by the remolding of political alliances within the state. But this is not to argue that the communist movement in West Bengal is of recent origin or that the Communists can be understood without reference to India's past associational life. All of the successful political parties that have been founded in India during the last few decades have been led by people with previous organizational experience, and most of them were made up of factions from older, better-established political groups. Therefore, in order to understand the success of the communist movement, it is essential to analyze its sources of recruitment and the patterns of political participation that have affected its growth.

Communism in West Bengal has always been elitist. The leadership of the movement has been drawn from rich, influential, and highly respected Bengali families, and its most consistent followers have come from groups that are relatively well established in the social structure. While attempts have been made to gain support from the poor, the low castes, and the illiterate, every available piece of evidence would indicate that the Communists in West Bengal have not succeeded in bringing members of low-status groups into leadership positions in the party or in securing the unquestioned backing of such groups. In the words of a Central Committee document published by the CPM in 1967,

. . . a good portion of the members of top and leading committees has inevitably come forth from Communists of bourgeois and petty bourgeois class origins. . . . The intellectuals coming from the propertied classes, . . . belonging to the social status of either the bourgeoisie or the petty bourgeoisie, who study and accept Marxist-Leninist theory and practice, have come to occupy a dominant position in the leadership of the policy-making committees.[2]

While the communist movement in other parts of India has also been led by elites, the Communists in West Bengal are distinguished by the fact that they have come to power on the basis of an elite leadership with essentially an elite following. The only other state in India where Communists have succeeded in capturing a dominant influence in a state ministry is in Kerala, but the growth of the movement in Kerala has depended on considerable support from low-status groups (principally the Ezhava caste), and Kerala's Communists have therefore been able to secure a larger portion of the vote than West Bengal's.

Because of these anomalies, the question arises as to the nature of the social groups that have provided the leadership and much of the following for the communist movement in West Bengal. Why did the sons of wealthy and influential families become Communists? Why is it that the best-established Bengali families have provided the bulk of the recruits for Communist leadership positions?

The Bhadralok in Twentieth-Century Bengal

The elite from which the Bengali Communist and Marxist Left parties have drawn their leadership (and much of their following) is the Bengali *bhadralok*, an elite that is unique to the Bengali-speaking area. Neither a single class nor a single caste, the *bhadralok* (literally "respectable people," or "gentlemen"; sometimes called just *borolok* or "big people") are a privileged minority most often drawn from the three highest castes (Brahmins, Kayasthas, and Vaidyas), usually landed or employed in professional or clerical occupations, extremely jealous of their social positions (which they have maintained by caste and ritual proscriptions and by the avoidance of manual labor), very well educated, very proud of their language, their literacy, and their history, and highly skilled in maintaining communal integration through a complex institutional structure that has proved remarkably adaptable. Broomfield, who has analyzed this elite in great detail, has described the position of the *bhadralok* at the beginning of the twentieth century as follows:

> In city, town, and village there was one group of Bengalis who claimed and were accorded recognition as superior in social status to the mass of their fellows. These were the *bhadralok* . . . distinguished by many aspects of their

[2] *Our Tasks on Party Organisation*, a report adopted by the Central Committee of the Communist party of India–Marxist, at its Calicut session, October 28–November 2, 1967 (Calcutta: CPM, 1967), pp. 28–29.

behavior—their deportment, their speech, their dress, their style of housing, their eating habits, their occupations and their associations—and quite as fundamentally by their cultural values and their sense of social propriety.[3]

During the nineteenth century the *bhadralok* experienced a cultural renaissance that Bengali scholars frequently liken to the Italian Renaissance of the thirteenth and fourteenth centuries: a flurry of activities in literature, art, politics, and economics that placed Bengal firmly in the forefront of almost all Indian associational life.[4] By the end of the century Calcutta was second only to London among the great cities of the British Empire, Bengali poets and writers were distinguished as leading international literary figures (Tagore won the Nobel prize in 1913), and Bengalis were prominent among the Indian professional classes and in government circles in regions as distant as Sindh in the northwest and Burma to the east.

In the twentieth century, however, this elite witnessed a series of dislocations that restricted the influence of its members outside of the Province of Bengal, while fundamental cleavages developed among social groups within the elite itself. As a result, a considerable portion of the *bhadralok* adopted Marxism as a political creed in the 1930s, and their numbers have expanded since. These events were in large part the outcome of the inability of the *bhadralok* to confront three powerful political protagonists during the course of the twentieth century, each of whom was a threat to the extension of *bhadralok* dominance, whether in Bengal or in the rest of India. The first of these were the British rulers of India, who were themselves divided as to the kind of political strategy they should pursue in Bengal; the second were the Muslims; and the third were the nationalist politicians loyal to Gandhi.

In the late nineteenth century, one section of British opinion (led by Lord Ripon and Lord Dufferin) favored the extension of *bhadralok* opportunities in British administrative positions, in local self-government bodies, in the courts, and in the legislative councils. But around the turn of the century this section of British officialdom was submerged by the majority feeling that the Bengali "baboos" (a derogatory word for *bhadralok*) had "lost touch with the people—the real Indian people" and that they were likely to "use any local body we [the

---

[3] John H. Broomfield, *Elite Conflict in a Plural Society: Twentieth-Century Bengal* (Berkeley: University of California Press, 1968), pp. 5–6. Broomfield's work is by far the most valuable history of Bengal in this century.

[4] For an exploration of the Renaissance theme in a study of nineteenth-century Bengal, see David Kopf, *British Orientalism and the Bengal Renaissance* (Berkeley: University of California Press, 1969).

British] appoint as an instrument of oppression."[5] Lord Curzon, viceroy of India from 1898 to 1905, tipped the scales irrevocably in favor of the latter opinion when he declared in June 1903 that initiative for his administrative reforms would have to "spring from the Supreme [British] Government—because there is no other fountain of initiative in India." Curzon therefore set out to "cleanse" Bengal of its "antiquated bureaucratic procedures" and its "proliferation of secondary political structures," in all of which the *bhadralok* were prominent. Despite protests from *bhadralok* political leadership, Curzon proceeded with a reform of Calcutta Corporation that reduced the elected element in the corporation and entrusted executive functions to a committee with a British majority. He next set out to reform Calcutta University, since in his view it had "fallen into the hands of a coterie of obscure native lawyers who regard educational questions from a political point of view," and he climaxed his years in India with the partition of the Province of Bengal in 1905, which was clearly intended "to cut short *bhadralok* nationalist attempts to find allies in other communities."[6]

Bengali *bhadralok* politicians at first responded to the partition of 1905 with the political weapons they had developed in the nineteenth century—press articles, public protest meetings, petitions, and deputations—and when these failed they gradually escalated to a boycott of British manufactured goods and encouragement of *swadeshi* (indigenously manufactured) products, the foundation of national educational institutions, the organization of volunteer brigades, trade unions, and *akharas* (gymnasiums) that could be used for agitational purposes, and eventually to a glorification of violence through conspiratorial organizations. With these methods the *bhadralok* were able to achieve the reunification of Bengal in 1912, but at great cost to themselves. The partition agitation convinced the British that it was time to shift their capital to the traditional center of imperial rule in Delhi, and it also revealed the unpopularity of the Bengali *bhadralok* with the communities (Oriyas, Biharis, and Muslims) that had welcomed partition. In the decades following 1905, Bengal witnessed the growth of an independent Muslim elite in Bengal, a rapid increase in communal tensions (between extremist Hindu *bhadralok* and Muslim extremist politicians), and in 1926 the loss of many local bodies and

[5] The words are those of Robert Carstairs, an Indian District officer stationed in Bengal at the beginning of the twentieth century, quoted in Broomfield, *Elite Conflict*, p. 25.

[6] The quotations are from the writings of Lord Curzon and from minutes written by members of his administration, quoted in ibid., pp. 26–28.

the Provincial Legislature itself to a new Muslim political majority, now allied with the non-Bengali communities and the British.

Although the Muslim community in the Bengali-speaking areas of the province was in a majority at the turn of the century,[7] the social position of the Muslims and their political and economic influence had never matched that of the Hindu *bhadralok*. Bengal's large Muslim population, unlike the Muslim population in other parts of India, was the result of local conversion. Since Bengal had always been on the periphery of the great Brahmanic cultures, orthodox Hinduism had always been challenged among the lowly in Bengal—by Buddhism, Jainism, Vaishnavism, and finally by Islam—but the *bhadralok* had nevertheless maintained their dominant position for a number of centuries before the British invasion. By origin the Muslims of Bengal were low-caste Hindus, and in many ways they were indistinguishable from their former caste fellows throughout the nineteenth century, since their backwardness was less a consequence of the decline of Muslim power and the rise of the British than it was the "result of the poverty and lowly status of Bengali Muslims since time out of mind."[8] With the exception of a small clique of scholars in Persian, a few landlords who had adopted *bhadralok* customs, and a small scattering of educated Muslim elites, the Muslim community during the nineteenth century remained illiterate, unorganized, and poor.

In the twentieth century, however, the leadership of the Muslim community launched a series of successful political maneuvers that brought them into political power in the province from 1926 until 1947, when Bengal was finally partitioned between two international states and most of the Muslim political leadership went over to East Pakistan. Before 1926 the Muslim community allied itself first with the British, in an elaborate system of patronage that lasted until 1911 and gained for the Muslims the extremely valuable institution of communal electorates in 1909. Then, under a newer and younger leadership led by A. K. Fazlul Huq, the Muslims entered into an alliance with the Hindu *bhadralok* in the legislative councils and eventually out-maneuvered their new allies. Using their positions in the provincial government and forming coalitions after 1926 with the Europeans and the low-caste Hindu communities, the Muslims gained unquestioned control of Bengal's institutional life in the 1930s and early 1940s.

[7] An excellent statistical account of the place of the Muslim community in Bengali society is given in Anil Seal, *The Emergence of Indian Nationalism: Competition and Collaboration in the Later Nineteenth Century* (Cambridge: Cambridge University Press, 1968), pp. 37–38, 300–315.

[8] Ibid., p. 38.

In this atmosphere *bhadralok* political leaders had little alternative but to try to consolidate the members of their own community and to mobilize the *abhadra* (non-*bhadralok*) in order to gain a political base. In doing so they alternated among various strategies and eventually became divided among themselves. Some of the *bhadralok* sought to continue their dominance of the liberal institutions imported by the British raj—the bureaucracy, the educational establishments, the legal apparatus, and the legislatures—but they were outmaneuvered (until 1947) by the British government and the Muslim majority led by Fazlul Huq. As Broomfield points out, this turn of events was largely a result of the failure of the *bhadralok* to adapt to the mass electorates that were introduced in Bengal in the 1920s: "The problem the *bhadralok* faced . . . very crudely . . . was the problem of thoroughly literate men trying to make themselves understood by the unlettered, of a written tradition confronting an oral tradition."[9] Because they failed to gain legislative majorities in the 1920s and 1930s the *bhadralok* lost their control of institutional life in Bengal, and many of them became permanently disenchanted with electoral politics.

The effect of this disenchantment was that the majority of the *bhadralok* surrendered the liberal, secular, and parliamentary democratic movements to the Muslims and *abhadra* groups, and many of them took to Hindu revivalism in an effort to consolidate their positions. In the 1920s and 1930s Bengali high-caste communal associations grew in number and influence, lending their support to the terrorist movements and secret societies that flourished during these decades, and ultimately rallying behind Subhas Chandra Bose, the undisputed leader of the *bhadralok*. But this school was also unsuccessful in gaining a mass following, since the various Hindu revivalist movements only tended to create factionalism within the society, and since all of them made for greater and greater exclusiveness on the part of the high castes. Many of them even alienated the vast majority of the people living in Bengal. Most of the Hindu revivalist groups were based on the worship of the Mother Goddess (*Durga*) as the embodiment of strength, but only a few sections of the high castes in Bengal are *Sakta* (the Hindu sect in which worship of the Mother Goddess is prominent). In a society where most of the people were Muslims or Vaisnava Hindus, the myth of the Mother Goddess was "an exclusive myth," largely irrelevant even to most Hindus living in Bengal.[10] Thus, Hindu revivalism in Bengal failed to serve as a rallying point for large-scale

[9] *Elite Conflict*, pp. 321–322.
[10] Ibid., pp. 16–17.

political organizations, and Bengali politicians abandoned strictly communal political organizations. Ever since Independence, the avowedly communalist parties that are so prominent in other parts of India have been all but extinct in West Bengal.

In addition to the loss of their dominant political position within Bengal, the *bhadralok* experienced a number of other dislocations. Earnings from land began to diminish throughout India in the late nineteenth and early twentieth centuries, and the landed gentry of Bengal were among the most severely affected by this development. Educated unemployment on a large scale began to be felt in and around Calcutta at the turn of the century, just as the leadership of the nationalist movement was shifting from Bengal to Gandhi and the Hindi-speaking Brahmanic heartland. The dominance of Bengalis in the Indian Civil Service receded as other areas gained in higher education, and business in Calcutta came increasingly to be dominated by non-Bengali Indians and British industrialists. All of these factors grew in intensity right up until the 1940s, when Bengal witnessed in rapid succession a major famine (in 1943), the activities of 200,000 Allied troops in and around Calcutta during World War II, the partition of 1947 and the communal riots that accompanied it, and finally a trade war between West and East Bengal that was accompanied by the influx into West Bengal of millions of Hindu refugees.[11]

By the late 1930s a number of Bengali *bhadralok* politicians were ready for Marxism. Marxism appealed to the *bhadralok* because it rejected electoral politics, which had led to the loss of *bhadralok* dominance; because it denigrated orthodox Hindu ideas and behavior at a time when Bengalis were becoming disenchanted with Hindu revivalism; because it promised the overthrow of the hated British and the anglicized ruling and commercial groups who were guided by their ideas (and who controlled Calcutta); because it promised a modern society in which the intellectual would have a more prominent position; because it legitimized the terrorist and conspiratorial activities on which the *bhadralok* had staked their reputations for three decades; and because it denied the usefulness of *banyas* (traders) and merchants, caste groups who had begun to rise in status in the twentieth century and who in Bengal were almost all *abhadra*.[12] In the late 1930s, four Marxist Left parties were founded by *bhadralok* leaders

[11] These factors are explored in greater detail in my article on "West Bengal," in *State Politics in India*, ed. Myron Weiner (Princeton: Princeton University Press, 1968), pp. 247–318.

[12] An excellent description of the rise of these castes in Bengal before Independence is offered in a novel by Tarasankar Banerjee, *Panchagram* [Five Villages] (Calcutta: Calcutta Publishers, 1943). I am working on a translation of this book in collaboration with S. K. Chatterjee.

(the Revolutionary Communist party of India, the Bolshevik party, the Revolutionary Socialist party, and the Forward Bloc), all of which are still in existence and were in the United Front governments dominated by the Communists in the late 1960s. The transformation of the Bengali *bhadralok* from a strategy of participation in British institutions to the adoption of Marxism as a creed can be seen most clearly in the political evolution of Subhas Chandra Bose over the course of the 1920s and 1930s. In 1924 Bose was elected the chief executive officer of Calcutta Corporation as a leading figure in the Swaraj party, which controlled the Provincial Legislature and the Calcutta Municipal Corporation. By 1934 he was outside the legislature and the higher councils of the corporation, encouraging Hindu revivalism and supporting the wave of revolutionary activities that had begun with the Chittagong Armoury Raid in 1930. In 1939 Bose formed the Forward Bloc, a Marxist political party that sought to consolidate all of the small Marxist Left parties that had come into being with the failure of revivalist terrorism.[13]

Communism and the Bhadralok

The communist movement in West Bengal can trace its origins back as far as 1921, when a number of Bengalis established working relations with the Comintern, but the growth of the party as a significant factor in provincial and state politics dates from the late 1930s. As a result of a successful recruitment drive in the jails during the 1930s, the CPI was able to absorb a large number of the *bhadralok* terrorists who had been active in Bengal since the first partition of the province in 1905. These recruits were later joined by Bengali intellectuals returning from England, by graduates of the colleges and universities in Bengal during the 1940s, and eventually by a large section of the urban *bhadralok* living in and around Calcutta and the West Bengal industrial belt. The growth of the movement has been somewhat sporadic, with significant declines in membership taking place in 1948 and 1963, but despite these temporary setbacks it has on the whole grown fairly steadily. According to membership figures given by party leaders, the CPI in pre-Independence Bengal grew from 37 members in 1934 to more than 1000 members in 1942 and to almost 20,000 members in 1947.[14] The partition of Bengal in 1947 divided the party between two international states, with more than half of the membership going over

---

[13] Bose's shifts in strategy are detailed in Subhas Chandra Bose, *The Indian Struggle*, *1920–1942* (Calcutta: Asia Publishing House, 1964); see especially pp. 275, 357–358.

[14] These estimates of party membership are taken from Abdul Halim, *Where Are We Now?* (Calcutta: n.p., 1934), p. 6; from interviews with party leaders, and especially with Muzaffar Ahmad in March 1969; and from estimates published in party newspapers.

to East Bengal in Pakistan. From a membership of less than 10,000 in 1947 the party in West Bengal grew to more than 12,000 members in 1954 and to 17,600 in 1962. At present there are approximately 17,000 members in the CPM (which broke away from the CPI in 1964) and 8000 members in the regular CPI.

The communist movement is still led by educated, high-caste Bengalis from *bhadralok* families who are well established in the social structure, as the following figures show.[15] Of the 33 members of the State Committee of the CPM in 1969, 24 (or 73 percent) belonged to the three highest castes in Bengal (Brahmins, Kayasthas, and Vaidyas), and all but 2 had been to college for at least a year.[16] Only 3 of the 33 members had ever engaged in manual labor for their livelihood; most of them were sons or relatives of landholders and professionals (lawyers, doctors, and teachers). Similarly, 8 of the 9 members of the CPI State Secretariat in 1969 were from high-caste families (the other being a Muslim), all had been to college or beyond, and all came from respectable and fairly wealthy families.

This elite leadership is by no means homogeneous, however, and the differences in interests among the upper echelons of the movement have been evident whenever major questions of strategy and tactics have had to be resolved. All political movements in India seem to be plagued by an intense factionalism that runs the gamut of possible interest rivalries, and the communist movement is hardly an exception. At the risk of grossly oversimplifying the factional interests involved in the movement, it is possible to distinguish three major groupings among the older leadership, each with its own interests and following, and each with its own set of ideas about revolutionary change. One of them is now centered in the organizational apparatus of the CPM, another forms the basis for the regular CPI, and the third is clustered around the electoral machinery of both parties. To a great extent these factional groupings are the result of party recruitment from three divergent sources during the past four decades.

The Terrorist Movement and the Communists

The leadership of the organizational apparatus in West Bengal has been drawn for the most part from former terrorists. The head of the

---

[15] A detailed study of political leadership in West Bengal, based on data gathered for 408 leaders of the major political parties, is provided by Myron Weiner, "Changing Patterns of Political Leadership in West Bengal," in *Political Change in South Asia* (Calcutta: Firma K. L. Mukhopadhyay, 1963), pp. 177–227.

[16] Data on the leadership of the Communist parties was collected by the author in interviews with present and former members in 1962–1964 and 1968–1970, and from biographical data furnished in *Who's Who*s, newspapers, and articles.

state CPI office from 1951 until 1964 was Pramode Das Gupta, a former member of the largest of the pre-Independence terrorist groups, the Anushilan Samity. Das Gupta, who is currently state secretary of the CPM, was one of the many members of the Anushilan Samity who were converted to communism in the jails in the 1930s, and most of his closest associates in the party headquarters and in the districts are either former members of the Samity or of other terrorist groups. The organizational transition from the older terrorist groups to the communist movement in Bengal is indicated by the way in which the Communist parties have been able to adapt the organizational structures that were used by the terrorists after the founding of the Samity in 1902. Like the Anushilan Samity, the Communist parties are now centered in large urban areas, structured around a small group of leaders, with subordinate units in each of the districts and village units in areas where the party is most active. As in the Samity, party discipline, secrecy, and democratic centralist lines of authority and responsibility are enforced. New members are carefully screened and have to pass through candidate memberships and periods of indoctrination. Communist party members, like the members of terrorist societies, are required to take oaths pledging their loyalty to the party and promising never to engage in factionalism, and their attempts to establish training schools and educational bodies in which theoretical issues can be discussed and inner-party debates carried on are similar in many respects to the activities of the terrorists during the first few decades of the century.[17]

The terrorist movement in Bengal was dominated by two large federations of terrorist groups, one of which was the Anushilan Samity and the other Jugantar, also founded in the first decade of this century.[18] In every town of any size, and in many of the villages as well, there

[17] The structure of the Anushilan Samity is analyzed in great detail in James Campbell Ker, *Political Trouble in India, 1907–1917* (Calcutta: Government Printing Office, 1917), pp. 154–169. Sir James Ker was personal assistant to the Director of Criminal Intelligence, Government of India, from 1907 until 1913.

[18] Almost every Bengali is his own expert on the terrorist movement, but one whose accounts are acknowledged as more accurate than those of others is Kali Charan Ghose, who is now in his middle seventies, and who has written a number of books on the movement. See especially his *Role of Honour* (Calcutta: Vidya Bharati, 1965) and his series of articles in *Prabasi* (October 1968 through November 1969). See also Suparna Home, *Our Bengal* (Calcutta: Paramita Prakasani, 1950) and Satish Chandra Samanta, *August Revolution and Two Years' National Government in Midnapore* (Calcutta: Orient Book Company, 1946). Unfortunately, a major work on Bengali terrorism and Marxism by David M. Laushey was not available at the time of writing. See David M. Laushey, "The Bengal Terrorists and Their Conversion to Marxism: Aspects of Regional Nationalism in India, 1905–1942," Ph.D. dissertation, University of Virginia, 1970.

were small terrorist bands that maintained contact with the leadership of the two large federations, occasionally receiving help from them in the form of money or literature, though in most cases it was simply moral support. In addition, there were at least two dozen other small terrorist societies that operated independently of the Anushilan and Jugantar groups, each being confined to small local areas and remaining separate from the larger terrorist groups because of personal and factional differences. The periods of greatest activity for the terrorists in Bengal were 1908–1912 (when six known murders and twenty-three other known "outrages" were committed) and 1930–1934, a period that began with the Chittagong Armoury Raid of 1930. Terrorist incidents were reported by British officials for every year between 1908 and 1947 as well, and the members of the revolutionary and terrorist bands that operated in Bengal during this time were constantly in and out of jail or absconding from the police.

The Chittagong Armoury Raid was perhaps the most successful of the terrorist acts carried out in Bengal, but its outcome was instrumental in convincing many terrorists of the need for a more enduring political movement. The raid took place on April 18, 1930, in the city of Chittagong, a seaport in East Bengal near the Burmese border. During the night a group of *Jugantar* revolutionaries, dressed in official khaki police uniforms, moved on the armory at Chittagong, killing the guards and destroying the telegraphic and telephonic communications systems. Declaring themselves the independent provisional government of a free Bengal, the raiders held the armory for three days and looted innumerable weapons. While they were eventually subdued by British troops, their activities set in motion widespread violence throughout Bengal during the next four years. In addition to attacks on armories, transport, and communications systems, attempts were made on the lives of at least seven senior police and prison officials (in Dacca, Calcutta, Rajshahi, and Chittagong), four of them resulting in the deaths of the officials involved. In addition, two attempts were made on the editor of *The Statesman* (a British daily in Calcutta), forcing his early retirement, and two successive governors of Bengal (Sir Stanley Jackson and Sir John Anderson) narrowly escaped the bullets of revolutionary assassins.

As a result of the Chittagong raid and the ensuing violence, the British government detained almost all the Bengal revolutionaries during the late 1930s, placing most of the leadership in jail and banishing the others to remote outlying districts of the province. But because of the nature of earlier movements, the British were not as concerned with the ideological notions of the terrorists as they were with the technical expertise they had acquired in their pursuit of violence. British jail officials would therefore not allow any literature on chemistry, warfare, and related topics (which the terrorists might use to learn the art of making bombs), but philosophical writings (including almost everything written by Marx and Lenin) were permitted. In fact, since some of the prisoners in the jails claimed to be Marxists or Communists, and since they were charged by the British with conspiracy, they were frequently allowed to purchase Marxist literature from England *at government expense*, in order that they be given every opportunity to defend themselves.[19] Moreover, they were allowed to maintain contact with one another, to read books, to do research, and to engage in their own cultural and sports activities, so long as they did not disturb prison officials or interfere with the operation of normal prison life. As a result of this atmosphere a number of warm and intimate relationships developed among the prisoners in the jails, and a number of them were won over to Marxist-Leninist ideas.

Perhaps a majority of the terrorists who were imprisoned in the late 1930s either left politics after their release or joined the Congress party after Independence. According to government records and the

[19] An attempt to draw together many of the statements that Communists prepared from this literature in the jails is provided in Muzaffar Ahmad, *Communists Challenge Imperialism from the Dock* (Calcutta: National Book Agency, 1968). The effect of communist propagandizing in the jails on a young Bengali woman (Kalpana Dutt) who had been involved in the Chittagong Armoury Raid and converted to communism in the jails (and who later married the eminent Indian Communist P. C. Joshi) is described in her own words as follows:

. . . I could hear about Communism from time to time, and from them [CPI members] too came to me books of Socialism and Communism by Joad, Cole and Shaw.

The arguments and the approach of these books began to stir the mind and forced me to ponder over the difference that these have with the revolutionary literature in which I had been steeped so long. The narratives of revolutionary deeds, the lives of Khudiram, Kanailal, Bhagat Singh, no doubt stirred us to the very core, teaching us to defy death; but these writings on Socialism and Communism could not be set aside as irrelevant, and so the faint rumblings of a new battle could be heard within myself.

These I began to read avidly, but understood in my own way, fitting them into the trend of my own thoughts; and so it seemed that Communism was all right and that there was no difference between it and our own ideas. When someone would say that the Communists looked upon the terrorists as opponents, I would just laught it off and could never believe it. If our ideals were the same and both of us had dedicated ourselves to the cause of freedom, then we were but fellow-travellers and could never be opponents. And yet I could not help confessing to myself that the Communists were more widely read and knew a lot more than us of men and things, of the world at large and of the people and their past, and so I nurtured a sneaking admission of our own inferiority.

Quoted from Kalpana Dutt, *Reminiscences* (Bombay: People's Publishing House, 1945), pp. 87–88.

recollections of the terrorists themselves, there were literally thousands of them in the jails during this period; estimates range upward of ten or twelve thousand. Congress made a sincere attempt to recruit these people, especially after Independence, when many of them were offered jobs, ministries, or other forms of patronage. In the early years of Congress rule, special consideration was given to "political sufferers": entrance fees were waived for their children in the schools and colleges, standards were relaxed when they applied for jobs, and relief facilities were set up for those who had no incomes. Streets, parks, hospitals, and other public facilities were named after revolutionary leaders, and in recent years an old-age home has been established specifically for elderly people who took part in the nationalist movement in Bengal.

But Congress was unable to recruit all of the revolutionaries, either before or after Independence, and a good many of them went into the Communist and Marxist Left parties. Their reasons for opposing the Congress are varied, but for the most part they derive from the opposition of Bengalis to Gandhi[20] and the mainstream of the Indian nationalist movement throughout the pre-Independence period. Gandhi's emphasis on nonviolence was seen as weakness by most Bengalis, and his restraint in dealing with the British was interpreted as cowardice. When he was defeated by Subhas Bose in the contest for Congress president in 1939, most of the Bengali revolutionaries considered it a sign that India was on the side of Bengal, not of Gandhi, and they therefore followed Subhas Bose out of the Congress party when he was expelled in 1941. The split between the terrorists and Congress became complete in 1947 when Gandhi and Nehru accepted the partition of India, which divided Bengal between two nations. Most Bengalis still blame Gandhi and Nehru for the partition of 1947, and in every election campaign its consequences are invoked as reasons for opposing the Congress.

A second reason for the rift between Congress and the terrorist leadership in Bengal has to do with the nature of the support generated by the Congress party with the advent of Gandhi. Gandhi and the leadership around him were especially skillful in creating a political party that could combine a great many interests and social groups. Even before Independence, the Congress made a series of alliances with powerful local leaders who were established in the Indian social structure: rajahs, zamindars, jotedars, and other titled powerholders;

---

[20] Bengali attitudes toward Gandhi are summarized in a paper by Leonard A. Gordon, "Bengal's Gandhi: A Study in Modern Indian Regionalism, Politics and Thought," in *Bengal Regional Identity*, ed. David Kopf (East Lansing: Michigan State University Asian Studies Center, 1969), pp. 87–130.

journalists, lawyers, academicians, and administrators; and the small landholding rural gentry and the bazaar merchants in the towns. With these people acting as intermediaries in the social hierarchy, Congress was able to secure the support of landless laborers, tenant farmers, sweepers, and other politically passive groups, both before and after Independence.[21] In Bengal, however, these Congress alliances were based almost entirely on the non-Bengali communities and the rural gentry, to the detriment of the *bhadralok* and the urban complex around Calcutta. Terrorist leaders who were established in the social structure could (and often did) move into the patronage system and become Congressmen, but a great many of the terrorist leaders (those from East Pakistan, or those who were from poorer families, for example) were without an electoral base, and many of them refused to have anything to do with the electoral system established by the Congress. Those who had surrendered their opportunities for higher education, for good-paying jobs, or in some cases even their landed wealth, in order to devote themselves to nationalist and terrorist activities, were particularly hostile to a regime that was increasingly dominated by landed, wealthy, and educated non-Bengalis and (especially in the case of the bazaar merchants in the towns) the *abhadra*. It is no coincidence that the leaders of the Communist and Marxist Left parties consider themselves greater intellectuals than their counterparts in the Congress, while they are in fact not as well educated (in terms of degrees) as Congressmen.[22]

Perhaps as many as a thousand of the former terrorists joined the Communist party during the "Communist consolidation movement" in the jails of Bengal during the 1930s. They joined because of their opposition to Gandhi and because of their belief in the efficacy of revolutionary movements and conspiratorial organization. After the failure of the Chittagong Armoury Raid, many of the Bengali revolutionaries became disillusioned with terrorism. The Chittagong raiders had been able to capture an armory and to secure a great many weapons, but the British had been cautious enough to store the ammunition in armories scattered throughout the province. A small band of revolutionaries would have had to move on a large number of British armories with amazing precision to achieve success, and the

[21] Congress party strategy in West Bengal is analyzed in Myron Weiner, *Party-Building in a New Nation: The Indian National Congress* (Chicago: University of Chicago Press, 1968), pp. 321–355. See also Marcus F. Franda, *West Bengal and the Federalizing Process in India* (Princeton: Princeton University Press, 1968), pp. 179–224.
[22] This is pointed out in Weiner, "Changing Patterns of Political Leadership in West Bengal," pp. 188–189.

organizational apparatus necessary to carry out such an operation would have had to be extremely well established in the Bengali countryside. The severely repressive measures taken by the British after 1930 convinced many terrorists that a successful revolutionary organization had to have outside support and be able to mobilize the masses in cities and villages all over India. While few of the terrorists in Bengal ever became party theoreticians of any stature, they were impressed by the extent to which Marx (and particularly Lenin) had discussed situations of this kind, and they were encouraged to join the communist movement by older members who had been in contact with international communism since 1921. In the 1940s the former terrorists in the party became more and more committed to the CPI as they engaged in agitational and revolutionary activities; by the 1950s the organization had acquired an institutional personality of its own.

The prevalence of former terrorists in positions of leadership in the organizational apparatus has done much to determine the interests of the cadre as opposed to other factional groupings within the Communist parties in West Bengal. The leaders of the regular party organization in the united CPI entered the movement because of their belief in the effectiveness of revolutionary and conspiratorial activities. While they learned some of the rhetoric of Marxism, they did not join the party because of their knowledge of or even their belief in Marxist theoretical arguments. Many of the men who pride themselves on being members of the inner councils of the movement still confess to an ignorance of Marx and to a lack of interest in theoretical debates. Their concern is with the political situation in West Bengal and India and with the ways in which it might be exploited to capture power. They have always been prominent in the agitational activities of the party, they were deeply influenced by the "insurrectionist" line in the period 1948–1951, and their own factional unity has been forged largely in the jails, where they have spent much of their lives (both before and after Independence) discussing revolutionary situations. Not surprisingly, the regular party organization of the united CPI has been the backbone of the older Left Communist faction.

Intellectual Communism in West Bengal
In contrast to the terrorists, a number of people did join the CPI in the 1930s and 1940s because of their commitment to intellectual Marxism and socialism. Older party members in West Bengal now argue that the state party had only three theoreticians of any stature in the 1930s: Reboti Borman, who published a commentary on *Das Kapital* in

Bengali in 1938 (but who contracted leprosy a short time later and died in the 1940s); R. Palme Dutt, the son of a Bengali doctor and a Swedish writer and nephew of the present prime minister of Sweden, who has lived in Cambridge, England, all his life but has published widely in India during the past five decades; and Bhowani Sen, the present secretary of the CPI. In addition to these leading figures, however, there were a number of other Bengalis who came into contact with the intellectual content of Marxism and communism in the 1930s, most of whom joined the party in the period following 1942, when the legal ban on the party was lifted because of CPI support of the British war effort. The orientation of the Bengali Marxist intellectuals, unlike that of the terrorists, reflects positions taken by the international communist movement and the tradition of Marxist scholarship in Bengal. Thus, in order to explain the broad differences in outlook between the two groups,[23] it is necessary to have a grasp of the historical growth of intellectual Marxism and communism in the province.

Communism and socialism have been debated among intellectuals in Bengal for at least a century. In 1870 an examiner at Calcutta University asked M.A. students in history to discuss the goals of communism in their examinations,[24] and in 1879 the renowned Bengali nationalist novelist, Bankim Chandra Chatterjee, wrote an essay on European communist and socialist ideas in which he advocated a synthesis of European socialism and revivalist Hinduism.[25] Swami Vivekananda, who had an enormous impact on Bengali thought in the late nineteenth century, described himself as a socialist and prophesied that at some future date "Socialism of some form is coming on the boards."[26] It was through the writings of Bankim Chandra, Vivekananda, and a few others that the earliest members of the twentieth-

[23] There is some overlap between intellectuals and former terrorists in the Bengali communist movement, although not as much as one might expect. Bhowani Sen is the only noteworthy example of a Bengali Communist leader who took part in terrorist activities and later became a leading party theoretician. But Sen's case is unusual, for he spent most of his years in jail working toward an M.A. degree and writing scholarly articles on Marx, as a result of which he quickly established himself as a leading intellectual. None of the other terrorists in the party has achieved a reputation for intellectual endeavors that is even remotely comparable.

[24] Listed in the Calcutta University calendar, 1870–1871, and quoted in Biman-behari Majumdar, *History of Indian Social and Political Ideas* (Calcutta: Bookland Private Ltd., 1967), p. 185.

[25] Bankim Chandra Chatterjee, *Samya* [Equality], originally published in 1879 and reprinted by the Bangiya Sahitya Parishad (Literary Academy of Bengal) in 1938. *Samya* is still in print and is available from the Parishad in Bengali.

[26] Swami Vivekananda, *Caste, Culture and Socialism*, a collection of Swami Vivekan-anda's writings on socialism compiled by Swami Chidatmanada (Calcutta: Advaita Ashrama, 1965), p. i.

century terrorist movements in Bengal learned something of socialism, though perhaps less about Marxism and communism. Many of them in turn tried to establish contact with anarchists and nihilists as well as Socialists and Communists in a number of European countries.

The connections between Bengali *bhadralok* intellectuals and the early communist and socialist movements in Europe have yet to be satisfactorily traced, but there is sufficient evidence to indicate that Bengalis were attracted to socialism and had some contact with it at the beginning of the century.[27] It is known, for example, that Swami Vivekananda met Peter Kropotkin at the Paris International Exhibition in 1900, and it is widely believed that he also talked with some of Plekhanov's supporters in England around the same time. Swami Vivekananda's brother, Bhupendra Nath Dutt, was a member of the Anushilan Samity and later flirted with communism when he came into contact with the international movement in Europe. Bengalis also met informally with a number of Socialists through the revolutionary societies of Indian students in London (especially the Home Rule Society, which was founded in 1905 and communicated with the Anushilan Samity through Bepin Chandra Pal in Calcutta), and there is some evidence that Bengali terrorists were educated in the use of bombs and other weapons by a Russian anarchist named Safranski in Paris as early as 1907.

Despite the romantic attachments of many modern-day Marxists to this earlier period in Bengal's history, the organization of the Communist party in Bengal did not begin until the 1920s. During World War I Bengali terrorists had received arms and money from Germany in support of their many plots against the British, but with the defeat of Germany in 1918 they began to look for new sources of financial support, and it was at this time that they began to explore their mutual interests with the Bolsheviks. The Communist International became seriously interested in India when Lenin's colonial thesis was adopted at the Second Congress in 1920 (the International was established in 1919), and its immediate concern was to find a number of Indians who could live in India and carry out propaganda and organizational work. With regard to Bengal there were two sets of leaders considered by Moscow in the early years. One of them consisted

---

[27] Some feeling for the curious mixture of revivalist Hinduism, European socialism, and conspiratorial terrorism that pervaded the terrorist groups in Bengal at this time can be found in a novel by Rabindranath Tagore, *Char Adhyaya* [Four Chapters], written in 1938 and translated into English by Surendranath Tagore (Calcutta: Visva Bharati, 1950).

of Bengali émigrés living in America and Europe, the most prominent of whom was M. N. Roy. Roy was a Bengali Brahmin (born Narendra Nath Bhattacharya in 1886), a member of a landed *bhadralok* family who grew up in the village of Arbalia in West Bengal.[28] Like most of the other Bengali émigrés living in Europe or America at that time, Roy had been deeply influenced by revivalist terrorism at an early age, had traveled abroad to escape arrest and to seek arms for revolutionary movements, and had come into close contact with the Communist International as a result of a mutual interest in promoting revolution. Roy gained considerable prominence at the Second Comintern Congress when he took the "leftist position" (against cooperation with the national bourgeoisie) in opposition to Lenin, but Roy was not the only Bengali who went to Moscow to seek the assistance of the International in the 1920s. In fact he waged a constant battle against fellow Bengali émigrés who were competing for the confidence and financial support of a potentially powerful ally. Almost all of the Bengalis who traveled to Moscow in these early years, however, were from Hindu *bhadralok* families, and most of them had also been involved in the revivalist terrorism that swept Bengal in the first two decades of the century.

In Bengal itself the work of the CPI in the 1920s was carried out by an entirely different kind of leadership, consisting largely of young Muslim activists who had come into contact with international communism through the Khilafat agitation that took place in India following the Treaty of Sèvres in 1919. Muslims in Bengal (as in other parts of India) had great spiritual feeling for the Caliphate, the highest religious office in the Islamic world, and when Turkey was defeated in World War I and the office of the caliph disbanded, a powerful politico-religious movement was launched in India, headed by Mohammed and Shaukat Ali. As a result of this movement, nearly 18,000 Muslims left India to fight on the side of Turkey in an effort to restore the Caliphate. The vast majority of these potential guerrillas

---

[28] Manabendra Nath Roy (born Narendra Nath Bhattacharya) is one of the most fascinating of the earlier revolutionaries in Bengal, and his life and work have engaged the attention of historians studying communism in India. For example, Gene D. Overstreet and Marshall Windmiller, in *Communism in India* (Berkeley: University of California Press, 1959), devote more than a quarter of their volume to the activities of Roy. Two younger scholars, Samaren Roy and Leonard Gordon, have recently been doing research on Roy's activities, with emphasis on his Bengali origins and his involvement in terrorism. See Samaren Roy, *The Restless Brahmin: The Early Life of M. N. Roy* (Calcutta: Allied Publishers, 1970), and Leonard Gordon, "Portrait of a Bengali Revolutionary," *Journal of Asian Studies* 27 (February 1968): 197–216.

were from Sindh and the Punjab in the northwest. Bengali Muslims did not join the exodus from India, but many of them did take part in the Non-Cooperation Movement that was launched in India by Gandhi in 1920, since it was at least in part directed toward the preservation of the Caliphate. Many Bengali Muslims also maintained contact with their coreligionists who had left India.

The three principal founders of the CPI *within* the Province of Bengal —Muzaffar Ahmad, Abdur Rezzak Khan, and Abdul Halim— entered politics during the Khilafat agitation, and throughout the rest of their lives they continued to maintain contact with Muslims who had left India during the Khilafat exodus. The nature of their first contacts with the Communist International are disputed, but it is certain that they had opportunities to learn about Marxism (and about the International) from their fellow Muslims who had left India, many of whom found their way to the Soviet Union and joined the CPI in Russia, and from M. N. Roy. Muzaffar Ahmad has consistently argued that he was a confirmed convert to the international communist movement when he began to communicate with M. N. Roy in Moscow in 1921, and he has also indicated his close relations with the Khilafat pilgrims. One might assume, therefore, that his initial decision to join the Communist International was heavily influenced by the Khilafat incident. He also argues that the Communist party of India was formed abroad by Muslims who left during the Khilafat agitation.[29]

The initial contacts between Bengalis and the Comintern did not lead to immediate political success in the province. Conflicts developed between Roy in Moscow and the members of the party working in Bengal; Roy eventually became disenchanted with international communism and quit the party in the 1930s; and the CPI unit in Bengal remained woefully small during the first decade and a half of its existence. As late as 1934 there were only thirty-seven members of the CPI in Bengal, and the party had failed throughout the 1920s either to ally itself with the Congress or to create a base of its own. There was a small branch of the Red Trade Union in Calcutta that functioned under CPI leadership from the late 1920s, but the party had no permanent publishing facilities and no branch of the Young Communist League, and its most dedicated and able leader (Muzaffar Ahmad) languished in jail throughout most of these early years merely because of his undisputed association with the Comintern. The CPI continued to function in Calcutta when Muzaffar Ahmad was in jail,

[29] Muzaffar Ahmad, *The Communist Party of India and Its Formation Abroad* (Calcutta: National Book Agency, 1962), pp. 55–96.

usually under Abdul Halim, but it did so within the letter of the law and was "satisfied with publishing workers' newspapers and conducting Marxist study clubs. . . ."[30] In fact, with the exception of a small flurry of activity in 1927 and 1928 prompted by the Calcutta visit of organizers from the Communist party of Great Britain (CPGB),[31] the CPI did not engage in any agitation or demonstrations in Bengal until the late 1930s.

In retrospect, however, the CPI did make some gains during these years. Of particular importance to the future growth of the party was the translation into Bengali of a large quantity of Marxist literature and the publicity given to the leaders of the communist movement during the lengthy Cawnpore and Meerut conspiracy trials. Much of the early activity in Bengal was centered on Muzaffar Ahmad, the son of a respectable rural Muslim family born in 1889 on the island of Sandvip in the Bay of Bengal. In his writings he recalls that he was deeply influenced by the sailors of the many oceangoing vessels that found their way to Bengal at the beginning of the century, although it was not through the sailors that he became attracted to Marxist ideology. He was educated in primary schools in East Bengal, attended high school in Noakhali (in East Bengal), and entered Hooghly College (in West Bengal) in 1913, later transferring to Bangabashi College in Calcutta. When he failed his intermediate examinations, he dropped out of college and joined a literary association, in which he established a great friendship with the famous Bengali nationalist (and later socialist) poet, Kazi Nazrul Islam. Muzaffar Ahmad decided to enter politics in 1920, when he and Kazi Nazrul became joint editors of a Bengali evening paper, *Navayag* [New Age], published by the prominent Muslim political leader A. K. Fazlul Huq.

Muzaffar Ahmad's description of how his early activities led him to adopt the party shows how limited the Bengalis' acquaintance with Marxism was in the early 1920s:

Navayug was distinct from the other Bengali dailies in that it contained much more news about workers and peasants. Far from objecting to it, Mr. Fazlul Huq used to encourage this feature. One of my friends, who was not a political worker, told me: "Bengali papers are excessively sentimental. Do write something about the common people, especially about the workers and peasants". . . . I readily responded to this suggestion. . . . I especially focused [on] the problems of the sailors in Navayug [but] I could not even

[30] Overstreet and Windmiller, *Communism in India*, p. 146.
[31] For an account of these two years of activity by one of the organizers from the CPGB, see Philip Spratt, *Blowing Up India* (Calcutta: Prachi Prakashan, 1955), pp. 39–46.

imagine that I was being slowly drawn towards the Third Communist International through these writings in the paper.

[By 1921, however,] our aim was to build up the Communist Party in India. . . . My knowledge of Marxism was very superficial. But when I took the leap into the unknown, I counted on two things—my faith in the people and my unquestioned loyalty to the directives of the Communist International.[32]

The writings of Muzaffar Ahmad and Kazi Nazrul Islam (who never joined the party) were quickly followed by other writings by Bengalis which attempted to interpret India in terms of Marxist ideas.[33] In 1921 M. N. Roy and Abani Mukerji published *India in Transition* in Geneva, and from 1923 to 1925 the European correspondent of the Bengali daily *Forward*, Benoy Sarkar, began to publish translations of Marxist and socialist writings in Bengali: *Parivar, Gosthi O Rastra* [Family, Clan, and State], consisting of translations from the German writings of Marx and Engels, was followed by *Dhana-daulater Rupantar* [Transformations of Wealth], translations from the French of Paul Lafargue, and *Navin Rushiyar Jivan-Prabhat* [Life's Dawn in New Russia], based on Trotsky's *Russische Revolution, 1905*. Since all of these works were first serialized in *Forward* and other journals and were later published in three volumes, they were circulated among a number of Bengali intellectuals. The fact that they were published in *Forward*, which was edited by Chittaranjan Das and managed by Subhas Bose (the two leading figures in Bengal's nationalist movement at the time) is an indication that Marxist ideas were already being seriously considered by the mainstream of Bengal's intellectual and political leadership. From this point on, Marxist and Communist writings (both in Bengali and in English) increased in volume with each passing year.[34]

---

[32] Muzaffar Ahmad, *Communist Party of India: Years of Formation, 1921–1933* (Calcutta: National Book Agency, 1959), pp. 6–8. See also *Myself and the Communist Party of India* (Calcutta: National Book Agency, 1970). This is his autobiography, unavailable at the time of writing.

[33] In compiling this section on Marxist writings in the early twentieth century, I have drawn heavily on my own readings in Bengali, but I have also consulted with profit Indira Sarkar, *Social Thought in Bengal (1757–1947): A Bibliography of Bengali Men and Women of Letters* (Calcutta: Calcutta Oriental Book Agency, 1949), pp. 7–56.

[34] Muzaffar Ahmad has written of the 1920s: "In those days, Marxist literature was hard to get in Calcutta. If anything was available at all, we did not have the means to buy it. Qutubuddin Ahmad [coeditor of two Urdu weeklies, along with Maulana Azad, a prominent Congressman] used to buy as well as read a lot of books. It was because of him that I could read *My Reminiscences of the Russian Revolution* by Phillips Price. It was the first book on the Russian Revolution that I read. We could never have bought this book, which was priced at 18 shillings." *Years of Formation*, p. 9.

In addition to the interest in communism that the CPI evoked in Bengal in the early 1920s, the party was also successful in gaining the confidence of the Comintern and became formally affiliated with the Communist International in 1930. Moreover, by the late twenties Muzaffar Ahmad and Abdul Halim had established contact with the leaders of the CPI in the United Provinces, Punjab, Bombay, and Madras, and they had gained the respect of the CPGB. Most important, they had applied themselves to the study of Marxism, and their resolve to promote the interests of the international communist movement had been tested in the jails. When Bengalis with Marxist ideas began to return from England in the 1930s, they were therefore willing to join the party, convinced that they were associating themselves with truly dedicated Marxists, and when Marxist study groups became the fashion in the jails during the 1930s, the members of the CPI could overwhelm and impress their colleagues with their knowledge of Communist ideas on organization and their contacts in the international movement. All of this stood them in good stead, for in the 1930s the CPI began to grow, and the members of the party who were converted or accepted into the party in the 1930s were for the most part men who had received some Marxist education and a fairly rigorous training in Leninist ideas of party organization.[35]

The discipline and training of the other Marxist Left parties formed in Bengal in the late 1930s were not nearly so good. Party splits were more common than unity, discussion groups rambled, knowledge of Marxism was confused at best and lacking entirely on many occasions, and communal feelings and family and caste conflicts frequently took

---

Press censorship and lack of funds forced Muzaffar Ahmad and others constantly to shift their publication offices and change the format of their journals, which appeared somewhat infrequently, but despite this he and Saumyendranath Tagore (the grandnephew of the great poet) managed to introduce Marxist literature *in Bengali* in the 1920s, through the pages of *Langal* [The Plough], a weekly founded in 1925 and *Ganavani* [The Voice of the Masses], a weekly that replaced *Langal* in 1927. The first year that a number of books on communism were published in Bengali was 1931, when four volumes appeared: *Samyabad* [Communism] by Somnath Lahiri; *Karl Marx* (in Bengali) by Monimaya Pramanik; *Marxvad* [Marxism] by Anil Roy; and *Soviet Russia* (in Bengali) by Jaharlal Bakshi.

[35] In addition to Kalpana Dutt, *Reminiscences*, see Jogesh Chandra Chatterjee, *In Search of Freedom* (Calcutta: Firma K. L. Mukhopadhyay, 1967), pp. 242–243, for an impression of the CPI in the jails in the 1930s. A novel by Satinath Bhaduri, *Jagari* [The Vigil], written in 1944 and published in 1946, translated into English by Lila Ray (Calcutta: Asia Publishing House, 1965), offers a description of the intellectual atmosphere in the jails, but *Jagari* is anticommunist. For a Communist interpretation of life in the jails, see Gopal Haldar, *Ekada* [Once], 6th ed., written in 1933 and published for the first time in 1939 (Calcutta: Bengal Publishers Private Ltd., 1960).

precedence over dedication to the class struggle.[36] Only one of these parties, the Bolshevik party, ever had a significant number of Muslims within its ranks, and the Bolsheviks were never a force.[37] The Forward Bloc, the RSP, and the other Marxist Left groups were simply *bhadralok* parties, and the warring factions among them indicated the confusion that prevailed among the *bhadralok* about how they might use Marxism to capture political power. The largest of the non-communist Marxist Left parties, the Forward Bloc, was without leadership throughout World War II, since Subhas Bose had abandoned the party to join with the Axis powers in a plan to invade India and free the subcontinent from foreign domination. The closest Bose ever came to defining the objectives of the Forward Bloc was to state that he wanted a synthesis between fascism and communism,[38] but he was killed in a plane crash before he could ever bring his elaborate political program into being.

The CPI was not without its own factional disputes in the thirties, but in contrast to the Marxist Left parties, the CPI in Bengal acted with dedication, resolve, and unity from the 1930s right up until Independence. In January 1936 it was accepted into the Congress Socialist party, and through its "consolidation movement" it began to take over established Congress trade unions and peasant organizations. Party members literally invaded the colleges to teach Marxism in class and to recruit Communists in the coffeehouses. The CPI in Bengal also began to organize innumerable front organizations in the late 1930s—the Indian People's Theatre Association, the Progressive Writer's Workshop, Friends of the Soviet Union, the Mahila Atma Raksha Samiti (a women's organization), children's societies, study clubs, gymnasiums, relief committees, and a host of other cultural and sports groups. It was through these activities that the educated *bhadralok* became involved with the party for the first time. Membership in the

[36] For representative discussions of ideological disputes within the Forward Bloc in the period of its formation, see Nemai Nag Chowdhury, *Subhas Chandra and Socialism* (Calcutta: Bookland Private Ltd., 1965); Durlab Singh, *The Rebel President: A Biographical Study of Subhas Chandra Bose* (Lahore: Hero Publications, 1946); and Sita Ram Goel, *Netaji and the CPI* (Calcutta: Society for the Defence of Freedom in Asia, 1955).

[37] One Muslim member of the Forward Bloc, Ashraf-ud-din-Chaudhury, held the position of chairman of the party in the 1940s, but with partition he chose to remain in East Bengal (Pakistan). Muslim involvement with the communist movement in West Bengal is examined in some detail in Marcus F. Franda, *Marxism and the Bengali Elite* (Cambridge: M.I.T. Center for International Studies monograph, forthcoming).

[38] Jayantanuja Bandhopadhyaya, *Indian Nationalism versus International Communism* (Calcutta: Firma K. L. Mukhopadhyay, 1966), pp. 335–336.

Bengal CPI grew from 37 in 1934 to more than 1000 in 1942, and the support of fellow travelers and nonparty members grew apace. By the late 1970s a Soviet article pointed out that Bengalis were celebrating May Day, Anti-War Day, Lenin Day, November Resolution Day, Palestine Day, Spain Day, Saklatvala Day, Subhas Bose Day, and Political Prisoners Day, in all of which the CPI now played a prominent part.[39]

These activities were intensified during the war. The CPI in Bengal broke with the Forward Bloc and the Congress Socialists in March 1940, allying first with the regular Congress (until December 1940) and later with the British government in support of the Allied war effort. By December 1941 CPI members had captured the All-India Students Federation; by October 1942 they had complete mastery over the All-India Kisan Sabha (India's largest mass peasant organization); and by the late 1940s they had taken over the All-India Trade Union Congress. These three organizations, each the largest of its kind in India at the time, gave the party a mass base for the first time, particularly in Bengal, where all three organizations were strong. With its members released from prison in July 1942, the CPI in Bengal launched into relief work during the famine of 1943,[40] hardened its cadre with innumerable study groups, discussions, and party meetings, and even gained some training in guerrilla warfare when the British recruited a guerrilla unit from among CPI members to fight against Bose in the Northeast Frontier areas.[41] The party was not without its stresses and strains throughout the period preceding and following World War II, but the discipline of its members was demonstrated by the fact that the Bengal CPI followed the all-India party in maneuvering itself through almost innumerable strategic and ideological shifts between 1936 and 1947,[42] during which time there were few defections from the party and party membership continued to increase.

Most of the people who are now regarded as leading intellectuals or theoreticians in the communist movement in Bengal joined in the period following 1942, when the legal ban on the party was lifted; a few of them joined earlier. Of the intellectuals in the party who were interviewed in 1969–1970, the vast majority traced their initial interest in Marxism back to Indian intellectual movements and their

[39] Overstreet and Windmiller, *Communism in India*, p. 175.
[40] For a description of the famine relief activities of the CPI in Bengal during the war, see "People's Fight against Epidemics in Bengal," *Marxist Miscellany* (Bombay) 7 (April 1946): 82–93.
[41] Overstreet and Windmiller, *Communism in India*, p. 206.
[42] For a discussion of these shifts, see John H. Kautsky, *Moscow and the Communist Party of India* (New York: John Wiley & Sons, 1956), pp. 6–24.

leaders: to Bankim Chandra, Vivekananda, Sarat Chandra Chatterjee (a novelist writing in the early part of the century), and especially to Jawaharlal Nehru and Rabindranath Tagore. Nehru rejected Stalinism throughout his life but spoke in very glowing terms about many aspects of Marxism and intellectual communism in his autobiography and other writings of the 1930s.[43] Tagore also rejected communism, but when he returned from his trip to the Soviet Union in 1930 he did write a number of articles (both in Bengali and in English) in which he praised the socialist experiments he had witnessed.[44] The present generation of Marxist intellectual leaders in Bengal was introduced to socialist ideas through the works of Tagore, Nehru, and other Indian writers as students in the 1930s, and most of them coupled this intellectual tradition with an extensive reading of British socialist writers (particularly Harold Laski and John Strachey), as well as commentaries on Marx, Engels, and Lenin or occasionally the writings of Marx and Lenin in English translation. One author who has been universally read by Bengali Communists is R. Palme Dutt, who was born in 1896 in Cambridge, England, was a founding member of the CPGB in 1920, and has been a major advisor to Indian Communists ever since. Although Dutt has been to India only once (in 1946, when he covered the Cabinet Mission for the London *Daily Worker*), he has tutored innumerable Bengali (and other Indian) Communist intellectuals at his "study circles" in Cambridge, which he started in the 1920s. His *India Today* (which is currently being revised for the sixth time) is still the basic Communist primer on Indian politics, and his voluminous shelf of other writings has also been widely read.

This reading list could be expanded, but the names already mentioned are representative of the intellectual orientation of the Bengalis who joined the party in the 1930s and 1940s. The list points to the fact that intellectual Marxism in Bengal has been led by Western-educated "gentleman Communists," a phrase that is frequently used by the intellectual community in Calcutta to describe the Marxists. These are people who are well read; most of them have friends in the communist, socialist, and labor movements in Great Britain, and many of them have traveled to the Soviet Union and Eastern Europe. Very few members of the older generation of Marxist scholars in Bengal have ever studied Marx himself in any depth, and most of them confess to great difficulty in getting through *Das Kapital* or other

[43] See especially Chapter 67 of the original Bodley Head edition of the *Autobiography* (1937), which is still widely quoted by CPI theoreticians in Bengal.

[44] Many of these writings on Russia have been collected in Rabindranath Tagore, *Letters from Russia*, trans. Sasadhar Sinha (Calcutta: Visva Bharati, 1960); see especially pp. 117 ff.

highly theoretical works.[45] Few of them have ever read Mao, and when they have done so they have read him in English translation, invariably with the aid of commentaries in English. Party members are the first to admit that the communist movement in Bengal has never been able to boast a truly original Marxist theoretician, despite the presence of many brilliant scholars in the party.

Intellectual Marxism in Bengal derives its sustenance from the atmosphere of the highly educated *bhadralok* in Calcutta, and its leading adherents are drawn from wealthier and better established families than those of the terrorists in the organizational apparatus of the movement. Most of the intellectuals remained outside the terrorist movement in the 1930s in order to complete their education. Many of them traveled to England to secure higher degrees. Since all of the leading members of the older generation of Marxist scholars in West Bengal are now in the regular CPI, the difference between the leadership of the CPI and the CPM is essentially the difference between the intellectual leadership of the movement, on the one hand, and the organizational leadership (dominated by former terrorists) on the other. Of the 33 members of the CPM State Committee in 1969, only a third had college degrees, since most of them had interrupted their education in the 1930s to join with revolutionary parties. In contrast, all of the 9 members of the CPI State Secretariat in 1969 were college graduates, and 6 of the 9 had advanced degrees. Most members of the CPM State Committee (18 of the 33) stemmed from rural backgrounds, with almost half of them (15) coming from families of middle peasants (landholders owning less than 10 acres), while 7 of the 9 members of the CPI State Secretariat were born into families with ancestral homes in Calcutta, and all of them thought of themselves as coming from relatively wealthy backgrounds.

Some idea of the orientation of the leading intellectuals in the communist movement in Bengal can be gained from the writings of Professor Hiren Mukherjee, who is now one of the major theoreticians of the regular CPI, a prominent member of the state leadership of the party, and the leader of the CPI parliamentary party in the Lok Sabha. Mukherjee was born into a respected Brahmin family in Calcutta in 1907,

. . . a modest middle-class Bengali home, urban but without luxuries, where every living room had its clutter of books in three languages, Bengali, Sanskrit and English, and masses of newspapers filed for reference purposes and cardboard-bound hunks where cuttings were pasted, and where on Sundays the

[45] *Das Kapital* has been translated into three Indian languages (Marathi, Hindi, and Malayalam) but never into Bengali. See *Das Kapital: Centenary Volume*, ed. Mohit Sen and M. B. Rao (Delhi: People's Publishing House, 1968), pp. 228–229.

sitting-room, whence we were banned till we grew up, would resound for hours to loud and perhaps exciting talk on politics and literature and heaven knows what other subjects. We came thus to inhale, with the very air we breathed, a sort of interest in public affairs and in learning—an interest which pervaded the atmosphere, so to speak. . . .[46]

Mukherjee's hero during his adolescence was Gandhi, and though he had great respect for the terrorists, he chose to go abroad for his education rather than participate in a revolutionary student group. Educated at Calcutta University and Oxford, he has three advanced degrees (M.A., B.Litt., and Barrister-at-Law) and was the chairman of the Department of History at a Calcutta college before he decided to work full time for the party. As recently as 1964, Mukherjee wrote eloquently of his respect for Nehru:

I have had the good fortune of being admitted to the affections of Jawaharlal Nehru. It is something that I hesitate to speak about. When he was alive we would often write to each other, but it was entirely personal and almost always it was far removed from the stink of day-to-day politics. If from a railway carriage window the Supreme Court building hurt my eyes till the sight of Humayun's tomb soothed them, I would tell him about it but not whisper a word to others who would not understand. . . . If I was a good enough Marxist, which I fear I am not, I would have written differently. I have written as the bent took me, for I could not do otherwise.[47]

Since 1964, the interests of the state CPI have been conditioned by the social backgrounds of the intellectual leadership. Unlike the former terrorists in the organizational apparatus of the CPM, the intellectuals in the communist movement in West Bengal gave way to their nationalist feelings during the Sino-Indian border dispute of 1962 and have consistently advocated solidarity with the Soviet Union during the course of the Sino-Soviet rift.[48] With the exception of the Zhdanov period immediately following Independence, the intellectual leadership has always advocated a position of support for Nehru's foreign policy and a more orthodox conception of the dictatorship of the proletariat than the rest of the organization has thought practical,

[46] Hiren Mukherjee, Gandhiji: A Study, 2nd rev. ed. (New Delhi: People's Publishing House, 1960), pp. 2–3.

[47] Hiren Mukherjee, The Gentle Colossus: A Study of Jawaharlal Nehru (Calcutta: Manisha Granthalaya Private Ltd., 1964), p. v.

[48] An excellent discussion of intellectual Marxism in India, in which the communists are compared to the socialists, democratic socialists, and radical humanists, is provided in Sibnarayan Ray, "India: Urban Intellectuals and Rural Problems," in Revisionism: Essays on the History of Marxist Ideas, ed. Leopold Labedz (London: Allen & Unwin, 1962), pp. 374–386.

at the same time as it has opposed members of the organization who advocate the Maoist or Left Communist strategies that have frequently been discussed in inner-party debates. While the intellectuals have worked effectively in constitutional and electoral bodies, especially at the central government level, they have never been able to wrest control of the electoral machinery of the party from the organizational cadre. Intellectuals have been prominent in urban labor unions, particularly in the engineering industries, and have also been active in cultural front groups and student associations. Where they have taken an interest in the peasantry, they have preferred to work through the electoral machinery rather than the peasant organizations, which are based on class conflict, and which are dominated by the organizational cadre.

Electoral Politics and the CPI

The first elections contested by the Communist party in Bengal were the elections to the prepartition United Bengal Assembly, which took place in 1946. During the previous elections in 1935 and earlier, the CPI had always been much too small even to consider contesting, and in the years between 1935 and 1946, when the CPI began to grow in numbers and influence, elections were suspended because of the war. The elections of 1946 were therefore especially important, both for the province and for the party, since they were to choose the first Provincial Legislature of postwar Bengal, as well as the makeup of the All-India Constituent Assembly that was to draft a postwar constitution for India. In the elections of 1946, twelve parties contested 250 seats, 89 of which remained within West Bengal after partition, with the other 161 going over to East Pakistan.[49] The CPI contested 3 of these seats and succeeded in winning all of them, so that the party gained at least token representation in the first Legislative Assembly in independent West Bengal. In the pluralist electoral system used by the British in 1946, the CPI won seats from very diverse constituencies: the Railway Trade Union constituency, where the CPI won 87 of 166 votes (52.4 percent); the Darjeeling Tea Garden constituency, where it won 1120 of 1322 valid votes (84.7 percent); and the Dinajpur Rural constituency, where it won 35,127 of 54,626 valid votes (64.1 percent). As a result of these elections, the CPI in West Bengal was able to elect the only Communist representative (Somnath Lahiri) to the Constituent Assembly, which was ultimately responsible for drafting the

[49] Complete returns for the 1946 election in West Bengal are available in West Bengal, Provincial Statistical Bureau, *Statistical Abstract, West Bengal, 1947* (Alipore: West Bengal Government Press, 1948), pp. 59–69.

Indian Constitution, and which served as the central legislature for all of India until 1952. The elections also made it possible for the legislative leader of the CPI in West Bengal (Jyoti Basu) to establish himself in state politics.

The legislative experience of the CPI between 1946 and 1952 (when the first General Elections were held in independent India) was extremely important for the growth of the CPI in West Bengal, since the Communists were the only organized political party besides the Congress that remained in the Legislative Assembly throughout the post-Independence period. The other political parties that had run against the Congress in the 1946 elections either went over to Pakistan or eventually merged with the Congress, so that its principal opposition during the first five years of Independence was provided by the CPI and a handful of independents. Moreover, the eloquence and parliamentary conduct of Jyoti Basu, who was initially the leader of the CPI legislative party and eventually the leader of the entire opposition in the state assembly, was widely praised, both by his supporters and by his opponents. Even *The Statesman*, which has always been editorially anticommunist, praised Basu often as the only person who stood in the way of monopoly rule by Congress in the early years of the state legislature.[50]

The electoral support that the CPI was able to generate in West Bengal during these early years was shown by the success of the party in the elections that took place in 1952, when the party secured 28 seats in a Legislative Assembly of 238, establishing itself as the largest opposition party in West Bengal. The electoral supporters of the Communists in these early years were drawn almost exclusively from the urban areas in and around Calcutta, while the leadership of the electoral apparatus of the party came for the most part from the intellectual community and the organizational cadre dominated by former terrorists. Support of the CPI by the *bhadralok* in the period before 1952 was retained by the superior organization of the CPI over the other opposition parties and reinforced by the role of the Communists in the agitation directed against the West Bengal Security Bill of 1948.

The principal purpose of the West Bengal Security Bill, in the words of the first Chief Minister of West Bengal, was to "make special provision for the suppression of subversive activities."[51] As a result

[50] See, for example, the editorial in *The Statesman* (Calcutta daily), March 31, 1948.
[51] *Ananda Bazaar Patrika* (Calcutta daily), December 9, 1947.

of World War II and the partition of 1947, West Bengal was in a state of chaos, and there existed a number of organized groups who had secured arms and ammunition from a variety of sources. Many of the 200,000 Allied troops who had been stationed in and around Calcutta during the war had sold their weapons to private individuals, and many weapons had been smuggled or stolen from army camps by Indian citizens. In addition, members of Bose's Indian National Army (INA) returning from the campaigns in Burma were able to bring their weapons into India illegally, and many of the terrorists still had their own supplies of arms and ammunition accumulated during the previous half century. Calcutta had been the scene of two violent upheavals just before Independence, one a period of almost three months of continuous agitation directed against the British in 1945–1946, when the government of India placed the members of the INA on trial for treason, and the other in mid-1946, when countless numbers of people were killed in the communal rioting after the decision to partition Bengal. Calcutta had witnessed massive communal riots previously, in 1910, 1918, and 1926, and great nationalist bloodshed in 1921–1922 and 1930–1931, but the INA agitation and the Great Calcutta Killing of 1946 were unprecedented in their ferocity.[52] Hindu and Muslim extremist groups, private armies of various kinds, and many of the leftist political parties increased their stores of arms and ammunition during this period, and most of them acquired a great deal of experience in the use of their arsenals in the two years preceding the partition.

The first Chief Minister of West Bengal, Prafulla Chandra Ghosh, argued that he needed special emergency powers from the Legislative Assembly to deal with the explosive situation that had arisen as a result of Calcutta's violent past and its uncertain future. In a plaintive speech to the Legislative Assembly in November 1947, the Chief Minister said,

> Robberies are rampant in Calcutta and elsewhere. There are arms and ammunition in the hands of many people, both Hindus and Muslims. I have not been able to recover them even with the help of ordinances. What am I to do?[53]

[52] Bengalis have shied away from writing about the rioting that went on in Bengal during the years 1945–1946. There is nothing comparable for Bengal to Manohar Malgonkar's *A Bend in the Ganges*, or Kushwant Singh's *Train to Pakistan*, both of which deal with events surrounding the partition of Punjab. For an eyewitness account by a Britisher, see Francis Tuker, *While Memory Serves* (London: Cassell, 1950).

[53] *West Bengal Legislative Assembly Debates*, November 27, 1947.

As the police fired thirty rounds of ammunition outside the Legislative Assembly to disperse a crowd of protesters, Chief Minister Ghosh introduced the West Bengal Security Bill on December 10, 1947.[54] The bill allowed the West Bengal government to detain persons suspected of subversive activities for a period of three months, which was renewable, and to do so without informing the individual involved even of the grounds of his detention for a period of fifteen days. This legislation was in many ways an extension of British legal codes having to do with "preventive detention," and much of it was eventually superseded by the preventive detention clauses adopted by the Constituent Assembly of India.[55] But West Bengal was the only state in the Indian Union to make wide use of such legislation immediately after Independence.

The CPI led the opposition against the West Bengal Security Bill, which had been labeled by the other Marxist Left parties in Bengal as a "black act" and a "totalitarian subterfuge."[56] Jyoti Basu described the emergency powers as "pernicious, . . . contrary to democracy, and in sheer violation of all that the Congress has stood and fought for for so many years."[57] Using every parliamentary tactic that he knew, Basu moved innumerable amendments to the bill in the Legislative Assembly, losing on every occasion and often voting alone against a particular clause. Yet in the end he delayed the legislation for a considerable period of time and gained a reputation for legislative leadership and courage among the urban *bhadralok*. In the years between Independence and the first General Elections in 1952, communist intellectuals and front groups staged innumerable meetings and demonstrations, protesting against the Security Bill and particularly against the government's use of it to declare the West Bengal CPI illegal.

The CPI was banned on March 27, 1948, and most of the leadership of the party spent the next four years in prison. There is no question that from 1948 to 1951 the party was engaged in a movement designed to overthrow the state government by the use of revolutionary violence as prescribed by the Zhdanov line, taking advantage of the chaotic conditions that prevailed after the war and after partition. But the Congress in West Bengal was not persuasive in stating its case for a

[54] *Hindusthan Standard* (Calcutta daily), December 11, 1946.

[55] For an analysis of this type of legislation in India, see David Bayley, *Preventive Detention in India: A Case Study in Democratic Social Control* (Calcutta: Firma K. L. Mukhopadhyay, 1962).

[56] The words are those of Sarat Chandra Bose, the elder brother of Subhas, and Mrinal Kanti Bose, president of the Bengal Provincial Trade Union Congress. See *The Statesman*, December 8, 1947, and December 12, 1947.

[57] Quoted in ibid., November 28, 1947.

ban on the party, particularly in the early years, and the intellectual community and the opposition political parties were for the most part outraged by what they considered a far too repressive policy. One member of the opposition in the Legislative Assembly argued that "blaming Communists was only a convenient way of explaining away the defects of the government," and another (who eventually joined the Congress) said that "by blaming Communists for everything the Government is only strengthening them, and though people are not willing to accept communism, it is being forced on them."[58] Jyoti Basu, when he was not in jail during this period, was extremely effective in challenging the government to provide evidence of Communist subversion, and Communist cultural front groups and the Marxist Left parties of West Bengal became increasingly outspoken and active in their opposition to government arrests.

The extent to which the urban intellectual and political leadership of Calcutta was united in opposition to the Security Bill was indicated in a 1949 by-election for the Legislative Assembly in South Calcutta constituency. In this election the Marxist Left parties united behind the candidacy of Sarat Chandra Bose, the elder brother of Subhas, and took the side of the CPI on the issue of preventive detention. Prime Minister Nehru himself, during one of his frequent trips to Calcutta, presented the position of the Congress government in an unusual preelection appeal to the voters:

I have generally avoided during recent years interfering in any election contest. But in the present instance I feel that the issues raised are such that I should make it perfectly clear what I feel in the matter. I regret that Mr. Bose should associate himself with a disruptive policy which could only be termed antinational. Not only has he allied himself with all these antinational elements, he is also being exploited by them. Under which flag does Mr. Bose stand, to which flag do his associates give allegiance?[59]

Sarat Bose countered Nehru's appeal with an election statement that summarized the feelings of a large portion of the urban *bhadralok*. Bose argued that he too was anticommunist, but that Nehru and the Congress had "compromised with British imperialism in 1946" and had accepted "the British game of dividing the country." He pointed out innumerable instances of what he described as "the deterioration in administration and . . . the rise of nepotism, corruption and favoritism" in the state government, and argued that West Bengal

[58] *West Bengal Legislative Assembly Debates*, January 21, 1949. The statements are by MLAs Khuda Bhaksh and Abul Hashim.
[59] Nehru's statement is printed in full in *The Statesman*, June 9, 1949.

was being run by "a handful of capitalists." The press, Mr. Bose argued, had been "gagged," civil liberties had been "done away with," and "demands [had] been met by . . . lathis, tear gas, batons, bayonets, and bullets, as in British times."[60] In the election the Congress was defeated by a massive margin of almost four to one, as Bose garnered 19,030 votes to his opponent's 5780.

The CPI was the most successful opposition party in the 1952 elections in West Bengal, not only because it was better organized and more realistic in assessing the number of constituencies in which it could challenge the Congress, but also because of the halo of martyrdom that it had acquired in the eyes of the urban *bhadralok* as a result of its four years in jail. When the CPI contested the elections in 1952, more than 250 party members were still political prisoners, and 5 of the 28 CPI candidates who won were elected despite the fact that they were still under detention.[61] In succeeding elections support for the CPI increased steadily, and the Communist parties were able to form a series of leftist electoral alliances that eventually placed party members in positions of power and influence in the ministries. During the last two decades, however, the Communists in West Bengal have never been able to win more than 25 percent of the vote for the Legislative Assembly, and attempts to devise electoral strategies have frequently resulted in intense factionalism. The conflicts within the party have mainly been the result of disagreements regarding the role of party leaders prominent in election campaigns.

Congress was able to win the first three general elections in West Bengal because of its success in putting together a coalition of urban businessmen, influentials, and rural leaders from a variety of social groups. Using the patronage that the party commanded through its position in the government, Congress was able to attract men who had influence in their own localities and who could sway large portions of the electorate; the party was subsequently able to advance the positions of members who had helped perpetuate the patronage system it had created. But the support of the opposition parties in West Bengal came from discontented urban intellectuals and former terrorists, groups far too small to present a challenge to a well-organized aggregative political party. The opposition parties clearly had to devise a strategy that would enable them to attract more widespread support, but on this issue the Communist party was more seriously divided

[60]Ibid. For an expanded version of Bose's views on independent West Bengal, see *I Warned My Countrymen: Being the Collected Works 1945–1950 of Sarat Chandra Bose* (Calcutta: Netaji Research Bureau, 1968), pp. 181 ff.

[61] *Ananda Bazaar Patrika*, February 16, 1952.

than on any other. One section, led by some of the most influential members of the organizational cadre, argued that the party had no business contesting elections and opted for a more revolutionary strategy. Another section argued that electoral support would be forthcoming among the disadvantaged in West Bengal if the party were only able to foment "class struggles" in the countryside, undercutting the power of local influentials by turning peasants against landlords, the landless against the landed, workers against management, and so forth. A third section of the party, generally led by the intellectuals within the movement, sought to work within the existing social structure in order to beat Congress at its own electoral game, leaving open the possibility of continuing with other, more revolutionary activities at the same time.

The factional conflicts that have developed over this issue are still unresolved, but during the course of the last two decades the state communist movement has clearly recruited an electoral following quite distinct from the regular cadre and the intellectuals. This section of the movement is composed of people who are usually much better established in the present social structure of West Bengal than the members of the regular party organizations: doctors, lawyers, journalists, teachers, landholders, traders, merchants, even managers and businessmen and former princes. Frequently lacking an intellectual commitment to Marxism, they have joined the communist movement because of their mutual interest in besting the Congress in electoral contests, an interest with a variety of motives. Because they are committed to the support of the Communists in electoral contests, and because the cadre controls the electoral machinery of the party, these people have usually sided with the organizational apparatus rather than the intellectuals in party disputes. They are distinguished from the rest of the organizational cadre, however, by their greater interest in the electoral contests in which the party has been engaged and by their exclusion from the inner councils of the party apparatus dominated by the cadre. They are also distinguished by the fact that they have generally served shorter prison terms than the leading members of the cadre; most of them have never been to jail. A few of the leading electoral communists are now members of the State Committee of the CPM, but the extent to which they are outnumbered on the committee is indicated by the fact that 12 of its 33 members have never contested elections and another 7 have tried once and been defeated. Only 1 member of the State Committee of the CPM has been in the legislatures throughout the period since Independence, and only 7 have won more than two terms.

The unquestioned leader of the electoral wing of the CPM is Jyoti Basu, who was born in Calcutta in 1914, the son of one of the wealthiest and most respected homeopathic doctors in West Bengal. Basu was educated at the best English-medium schools and colleges in Calcutta (St. Xavier's and Presidency College) and spent a number of years in England in the 1930s, where he secured a Barrister-at-Law degree from the Middle Temple in London. Jyoti's elder brother, now a famous doctor in Calcutta, married into the Jalpaiguri Raj family, one of the oldest of the princely families in West Bengal, and it was through his brother that Jyoti first came into contact with the family he married into. His first wife was the daughter of a Jalpaiguri tea plantation owner who had also become something of an entrepreneur in manufacturing and industry, and his second wife is the younger sister of the first. Jyoti Basu joined the CPGB in Britain in 1937 and was active in the Indian League and the Indian Seaman's Club in London in the 1930s. Upon his return to Calcutta in 1940 he was enrolled as an Advocate of the Calcutta High Court, but he eventually chose to devote his life to politics rather than law. In the early 1940s he was extremely active in the All-India Railwaymen's Federation, one of the largest of India's labor unions, but after his election to the Legislative Assembly in 1946 his political activities became focused almost exclusively on electoral politics, in which he has been highly successful. He has won every election to the Legislative Assembly that he has entered, usually by large margins, and until 1967 was the unquestioned leader of the opposition in the state assembly. In the first United Front government in 1967 he became the Finance Minister, in the second he was placed in charge of the major portfolios in the Home Ministry (Constitution, Elections, Special and General Administration, Police, and Press). In both United Front governments he was the Deputy Chief Minister.

Basu's interests clearly revolve around electoral politics, as do those of a great many of the leaders of the CPI and the CPM. With his educational background he could easily have become a leading theoretician in the party, but he has in fact published almost nothing, because of the risk of alienating some of his supporters. Basu's dominance of the electoral organization of the state party has led to his inclusion on the most powerful party committees, both at the central and at the state levels, but he has also complained often that he was being excluded from "inner party cells" and has thus far been unable to gain control over a significant portion of the organizational cadre. Even during the eight years when Basu was secretary of the State Council of the CPI (1951–1959), the party office was run by the leader of the organizational cadre, Pramode Das Gupta, and

Basu himself was frequently disciplined by party headquarters for what would normally be considered rather routine parliamentary behavior. On one occasion he was subject to party discipline when he participated in a Hindu festival (*Vana-Mahotsava*) with which Congress was identified, and at other times the party has required him to confess openly to "mistakes" in the Legislative Assembly and to request the Speaker of the assembly to expunge from the published debates utterances that were unacceptable to the cadre. Because of his dependence on the leadership of the cadre for support in electoral politics, Basu has subjected himself to party discipline on all of these occasions.[62]

Elite Recruitment and Communist Ideology

The elitist nature of the Communist leadership in West Bengal and its factionalism are matched by similar phenomena in other Communist parties in Asia. Communist ideology, as opposed to the movement itself, has had little appeal to the general public in Asia—in fact it is probably incomprehensible to most citizens of Asian nations— and Asian Communists have therefore refrained from any attempt to indoctrinate the masses in countries where they are still struggling for power. Most Asian Communists have devised a mass appeal that is based on a number of remarkably similar popular issues (corruption, excessive bureaucratism, imperialism, land reform, and so forth), while the ideology has remained the preserve of the party leadership. The ideology has been used to determine "the nature and objectives of the movement, its operational techniques, the types of persons it recruits, how it trains them, and how they should be deployed over a broad front to create a situation favorable to a Communist revolution."[63] India has been no exception to this general trend, and in West Bengal (where the gap between the literate high-caste elite and the illiterate masses is greater than in other parts of India)[64] the tendency is perhaps even more marked.

The ideology of communism can be (and frequently is) a unifying factor among Asian elites. Because it provides both a world view and methods of organization that are the product of the thinking

[62] These incidents are elaborated in N. C. Bhattacharya, "Leadership in the Communist Party of India," in *State Politics in India*, ed. Iqbal Narain (Meerut: Meenakshi Prakashan, 1967), pp. 544–545.

[63] Goh Keng Swee, "The Nature and Appeals of Communism in Non-Communist Asian Countries," in *Communism in Asia*, ed. John Wilkes (Sydney: Angus and Robertson, 1967), p. 41. See also *The Communist Revolution in Asia*, ed. Robert A. Scalapino, 2nd ed. (Englewood Cliffs, N.J.: Prentice-Hall, 1969).

[64] This gap is largely owing to the absence of the intermediate castes that usually act as a bridge between high and low in other parts of India. See Broomfield, *Elite Conflict*, p. 6.

and experience of Communists in many countries for more than a century, it offers a model that can be used to gain cohesion among political leaders who might otherwise have a wide variety of divergent interests. "Whatever the gap between [the] concept and practice [of communism]—and there is increasing reason to believe that it has always been substantial—this organizational system has been far superior to most competitive systems available in Asia."[65] The greater unity and cohesion achieved by the Communists in West Bengal compared to the Marxist Left parties has been in large measure a result of their greater ideological commitment.

But the ideology of communism can also be divisive, and West Bengal provides an almost classic example. Communist ideology can be divided into at least two major parts. One is the theory (or perhaps more accurately the metaphysics), the "science" of dialectical materialism expounded by Marx and Engels, which envisages the development of human society in a series of quantum changes. The other is the doctrine (as used in the political rather than the metaphysical sense), a set of principles underlying organizational and operational methods, the most basic of which are usually traced to Lenin and, especially in Asia, to Mao Tse-tung.[66] Ideally, Communists should interest themselves both in theory and in doctrine, and those who are extremely well versed in one or the other should be able and willing to function effectively together, each contributing his particular expertise for the well-being of the party and each subjecting himself to party discipline and democratic centralist rules of political organization. In practice this has happened perhaps more often than not in West Bengal, which accounts for the greater relative unity among the Communists there. But the communist movement in West Bengal has had its share of factionalism too, particularly since the Sino-Indian border clashes of 1959 and 1962, and for the most part this has been the result of ideological differences among various party elites.

Both former and present members of the Communist parties in West Bengal distinguish sharply between party leaders who are interested in organizational (doctrinal) questions, those who are prominent in theoretical debates, and those whose principal interests lie in the legislative arena. Since the leaders themselves frequently describe their activities as falling into one or another of the three categories, it is not difficult for an outsider to determine them. Few

[65] Robert A. Scalapino, "The Nature of Communist Regimes in Asia," in *Communism in Asia*, p. 4.

[66] This distinction is made in Swee, "Communism in Non-Communist Asian Countries," pp. 41–43.

Asian societies have experienced with the same degree of intensity the three major movements that over the last century have produced distinct leadership sets among Bengali Communists: a terrorist movement led by highly institutionalized terrorist federations; a burgeoning of intellectual activities in which both Western and indigenous traditions were prominent; and an experience with electoral democracy that dates back to the 1880s.

While communist ideology and recruitment patterns have combined to produce well-defined factions among the leadership of the movement in West Bengal, the factions themselves have derived much of their sustenance from the nature of the social and political systems that have prevailed in India in recent times. In a society where hierarchical forms of social organization have existed for so long, and where men established in positions of authority can expect a kind of deference that is almost unknown in societies that place less emphasis on status, there is often an intense competition among those in leadership positions to gain the support of followers and subordinates. This competition is reinforced in most Indian political parties by frequent struggles among party leaders to secure the position of leadership in their own factions.[67] Furthermore, in political parties that contain a number of people who have been alienated from the rest of society and who have suffered repression, there is a greater than usual need for social integration between party leaders and their followers.[68] All of these factors have resulted in a high degree of identification between the membership of the Communist parties in West Bengal and particular sets of factional leaders.

Conflicts among elite Communist leaders in West Bengal have covered the spectrum of personal and other factional differences but have usually centered on fundamental questions of strategy. What kind of strategy should a Communist party pursue in a pluralist and hierarchically organized society, in a developing nation in which electoral politics is highly institutionalized, and which has recently been dominated by largely rural interests? There are no neat Marxist, Leninist, or Maoist formulations that can answer this question, and the cleavages that have taken place within the movement have revolved around the attempt by various leadership groups merely to

[67] The theme of factionalism among Bengali Communists is discussed in Chapter 3, and especially in the concluding chapter. For contrasting data from another Indian region, cf. Paul R. Brass, *Factionalism in an Indian State: Congress Party Politics in Uttar Pradesh* (Berkeley: University of California Press, 1967), pp. 235–243.

[68] See Myron Weiner and Joseph LaPalombara, "The Impact of Parties on Political Development," in *Political Parties and Political Development*, ed. Joseph LaPalombara and Myron Weiner (Princeton: Princeton University Press, 1966), p. 405.

reach some kind of minimal agreement. The following chapter explores some of the problems Communists have faced in devising an appropriate strategy in West Bengal, focusing on the period before the split in 1964.

3

FACTIONAL CONFLICT AND
PARTY ORGANIZATION

Factional alignments that were present among Bengali Communists at the time of Independence have shifted considerably since 1947. The pro-Soviet intellectual leadership of the movement, which was dominant in the state party throughout World War II and the immediate post-Independence period, continued to support the CPSU and the national leadership of the CPI in the 1950s and 1960s. But this faction has been increasingly opposed at the state level by former terrorists and electoralists within the party who have been able to recruit large numbers of state supporters in recent years. Conflicts between the older intellectuals and the other leadership sets in the West Bengal movement culminated in a split in the CPI in 1964, with the state intellectual leadership being isolated in the Soviet-backed CPI, now arrayed against former terrorists and electoral Communists allied with each other in the CPM.

On the national level there is perhaps no country in Asia and Africa where Communists have been more divided over strategy. Indeed, the Indian movement is frequently cited by Communists and noncommunists alike as an almost classic example of a poorly organized, ideologically confused, and politically impotent movement, particularly in comparison with the Asian Communist party that has succeeded in capturing power in China. In contrast to the Chinese Communists, the Indian Communists have never been able to decide what combination of forces they should try to organize from among the peasants, the proletariat, the anti-imperialists, and the bourgeoisie. Frequently they have been unable even to agree on which segments of Indian society come under these headings, and perhaps more often than not, party theoreticians have created so many subdivisions that Indian society becomes all but unrecognizable to a membership that wants a clear formula for political action. Even when there has been general agreement on the identification and definition of the various classes, the parties have often found themselves unable to decide whether to form alliances with them or to oppose them. Indian communism has therefore vacillated between an insurrectionist strategy toward certain classes, an electoral strategy toward others, and a host of combined strategies in which insurrection and constitutional communism have sometimes been pursued simultaneously. The frequent shifts in the leadership of the national movement in India, especially when compared to Mao's dominance in China, points up in a dramatic way the lack of continuity that has characterized the growth of Indian communism.

The divisions that have plagued the communist movement in other parts of India have also been present in West Bengal, and yet communism has been more effective in West Bengal on a regional basis than it has on the national level. Indeed, the challenge of the communist movement in India derives not from its nationwide strength but rather from the way it has periodically become entrenched in certain strategic regions of the country (particularly the Telengana and Srikakulam regions of Andhra, large portions of the state of Kerala, and the southern districts of West Bengal). The strength of communism in particular regions is at least partly the result of agreement—or perhaps more accurately, accommodation— on strategy. While questions of strategy on a national level have frequently created serious factionalism in the all-India party, between regional units as well as within them, accommodation of differences has often been achieved within regional units in a way that has not been possible nationally. In West Bengal, essentially the same leadership dominated the state party organization of the CPI from 1951 to 1964, a leadership that now controls the largest of the two parties presently existing in the region.

One obvious reason for the greater degree of continuity in the regional units is provided by the nature of the Indian political system and the society in which it operates. Indian politics and society could perhaps best be described as consisting of segmented, pluralist units, divided among themselves on the basis of language, caste, culture, and other fundamental differences. Each of the various linguistic-cultural units has its own peculiar social structure, each has been subject to different patterns of economic development, and each has evolved politically in response to factors that are often peculiar to only one or two of India's many regions. This is not to argue that the regions can be understood without reference to national and international factors, but it does point up the nature of the organizational problems posed by India's great diversity, especially for a political party that aspires to unity and cohesiveness.

Party Unity and an Insurrectionist Strategy

In contrast to the CPI on the national level, the CPI in West Bengal was most unified during the three-year period between Independence and the promulgation of the Indian Constitution in 1950. This is explained by the political situation in the newly independent state of West Bengal, which was unlike that in other parts of India. Partition split the economy of West Bengal into two parts; it was accompanied by massive movements of people across a recently defined international border; it was conceived and carried out in an atmosphere of widespread rioting and violence; and in West Bengal it created enormous resentment, bitterness, and hostility. Moreover, the governments that were created after partition, both in East Pakistan and in West Bengal, were decidedly more unstable than the governments in other parts of India and Pakistan. The Muslim majority that had ruled Bengal before Independence went over to Pakistan, where Muslim political leaders found themselves without an administrative apparatus and without much of a police force.[1] While West Bengal did have an administrative cadre of proven skill and a much better police force than East Pakistan, in order to create a legislative government for the newly defined state, political alliances had to be completely restructured. This led to factional infighting within the Congress government and a two- or three-year period of instability. Food and other consumer goods were scarce in 1947 and 1948, there was great tension between the various Hindu and Muslim (and non-Bengali and Sikh) "resistance groups" that had been formed to protect communal interests, and there was even the possibility that the Indian Army might become disenchanted, owing to the treatment of the Indian National Army of Subhas Bose, the response of the government to the Bombay naval mutiny in 1946, or the general disorder and lack of direction that seemed to prevail almost everywhere in divided Bengal.[2] In short, there were compelling reasons for the Bengali Communist belief that war and partition had created a state of affairs in which violent revolution might be successful.

[1] The effect of partition on the administrative cadres and police services of West Bengal and East Pakistan is described in detail by Ralph Braibanti, "Public Bureaucracy and Judiciary in Pakistan," *Bureaucracy and Political Development*, ed. Joseph LaPalombara (Princeton: Princeton University Press, 1963), pp. 365 ff. See also David Bayley, *The Police and Political Development in India* (Princeton: Princeton University Press, 1969), pp. 50 ff.

[2] Some appreciation of the expectations of Bengali leftists immediately after Independence can be gained from Balai Chandra Dutt, *Nau Bidroha* [The Naval Revolt] (Calcutta: Compass Publications, 1969). The author was a participant in what the British called the Bombay naval mutiny, but what the leftists call the naval revolt of 1946.

The CPI in West Bengal did not take part in India's Independence Day celebrations. Unlike their party colleagues in other parts of India, who embraced Congressmen publicly in the wave of emotion that came with Independence, the CPI in West Bengal was almost unanimous in its assessment of the Congress party as the enemy of the Communists. When the Central Executive Committee (CEC) of the CPI rallied behind Nehru after Independence and appeared to be on the way toward evolving a party line calling for an alliance with "progressive elements in the Congress," the CPI unit in West Bengal stood in opposition to central party leadership and was eventually successful in shifting the headquarters of the national party to Calcutta, where an insurrectionist strategy was adopted at the Second Party Congress in March 1948. Adoption of the new line supporting an insurrectionist strategy was possible in 1948 for a variety of reasons. Not only did the time seem ripe for revolution in West Bengal, it seemed so in many other parts of the world as well, and there was great support for extremist policies from Moscow during the Zhdanov era. Many Bengali Communist intellectuals who might otherwise have shied away from an insurrectionist policy therefore felt that they were taking part in a worldwide movement of great significance, and many of those who believed that India was incapable of maintaining a unified political system in the absence of British rule felt at the same time that only the best-organized violent revolution would succeed in producing successor governments to the British. With support from Moscow, and with the example of China assuming greater proportions as Mao's armies marched toward Peking, the CPI threw itself whole-heartedly into two years of violent struggle.

The most intense party activity in West Bengal took place during an eighteen-month period that extended from October 1948 until March 1950, during which time innumerable trams, buses, trains, and build-ings were either bombed or set on fire, demonstrations by students, mass organizations, and cultural front groups took place at the rate of at least one or two a week in Calcutta, and deaths from the activities of revolutionaries were estimated in the hundreds. Acts of sabotage officially traced either to the CPI or to a faction of the Revolutionary Communist party of India led by a close relative of Pramode Das Gupta (Pannalal Das Gupta) include the following: an arsonist's attack on the home of Labour Minister K. P. Mukherjee (the house was doused in gasoline and kerosine and set on fire); an attack with "crackers" (small bombs) at a meeting presided over by the same Labour Minister; the complete destruction by fire of the Calcutta Telephone Exchange in October 1948 and an attempt to blow up the Calcutta Water Works in January 1949; raids on the home of the president of the state Congress party, S. M. Ghosh, and raids on a number of Congress party offices; attacks on Prime Minister Nehru in Calcutta and on the automobile and home of Chief Minister B. C. Roy; and large-scale raids on Dum Dum airport, as a result of which men and officers of Jessops and BOAC airlines were killed and the bodies of two European plant managers were thrown into blast furnaces.[3] During one three-week period in early 1950, a total of 79 policemen were injured by CPI bomb attacks, and eventually many Republic Day functions planned for Calcutta in January 1950 (when the new Constitution was promulgated) had to be postponed.[4] Later in 1950, during a period of almost seven weeks, Calcutta and its surrounding areas were rocked by a massive wave of communal violence, in which some CPI units were reportedly active.

The high point of insurrectionist activity in West Bengal during the Zhdanov period was mid-1949, when the massive defeat of the Congress by Sarat Bose and the leftist electoral alliance convinced many people in the communist movement that a strategy of violent agitation against the government could generate popular support. On June 15, 1949, shortly after the election of Bose, the CPI staged a series of attacks on Congress party offices, police stations, and jails. More than 250 security prisoners in West Bengal began a two-week fast protesting conditions inside the jails, and party units began to expand their activities in the countryside to such an extent that Section 144 of the Criminal Procedure Code (which prohibits assembly of more than five persons) had to be invoked throughout two large districts (Hooghly and Howrah) bordering on Calcutta. With Chief Minister B. C. Roy in Switzerland undergoing treatment for a serious eye ailment, the acting Chief Minister of the state, Nalini Ranjan Sarkar, made a number of concessions to the Communists, including a promise that cases against some prisoners would be dropped by the West Bengal government and that Section 144 would be withdrawn from some areas in Calcutta. The seriousness with which the events in West Bengal were viewed by the central and state governments is indicated by the fact that

[3] An official description of CPI terrorist incidents and literature during the insurrectionist period 1948–1951 is contained in India (Dominion), Ministry of Home Affairs, *Communist Violence in India* (New Delhi: Government of India Press, 1949). For the views of Chief Minister B. C. Roy, see his speeches in the *West Bengal Legislative Assembly Debates*, March 30, 1948, January 21, 1949, March 4, 1949, and April 16, 1949. See also the speech by Home Minister Kiron Shankar Roy in ibid., September 27, 1948.

[4] *The Statesman* (Calcutta daily), January 7, 1950, January 8, 1950, and January 28, 1950.

Prime Minister Nehru made a special trip to Calcutta to plead publicly with the people of the state for support in the face of what he now called "the conspiracy of the Communists,"[5] while Acting Chief Minister Sarkar went on All-India Radio with a special government broadcast in an attempt to impress the citizens of the state with the severity of the political crisis. In the concluding portion of his speech, he warned,

> When a country lapses into chaos, anarchy and disorder, the police alone cannot be expected to maintain law and order unless they have behind them public cooperation and support. . . . It is time that my countrymen forsook their complacence and pondered deeply whether the present distraction, the orgy of violence and disorder, will serve their best interests and lighten the burden of their sufferings. . . . The time for sitting on the fence and inactivity is gone and nobody can assume a middle-of-the-way attitude except at his own peril. . . . The fire which is being deliberately kindled by the forces of evil is bound to engulf them sooner or later—sooner, I imagine, than later.[6]

Encouraged by their success in Calcutta, yet subject to greater and greater repression and more effective police work by the West Bengal government, members of the party turned their attention to the rural areas in the latter half of 1949,[7] concentrating on five southern districts of Bengal in close proximity to Calcutta: Bankura, Burdwan, Midnapore, Howrah, and 24-Parganas. The CPI had been active before World War II in many of these areas through its involvement in a *tebhaga* (literally, "three shares") movement among sharecroppers, which advocated that two-thirds of the crop be given to the sharecropper and one-third to the landlord, instead of the usual arrangement in which it was divided equally between landlord and sharecropper. In 1949, however, the CPI became even more extremist, now advocating that *all* land and *all* produce from the land be given to those who cultivated it and encouraging all cultivators (sharecroppers as well as other landless and poor peasant cultivators) to seize harvested crops, loot wealthy homes, and raid government food stocks.[8]

---

[5] Ibid., June 9, 1949.

[6] The full text of this speech appears in ibid., p. 1.

[7] The shift to an emphasis on rural areas coincided with a similar shift in emphasis by theoreticians in Moscow at this time. See V. Balabushevich, "Novyi etap natsional-no-osvoboditelno borby narodov Indii" [The New Stage of the National Liberation Struggle of the People of India], *Voprosy Ekonomiki*, no. 8 (1949), pp. 42–43, quoted in Morton Schwartz, "The Wavering 'Line' of Indian Communism," *Political Science Quarterly* 70 (December 1955): 556.

[8] There is almost no published record of the *tebhaga* movement of the CPI in Bengal, despite the way in which it is constantly recalled in the most romantic terms by party leaders. For a brief Communist account of the movement, see Hiren Mukherjee,

In 1949 the party concentrated especially on tribal and other poorer cultivators living near inaccessible areas, such as the Laiks in Bankura District, whose familiarity with jungle tracts made it possible for them to loot or seize food crops from landlord and government warehouses and then disappear into the jungle. The areas of the most intense rural activity were the Kakdwip, Lyalgunge, Sandeshkhali, and Canning regions of 24-Parganas, extremely poor areas of the state that are virtually inaccessible during the rains. These are also areas surrounded by forests and the deltaic portion of the Bay of Bengal, where local residents had a distinct advantage over outside policemen in any chase or search. In 24-Parganas especially, CPI leaders would frequently supply arms to local tribals and poor cultivators or encourage them to arm themselves with their own tribal weapons (bows, arrows, lathis) in an attempt to organize them on a large scale for occupation of the land by force. The movement in 24-Parganas was clearly modeled after the Telengana movement in Andhra Pradesh, involving a number of murders of those who resisted, and a large number of booklets entitled *Sishu Telengana* [Infant Telengana] were distributed in the areas where the CPI was active.[9]

Both the rural movement and the movement in Calcutta were eventually more successful in terms of individual acts of terrorism than they were in creating a mass revolutionary upsurge. The West Bengal government countered the rural movement with police hunts and organizations of village welfare workers (*Seva Dals*) who knew the terrain and were occasionally armed, and by late 1950 almost all the organizers of the movement had been arrested. By this time most members of the party were ready to admit defeat, and Jyoti Basu was subsequently able to preside over a public meeting in Calcutta in early 1951 at which the party passed a resolution pledging that it would "learn from its mistakes, re-establish links with the people, and do everything in its power to unite all leftist parties to form a dem-

India's Struggle for Freedom, 3rd rev. ed. (Calcutta: National Book Agency, 1962), pp. 280–281. For a West Bengal government account, see the statements by the state lawyers who prosecuted the case against thirty-six members of the CPI accused of fomenting the "Kakdwip Tebhaga movement" in 1949–1950, in *The Statesman*, May 6, 1951, and December 12, 1953. A more detailed Communist account of the earlier stages of the movement is available in a thirty-six-page pamphlet by Krishna Binod Rai, *Tebhagar Lorai* [The Tebhaga Struggle] (Calcutta: Bangio Pradeshik Krishak Sabha, 1939).

[9] An excellent analysis of social and political change in the West Bengal district of 24-Parganas is Ashim Mukhopadhyay, "The Peasants of the Parganas," *Frontier* (Calcutta weekly), serialized in the six issues from December 20, 1969, to January 24, 1970.

ocratic front to fight the present government."[10] In an impressive display of party discipline, especially for an Indian political party, the CPI in West Bengal regeared its organization for electoral purposes, and by late March 1951 it was able to participate in a coalition of leftist parties that defeated the Congress in the Howrah municipal elections. Arguing now that it was the police who had "terrorised the people" and not the Communist party, the CPI joined with the other Marxist Left parties to demonstrate against food shortages and the lack of adequate relief programs for refugees. In the 1952 elections it was able to unite with the Socialist Republican party (founded by Sarat Bose) and the Forward Bloc, the two largest Marxist Left parties at that time, in the only successful opposition electoral alliance against the Congress. The CPI not only gained the most seats among the opposition, it also scored the most impressive prestige victories in the state, defeating Labour Minister Kalipada Mukherjee in a predominantly working-class constituency, as well as the Judicial Minister who had drafted the West Bengal Security Act. In addition, CPI candidates defeated the Education Minister (H. N. Chaudhuri) and the Revenue Minister (B. C. Sinha), both of whom were *zamindars* (large landholders) running in their own *zamindaris*.

Party Factionalism and Electoral Politics

While it is generally argued that the insurrectionist policies of the CPI in the years between 1948 and 1951 gave birth to much of the factionalism that existed in the all-India party throughout the 1950s, in West Bengal the combination of insurrectionist activities and the outcome of the 1952 elections intensified factional differences. The 1952 elections surprised almost everyone in the state unit of the CPI as well as most observers, for it was generally expected that the democratic socialist and Marxist Left parties would fare much better than the Communists. In fact, this was the case in terms of the popular vote—the democratic socialist and Marxist Left opposition parties gained a combined percentage of 19.96 percent of the vote for the state Legislative Assembly in 1952, compared with 10.76 percent of the vote for the CPI—but the vote of the noncommunist Left opposition was so divided that the Communists emerged with as many seats (28) as all six of the Left parties combined. Congress easily carried the elections with 38.93 percent of the vote and 150 of 278 seats.

---

[10] *The Statesman*, January 14, 1951. For the timing of this decision with similar decisions made in other parts of India, see Ruth Fischer, "The Indian Communist Party," *Far Eastern Survey* 22 (June 1953): 79–84.

Before the 1952 elections the state party had witnessed a number of small factional quarrels: between rural and urban District Committees over questions of status; between one section of the party that was in jail and another whose members were accused of "purchasing their freedom" by refusing to adhere strictly to the party line as laid down by the Second Party Congress in 1948;[11] and, in the later stages of the insurrectionist movement, between some of the trade unionists and the leaders of the regular party organization over questions of trade union organization. But these factional quarrels had involved the allocation of party resources rather than the fundamental questions of strategy that came to the surface after the elections of 1952. While earlier factional quarrels could be solved by the expulsion of a few members or by relatively minor adjustments within the framework of the current policy, the disputes that arose within the party after 1952 led to intense inner-party debate and eventually to a split.

Most of the seats that the West Bengal CPI won in 1952 were located in precisely the areas where the party had been most active during the insurrectionist period. Four of the party's successful candidates ran in constituencies located in Calcutta, while another 10 came from urban constituencies in the 5 large southern districts surrounding Calcutta (Howrah, Burdwan, 24-Parganas, Hooghly, and Midnapore); 12 of the remaining 14 seats came from rural constituencies in the same 5 districts. The party won only 2 seats in the remaining 8 predominantly rural districts, one an urban constituency (Kalimpong) in Darjeeling and the other a rural constituency (Gazole) in Malda. Especially because they were so unexpected, the results of the election were subject to a great many interpretations, both within the party and outside. They could be interpreted to mean that the party needed to devote more attention to electoral strategy in the urban areas and particularly in Calcutta (one of the few areas where it had not done as well as expected), but they could also be read as encouragement for a rural electoral strategy. They were interpreted by many as an endorsement by the people of West Bengal of a strategy of insurrection and particularly of rural insurrection, since the party had scored its most striking and unexpected victories in rural areas where it had engaged in "mass struggles." The 1952 elections, which followed the insurrectionist period of 1948–1951 so closely, were to provide subject

[11] For a list of those purged from the party in West Bengal for failing to support the insurrectionist line wholeheartedly, see *The Statesman*, February 4, 1949. A more complete discussion of the numerous disputes within the CPI during the early years of Independence is provided in Jean A. Curran, Jr., "Dissension among India's Communists," *Far Eastern Survey* 19 (July 1950): 132–136.

matter for protracted state and national party debate for at least the next decade.

The debates within the CPI in West Bengal in the 1950s took place in an environment in which the national party was dominated by a vacillating and divided leadership led by Ajoy Ghosh, torn between various factional and regional groupings within the communist movement in India, and frequently uncertain of its stance in international communist disputes. While Ghosh was always able to effect some form of compromise that kept the CPI from an open split, he could do this only by allowing a great deal of independence to local units and by almost constant recourse to international Communist authorities centered in Moscow and in England. An understanding of the factionalism that plagued the CPI in the 1950s must therefore take into account the significant role played by the CPSU and CPGB throughout this decade.

Ajoy Ghosh became general secretary of the national CPI on June 1, 1951, on the basis of support from Moscow relayed to CPI members through an open letter written by R. Palme Dutt of the CPGB.[12] Dutt argued that the insurrectionist policy of the Zhdanov era had been premature and that while revolution in India might eventually have to take the form of an armed struggle, this could only be done when the party was strong enough to pursue it to final victory. For the present, Dutt argued, the Indian government was well established, and the CPI would have to formulate party strategy on the assumption that the Congress government in India was not about to lose control. Dutt then proceeded to point to "new opportunities" for the CPI to influence political developments in India. Congress, he argued, was composed of two groups, one seeking outright alignment with the British and the Americans and therefore opposed to world socialism, the other inclining toward a more cautious policy. While he saw the Congress party government as being generally representative of big business interests, this did not necessarily mean that either the government or the Indian bourgeoisie would support "Anglo-American

---

[12] Dutt's letter is analyzed and quoted extensively in M. R. Masani, *The Communist Party of India* (London: Derek Verschoyle, 1954), pp. 108–111. Minoo R. Masani was a joint secretary of the Congress Socialist party (CSP) in the 1930s, during the period when the CSP was allied with the CPI. As a result of this experience Masani became bitterly anticommunist and has played a major role in the work of the Democratic Research Service (DRS) of India, which has published a number of CPI inner-party documents. Two of the volumes published by the DRS are standard collections on the Third and Fourth party congresses (held at Madurai in 1953 and Palghat in 1956). See *Communist Conspiracy at Madurai* (Bombay: Democratic Research Service, 1953) and *Communist Double-Talk at Palghat* (Bombay: Democratic Research Service, 1956).

imperialism." The Indian government, in Dutt's view, was oscillating, and it was the duty of the CPI to convince it to take an increasingly anti-British and anti-American stance. Dutt's letter was supported by a number of other statements and articles emanating from Moscow at about the same time.[13]

The thrust of the arguments of the CPGB and the CPSU in the early 1950s was to convince the CPI that it should ally itself in "close collaboration" with the bourgeoisie, forming "a bloc or even an alliance" with bourgeois organizations if necessary.[14] This policy, which was pursued with some modifications throughout the 1950s, was similar to the united-front line of 1935–1939, when the CPI entered the Congress Socialist party and eventually took over a number of former Congress organizations. In the 1930s the CPI had been asked to mobilize against fascism; in the 1950s it was asked to mobilize against the Western powers.[15] The Soviet Union, which was the principal instigator of the policy in both instances, was acting in the 1950s out of a profound appreciation of Nehru's neutralism, which after Stalin's death the USSR came more and more to see as an opportunity either to draw India into the communist camp or to isolate it from the Western bloc. Friendship between Nehru and the Soviet Union grew after 1953: Nehru, Bulganin, and Khrushchev exchanged visits in 1954 and 1955; Nehru's books were translated into Russian and reviewed critically but favorably; even Gandhi's role in the early period of Indian nationalism was praised in Soviet journals; and by 1956 Soviet spokesmen were approving not only Nehru's foreign policy (neutralism) but also much of his domestic program (socialism and planning). Following Nehru's visit to Moscow, large-scale aid programs and trade agreements were signed, the USSR made a gift of a Soviet passenger aircraft to serve as Nehru's personal transport plane, and hundreds of cultural delegations each year began to travel between

[13] A major review of Soviet policy toward India was undertaken at a meeting of the Institute of Asian Studies of the Soviet Academy of Sciences in November 1951, as a result of which E. M. Zhukov wrote an article that has since been regarded as the first systematic statement of a major turning point in Soviet attitudes toward free India. See E. M. Zhukov, "O kharaktere i osobennostiakh narodnoi demokratii v stranakh vostove" [On the Character and Attributes of People's Democracy in the Countries of Asia], *Izvestia Akademii Nauk SSSR, Seria Istorii i Filosofii* 9 (January–February 1952): 80–87, quoted in Gene D. Overstreet, "Soviet and Communist Policy in India," *Journal of Politics* 20 (February 1958): 191–192.

[14] Zhukov, "O kharaktere . . . ," p. 86. For the overall revision of Soviet foreign policy in the last years of Stalin's rule, see Marshall Shulman, *Stalin's Foreign Policy Reappraised* (Cambridge: Harvard University Press, 1963).

[15] The comparison to the earlier united-front period is made explicit in R. Palme Dutt, *The Way Forward for the Countries within the Sphere of British Imperialism* (Calcutta: National Book Agency, 1955), pp. 31 ff.

New Delhi and the communist capitals of the Soviet Union and Eastern Europe.

To the extent that the CPI cooperated with the new policy of the Soviet Union, it was increasingly forced to moderate its attitudes toward the Nehru government and the Congress party. And the central leadership of the CPI, lacking any agreement on alternative strategies, eventually had recourse to Soviet strategy on almost every issue. In the early 1950s Ajoy Ghosh evolved a policy that allowed the party to shift the focus of its activities to the state level, making it possible for it to soften its attacks on the central government while addressing itself to local issues and appealing to regional emotions and interests.[16] By November 1954 the Central Executive Committee of the party had voted to abandon the foreign policy stance adopted in 1948, and party units were asked to cease referring to Nehru as "the lackey of the British" and to his foreign policy as dictated by "imperialists." Party members were also instructed to join in celebrations of Independence Day and Republic Day and to stop organizing "Quit-Commonwealth" movements.[17] By the time of the Fourth Party Congress at Palghat (April 1956), the central leadership of the party had moved toward a recognition not only of the positive aspects of Nehru's foreign policy but also toward a relatively favorable assessment of some Congress government domestic programs.[18] Two years later, at the Fifth Party Congress at Amritsar (March–April 1958), the CPI followed the lead given by Khrushchev at the Twentieth Congress of the CPSU in 1956 and committed itself publicly to constitutional communism, the "peaceful transition to socialism."[19]

The intellectual leadership of the CPI in West Bengal—Bhowani Sen, Somnath Lahiri, and others—sided with Ajoy Ghosh and the central leadership of the party throughout the 1950s, either defending CEC decisions and the CPSU in party meetings or abstaining on crucial votes in order to preserve a semblance of party unity. But the leadership of the organizational apparatus gradually became allied with the electoralists in opposition to central party directives. In what was somewhat of a misnomer, the intellectuals in the state party were

---

[16] This shift in focus is traced out in some detail in Overstreet, "Soviet and Communist Policy in India," p. 199, and is analyzed at length in Selig S. Harrison, "The Dilemma of the CPI," *Problems of Communism* 8 (March–April 1959): 27–35.

[17] Randolph Carr, "Conflicts within the Indian CP," *Problems of Communism* 4 (September–October 1955): 11.

[18] Marshall Windmiller, "Constitutional Communism in India," *Pacific Affairs* 31 (March 1958): 26.

[19] Gene D. Overstreet, "The Communists and India," *Foreign Policy Bulletin*, November 1, 1959, pp. 29–31.

generally dubbed the Right faction, while those opposed to central party directives were labeled as leftists. Actually, the faction headed by the state's older intellectuals did not always opt for a classical Right Communist strategy; what tied it together was its mutual interest in maintaining the backing of the CPSU. Similarly, the Left faction contained some members who advocated a classic Left Communist strategy, but they were by no means in a majority. Most of the members of the Left faction agreed with R. Palme Dutt and others that the insurrectionist policy of the Zhdanov era had been premature, but they did not conclude, as Dutt did, that this necessitated an alliance with bourgeois forces, particularly with the Congress. Like the Andhra Communists, who began to argue in 1951 that the insurrectionist policy of the Zhdanov era had indicated the great potential of the Indian peasantry for revolutionary movements, the Left faction in West Bengal was initially interested only in exploring the relevance of the Chinese communist movement as an alternative to the CPSU model.

A number of reasons can be adduced for the inclination of the CPI organization in West Bengal to adopt either a classic Left Communist or a "neo-Maoist" strategy in the 1950s.[20] For many people the geographic location of West Bengal after Independence suggested the possibility of guerrilla warfare and large-scale peasants' and workers' organizations that could be mobilized for revolutionary activities. West Bengal borders on two foreign nations (East Pakistan and Nepal) and on two border kingdoms (Sikkim and Bhutan) that are nominally independent but are tied by treaties and subsidies to India, and it is less than thirty miles from Tibetan China. At one point in Darjeeling District the "Siliguri corridor," only fourteen miles wide, connects the main portions of India with its northeastern states and territories (Assam, Northeast Frontier area, Nagaland, Manipur, and Tripura). Moreover, much of this area consists of mountainous and hilly terrain, covered with jungles and dotted with rivers, marshes, and swamps, an area particularly difficult to cross during the monsoons. A large part of the population of West Bengal (25.7 percent according to the 1961 census) belongs to scheduled tribes and castes that consist for the most part of landless day laborers and plantation workers, and another large part of the population

[20] The Bengali Communists' understanding of the classic Right and Left Communist strategies, as well as the "neo-Maoist" or "Maoist Right" strategy, will be explored in detail in Chapters 6, 7, and 8. For a concise description of the three strategies as ideal types, see Donald S. Zagoria, "Communist Policy and the Struggle for Developing Countries," *Proceedings of the Academy of Political Science* 28 (April 1965): 69–73.

(almost 17 percent in 1961) lives in cities of 50,000 people or more, all of which are overcrowded with international refugees. Large portions of Calcutta and the metropolitan area that extends up and down the Hooghly River are as squalid and lacking in public facilities as any urban slum in the world.

The possibility of guerrilla warfare in West Bengal in the 1950s was diminished, of course, by a number of factors, including the lack of weapons available to politically interested groups and the presence of highly skilled and extremely loyal administrative, police, and military services in the Indian and West Bengal governments. Most party leaders could therefore agree that the CPI was not ready to launch a guerrilla movement, but a small segment of the party did argue for a strategy that would provide some training for future guerrilla activities in key areas of the state. While information about such activities is almost impossible to acquire, it is an open secret that the party in West Bengal did maintain some "tech cells" (technical cells) in the period before 1954, in which party members were given experience in stimulating peasant revolts, trained in guerrilla techniques, and educated for recruitment drives in the more remote regions of the state and in the northeastern portions of India.[21] Both the government of India and the government of Pakistan have on occasion arrested Communist party members on the suspicion that they were again preparing for such activities,[22] but it is more than likely that guerrilla units trained by the CPI or by the CPM no longer exist, or if they do exist, they have either not progressed very far or are an unusually closely guarded secret.

Reasons that are much less speculative can be adduced for the inclination of West Bengal's CPI leadership toward Left communism or neo-Maoism in the 1950s. In many ways the attitude of the state

[21] Several former party members interviewed in 1968–1970 mentioned the existence of "tech cells" in the years following Independence, but all of them agreed that such cells had ceased to exist in the united CPI in 1954. In April 1969 a portion of the Left faction in West Bengal established the Communist party of India–Marxist-Leninist, or CPML, which has as its avowed goal a guerrilla strategy on the lines of Mao Tse-tung's. The activities of the CPML are discussed in detail in Chapter 6.

[22] In July 1960, for example, President Ayub Khan of Pakistan issued a series of statements from East Bengal claiming that Communists "operating out of Calcutta" were carrying on a campaign for "a weak federal structure, Parliamentary democracy, too many provinces, and an ineffective government for Pakistan." Ayub justified his arrests of Communists by arguing that South Asian Communists eventually hoped to wage a guerrilla war to realize "their desire to organize a state under their control comprising Assam, West Bengal, and East Pakistan." See *The Statesman*, July 26, 1960. Essentially the same justifications were used for arrests of Communists by Yahya Khan in 1969. For a similar report emanating from the Home Ministry in New Delhi, see the *Hindusthan Standard*, May 3, 1964.

leadership can be viewed as a negative reaction to central party directives rather than a positive attraction to guerrilla warfare. Most of the former terrorists in the CPI in West Bengal entered the communist movement because of a serious and deep-seated disenchantment with electoral politics, motivated by opposition to the Congress party and by resentment of the non-Bengali business interests and landed gentry that dominated the Congress in the state. That the CPI in West Bengal should be asked to soften its attitude toward Nehru and the Congress was therefore personally galling to many Communist leaders, and particularly to former terrorists. Moreover, a more moderate policy toward Nehru and the Congress party ran the risk of alienating many Communist supporters in the state, particularly among the urban middle-class and *bhadralok* refugees from East Bengal. In contrast to most other areas of India, in West Bengal the CPI has always had to worry about the possibility of the Marxist Left parties' cutting into Communist support by becoming more militant on issues that affect middle-class elites. In this atmosphere, the experience of the CPI in West Bengal between 1947 and 1952 was sufficient to convince both former terrorists and electoralists that militant, mass agitational movements were the key to future electoral victories in West Bengal, while alliance with the Congress could only lead to the eventual entrapment of the CPI in the web of Congress bourgeois democracy.

Because of their mutual opposition to alliance with the Congress, the former terrorists and the electoralists in the state party were able to unite in resistance to the central leadership's attempts to moderate the CPI stance toward Nehru and the Congress party. At the Third Party Congress of the CPI in Madurai (December 1953), most of the delegates from West Bengal joined with the delegates from Andhra in abstaining from the vote on the political resolution placed before the Congress, indicating their disagreement with the strategy that had been outlined by the Central Committee.[23] Throughout the 1950s the leadership of the state organization continued to oppose CEC formulations, for the most part effectively enough to obtain some compromises. The problem that plagued the dissidents from West Bengal and Andhra, however, was their own lack of agreement on an alternative strategy. In the words of one of the members of the State Committee at this time, who was interviewed in June 1969: "We always knew very clearly what we did not want, in a negative way, but we could never agree on what we did want—on a positive program." As a result of internal divisions, the party in West Bengal was unable even

---

[23] Carr, "Conflicts within the Indian CP," p. 10.

to propose an alternative to the policies of the Central Committee, and the leaders of the electoral and Left factions therefore followed the party line rather halfheartedly while devoting themselves to strengthening their own factional positions in the state.

Membership Recruitment and the Decline of the Right Faction

The declining influence of the West Bengal Right Communist faction in the 1950s and 1960s is related to a host of factors, but mainly to the inability of the intellectuals to maintain their previous sources of party support. The intellectual leadership of the communist movement in West Bengal derived its strength from its ability to attract students in the colleges of Bengal (and in England) in the 1930s and 1940s, but the nature of the student leadership recruited by communists in the last two decades has changed considerably. Bengali students who entered the communist movement after 1947 increasingly gravitated to the electoral organizations and to the Left faction. Both the nature of student politics in independent West Bengal and the activities of the Communists themselves have determined these developments.

Most party leaders agree that the colleges of West Bengal continued throughout the 1950s to provide a larger number of new party members than any other source; estimates range upward of 40 or 50 percent of total recruits each year. In this respect West Bengal appears to be somewhat unusual, since the role of colleges as a source of Communist party recruitment has apparently been declining elsewhere in India.[24] Political activities on the part of college students in other parts of India have been affected by the attitudes of India's political leadership toward student demands, since activities that in the pre-Independence period were considered indications of "loyalty and devotion to the nation's cause" suddenly in 1947 became manifestations of "rowdyism" and "anti-social behaviour" in the eyes of many politicians (and particularly those in the ruling Congress party). Much of the thrust of governmental, parental, and educational authority has therefore been directed toward a depoliticization of student life, and a number of Indian college and governmental officials have been involved in attempts to dissociate student activities from the work of political party organizations.[25]

[24] Based on interviews with Communist leaders in New Delhi, Kerala, Bombay, and Madras in 1962–1964 and 1968–1970.

[25] Perhaps the best statement of the official position is the *Report on the Problem of Student Indiscipline in Indian Universities* (New Delhi: University Grants Commission, 1960).

While this factor has been operative in West Bengal since Independence, its effect on student politics has been blunted by a number of countervailing forces. Student movements in West Bengal have received considerable support from political parties and influential individuals—even from the Congress party[26]—because there is a widespread feeling in West Bengal that the plight of the student population is merely a reflection of the declining power and cultural significance of the entire Bengali region. Indicative of this decline is the dramatic shift that has taken place since Independence in recruitment to the Indian Administrative Service (IAS, formerly the Indian Civil Service). In 1948 Calcutta University ranked second only to Madras among the five major universities responsible for more than two-thirds of India's IAS candidates, but by 1960 Calcutta no longer even ranked in the top five; it had been replaced by the major universities in Delhi and in Punjab.[27] In this atmosphere Bengali political and social leadership has been reluctant to blame student demonstrations on "rowdyism" and "indiscipline" and has often sided with the students in order to draw attention to the educational needs of the state. On a number of occasions teacher and student groups in Calcutta have even joined in making demands on the central and state governments, and both teachers and college administrators have actively recruited Bengali students into political movements.[28]

Outside West Bengal the Calcutta student body has gained a reputation for being "flamboyantly undisciplined and violent," and the Communist and Marxist Left parties have often been blamed by national politicians, educators, and observers alike for the militancy

[26] Student unions led by the Communist All-India Student Federation (AISF) in Calcutta, for example, have built a Health Home for students and a number of hostels, all with financial support from Calcutta University, Calcutta Corporation (even when it was dominated by the Congress), membership donations, and private contributions. See Myron Weiner, *The Politics of Scarcity: Public Pressure and Political Response in India* (Chicago: University of Chicago Press, 1962), p. 168. For other evidence of supportive feelings collected by a Bengali Member of Parliament and former central government minister, see Humayun Kabir, *Student Unrest: Causes and Cure* (Calcutta: Orient Book Company, 1958).

[27] R. K. Trivedi and D. N. Rao, "Regular Recruits to the Indian Administrative Service," *Journal of the National Academy of Administration* 5 (July 1960): 52–80, and "Higher Civil Service in India: A Sample Survey," ibid., vol. 6 (July 1961): 33–64. Quoted in Joseph R. Gusfield, "The Academic Milieu: Students and Teachers in India and the United States," in *Turmoil and Transition: Higher Education and Student Politics in India*, ed. Philip G. Altbach (Calcutta: Lalvani Publishing House, 1968), p. 119.

[28] "Bengal Provincial Students' Federation Celebrates Silver Jubilee," *New Age* (CPI weekly), October 11, 1964, p. 6; see also *A Brochure on Police Action in Raja Peary Mohan College* (Uttarpara: Raja Peary Mohan College Teachers' Council, 1967), pp. 1–14.

and volatility of Bengali student life.[29] At the same time, however, many Communist and Marxist Left party leaders, particularly the intellectuals in the movement, have themselves been concerned with the changes that have taken place in Bengali student politics, and especially with the decline in the *quality* of the students whom the leftists have been able to attract (a decline frankly admitted both by party leaders and by educators). In the 1930s and 1940s the Communists had a reputation for attracting many of the best students in the colleges and universities, and the party made a special effort to encourage this by tutoring students who had fallen behind in their studies because of party involvement and by providing informal guidance programs for students with personal and family problems, as well as study circles during examination periods.[30] Communist parties still engage in such activities, perhaps more so now than before Independence, but for a variety of reasons the academic excellence of students involved in the communist movement has dropped. Since Independence the Communists have been much more heavily involved in agitational activities than they were in the 1930s and early 1940s, and students have been increasingly used by the parties both to mobilize and to take part in Communist demonstrations. Such activities are not only distracting for students; perhaps more important, they appeal to entirely different kinds of student activists than the ones who joined the party before Independence. Moreover, the idealistic students of the thirties, who were interested in intellectual pursuits and frequently inspired by the nationalist movement and by the writings of Marxism-Leninism, have now given way to a student body disillusioned with events since partition and particularly with the diminishing opportunities for educated Bengalis compared with the college-trained in other parts of India.

In this atmosphere many of the better students (and there is some evidence that this is particularly true for those in the sciences and in engineering) have consistently refused to have anything to do with politics, and it is likely that most students are fundamentally opposed to the present structure of political authority.[31] Some students may take

---

[29] For comparisons of the AISF in Calcutta and elsewhere, see Philip G. Altbach, "Student Politics and Higher Education in India," in *Turmoil and Transition*, p. 47.

[30] See Philip G. Altbach, *Student Politics in Bombay* (Calcutta: Asia Publishing House, 1968), p. 127, for a description of the communist student movement in the pre-Independence period.

[31] These generalizations emerge from my own interviews with 108 college graduates in Calcutta in 1963–1964; see "Perceived Images of Political Authority among College Graduates in Calcutta," in *Urban Bengal*, ed. Richard L. Park (East Lansing: Michigan State University Occasional Papers on South Asia, 1969), pp. 87–116.

a great interest in political affairs—even in Marxism, Maoism, and communism—and many of them may also take part in agitational activities and demonstrations, but in doing so an increasing number of them prefer to work outside the context of the existing party structure, since in their view *all* of the present political parties are "corrupt and self-seeking, the Communists and the Congress included."[32] Those who do join political parties frequently do so only to secure financial support and publication facilities for the student organizations they lead, but they too are often critical of a political system in which they are forced to ally with parties for which they have little respect.

Throughout the 1950s the intellectuals in the CPI attempted to deal with such disillusionment by involving students in a wide variety of activities, ranging from participation in mass movements to study circles, constructive work, and international student conferences. By the late 1950s there was no student demand that had not been championed by the Communists at one time or another, and on the whole the party had been generous in providing students with funds and facilities for their national, state, and international projects. In addition to agitational activities, Communist students in West Bengal have constructed a Health Home for students in Calcutta, built a number of small libraries and hostels, established primary schools, and participated in numerous relief programs, all with party support. Most of these projects have been undertaken by the All-India Students Federation (AISF), which has dominated student politics in Bengal until recent times. Between 1947 and 1959 the AISF controlled the majority of the student unions on Bengali campuses in every year except 1956, when the Congress student federation was temporarily able to win leadership positions in a majority of them,[33] but since 1959 the increasing factionalism within the communist movement has led to serious splits in the AISF, with a consequent decline in the hegemony of any one Communist student faction.

It is clear, however, that the Right faction in the state communist movement has suffered the greatest losses in terms of student support. Whereas the older intellectual leaders in the movement dominated almost all the student unions on Bengali campuses before Independence,[34] by 1969–1970 Right faction student groups (those supporting

---

[32] For an excellent study of student politics in three Calcutta colleges, in which relations with political parties are described in detail, see an unpublished manuscript by Jaladhar Hazra, "Undergraduate Students and Politics in Calcutta."

[33] *The Statesman*, January 17, 1959.

[34] For a short history of the student movement in pre-Independence Bengal, see Amarendra Nath Roy, *Students Fight for Freedom* (Calcutta: Gupta Bhaya, 1967).

the postsplit CPI) could gain a majority on only 10 of 153 campuses, while other Communist student groups controlled 107 of the remaining unions, either in coalition with one another or in coalition with other noncommunist groups.[35] Support for the CPSU and the CPGB, the dominant theme of the Right faction, has had little appeal for students increasingly conscious of conflicting regional and national interests, while the Right faction strategy of allying with "progressive elements in the Congress" has been even less successful in evoking a positive response. Students who have participated in politics since Independence have been much more concerned with immediate demands (particularly jobs and degrees) than with ideology, and they have therefore preferred to work with the most militant parties and groups.

Agitational Politics and the Left Faction

The Left Communist faction in West Bengal has appealed to new party members precisely because it has been more militant than the Right faction, and its militance has in turn made it possible for Left faction leaders to dominate the state party organization. In the period before the split in 1964 the leadership of the Left faction was centered in the headquarters of the state party, dominated by the staff of the state party organization headed by Pramode Das Gupta. Before 1958 the people who staffed the headquarters in Calcutta were in theory subordinate to the state party secretary, the State Politbureau, and the State Committee of the party, all of which were in theory elected by delegates from local cells who met every other year in a state party conference. After the Amritsar party congress in 1958, "cells" came to be designated as "branches," the size of state (and central) party committees was enlarged, and the nomenclature for these committees was changed in keeping with the transition to constitutional communism. On paper the staff of the state party headquarters then became subordinate to a state party secretary, who was now assisted by a Secretariat (instead of a Politbureau), a State Committee, and a new body of approximately one hundred members, which was called the State Council of the party. As in the previous organizational structure, each of these committees was now elected by delegates from the state party "branches" meeting in conference every other year.[36]

In practice, however, the staff of the organizational headquarters in Calcutta dominated the party throughout the 1950s and has

[35] *The Statesman*, April 18, 1969, and May 1, 1969. See also the *Hindusthan Standard*, April 9, 1969, and the *Times of India* (New Delhi), November 11, 1969.

[36] The organizational changes in the CPI in 1958 are described in Gene D. Overstreet and Marshall Windmiller, *Communism in India* (Berkeley: University of California Press, 1959), pp. 540–546.

continued to exert enormous influence as a faction within the CPM since the split in 1964. The party secretary from 1951 until 1959 was Jyoti Basu, whose involvement in legislative politics left him little time for organizational work, and who therefore delegated his authority to members of his staff headquartered in Calcutta. Since both the state and central offices were located in Calcutta from 1947 until 1952, and since Basu was also very much involved in central party affairs during these years, it would have been impossible for him to have devoted much of his time to the state party organizational apparatus without neglecting his work in the legislature, in the electoral machinery, and in the Central Executive Committee. The organizational apparatus therefore came to be controlled by the staff of the party headquarters in Calcutta, headed by Pramode Das Gupta, and in 1959 Das Gupta's position was formally recognized when he was elected state party secretary in place of Basu.

Pramode Das Gupta was born in 1910, the son of a Sub-Assistant Surgeon in the Bengal Provincial Medical Service, in Barisal District of what is now East Pakistan. He entered politics in 1930, when he joined the Anushilan Samity as a college student, and spent most of the 1930s in various jails and detention camps.[37] Das Gupta joined the Communist consolidation movement in the jails fairly early, was put in charge of the party's underground technical apparatus when he was temporarily released from prison in 1935, but was rearrested in 1936 and sent to the Hijli detention camp (in Midnapore District of West Bengal) until the British released almost all of the members of the CPI in 1942. At Hijli, Das Gupta was in charge of the CPI Jail Committee. He advanced in standing within the party when he successfully arranged for the escape of two leading underground party members (Panchu Gopal Bhaduri and Nripen Chakravarty). Upon his release in 1942 he was put in charge of the party's anti–Fifth Column activities in Bengal and the Northeast Frontier area, working with American and British military intelligence units to gather information on Indian political parties opposing the war effort.[38] Das Gupta and Khoka Roy (who rose to prominence as a Communist leader in East Bengal

[37] Data on Pramode Das Gupta was obtained from a variety of interviews and other sources, but I am especially indebted to a colleague in Calcutta for the use of a biographical sketch on Das Gupta which he compiled through interviews. Our understanding of communism in Bengal will be greatly enriched when it becomes possible for this colleague to publish the rich store of materials he has collected.

[38] For a nationalist description of the CPI's anti–Fifth Column campaign during World War II, see V. B. Sinha, *The Red Rebel in India: A Study of Strategy and Tactics* (New Delhi: Associated Publishing House, 1968), pp. 33 ff. A CPI anthology of articles and poems published during the campaign is contained in *Anti-Fascist Traditions of Bengal* (Calcutta: Indo-GDR Friendship Society, 1970), pp. 45–104.

after partition) were especially active during World War II in recruiting and training party members for specialized intelligence work that could be used by the British and in training other party units in guerrilla warfare and sabotage. Many of these activities were supported (and sometimes sponsored) by the British government in India because of their potential usefulness in the event of an occupation of Indian territory by the Japanese (or by the Indian National Army of Subhas Bose).[39] After Independence Das Gupta became aligned with Jyoti Basu and Muzaffar Ahmad in a leadership struggle against the Right faction, as a result of which Basu became party secretary (in 1951) and Das Gupta was placed in unquestioned control of the party headquarters and the underground apparatus.

As has been indicated previously, the organization that Das Gupta created in the 1950s was similar in structure to the Anushilan Samity, the largest of the old Bengali terrorist organizations, in which Das Gupta and many of his most trusted subordinates had been introduced to politics. Party committees were organized in each of the districts in Bengal, theoretically by holding elections at conferences of delegates representing the cells in the districts. In practice the party had a large membership only in the five southern districts and in Calcutta, and the committees from the other districts of West Bengal were simply co-opted from among party members who were known and trusted by the leadership around Das Gupta. Elections were held more frequently in districts where there was a large party membership, but even here the state leadership played an important part in determining the makeup of the district organizations, since the headquarters of the state party in Calcutta was responsible for organizing district conferences, proposing slates of candidates, and assigning tasks to district secretaries and committees once they were elected. So far as state party members are concerned, democratic centralism has meant the unquestioned authority of state party leadership, to which they are accountable and which is theoretically responsible to them. With the exception of organized factions that became active in the party after the Sino-Indian skirmishes in 1962, the membership of the state party has been loyal to the state leadership rather than to the Central Committees of the party: members have obeyed central party directives when orders to do so have been issued by state head-

---

[39] British attempts to cope with Fifth Column activities in Bengal during World War II (especially those of Subhas Bose and the Forward Bloc) are described in Edgar Snow, *Glory and Bondage* (Bombay: Thacker, 1944), pp. 33–36, 48–53, 257–259. For a description of Indian Communist training in guerrilla warfare during World War II, see Overstreet and Windmiller, *Communism in India*, pp. 205–206.

quarters, but the central leadership of the party has not succeeded in bypassing the state leadership and going directly to the party membership in local areas.

The enormous influence of the Left faction leadership clustered around Das Gupta is due largely to the nature of the activities in which the party has been engaged since 1951, most of which have necessitated the organization of large numbers of people for agitational purposes. The Communists have not initiated all of the mass demonstrations that have taken place in West Bengal since Independence, but they have been able to exploit spontaneous demonstrations and those initiated by other parties in ways that have not been possible for other political organizations within the state. Moreover, the demonstrations that have been initiated by the Communists or taken over by them have invariably been the best organized and the most effective over the course of the past two decades.

Owing to a number of factors, organizing a political party that can exploit the tactic of mass demonstrations in an environment like West Bengal's since 1947 is a complex and difficult task. The police and administrative services have had a great deal of experience with mass action over the course of the last half century, and the intelligence and security branches of the state government have been imaginative and skillful in devising means for collecting information on political activists.[40] Especially in Calcutta, regularized procedures have been established for controlling crowds as large as half a million people or more, procedures that have generally favored the administration and the police in any confrontation with demonstrators. The courts, on the other hand, have defended the rights of citizens as sedulously as they do in most Western democracies, but because of the nature of the judiciary and the heavy load it carries, the actions of the courts have been more effective in securing redress of grievances by individual citizens than in altering day-to-day operations of government.

In addition to the problems posed by the administrative structure and the police, potential agitators who have attempted to organize on a large scale have been confronted with a host of problems that derive from the nature of the social structure. Most people in West Bengal remain deeply committed to a hierarchical social system in which authority relations between individuals and classes are well defined, in which the area of legitimate individual ambitions and

---

[40] For an excellent analysis of Congress government strategy and the role of the police in curbing violent movements in West Bengal, see Myron Weiner, "Violence and Politics in Calcutta," *Journal of Asian Studies* 20 (May 1961): 275–281. See also Bayley, *The Police and Political Development in India*, pp. 248 ff.

aspirations is carefully circumscribed, and in which the weight of almost all symbols of authority is on the side of obedience to caste, family, and village superiors. This pattern is reinforced by the wide economic gap between the low-caste cultivators and laborers on the one hand and the nonlaboring *bhadralok* on the other. As much as some members of the CPI (and other parties, including the Congress) have tried to break this pattern of relationships, they have been unable to do so in all but a few cases, with the result that agitational activities (like most other large-scale activities) have had to be organized in ways that are consistent with the existing structure of authority in Bengali society. The ability of the Communists to take advantage of movements initiated elsewhere has depended to an even greater extent on the capacity of the leadership to avoid coming into conflict with the formal and informal authority patterns that have confronted the Communists in the noncommunist movements they have sought to capture.

In this atmosphere it is not surprising that the Communists were initially much more successful in organizing the urban middle class— middle-class trade unions, teachers, students, engineers, and so forth— than they were in organizing either the peasantry or the poorer factory laborers.[41] Since the leadership of the CPI was drawn almost entirely from men of middle-class *bhadralok* origins, party leadership could define relations between leaders and led among the *bhadralok* more easily than when it had to deal with a following recruited from other social groups. The party did try at times to increase its influence among low-status groups by recruiting more and more of its lower-level leadership from among laborers and cultivators, but in this endeavor it met with a number of problems. The organization of the party in the 1950s was already top-heavy, and almost all leaders of the CPI now argue that there was little room in the organization for people aspiring to statewide positions unless the party expanded its sphere of operations considerably. In the 1950s the central leadership of the CPI did make efforts to turn it into "a truly mass party" by increasing the membership and by embarking on a number of new projects that demanded a larger membership.[42] But the state leadership of the CPI in West Bengal generally resisted expansion, arguing that it

---

[41] This discussion of party leadership is derived almost entirely from interviews with Communist and Marxist Left party members and leaders in 1968–1970. For a critical assessment of Communist leadership recruitment practices in West Bengal by a disenchanted Marxist, see Charan Gupta, "Calcutta Diary," *Frontier*, May 3, 1969, pp. 11–12.

[42] Overstreet and Windmiller, *Communism in India*, pp. 356 ff.

would mean less efficiency and perhaps even loss of control by state and central party committees. Moreover, expansion of the party was frequently associated with an electoral strategy, so that many state leaders therefore viewed it as a backhanded method of making the state party dependent on electoral politics.

Since recruitment of statewide leadership from among the laboring and agricultural classes in Bengal could be undertaken only by enlarging the party considerably or by going over the heads of high-caste Bengalis who stood in line for promotion to the top, such proposals met with great resentment in the united CPI. Moreover, recruitment among peasant cultivators and laborers might have led to the growth of a strong faction based on this new leadership, or at least might have deprived those who were established in the State Secretariat and State Council of some of their control over the party. For these reasons, too, state CPI leaders could not accept a large number of lower-caste cultivators and laborers into the higher councils of the party. State leaders also argue that low-status leadership was simply not forthcoming in the 1950s and that party members from low-status backgrounds did not have the requisite skills for state party leadership positions: people of low status were not able to read Hindi or English, they had little knowledge of areas beyond their own local regions, and they usually lacked interest in ideological and organizational matters. This may also be a significant factor in explaining the absence of people from low-status groups in the higher echelons of the state party, but it would be difficult to test this out without more research on members of the party who come from low-status backgrounds. At this point, however, it is clear that members of low-status groups are still not established in state party organizations and are seldom prominent even at the district level or below.

Because of CPI recruitment patterns, party movements that have involved low-status groups in West Bengal have depended on communication flows between men of high-status groups, usually centered in Calcutta, and the many low-status groups spread out over the state. These communication flows are made possible by a number of intervening brokers, who are either drawn from among high-status Bengalis who have befriended men of low status or from indigenous leaders of low-status groups who are trying to establish linkages between their own groups and a powerful state political organization. A small sample (35) of such brokers interviewed in 1969 consisted of the following types of individuals: (1) relief workers (usually of high status) who had endeared themselves to low-status groups because of their prominence in local relief activities; (2) trade union organizers of high status who supported the economic demands of union members, helped them with court cases or confrontations with the state bureaucracy, and secured party funds and publishing facilities for local trade union activities; (3) low-status leaders of tribal, village, and caste associations who had gone into opposition to the state government when rival low-status leaders had been favored with patronage dispensed by the Congress party; and (4) low-status leaders who had adopted *bhadralok* manners and customs and who viewed their involvement with intellectual Marxism as a sign of their "progressive and modern outlook on life." All of those interviewed were prominent in District Committees of the party, as well as branch units in villages, towns, or cities. None of these people was active in the statewide organs of the parties, although they all communicated with the state organizations for party purposes.

Regardless of whether political movements were staged by members of the middle class or by members of low-status groups during Congress rule, the leadership around Pramode Das Gupta was able to gain the compliance of other leaders in maintaining strict control over the people mobilized by the party. Operating in a democratic society and with a skilled administrative and police network, the Congress governments of West Bengal took the position that demonstrations and other agitational activities could not be completely repressed, but at the same time the state government established well-defined limits beyond which demonstrations were not allowed to go. The state government always argued that demonstrations had to be peaceful and nonviolent, but it did tolerate a fair amount of violence when its source could not be determined. Political parties could therefore organize even large-scale demonstrations so long as they could assure the state government that they would be peaceful, and so long as the state government was convinced that a demonstration that was originally planned as peaceful would not trigger mass violence. Before a demonstration would be allowed by the state government, political parties were often required to obtain licenses for the "use" of a park, a meeting ground, or more often for the large open space at the foot of Ochterlony Monument (now called the "Martyr's Column," or *Saheed Manir*) on the Calcutta *maidan*. Often government officials, police administrators, and the leaders of opposition parties would confer before a proposed demonstration was sanctioned.

In this atmosphere the CPI could pursue one of two major strategies, either of which could lead to various reactions on the part of those whom it sought to organize, and either of which would evoke a fairly predictable response from the state government. If the CPI (or any other group for that matter) sought to organize a large-scale movement that involved violence, the state government would invariably react with mass arrests of party members, usually carried out before the time appointed for the demonstrations and made possible by the West Bengal Security Act, the Preventive Detention Act, and, after 1962, by the Defence of India Rules. When the party sought to organize nonviolent demonstrations, it had to convince the state government that it had enough control over its own members and following to ensure the maintenance of a peaceful atmosphere, and at times the party was even asked by the government to promise that it would help to restore peace if sporadic violence should occur during the course of a demonstration. The party could promote violence on occasion, either by trying to take control of a sporadic and publicly supported outburst that had caught the state government unaware or by retaliating against "police brutality" when it had sufficient public support to make the state government wary of repression. In both of these cases, however, the party always risked the possibility that the state government would react to violence by placing a large number of its members in jail.

Under these circumstances it is not surprising that state party leaders and members (regardless of their factional interests) felt it necessary to maintain strict control over agitational activities during the period when the Congress was in power in the state. Since party control could only be assured by the existence of a disciplined cadre loyal to a small and cohesive leadership, decisions to initiate a demonstration or to attempt to capture the leadership of a demonstration were always made at the highest levels. Moreover, only a few leaders at the state and district levels of the party were briefed on overall strategy, with other key individuals being briefed only on the activities in which they were to be instrumental. The vast majority of party members played lesser roles in demonstrations, receiving their directions from people who were established in the leadership structure and being expected to carry out particular assigned tasks.

The need for organizational control in staging agitational activities was especially great when large-scale demonstrations were planned in Calcutta, for such demonstrations involved the coordination of a number of different mass organizations and opposition party organizations, many of whose followers came from the most depressed low-status groups of society.[43] Large-scale mobilization of these people not only

[43] This discussion depends mainly on interviews, but see also "Demonstrations: How to Stage Them," *The Statesman*, July 10, 1966.

involved the danger that they might become uncontrollable in a mob, it also placed on the party the responsibility of caring for them and transporting them to and from their homes. Big demonstrations, therefore, had to be planned well in advance, and this involved a large number of organizers at the lower levels. The call for a demonstration had to be made through party organs, circulars, pamphlets, and handouts, and the issues had to be publicized in as many newspapers as possible throughout the state. Party meetings had to be held at the lower levels to explain selected aspects of the program, to establish quotas of people to be mobilized by each unit in a given area, and to assign tasks. Each of the party units had to hold "gate meetings," in which party members in the organization contacted members in mass organizations at factory gates (from which the name derives), at college entrances, or in the fields and assigned duties and personal quotas. Meetings had to be organized at street corners, markets, and other public places to solicit funds and to test the extent of public support, and large-scale poster and leaflet campaigns initiated. District units had to be given subsidies for transportation to get demonstrators into Calcutta and other cities and voluntary and *para* (neighborhood) organizations had to be contacted to supply food for out-of-town demonstrators. Transportation to and from rallying points in the city had to be arranged. In short, the large-scale agitational movements that were so characteristic of West Bengal during Congress rule required a great deal of coordination, and the need for such coordination facilitated the growth of the leadership that controlled the organizational apparatus.

The need for a tightly organized cadre loyal to a small, elitist leadership is greatest during a demonstration, for there is always the risk that events will get out of hand. Therefore, the party in West Bengal usually established a clear division of labor within each unit and between the various units that were involved in the demonstration. Some people were designated to lead in the shouting of slogans, others were responsible for maintaining order, and still others were charged with the task of supervising "retaliation against police brutality" in the event of violence. In each participating unit there were also a few leaders (usually a leader and auxiliary leaders, who could take charge in the event of the arrest of the original leadership) who were responsible for the overall behavior of the unit. These people were expected to communicate with the leaders of other units and to direct the people within their own unit to follow instructions relayed by the leadership in charge of the entire demonstration. In practice, of course, chains of command frequently broke down, but the organization of demonstrations in this manner assured the party of more control over its agitational activities than might otherwise have been possible.

In an area like West Bengal, which has witnessed mass agitational movements and mass violence for more than half a century, there are a great many people who are skilled in the techniques required for leading mass movements. But both political leaders and observers in West Bengal agree that the most highly skilled leaders of such movements are now in the Communist parties, either in the regular party organizations or in the mass organizations that are controlled by the parties. Because the organization headed by Pramode Das Gupta was able to recruit such people and to give them experience in a number of movements launched in the 1950s, he and the small, cohesive leadership around him were able to gain control of an apparatus capable of initiating large-scale agitational movements on a statewide basis. Other leaders, not associated with state party head-quarters, could gain control over parts of the state machinery—over portions of the electoral apparatus, party journals and newspapers, particular trade unions, a district Kisan Sabha, and so forth—but the leadership that was ensconced at party headquarters after 1951 had access to virtually all party units and activities and, more important, could coordinate the work of the various units in mobilizing vast numbers of people behind party programs. When the split occurred in 1964, most CPI leaders therefore joined with Das Gupta and the CPM, for to do otherwise was either to risk the destruction of the most effective instrument that had been developed by the state CPI or to cut themselves off from the use of that instrument.

The Independence of the Electoralists

Most of the electoral organizations in the communist movement in West Bengal have allied with the Left faction in the past, largely because of the importance of mass organizations and agitation in Communist electoral stategy. There are significant differences, however, in the kind of controls exercised by the leadership over the various types of organizational units, and the need for strict authority and discipline is not nearly so compelling in the case of the electoral organizations as it is for the party organs that depend on agitational activities. Communist peasant organizations, trade unions, and student groups are concerned primarily with the pro-motion of class conflict, with making groups militantly conscious of class differences in order that they might become more effective instruments for opposing the "designs" of landlords, businessmen, and other "vested interests." These groups judge their effectiveness by their ability to mobilize large numbers of people behind demands and slogans, and in doing so they are heavily dependent on the skilled organizers of the party apparatus. The electoral organizations, on the other hand, are concerned primarily with winning elections, and while agitational activities are sometimes helpful in this endeavor, they are at other times either unnecessary or harmful. The possibility of the electoral organizations' establishing themselves in positions relatively independent of the party apparatus are therefore greater, and the friction between them and the apparatus controlled by the party leadership has at times assumed sizable proportions.

The electoral machinery of the Communists in West Bengal is organized around Constituency Committees, usually fairly large in number (a hundred people or more), composed of relatives, friends, influential supporters, and workers of the principal Communist candidates in the constituency, who may or may not be party members. While the District Committees of the party assign some members or branch units to work in each constituency, and a Communist candidate (who is always a party member) is bound to accept such assignees, the candidate is usually free to select his own close associates and to allocate responsibility in any way he chooses. Party members assigned to candidates by District Committees may therefore be used or neglected, or sometimes even replaced, according to the wishes of the candidate and his associates in the Constituency Committee. The state leadership of the party exercises some influence over the Constituency Committees by providing them with publication facilities (for election pamphlets, posters, and so forth), by raising funds for candidates through local branch units, and by furnishing famous speakers (including national party leaders like E. M. S. Namboodiripad or S. A. Dange) and noted performers.[44] But these forms of control are much less direct than the party's control of mass agitational activities. Responsibility for initiating political acts in the electoral sphere is portioned out to the District and Constituency committees; the chain of command is much less clear in electoral organizations than it is in the case of mass organizations; and far more people become involved in making party decisions in the electoral sphere than elsewhere.

The state party apparatus in the united CPI did try to maintain strict party control over the electoral organizations and to tighten the chain of command between party headquarters in Calcutta and the Con-

---

[44] Perhaps the most successful performer the Communists have ever had in the elections was Utpal Dutta, the noted dramatist from Calcutta, who in the 1967 campaign wrote a play (which took the form of a Communist lawyer "trying" the Congress regime) that toured Bengali villages and towns on behalf of the CPM. See "The Drama in the Poll Battle," *People's Democracy*, February 19, 1967, p. 10.

stituency Committees spread across the state. The regular party organization retained the power to determine party nominees in each constituency, and candidates who did not work well with the party organization occasionally lost their nominations in succeeding elections.[45] The state leadership also rigidly enforced party rules requiring that a certain percentage of members' earnings in the legislatures and the ministries be given to the party and required that large electoral contributions be made over to party headquarters rather than to Constituency Committees. All of these factors did help the state leadership to maintain some degree of control over the electoral organizations and to isolate the few party leaders who tried to make themselves independent of the regular party apparatus.

But there were major conflicts between the electoral organizations and the state party headquarters in the united CPI, particularly on the issue of the use of party funds, and charges of misallocation frequently resulted in bitter personal attacks on the leadership by party members. Most members of the party now argue that Pramode Das Gupta and Jyoti Basu were the only leaders who had access to secret sources of state party wealth in the years 1951–1964 and that this placed them in a position where they could control and supervise the overall financial arrangements of the party. Because of the nature of party funding (which has never been fully revealed or explained),[46] and especially because the party found it necessary to keep sources of funds the most closely guarded of secrets *even within the party*, Das Gupta and Basu could always argue that they had good reason for maintaining strict control of party finances. But in the late 1950s a movement against Das Gupta was launched within the state party (led by Right faction leader Bhowani Sen and supported by a number of state CPI parliamentary and legislative leaders), as a result of which he was openly accused of using party funds to enhance his personal wealth.[47] The dissidents argued at that time that they would have no confidence in any investigation of these charges that

[45] In 1962, for example, the CPI candidate Mohammad Abdul Latif narrowly lost to the Congress candidate in Chanditala constituency in Hooghly District. Despite this he was forced out of the party as a result of a dispute with Pramode Das Gupta and in 1967 was opposed in Chanditala both by the CPI and by the CPM. After defeating both Communist candidates handily in 1967, Latif was subsequently given the support of the United Front in the 1969 elections, when he again ran as an independent candidate, but he was not accepted back in the ranks of either Communist party. (Based on interviews with Latif supporters in Hooghly in 1969.)

[46] A balanced discussion of CPI party finances appears in Overstreet and Windmiller, *Communism in India*, pp. 354–356. See also Peter Sager, *Moscow's Hand in India* (Berne: Swiss Eastern Institute, 1966) for the role of party publications as a source of Indian Communist funds.

[47] See Chapter 3, fn. 37.

was carried out either by Jyoti Basu or the Control Commission of the party, since Das Gupta's influence and power over party leaders who were dependent on him for their positions would affect the outcome. The dissidents therefore requested an investigation of state party funds by a three-man Central Secretariat Committee, proposing the names of Ajoy Ghosh, B. T. Ranadive, and P. C. Joshi, three highly respected national leaders representing the party's major factions.

Das Gupta's strength within the united CPI was indicated by the fact that nothing ever came of these proposals for an investigation of state party funds, despite widespread support for the dissidents. Indeed, Das Gupta has since been able to reinforce his position within the CPM, despite his continuing unpopularity with the membership. Many party members now describe Das Gupta as an extremely crude and rough-mannered man, who has a habit of shouting at almost everyone on the slightest pretext, and he is almost universally considered excessively bureaucratic in his handling of party affairs. The luxuries enjoyed both by Das Gupta and by Jyoti Basu (the use of a car, air-conditioning, trips to Darjeeling in the summer, a clean *dhoti* every day, cigars) are generally resented by members of the party who are convinced that the leadership has been paying itself more than it should. But while Basu is often forgiven for his style of living, Das Gupta is usually denounced. Basu comes from a wealthy family, has a law degree from the Middle Temple in London, and has married into a family that is perhaps wealthier than his own, which means that he could probably afford to live as he does (in fact, he might even live better) without the party. Since Das Gupta comes from much humbler origins and has little money of his own, he is accused by some party members of an attempt to raise his social status with the aid of party funds.[48] Perhaps the harshest denunciation of Das Gupta is contained in the description of him by some party members as "a Communist version of Atulya Ghosh."[49]

Aside from party funding and personal differences, the major sources of conflict between the electoral organizations and the state party

[48] Das Gupta is also accused of nepotism by some party leaders, since two of his relatives have been promoted to the State Committee of the CPM, and one of them (Krishnapada Ghosh) was the state Labour Minister in the 1969–1970 United Front government. In Bengali mythology *Vaidyas* are especially prone both to nepotism and to status seeking, making the charges against Das Gupta (who is a *Vaidya* by caste) all the more plausible in the eyes of many Bengalis.

[49] The reference is to the leader of the state Congress party, who has long been denounced by the Communists as an uncultured, status-seeking, corrupt politician—precisely the same image CPI and CPM party members have of Das Gupta. For a more detailed description of this image of Atulya Ghosh, see Marcus F. Franda, "The Political Idioms of Atulya Ghosh," *Asian Survey* 6 (August 1966): 432–433.

apparatus in the united CPI have had to do with the role of elections in overall Communist strategy. And yet the leadership of the electoral organizations have not dealt with these issues as vigorously as the party's intellectual leadership, with the result that the principal conflict over party strategy in the united CPI has been between theoreticians on the one hand and the organizational apparatus on the other, each contesting for the loyalty and allegiance of the electoral organizations. This pattern of factional conflict is best illustrated by the debate that has raged among peasant leaders in the state over the strategy to be pursued regarding two potentially powerful rural elements, the small landholders and the landless.

Ideally a Communist peasant organization might be able to secure the support both of the landless and of the small landholders, and some Communist electoral leaders have argued for strategies designed to do this. But most Communists argue that a single party cannot realistically appeal to both: effective organization of landless laborers in the rural areas has generally hurt small landholders more than anyone else and has therefore alienated this significant segment of the rural population; on the other hand, party attempts to gain the support of small landholders has usually made it impolitic to organize the landless at the same time, thereby depriving the party of support from a segment of the rural population that is potentially the most revolutionary in all of India. In the state unit of the party the Right faction has generally opted for a strategy designed to woo small landholders first, and perhaps the landless later, while the Left faction has sought to organize the landless.[50] But the electoral organizations in the party that have become involved in this debate have merely tried to mediate between the Right and Left factions and have used both Right and Left faction leaders to strengthen the party's position in electoral politics.

The strategies that have been formally adopted to meet this issue at the state and national levels have shifted considerably over the years, with Left faction views generally prevailing in party documents before 1957 and those of the Right faction from 1957 until the split in 1964. In

---

[50] The position of the Right faction is stated rather laboriously in Bhowani Sen, *Indian Land System and Land Reforms* (Delhi: People's Publishing House, 1955), pp. 111–129, and Bhowani Sen, *Evolution of Agrarian Relations in India* (New Delhi: People's Publishing House, 1962), pp. 280–288. The most concise statement of the Left faction position appears in *Decision and Resolutions of the 19th Session, All-India Kisan Sabha, Madurai, January 26–28, 1968* (New Delhi: AIKS, 1968); see especially the speech by President A. K. Gopalan, in which he states that "reluctance to take up their [agricultural laborers'] specific demands, fearing that this will drive the rich and middle peasants away from us, will have to be given up" (p. 7).

West Bengal, the Right faction in the Kisan Sabha gained at least a token victory over the Left faction in the peasant movement in 1957, when the state All-India Kisan Sabha (AIKS) adopted a strategy designed to court small landholders. According to Weiner,

> The fifteenth provincial conference, meeting in 1957, announced that the Kisan Sabha favored compensation for those small intermediaries whose holdings were confiscated by government. It further declared that the organization would launch agitations for agricultural loans, improved irrigation facilities, manure, education, health, and drinking water, and would continue agitation against excessive irrigation taxes and other taxes, including a proposed development tax. The Sabha also announced that it would work within the existing legislative framework, would take the initiative in forming panchayats [local government councils] under the new Panchayat Act, and would support credit cooperatives, marketing societies, handicraft cooperatives, and even the government's Community Development Program and National Extension Service. In short, the Kisan Sabha proposed to minimize agitations and maximize the benefits peasants (and the Kisan Sabha) might receive by working within existing legislation, while at the same time putting pressure on the state government for greater rural expenditures. Rural harmony rather than class conflict was the new theme of the West Bengal Kisan Sabha.[51]

But the victory of the Right faction in the state AIKS in 1957 was clearly a "paper victory" that had little effect on the day-to-day operations of state party workers in the Bengal countryside. Both before and after 1957 party activity in the rural areas was highly fragmented and localized, with party members organizing the landless laborers for mass struggles in areas controlled by the Left faction, while the 1957 resolution was pursued in areas controlled by the Right faction.

In the districts of 24-Parganas, Howrah, Hooghly, and Burdwan, where the Left faction has been in control since Independence, the Communists have always concentrated on the organization of tribals and other landless laborers in preparation for "mass struggles" against the landed. In Midnapore District, however, the Right faction has had control of the district party organization, and Midnapore AIKS leaders have made a much more serious attempt to implement the 1957 resolution. The extent to which indiscipline has characterized the state Communists with regard to the question of a rural strategy is indicated by the resolutions of the State Council of the united CPI (dominated by the Left faction) on agrarian questions between 1957 and the split in 1964, many of which clearly contradicted the 1957 resolutions of the state and national AIKS.[52] Such indiscipline has

---

[51] Weiner, *Politics of Scarcity*, p. 147.
[52] *The Statesman*, April 13, 1969.

made for a rather checkered history on the part of the state Kisan Sabha, with membership varying considerably from year to year (depending on the activities of one or another faction)[53] and with all factions complaining of the lack of overall improvement on the part of the Communists in the rural areas.

In this situation the electoral organizations have gained more than either the Left or the Right by simply using the efforts of both factions for electoral purposes. From the point of view of the electoral Communists in West Bengal, a strategy appealing to urban interests and the landless (the strategy of the Left faction) is highly desirable in 24-Parganas, Howrah, Hooghly, and Burdwan, since in all four districts these two highly discontented segments of the population are numerically strong. As Table 1 shows, urban dwellers and agricultural laborers together constitute 80.48 percent of the population of Howrah, 67.81 percent of 24-Parganas, 65.36 percent of Hooghly, and 56.60 percent of the population of Burdwan. In Midnapore, however, a

TABLE 1

RURAL, URBAN, AND AGRICULTURAL LABOR COMPOSITION OF
WEST BENGAL'S FIVE SOUTHERN DISTRICTS

District	Total Population	Rural (% of Total)	Urban (% of Total)	Agricultural Laborers (% of Rural)
Howrah	2,038,477	1,213,385 (59.52%)	825,092 (40.48%)	485,354 (40.0%)
24-Parganas	6,280,915	4,282,958 (68.19%)	1,997,957 (31.81%)	1,541,865 (36.0%)
Hooghly	2,231,418	1,652,135 (74.04%)	579,283 (25.96%)	650,941 (39.4%)
Burdwan	3,082,846	2,521,768 (71.80%)	561,078 (18.20%)	968,359 (38.4%)
Midnapore	4,341,855	4,007,569 (92.30%)	334,286 (7.70%)	1,074,028 (26.8%)

Source: Census of India, 1961 (New Delhi: Government of India, Bureau of the Census, 1963–1969), vol. 16, "West Bengal and Sikkim," Part I-A and Part II-B (ii). In the 1961 census, agricultural laborers were defined as "persons working on land as labourers for wages without holding any right upon the land."

[53] Membership figures published by the AIKS, for example, would indicate that the West Bengal unit had 185,389 members in 1954, 219,864 members in 1955, and only 143,247 members in 1956. See Twelfth Session of the All-India Kisan Sabha, Proceedings and Resolutions (New Delhi: AIKS, 1954), p. 59; Proceedings and Resolutions of the Thirteenth Session, All-India Kisan Sabha (New Delhi: AIKS, 1955), p. 53; and Fourteenth Annual Session of the All-India Kisan Sabha, Report (New Delhi: AIKS, 1956), p. 17.

strategy that appealed only to these two segments of the population would be aimed at a mere 34.5 percent of the total population of the district, and most state politicians agree that it would alienate the vast majority of the remaining segments.[54] By using the Right faction organizations of the party in Midnapore District and the Left faction organizations in 24-Parganas, Howrah, Hooghly, and Burdwan districts, the electoral organizations of the united CPI consistently did well in all five districts without getting involved in the substance of the ideological dispute except as mediators.

Factional Conflict and Electoral Politics

The question, "What have Bengali Communists attempted to accomplish since Independence?" has many answers. Most Communists in the state would agree that they are trying to do away with the regime that Congress has created, but major factional groupings within the state movement differ radically as to how this might be done and what might serve as an alternative to the electoral democracy that Congress has created. Since the failure of the insurrectionist strategy of the late 1940s, the communist movement in West Bengal has been so divided internally that it has been unable to find a strategy acceptable to all factional interests. The strategies that have been adopted have usually served merely as a framework within which various factional interests have pursued their own interests, and the factions have not been fettered by constraints imposed by state or national party leaders. The unity of the movement has therefore depended on the ability of state leaders to accommodate themselves to various factional points of view, and on the mutual interest of all factions in opposing the Congress party.

Because of the success of militant agitation directed against the Congress, the Left faction in West Bengal has gained considerable influence in the state organizational apparatus, while the position of the Right faction has been declining. But the Left faction has also had difficulty in adjusting to an electoral system, and electoral politics have therefore intensified factionalism within the Left faction itself. At one level the success of the Communists in state elections has led to a debate about the efficacy of participating in electoral politics, while at another it has led to constant disputes over what electoral strategies

---

[54] For an interesting correlation for all of India of demographic factors with the Communist vote by district, which substantiates the influence of segmentation on Communist voting patterns, see Donald S. Zagoria, "'Rice' and 'Feudal' Communism in India," paper prepared for the Columbia University Seminar on Modern East Asia, November 19, 1969.

would provide the quickest path to revolution and political power. While the Right faction, at the instigation of the cpsu, has advocated a strategy of alliance with bourgeois forces, the Left faction has continued to resist such a strategy. While the Left faction has improved its ability to engage in agitational activities, most of its efforts thus far have been directed toward electoral goals rather than toward the more revolutionary aims proposed by Left faction leaders. During the course of these developments, the electoral position of the Communists in the state has continued to improve, primarily because of the ability of the weakest faction in the party at the time of Independence (the electoralists) to use both of the older factions for electoral purposes. Since 1947 the electoralists in the West Bengal communist movement have increasingly threatened to dominate the entire movement.

Factional conflict within the state communist movement has also been intensified since Independence by the attachment of Bengali Communists to national and international political movements. As has already been indicated, the strength of the Right faction in the state has depended on the support of the central party leadership and the cpsu, both before and after the split in 1964, while the Left faction has also sought support from Communist factions outside West Bengal. The split that took place in 1964 was in fact a culmination of the conflicts between the Right and Left factions that had plagued the state party throughout the 1950s, as well as the product of a series of events in the national and international communist movement. Since the split in 1964, both organizational and theoretical differences have been infused with more intense emotions than in the 1950s, and they have also come to be related in much more complex ways to national and international politics and party affairs.

4

SINO-SOVIET CONFLICT AND THE SPLIT

The split between the CPI and the CPM is usually dated from April 11, 1964, when thirty-two of the sixty-five members of the party's National Council walked out of a party meeting being held in New Delhi. They eventually organized their own convention (at Tenali, in Andhra Pradesh) in July and their own National Congress (in Calcutta) in October, and they have continued to insist that they are the only genuine successors to the traditions of the Indian communist movement. While they have been able to attract at least as large a membership and following (both in India and in West Bengal) as the parent Communist party, they continue to be described as dissidents from the regular CPI by most people in India, and they have now accepted the party label (Communist party of India–Marxist, or CPM) that the Election Commission and Indian journalists have assigned to them.

Six of the thirty-two members who walked out in April 1964 were Bengalis: Pramode Das Gupta, Jyoti Basu, Hare Krishna Konar, Muzaffar Ahmad, Abdul Halim, and Saroj Mukherjee. They were all well known and were influential leaders of the party at the national as well as at the state level. Perhaps for this reason most accounts of the split have emphasized the important role that the West Bengal unit played in staging the walkout and in reorganizing the majority of the CPI membership under the banner of the CPM. Yet it is clear that the Bengalis in the united CPI were by no means a cohesive force at the time of the split. Indeed, the split in the national unit of the party was accompanied by serious cleavages within the statewide movement, and the regular CPI in West Bengal has been able to attract considerable support among Bengali Communists since 1964 despite its inability to outpoll the CPM in elections.

Throughout the 1950s the CPI in West Bengal took an active part in Indian ideological debates. As was pointed out in previous chapters, the Communist intellectual leadership in West Bengal consistently sided with Moscow and the CPGB during the course of these debates, deriving most of its theoretical inspiration from R. Palme Dutt of the CPGB in Cambridge, while the organizational apparatus of the state party opposed the pro-Moscow stance of Dutt on a number of occasions.

Lacking the theoretical support and unity needed to pursue alternative strategies, the organizational leadership of West Bengal had to content itself throughout the 1950s with a series of compromise formulas promulgated by the national leadership of the party headed by Ajoy Ghosh while it concentrated on building a more effective state organization. Factionalism within the state unit during this period did surface on a number of occasions, but party discipline was always sufficient to rally the membership around temporary compromise solutions.

In the late 1950s, however, the gap between the various factions in West Bengal began to widen, and most party leaders now trace the split back to a series of events—regional, national, and international—that occurred in 1959. The most widely publicized of these events resulted from the widening rift between the CPSU and the Chinese Communist party (CCP), a rift that had immediate repercussions in India because of the proximity of the Tibetan revolt and the Sino-Indian border dispute, both of which figured prominently in Sino-Soviet debates.[1] The conflicting models that the Soviet Union and China had presented to Indian Communists in the early 1950s were those of urban insurrection and peasant guerrilla warfare, but during the course of the 1950s the two Communist giants shifted ground considerably. By 1959 they had come to differ publicly on their assessments of the very nature of the Nehru government, and both now sought much greater influence over the strategies and tactics of the CPI.

In addition to events taking place in the international communist movement, the CPI in West Bengal was also influenced by the removal of the Communist regime in Kerala on July 31, 1959, and by the nature of the political environment in the state of West Bengal at that time. The CPI in West Bengal had been greatly encouraged by the results of the 1957 elections, since the party had improved its position considerably in the state legislature by increasing its number of seats from 28 to 46 (and its percentage of the votes from 10.76 to 17.82). Bengali Communists were also encouraged by the results of the election in Kerala in 1957, which had enabled the Kerala Communists to form a coalition government, the first state government to be dominated by Communists in independent India. In the words of one observer of Bengali politics,

E. M. S. Namboodiripad [the CPI Chief Minister of Kerala] had overnight become a hero in Bengal and the mammoth public meetings and receptions he was called upon to address during his visit to Bengal soon after becoming

---

[1] The role of the border dispute in accentuating the Sino-Soviet rift is described in William E. Griffith, *The Sino-Soviet Rift* (Cambridge: M.I.T. Press, 1964); see especially pp. 5–8, 56–59.

Chief Minister of Kerala, was [sic] indicative of the restlessness of the Bengali Communists to bring about a "second Kerala." Political life in the State became much more alive and active.[2]

The assumption of power by a Communist-led coalition government in Kerala had been a unifying factor in Bengal in the late 1950s for a variety of reasons. To begin with, the activities of the Left faction within the party became severely restricted with the formation of the Kerala ministry, since the party could no longer launch agitational movements on issues that threatened to undermine the Kerala government. The party could not easily demand, for example, such things as nationalization of industries without compensation, expropriation of foreign assets, or other such steps that the Kerala government was not willing to undertake itself. The victory of the Communists in Kerala therefore made it necessary as never before for the regular party organization in the state (which was dominated by the Left faction) to cooperate with the more moderate electoral and intellectual wings of the state party. Members of the CPI from all factions were now at least temporarily encouraged to view the possibility of a transition to socialism through parliamentary means in a much different light than they had previously, and the feeling among most Communists was that the Kerala government should at least be given a chance to prove or disprove the wisdom of joining a coalition government.

For these reasons, the declaration of President's Rule in Kerala on July 31, 1959, was especially significant for its effect on inner-party factional disputes. President's Rule in Kerala strengthened the factions within the CPI that had objected to the thrust of the 1958 Amritsar thesis (that the party could win and retain power through parliamentary means) at the same time that it freed the state organizational apparatus from the restraints under which it had been forced to operate during the period of Communist rule.   In West Bengal, factionalism within the CPI was also affected by the serious food crisis that had begun to develop in 1958 and that had reached a peak in late 1959. Food prices in West Bengal rose to new highs, and food grains were so scarce at times that there were rumors of famine. By September of 1959, the CPI in West Bengal had taken the lead in organizing a Price Increase and Famine Resistance Committee (PIFRC), which had succeeded in consolidating all but one of the state's leftist political parties in opposition to Congress food policy, and the PIFRC had in

[2] Aswini Kumar Ray, "Political Trends in West Bengal (1947–1962)," in *State Politics in India*, ed. Iqbal Narain (Meerut: Meenakshi Prakashan, 1967), p. 307.

turn succeeded in launching the most widespread food demonstrations West Bengal had ever witnessed.

Each of the four major events that took place in 1959—the Tibetan revolt, the first serious Sino-Indian border clashes, the declaration of President's Rule in Kerala, and the food crisis in West Bengal—served to widen the gap between the Right and Left factions in the state and national parties. At the national level, inner-party differences were papered over by a series of compromise measures until the death of Ajoy Ghosh in January of 1962, after which time the rightist faction in the party predominated until the split in April 1964. At the state level, however, the dominance of the Left faction in West Bengal was never seriously challenged until November 1962, when the leftists in West Bengal were imprisoned because of their refusal to condemn the Chinese. The rightists in the state party, almost all of whom remained out of the jails in 1962–1963, were then able to collaborate with the central leadership of the CPI in an attempt to rebuild state party units. Before their imprisonment in November 1962, the leftists in West Bengal used their dominant position in the state party to oppose the central leadership, attempting to find allies among Communists in other states of the Indian Union. After their release from the jails in December 1963, the leftists tried to recapture their dominant position, and when this failed they decided to split with the regular CPI.

During the five-year period from 1959 until 1964, CPI membership in West Bengal became almost institutionally divided between the three fairly well defined factions that had always existed in the party. The rightists were led by Bhowani Sen and Somnath Lahiri and counted among their leadership most of the intellectuals and theoreticians in the state party; the leftists were led by Pramode Das Gupta and Hare Krishna Konar and depended on the bulk of the regular party organization for support; and a third group, eventually termed centrist (because it tried to mediate between the two major factions), was nominally led by Jyoti Basu and Bhupesh Gupta and was heavily represented by leaders of the party's electoral organizations. Between 1959 and 1964 the leadership of each of these factions met separately on a number of occasions, each drafted its own inner-party documents which it distributed among the membership, and each sought support from like-minded members and factions in other states. After the split in 1964, the Right faction assumed control of the regular CPI, while the Left faction withdrew from the party to form the CPM. The centrists then divided themselves between both parties, with the bulk of the centrist leadership going over to the CPM. In this atmosphere, it is not surprising that several centrists eventually withdrew from party politics entirely as a result of the frustrations they had experienced while trying to mediate the almost constant disputes that plagued the state party during the years preceding the split.

The Role of the State Party Organization

By 1959 the leadership of the CPI in West Bengal had become accustomed to a fairly consistent pattern of relationships with the central leaders of the party and with the state's internal factions. On most issues the state leadership of the party opposed the rightists at the Center and sought alliances with other Left factions in other states of the Indian Union, and on most occasions it was eventually able to cajole the national leadership clustered around Ajoy Ghosh into adopting compromise measures designed to placate both factions. Within West Bengal, the leadership of the regular party organization was always faced with some dissent from intellectuals and leaders of the electoral organizations, but party discipline and an occasional compromise measure produced a semblance of unity. When the Dalai Lama fled to India in April 1959, after the Chinese suppressed the revolt by Khampa tribesmen in Tibet, this familiar pattern of relationships reasserted itself. The Chinese charge that the revolt in Tibet was being directed from the town of Kalimpong (in the northern district of Darjeeling in West Bengal) was immediately denied by Prime Minister Nehru, and CPI leaders both at the central and at the state levels subsequently became divided between those supporting Nehru and those supporting the Chinese. The central leadership of the party ultimately wavered, initially supporting the Chinese charges in a statement issued by the Secretariat of the National Council but later (when Moscow began to delete any references to Kalimpong from public statements) retreating from this position.[3] The state unit in West Bengal was therefore able to persist in its demand for an investigation of the Chinese charges and to emphasize in a series of meetings "the supreme importance of friendship between India and China" without strictly violating the party line at the center.[4]

But the state party organization was more concerned about the domestic political situation in West Bengal in 1959 than it was with

[3] The position of the CPI central leaders is outlined in *New Age* (CPI weekly), April 5, 1959, pp. 1, 20. For documentation, see *On Events in Tibet, Statement of the Secretariat of the CPI, New Delhi, 31 March, 1959* (New Delhi: CPI, 1959); *Strengthen Friendship between India and China, Resolution of the Central Executive Committee of the CPI, New Delhi, 9–12 May, 1959* (New Delhi: CPI, 1959); and *Incidents on Himalayan Borders, Statement of the Secretariat of the CPI, New Delhi, 30 August, 1959* (New Delhi: CPI, 1959).

[4] *The Statesman* (Calcutta daily), April 13, 1959.

international issues, since state politics had taken a sharp turn to the left with the formation of the Price Increase and Famine Resistance Committee in late 1958. In the eyes both of Left and of centrist faction leaders in West Bengal, the food agitation of 1959 had presented the party with entirely new opportunities to reinforce its position as the leader of the opposition to the Congress in the state. Bengali Communist leaders were mainly concerned that the party remain in a position to take advantage of the food issue and were well aware of the possibility that the other Marxist Left parties might seize the initiative. The position of the state party in 1959 was complicated, however, when Ajoy Ghosh returned from a trip that had taken him to Moscow (where he attended the Twenty-first Congress of the CPSU) and to Peking, on the basis of which he argued at a CEC meeting that "this is no occasion for change in CPI policy."[5] Ghosh and the CEC were even reported to have offered in February 1959 to assist the Congress party in the implementation of the Congress Nagpur resolution (which was adopted with strong support from Nehru and the left wing of the Congress party in January 1959, and which contained a strongly worded call for land reform).[6] The reaction of the state party to Ghosh's overtures to the Congress was much more immediate and intense than its response to events in Tibet.

At a meeting of the CPI State Council in early April 1959, the state party made no direct reference to the decisions of the CEC, but it did adopt a series of resolutions that were at odds with the thinking of the central leadership at this time. The leadership of the state party argued that the CPI had failed to take advantage of the political opportunities that had confronted it throughout the 1950s and that the state party should now take the lead in reversing this tendency. In the words of Jyoti Basu,

. . . popular movements mounted at a much faster pace than the party could comprehend [throughout the 1950s]. The result was that the party leadership degenerated into "tailism" [i.e., became a "tail" of the bourgeoisie]. The party associated itself with the struggles and movements which people started instead of being the guiding factor in them. That position must change.[7]

Following on this independent state assessment of the party's position, the state party decided that "a real people's front could be built on the basis of struggle alone," and it therefore called for a massive food agitation by all "democratic organizations," to be led by the Com-

[5] Ibid., February 22, 1959.
[6] Ibid., February 25, 1959.
[7] Ibid., April 14, 1959.

munists. Seeking to recruit a "volunteer force" of 50,000 people, the CPI pushed through the PIFRC the anti-Congress slogan, "Either accept our demands or resign," and in preparation for a "mass struggle" the PIFRC undertook the planning of three blatantly aggressive acts: (1) the detection and forced sale of hoarded rice stocks; (2) squatting, picketing, and defiance of the law throughout the state of West Bengal; and (3) resistance to arrest. The goal of the PIFRC, decided at a meeting in August 1959, eventually became the creation of "an administrative deadlock" that would "close down the city and the state with a continued general strike until demands are met," and the demands of the PIFRC included extreme degrees of price control, immediate redistribution of land vested in the state, confiscation of some privately held land without compensation, and state trading in food grains.[8]

As a result of the PIFRC's threat to engage in "a mass defiance of law," more than 250 Bengali leftist leaders were arrested in mid-August 1959, of whom 200 were members of the state CPI. Eventually many of the remaining leaders (including Jyoti Basu) went underground for a period of a month or so, and 12,845 people were arrested during a wave of violent demonstrations. After three weeks of rioting in Calcutta and the southern districts, 39 people had been killed in food demonstrations and 8 police stations had been attacked by mobs (the number of injuries to demonstrators and the number of food shops looted could not be officially estimated).[9] Only after some token concessions had been gained from the state government was the movement called off in late September.

The food agitation of the PIFRC in 1959 enhanced the position of the Left faction in West Bengal, for it demonstrated conclusively the ability of the state party organization to lead the other Marxist Left parties in the state and to wring concessions from the Congress. Since 1959 members of the Left Communist faction within the state have annually observed August 31 as Martyrs' Day, commemorating the deaths of the food demonstrators who lost their lives in the police firings on August 31, 1959, and the tactic of a massive food agitation was used by the leftist parties in West Bengal again in 1966, when the PIFRC was even more successful in securing the support of the Bengali populace.[10]

[8] Ibid., August 11, 1959.
[9] These are the figures announced by Chief Minister B. C. Roy in the *West Bengal Legislative Assembly Debates*, September 8, 1959.
[10] For a Communist version of the 1959 and 1966 food agitations, see *Report of the Non-Official Enquiry Commission on the Police and Military Excesses in West Bengal during the Period from 16th February, 1966 to 6th April, 1966* (Calcutta: Arun P. Chatterjee, 1967), especially pp. 3–11, 17–22.

Most observers now argue that it was the food agitation movements of 1959 and 1966 that brought about the demise of the Congress party in the 1967 elections.[11] But despite the success of the agitation in 1959, the central leadership of the party was extremely dissatisfied with the actions of the West Bengal unit. While no disciplinary action was taken against the state unit of the party, central party leaders did make known their feelings that the Bengali Communists had succumbed to "the mere needs of state politics" in organizing the food agitation. The position of the CPI central leadership was described by the correspondent of *The Statesman* as follows:

> They [central leaders] ask whether the party is for democracy, as defined in the Amritsar Thesis, or for revolution. If, by and large, the party is for constitutionalism, why then, they ask, was this preview of revolutionary strategy staged in Calcutta? If the object was as limited and parochial as it seemingly was, did not the Communist Party of Bengal use wasteful and unnecessary means? . . . [The food agitation] has engendered the fear that such acts might lead to the banning of the party for which most of its members are unprepared and unwilling.[12]

Under normal circumstances, the central leadership of the CPI might have been able to prevent the state unit of the party from participation in the food agitation of 1959, or it might have disciplined the state leaders responsible for the party's participation in the demonstrations. But the growing rift between the Soviet Union and China, whose relations turned into major hostility in the summer of 1959 (as a result of conflict on a whole range of issues involving atomic aid, de-Stalinization, policy toward the U.S., Soviet interference in Chinese party quarrels, and, for our purposes the most important, policy toward India), and the severe factionalism engendered in the Indian party by the rift made it impolitic for the central leadership of the CPI to attempt an exercise in discipline or control. Moreover, the Chinese had themselves precipitated a major crisis within the Indian party in August 1959 by moving into the Northeast Frontier Agency (NEFA) and occupying some of the territory around Longju that was considered by the Indian government to be an undisputed part of India. On September 3, 1959 (when the food agitation in West Bengal was at its peak), a Chinese Communist note to New Delhi accused India of "aggression"

---

[11] The food agitation of 1966 was especially significant in the assessment of the state Congress party leader Atulya Ghosh, who attributed Congress failures in 1967 to a lack of "real effort" on the food front. See Atulya Ghosh, *The Real Task* (New Delhi: All-India Congress Committee, 1967), pp. 4–5, 16–17.

[12] Mahesh Chandra, "Communists Prevaricate: Mission to Peking," *The Statesman*, September 30, 1959.

in the border area and demanded the withdrawal of Indian troops, and a later letter (dated September eighth), from Chou En-lai to Prime Minister Nehru, reiterated Chinese claims while professing a willingness to "negotiate" the dispute. Ajoy Ghosh had meanwhile traveled to Moscow, where he was meeting with Soviet officials when the now-famous TASS dispatch of September eighth announced the Soviet position of neutrality in the Sino-Indian border dispute, an event that helped to convince the Chinese of the need to launch a worldwide offensive against the line of the CPSU in April 1960.[13]

The interjection of the ideological debate of the two Communist giants into the internal debates of the Indian Communists created innumerable difficulties for all factions, but especially for India's Left Communists. The Left faction had been convinced throughout the 1950s that support of Nehru and Congress party policies was a mistake and had consistently pointed for evidence to the fact that the party was strongest in the areas of India (Kerala, West Bengal, and Andhra) where Left Communists had been strongest. Indeed, even in electoral contests the CPI had become a significant force only in the three Left faction strongholds of Kerala, West Bengal, and Andhra, as Table 2 shows. In eight of the remaining states (with the exception of Punjab in 1957, which was at that time dominated by the Left faction) the party had only polled between 5 and 10 percent of the vote. The leadership of the Left faction therefore had good reason to believe that the way to build party support was through a more militant stance toward the Congress, rather than through the moderate stance assumed by the national party throughout the 1950s at the urging of the CPSU.

Moreover, the leadership of the Left faction was always convinced that a larger portion of the membership of the CPI would ultimately support the Left faction rather than the Right, and this conviction was at least partially borne out once the party did split in 1964. Before the split, however, the Left faction was seriously disadvantaged by the system of representation on the Central Committees, which favored greater representation from a variety of state units (most of which were dominated by the Right faction), rather than a heavy concentration of representatives from states in which the party was strongest (where the Left faction predominated). The leadership of the Left faction was

---

[13] The effects of the Longju incidents are traced in Harry Gelman, "The Communist Party of India: Sino-Soviet Battleground," in *Communist Strategies in Asia*, ed. A. Doak Barnett (New York: Praeger, 1963), pp. 110–114. For the Sino-Soviet dispute, see Griffith, *The Sino-Soviet Rift* and *Sino-Soviet Relations, 1964–1965* (Cambridge, Mass.: M.I.T. Press, 1967).

TABLE 2

PERCENTAGE OF VALID VOTES POLLED BY COMMUNIST PARTIES IN
INDIAN STATE LEGISLATIVE ASSEMBLY ELECTIONS (1952–1969)

State	1952	1957	1962	1967		1969	
				CPI	CPM	CPI	CPM
Kerala	17.5	35.3	39.1	8.57	23.51	—	—
West Bengal	10.4	17.8	25.0	6.53	18.11	6.78	19.55
Andhra Pradesh	22.8	29.5	19.3	7.78	7.61	—	—
Orissa	5.7	8.4	8.0	5.26	1.16	—	—
Madras	9.8	7.4	7.8	1.80	4.07	—	—
Punjab	6.2	13.6	7.1	5.27	3.19	4.54	3.10
Bihar	1.1	5.2	6.3	6.91	1.28	10.30	0.95
Assam	2.4	8.1	6.3	5.15	1.97	—	—
Maharashtra	2.5	6.3	6.0	4.87	1.08	—	—
Uttar Pradesh	0.9	3.8	5.4	3.23	1.27	3.05	0.49
Rajasthan	0.6	3.0	5.4	0.97	1.18	—	—
Mysore	1.4	1.9	2.3	0.52	1.10	—	—
Madhya Pradesh	0.7	1.6	2.0	1.11	0.23	—	—
Gujarat	2.5	0.8	0.2	nil	nil	—	—
Harayana	—	—	—	0.90	0.54		

Source: Figures for the first three elections were obtained from Ralph Retzláff,
"Revisionism and Dogmatism in the Communist Party of India," in *The Communist
Revolution in Asia,* ed. Robert A. Scalapino (Englewood Cliffs, N.J.: Prentice-Hall,
1965), p. 315. Figures for the 1967 election were obtained from the official report of the
Election Commission and those for 1969 from the February 1969 issues of the *Times
of India* (New Delhi). Official election returns for 1969 were not available at the time
of writing.

especially critical of the Maharashtra and Uttar Pradesh units of the
party, both of which were dominated by leaders of the Right faction,
but which had failed miserably to secure support for the CPI within
their own states. While the Left faction had been unable to defeat the
Right within the party, it had been successful in preventing the Right
faction from gaining control of the national party organization, but
only by acceding to the compromises that had been engineered by
Ajoy Ghosh. By the late 1950s, therefore, the leadership of the Left
faction had staked its future on the hope that it would eventually be
able to gain control of the national party organization, and a number
of Left faction leaders were counting on the CPSU to revert eventually
to a Left Communist stance with regard to India. It was customary for
leaders of the Left faction, for example, to emphasize that neither
Nehru nor the Congress could last forever, and that the Left faction
of the CPI would be in a better position to take advantage of the

political situation when Congress was in a state of disintegration and there was no Nehru. In the eyes of the Left faction leadership, the Right Communists in India had taken an extremely short-run and opportunistic stance with regard to the domestic political situation by siding with the CPSU in support of Nehru's policies.

In this atmosphere the ideological rift between the Soviet Union and China created more difficulties for the Left faction, for it increasingly placed the Soviet Union in a posture that was opposed to Left communism, it led the Chinese to act toward India in a manner that made Left communism more and more untenable so long as it was supported by the Chinese, and it led to the adoption of a much more rightist stance on the part of a number of CPI leaders. Most disturbing was the reaction of Ajoy Ghosh to the embarrassing situation in which he found himself in October 1959. Ghosh had returned from China on the eighteenth to hold a press conference, where he spoke at great length of the assurances Mao had given him of the peaceful intentions of the Chinese People's Republic, and the press conference was reported extensively in the party organ *New Age* on October twenty-fifth. During the intervening week, however, Indian troops had again clashed with the Chinese in Ladakh, with some *jawans* (Indian soldiers) being killed and others taken prisoner by the Chinese army. Ghosh reacted to the outrage and indignation that was expressed throughout India by moving decidedly to the right, issuing a statement through the Central Secretariat of the party in which he argued that there was "no justification whatsoever" for the Chinese action. At subsequent meetings of the CEC and the National Council in November, Ghosh joined with the Right faction to push through the Meerut resolutions, endorsing the Indian government's claim to the McMahon Line for the first time and rejecting Chinese claims in the NEFA area.[14]

But Ghosh's reaction to the Sino-Indian border incidents of 1959 was not nearly so immediate as that of many other party leaders. In the words of one observer, the effect of the Chinese aggression was to "turn the CPI's gradual slide to the Right into a stampede."[15] In reaction to public sentiment, some of the most influential provincial organizations (including Maharashtra and Kerala), as well as a number of prominent party leaders (among them E. M. S. Namboodiripad,

---

[14] Almost the entire issue of *New Age* on November 22, 1959, is devoted to a discussion of Ghosh's trip to China, the press conference upon his return, and the drafting of the Meerut resolutions. See also *On India-China Relations, Resolution of the National Council of CPI, Meerut, 11 November, 1959* (New Delhi: CPI, 1959).

[15] John B. Wood, "Observations on the Indian Communist Party Split," *Pacific Affairs* 38 (Spring 1965): 51.

First Secretary S. G. Sardesai, and S. A. Dange), issued public statements supporting the Indian government position without authorization from any central party organ.[16] Eventually all of the members of the CPI in the Lok Sabha were instructed by the central leadership of the party to rally behind the Congress party position on the border dispute, and the CPI adopted resolutions that denied the legitimacy of the Chinese position.

In the face of extreme public pressure to condemn the Chinese aggression, the CPI unit in West Bengal resisted, while it worked within the party to slow the stampede to the right. On November 1, 1959, the State Council adopted a resolution demanding that Dange be brought before the Control Commission of the party for calling China an aggressor in a public statement, in contradiction to CEC resolutions.[17] While there was no formal inner-party debate in West Bengal in 1959, the state party organization did hold a series of informal meetings with all District and Branch committees, during which party leaders argued that "a Communist party cannot, under any circumstances, shed its proleterian internationalism to appease local popular feeling."[18] At these meetings the leadership of the regular party organization argued that Dange and Namboodiripad had "walked into the bourgeois trap" by supporting the Indian government stance. Party leaders invoked numerous examples of Communist leaders who had successfully resisted the temptation to adopt a "popular" political stance that was against the interests of international ideological communism (two of the most highly lauded were Otto Kuusinen, the CP leader in Finland who had defended the Soviet march on Finland in 1939, and Maurice Thorez of France, who had allegedly supported Algerian independence from French colonial rule). As a temporary measure, the CPI unit in West Bengal agreed that it would not defend the Chinese publicly, since that would only "antagonize public opinion,"[19] and the state party did eventually cancel a number of local meetings for fear of anticommunist demonstrations. At the same time, however, the state party organization refused to allow any state party members to criticize the Chinese position, either at party meetings, in public statements, or in the Legislative Assembly, and some rallies were held in late 1959 at which the party called for the negotiations between Nehru and Chou En-lai that had been proposed in Chou's letter of September eighth. When the Meerut resolutions were adopted by the

[16] Gelman, "The Communist Party of India," p. 114.
[17] *The Statesman*, November 2, 1959.
[18] Ibid., November 5, 1959.
[19] Ibid., November 12, 1959.

CEC and the National Council in November 1959, the West Bengal members of the CEC and the National Council were instructed by the state party to vote against them because they did not support the Chinese stand.[20]

By mid-November 1959 the rift between the Right and Left factions within the CPI had become so acute that Jyoti Basu was reported to have spoken of "a parting of the ways" at the Meerut meetings of the CEC and the National Council.[21] As the dispute progressed, however, the Left faction in West Bengal became even more committed to a militant, pro-Chinese stance. In February and March 1960, Nikita Khrushchev visited Calcutta on his way to and from meetings in New Delhi, and the Left faction in the state was highly discomfited by Chief Minister B. C. Roy's use of quotations from Khrushchev's speeches to demonstrate the progress that India had made under the Congress party.[22] The Left faction was especially irked by a speech that Khrushchev made in Calcutta, in which he was reported to have said,

Let the skeptics not believe in it [India's progress], let the pug dogs bark, but the Indian elephant will move forward along the path which it has selected for itself.[23]

In contrast to the icy silence exhibited by the CPI in West Bengal during Khrushchev's visit to Calcutta, the party organized official greeting ceremonies for Chou En-lai at Dum Dum airport when Chou stopped in Calcutta on his way to New Delhi for meetings with Prime Minister Nehru in April 1960.[24] By September of 1960 the state unit of the party had established independent contact with the Chinese Communists through Hare Krishna Konar, who traveled to the congress of the Communist party of North Vietnam and to Peking, in violation of instructions from the CPI Central Secretariat.[25] When Konar was censured by the Central Secretariat and asked to explain why disciplinary action should not be taken against him, the West Bengal unit of the party rallied behind him, arguing that censure of him amounted to censure of the entire state unit of the party.[26]

[20] Mahesh Chandra, "Communist Crisis Not Yet Over: Party Line in Bengal," ibid., December 30, 1959.

[21] Ibid., November 18, 1959.

[22] *West Bengal Legislative Assembly Debates*, March 2, 1960.

[23] *Ananda Bazaar Patrika* (Calcutta daily), March 3, 1960.

[24] *Hindusthan Standard* (Calcutta daily), April 20, 1960.

[25] For accounts of Konar's meetings in North Vietnam and China, see *Link* (New Delhi weekly), October 16, 1960, and *The Call* (monthly organ of the RSP), March 1967, p. 16.

[26] *The Statesman*, October 26, 1960, and November 3, 1960. See also *Indian Affairs Record* 6, no. 10, p. 229.

After Konar's visit to North Vietnam and China in 1960, the regular party organization in West Bengal was labeled by almost everyone, both within the party and outside, as the most vociferous pro-Chinese element within the party, a label that was both accurate and misleading. The leadership of the regular party organization in West Bengal did support the Chinese position in the ideological debate at the party center, but it would be difficult to attribute this support solely to the ideological convictions of the state's Left faction. Konar, the most outspoken of the pro-Chinese, was the product of Bengali revolutionary terrorism and the organizational wing of the state CPI, a peasant leader from Burdwan District who usually shunned ideological debate, both before and after his visit to China. The leading theoreticians within the state party were almost entirely on the side of the Soviet Union in the ideological debate, and the state unit of the party therefore depended for theoretical support on intellectual leaders from Maharashtra and Kerala (especially B. T. Ranadive and M. Basavapunniah). Most party leaders now argue that the predominant feeling within the state party in the years preceding the split in 1964 was one of great impatience with the debate itself and especially with the jargon used by theoreticians to explain their positions. After his return from China, Konar simply argued, in a very pragmatic way, that CPI adherence to directives from the CPSU had gone wrong on too many occasions in the past and had "led the Communist Party of India to ruin."[27] At meetings with party members Konar stressed the argument that the adoption of a pro-Chinese stance would present a challenge to the Russian "godhead," making it possible for the state unit of the party to gain greater flexibility, while encouraging the CPI to depend less on the CPSU and CPGB at the national level. This is not to argue that there were no genuine pro-Chinese elements within the regular party organization in the years before the split, but as later events were to point out in a very dramatic way, the leadership of the regular party organization was much more motivated by pragmatic considerations than it was by the wish to adopt a consistently pro-Chinese ideological stance. When in 1967 the leadership of the state party was faced with a choice between support of pro-Chinese elements in the state party and support of the electoral wing, it chose to support the latter, thereby alienating the CCP.

Even by 1961 the ideological debate in West Bengal had been caught up in the contest for factional advantage within the party. In January 1961 a state party congress was held at Burdwan (the

[27] *The Statesman*, October 26, 1960.

factional stronghold of Konar) which was attended by more than 500 members from all the districts of West Bengal. At this conference, the first to be held outside of Calcutta, the party membership listened to two reports on ways of reconciling the Sino-Soviet ideological dispute, one by E. M. S. Namboodiripad and the other by Bhupesh Gupta, but party members were not allowed to comment on the reports. The main task of the conference proved to be the election of a predominantly leftist slate of delegates to the Sixth National Congress of the CPI (held in April 1961 at Vijayawada, in Andhra Pradesh) and the determination of an electoral strategy for the 1962 elections.[28] Throughout 1961 the state party was concerned almost entirely with electoral politics, with the organization of demonstrations on the Assam-Bengal language controversy, and with internal factional politics, with the result that the involvement of state party leaders in the national and international ideological debates was reduced considerably.

The comparative calm that had returned to the party in 1961 was shattered once again by a series of events that took place in 1962, the most important of which were the death of Ajoy Ghosh in January, the election results in February, the death of Chief Minister B. C. Roy in July, and the large-scale attacks on Indian border posts by the Chinese in October and November. The death of Ghosh removed the only effective mediator between the Left and Right factions within the party and set in motion a struggle for party leadership positions, while the election results reaffirmed the view of the Left faction that they were gaining popular support. The death of B. C. Roy brought home to the Left that the period was fast approaching when the older leadership of the Congress (including Nehru) would all be gone, and this made it even more determined than before to maintain a posture of militant opposition to Congress policies. In the meantime, however, the Chinese attacks had again raised all of the old dilemmas for the Left faction, this time much more intensely than in 1959.

The Chinese military activities in the fall of 1962 amounted to a massive invasion of the territories that China had claimed, an invasion that lasted from October the twentieth until November the twenty-first and ended only when it was called off unilaterally by the Chinese as suddenly as it had begun. During a month of fighting, the Chinese struck both in Ladakh and NEFA, areas separated by 1000 miles of Himalayan mountains, supported on both fronts by artillery, mortars, mountain guns, and thousands of soldiers advancing in waves. India

[28] The state conference is reported extensively in *Swadhinata* (organ of the West Bengal CPI), January 22, 1961, and January 29, 1961.

claimed that China lost five soldiers for every Indian killed but that the Chinese nevertheless had seemingly inexhaustible reserves. Using techniques that had been developed in Korea, the Chinese overran all of India's forward positions in the northeast within the first week of fighting, paused for a few days to lure the Indian army forward, and then trapped the best of the Indian units in NEFA with a two-pronged offensive, part of which covered almost 100 miles in three days. The attacks proved conclusively that the Indian army at that time would have been unable to prevent the Chinese either from cutting off India's northeastern territories from the rest of India or from moving straight to Calcutta.[29]

The Chinese offensive was a significant turning point for the CPI's views on domestic politics and the international communist movement. Externally, the centrifugal tendencies in the CPI were strengthened, not only by the Chinese offensive but also by the increased Sino-Soviet tension over the October 1962 Cuban crisis and the increasing Chinese domestic extremism manifested at the September 1962 Chinese Tenth Central Committee Plenum. Internally, the party was faced with the choice of supporting the Indian government without equivocation or losing most of the popular gains that it had made since 1947, since failure to support the government in the face of the invasion would certainly have resulted in a nationwide ban on the party. National party leaders of the Right faction therefore immediately denounced the Chinese aggression publicly, and the National Council of the party eventually adopted a resolution that was so strongly rightist that it was unacceptable even to Moscow and the CPGB. For perhaps the first time in the history of the CPI, the party leadership disregarded advice both from Moscow and from London, pushing through a National Council resolution (the famous November 1 resolution) that called on all Indians to unite behind Nehru "in defense of the motherland against Chinese aggression." Even more extreme was the clause in the resolution to the effect that the CPI was not opposed to India's "buying arms from any country on a commercial basis," a clear acceptance of Nehru's attempts to find allies against China in the "imperialist" West. As a result of this resolution, the CPI was rebuked by the British party, the Czechs, and even by the "revisionist" Italian party, while within India the leadership of the Left faction resigned from the Central Secretariat in protest against the resolution, leaving S. A. Dange

[29] A very useful brief discussion of the Chinese attacks on India in 1962 appears in Pran Chopra, *Uncertain India: A Political Profile of Two Decades of Freedom* (New Delhi: Asia Publishing House, 1968), pp. 168–178. See also Kuldip Nayar, *Between the Lines* (Calcutta: Allied Publishers, 1969), pp. 169–275.

firmly in control of the national party.[30] Moreover, because of the refusal by the Left faction to support the National Council resolution, the Indian government decided to take legal action against the leadership of the Left under the Defence of India Rules, and during the course of November 1962 almost all the Left faction leaders were arrested.

The Right Faction Bids for Control

The extent to which the Left faction had dominated the regular party organization in West Bengal was indicated by the fact that almost two-thirds of the State Council (and all of the members of the State Secretariat) were arrested under the Defence of India Rules in 1962 for actively opposing the nationalist stance of the CPI National Council.[31] Because of the dominance of the Left faction in the regular party organization, the Right faction in the state party had been fairly quiescent before the Chinese invasion of 1962, confining criticism of the leftists almost entirely to inner-party meetings or else simply absenting themselves from public and private meetings with members of the Left faction. After the Chinese action in the Tibetan revolt in 1959, some of the leading rightists in the state party had even taken part in Indo-Chinese solidarity meetings and had also actively participated in the food demonstrations in September 1959 which had been championed by the Left faction. Thus the first indications of serious Right faction differences with the regular party organization came in late 1959, when an influential member of the Right faction, Snehengsu Acharya, labeled the Chinese actions on the border "an act of aggression."[32] Shortly after this, two other leading rightists (Renu Chakravarty and Bhowani Sen) defended Dange at meetings of the State Council, while several other Right faction leaders began to absent themselves from meetings.[33] In January 1960, a leading rightist (Somnath Lahiri) delivered a Republic Day speech in which he defended Nehru's foreign and domestic policies, and in March the Right faction was reported to have introduced into state party discussions a "syllabus" for party members which had been drawn up by

---

[30] The National Council resolution of November 1, 1962, and the reaction of other fraternal Communist parties to the resolution, are analyzed in some detail in Gelman, "The Communist Party of India," pp. 136–137. For the Sino-Soviet and Cuban aspects, see Griffith, *The Sino-Soviet Rift*, pp. 53–63, now to be supplemented by Mao's secret speech at the September 1962 CCP Central Committee Plenum, translated in *Chinese Law and Government* 1 (Winter 1968–1969): 85–93.

[31] *The Statesman*, November 22, 1962, and November 28, 1962.

[32] Ibid., September 9, 1959.

[33] Ibid., November 2, 1959, and December 30, 1959.

the central leadership.[34] In January 1961, at the state party's Burdwan Conference, the Right faction unsuccessfully advocated that the state unit work for a National Democratic Front with, among others, "progressive Congress elements."

While these actions of the Right faction in West Bengal revealed the tensions that existed within the state party, they were for the most part pursued within the limits of party discipline established by the central and state organizational leadership. After the Chinese attacks on India in October 1962, however, the Right faction began to assert itself in ways that posed a much greater threat to the leftist leadership in Bengal. For the first time in the history of the state party, the Right faction made a direct appeal to central party leaders for organizational support against the regular state party organization. On October 26, the day on which the Indian president proclaimed a State of Emergency, the Midnapore District Council of the state party passed a resolution condemning China's intrusion across "our national boundary" as "an attack on world peace," despite warnings from the regular state party organization to desist from doing so, and despite the fact that Biswanath Mukherjee, the leader of the Midnapore District unit, had attempted to raise the same resolution at a meeting of the State Executive Committee without success.[35] Following the lead of the Midnapore unit, the Right faction within the Calcutta unit drafted a similar resolution, and two leading rightist leaders from Calcutta (Bhowani Sen and Renu Chakravarty) publicly announced their unequivocal opposition to "acts of Chinese aggression." After the Left faction was jailed for its refusal to support the National Council resolution of November 1,[36] eight of the leading rightists and centrists in the state party were designated by the party center as the State Secretariat of a new Provincial Organizing Committee (POC), and Bhowani Sen was designated as the secretary of this committee (the other members of the POC were Somnath Lahiri, Biswanath Mukherjee, Renu Chakravarty, Ranen Sen, Indrajit Gupta, Jolly Kaul, and Biren Roy).[37]

With the Right faction in control of the state party organization outside the jails, the Left faction organized inside the jails, forming a

[34] Ibid., January 28, 1960, and March 7, 1960. Portions of this "syllabus" have since been included in *A Course of Party Education: Second Stage* (for Branch secretaries) (New Delhi: CPI, 1968); see especially pp. 141–168.

[35] *The Statesman*, October 27, 1962.

[36] A list of those arrested under the Defence of India Rules in late 1962 appears in *New Age*, February 24, 1963, p. 4.

[37] *Thought* (New Delhi weekly), January 26, 1963. For Dange's position on the formation of the POC, see *New Age*, February 17, 1963, p. 3.

group known as the PCZ (a set of code initials with no known referents), which issued a number of public statements labeling the Right faction as "the rival group" or "the revisionists." The first of these statements, issued in early January 1963, argued that "the police and the rival group are working together to hound all Communists who have refused to be agents of the Right reaction" and sought to dispel "the myth of support [for the Right faction] from international Communism."[38] The PCZ documents argued that neither the CPSU nor the CPGB was supporting the "Dange clique," pointing for evidence to information that Dange had not been able to meet with Khrushchev during his recent trips to Moscow except in the presence of two Bengali centrists (Bhupesh Gupta and Ranen Sen). The PCZ was also concerned with activating Left faction supporters outside the jails and was eventually successful in closing down the regular state party newspaper (*Swadhinata*) and replacing it with a new Left faction journal (*Desh Hitaishi*). Acting under instructions from the PCZ, Left faction members attended a number of party meetings in districts where Dange and Bhowani Sen were attempting to build support for the POC. Speakers of the Right faction were shouted down, booed, and condemned as "agents of imperialism."[39] Rumors had meanwhile emanated from inside the jails that the leadership of the regular state party organization was now advocating an open split.

In the face of a continued challenge from the Left faction, the leadership of the POC appealed to the National Council of the party for power to discipline those who violated the party line in Bengal, a request that was turned down by the National Council in June 1963 but finally granted by the CEC in September.[40] Using the disciplinary powers granted by the CEC, the state POC then suspended a number of Left faction leaders who had been working underground (outside the jails) to disrupt party meetings and sabotage election campaigns fought by the POC. The most prominent leftist suspended by the POC was Niren Ghosh, who had organized a "convention" of the Left membership of the state party in Calcutta in defiance of Dange and the POC.[41] The purpose of the PCZ convention was ostensibly to

---

[38] *PCZ Information Letter*, January 1963, pp. 3–5.

[39] *The Statesman*, January 21, 1963.

[40] The decision to grant disciplinary powers to the POC is analyzed in *Link*, June 30, 1963, p. 9, and July 7, 1963, pp. 9–10; see also *Indian Affairs Record* 9, no. 8, p. 259, and *Thought*, September 7, 1963, p. 4.

[41] The position of the Left faction in West Bengal with regard to holding a PCZ convention in September 1963 is stated in *Desh Hitaishi* (party organ of the CPM), September 26, 1963, pp. 1 ff. The position of the CEC is stated in "On West Bengal 'Democratic Convention,' " in *Resolutions of the Central Executive Committee of the National Council of the Communist Party of India, New Delhi 14–17 September, 1963* (New Delhi: CPI, 1963), pp. 11–14.

launch a fifteen-day agitation for the release of political detainees, and both the PCZ and POC subsequently sent deputations to see Chief Minister P. C. Sen in an attempt to secure the release of those in jail.

In early December the government began freeing the leadership of the Left faction, not only in West Bengal but throughout India, although not necessarily because either faction had been effective in pressing for their release. In an attempt to seize the initiative from the POC and to demonstrate their strength within the state, the leftists of West Bengal plunged into a by-election campaign in Burdwan District (the stronghold of the Left) immediately after their release from jail, where a prominent Left faction leader (Benoy Chowdhury) was running for the state legislature. When the National Council attempted to assist the campaign by sending a prominent member of the National Council Secretariat (Z. A. Ahmad) to speak on behalf of Chowdhury, the Left faction placed Ahmad under "party guard" and confined him to his bungalow, lest the National Council and the Right faction gain some credit for the election of a Left faction member. In an impressive display of Left faction strength in West Bengal, Chowdhury was elected by a margin of 17,858 to 14,505 against a strong opponent, while the CPI candidates in two other by-elections held at the same time (who were not supported by the Left faction in 1963) each finished fourth in a four-man race.[42]

Having demonstrated their organizational superiority over the Right, the Left quickly picked up the support of a large section of the centrist faction, which had been wavering ever since the Chinese attacks on India. The Left faction then threatened to break openly with the party if the West Bengal State Council was not revived, and the CEC quickly moved to restore the State Council under the leadership of Pramode Das Gupta. But in restoring the State Council, the CEC laid down three conditions that had to be met by the council before it would be "recognized" by the CEC: (1) the council had to propagate "sincerely and wholeheartedly" the decisions of the National Council of the party; (2) the State Council had to denounce the PCZ publicly; (3) none of the disciplinary actions of the POC that had been taken in concurrence with the National Council could be revoked. In effect, these three conditions would have forced the Left faction to recognize the legitimacy of POC and National Council resolutions on organizational and ideological questions, and, if met, would have restored at least a semblance of unity to the state party.[43]

[42] Reports on the election campaign and the results appear in *The Statesman*, December 24, 1963, and December 27, 1963.

[43] The conditions laid down by the National Council are detailed in *Fight against Revisionism (Political-Organisational Report Adopted at the Seventh Congress of the Communist Party of India* [Marxist]) (Calcutta: E.M.S. Namboodiripad, 1965), pp. 45–47.

When the revived State Council met in early February 1964, however, it soon became evident that the Left faction was unwilling to meet the conditions that had been laid down by the CEC. Both the Right and Left were inclined toward an open split. On the second day of the meetings, seventeen rightists, led by Bhowani Sen, walked out as a protest against the attendance of Niren Ghosh, who had been expelled by the POC. The Left faction then proceeded to violate all of the conditions laid down by the CEC, by pushing through a resolution withdrawing the disciplinary action that had been taken against Niren Ghosh and by refusing to denounce the PCZ.[44] From February until April 1964, both factions busied themselves in preparation for the split that was now inevitable. The Left faction reconstituted the four District Committees that had been captured by the POC (24-Parganas, Bankura, Birbhum, and Hooghly) as a result of POC disciplinary actions, while the Right faction arranged for the establishment of its own newspaper, publishing facilities, and bookstore.[45] By late March, West Bengal Left faction leaders had conferred with leftists from other states in India and prepared draft programs for a new party, as well as contingency plans for Left faction meetings. Finally, at an "emergency meeting" of the National Council called by the Central Secretariat to discuss disciplinary measures to be taken against the Left faction, the thirty-two Leftists walked out. The split was complete.[46]

The Right faction in West Bengal was almost entirely dependent on the pro-Dange national leadership of the party for support, from the time of the organization of the POC in 1962 right up until the split in 1964. Dange had established himself at the party center after the death of Ajoy Ghosh, when he was chosen as party chairman (a new position in the CPI, with ill-defined powers) and E. M. S. Namboodiripad was named general secretary, an unstable compromise that sought to deal with the succession issue.[47] The elevation of Dange as party chairman had been agreed to by the Left faction, since leftist leaders

[44] Reported in ibid., pp. 48 ff.

[45] In 1964 the Left faction was still in control of the National Book Agency in Calcutta, which had been the CPI bookstore since the early 1940s. The Right faction therefore consulted with S. A. Dange during his trip to Calcutta in February 1964 and arranged to establish a new bookstore (Manisha Granthalaya) at a location just around the corner from the National Book Agency, to be managed by Dilip Bose, a former personal secretary of R. Palme Dutt. After the split in 1964, the National Book Agency became the publishing and distribution center of the CPM in Calcutta, while "Manisha" now fulfills the same role for the CPI.

[46] The Left faction version of the events leading up to the split is *Repudiate Dange and His Group!* (Calcutta: CPI, West Bengal State Council, 1964), pp. 1–12.

[47] For details of the compromise, see *New Age*, May 6, 1962, pp. 8–9, and May 27, 1962, pp. 1, 4.

were given augmented representation on the Central Secretariat, but the Left was unable to bring its new powers to bear on the national party once the Chinese attacks on India began in the fall of 1962. After Dange succeeded in pushing through the November 1 resolution, the leading Left leaders in the Secretariat resigned their positions,[48] and by February of 1963 Namboodiripad had resigned as general secretary and editor of *New Age*, leaving the Dange leadership in sole control of the central organs of the party. Because the Right faction was so firmly entrenched in the most powerful committees at the central and state levels, the Left faction had to launch a concerted attack on both levels but especially on Dange himself, who had by now become the linchpin of the entire organizational apparatus.

The attack on Dange and the "Dangeites" by the Left faction in 1963 was merciless, bitter, and personal. It revolved for the most part around Dange's participation in the Cawnpore conspiracy (to deprive the King-Emperor of the sovereignty of British India) in 1924, including a series of letters by and about Dange at the time of the Cawnpore conspiracy trials. There is some evidence that the incident of the "Dange letters" was prompted by members of the CPGB, although the issue was first raised in the March 7 edition of *Current*, a right-wing anticommunist weekly published in Bombay. The principal letters quoted by the leftists to discredit Dange were dated July 26, 1924 (consisting of a petition by Dange to the Governor General of India), and another written by Colonel Cecil Kaye of the Central Intelligence Branch of the British government in India, in which he summarized his assessment of Dange's revolutionary potential.[49] In the first letter Dange had referred to a conversation with a British official named Stewart, in which Stewart had told Dange, "You hold an exceptionally influential position in certain circles here and abroad. Government would be glad if this position would be of some use to them." In his July 26 letter to the Governor General, Dange had quoted this conversation with Stewart and then added,

I think I still hold that position. Rather it has been enhanced by the prosecution [in the Cawnpore trials]. If your Excellency is pleased to think that I should use that position for the good of your Excellency's Govt. and the country I should be glad to do so, if I am given the opportunity by your Excellency granting my prayer for release. [50]

[48] *Swadhinata*, December 12, 1962, p. 1, and December 27, 1962, p. 1.
[49] The full text of the letters appears in *Dange Unmasked! Repudiate the Revisionists!* (New Delhi: CPI, 1964), pp. 1–12. Fifty-six pages of comments by Left faction members were also included in this pamphlet.
[50] Quoted from the account by Muzaffar Ahmad, *S. A. Dange and the National Archives* (Calcutta: Vanguard Publishers, 1964), p. 5.

In short, the July 26 letter indicated that Dange had offered himself as a "spy" for the British government in India. But even more damaging to Dange was the letter of Cecil Kaye, which indicated that the British Intelligence network held such a low opinion of Dange's own character that it would have been unlikely to have employed him as a spy. Kaye, for example, referred to Dange as a man of "personal cowardice" and "nervousness" and stated that "from all reports I conclude that Dange is only a worm; he is not worth the powder and shot" and that "no action need be taken against him; it is enough if he is called by an officer and given a severe official talking-to; that will frighten him."[51]

Dange argued that the letters were forgeries, although he refused to submit them to a party committee for analysis, but there is little reason to doubt their authenticity. Nevertheless, the Right faction in West Bengal defended Dange as a loyal party member who had served the party for more than forty years and who had suffered imprisonment on numerous occasions. One of the leading Right faction leaders in West Bengal, Renu Chakravarty, labeled the entire Dange "letter incident" as "a shabby attempt at *suppressio veri* and *suggestio falsi*, presenting the whole record in a slanted way."[52] Nevertheless, the Left faction continued to insist that "the question of Dange is an ideological one of prime importance . . . it is not at all a private affair of Dange's,"[53] and the Dange letters ultimately affected the way in which the split was carried out. Because of the evidence provided in the Dange letters, the Left faction had demanded that Dange step down as chairman of the CEC's meeting of April 9, preparatory to the meeting of the National Council scheduled for April 10, in order that a full discussion of the letters might take place. When Dange refused to vacate the chairmanship on April 9, twelve Left faction members of the CEC walked out, and on April 11 the thirty-two members of the National Council walked out in protest against the agenda that had been drawn up by Dange.

Centrist Attempts at Mediation

In retrospect, attempts to mediate the numerous disputes between the Right and Left factions of the CPI in 1964 seem like futile exercises, but they did not seem so to a number of party leaders at the time. The leaders of the electoral machinery of the party, in West Bengal and Kerala especially, were concerned that the party avoid the extremes toward which the two major factions seemed to be heading.

[51] Ibid., pp. 4–5.
[52] *The Statesman*, April 6, 1964.
[53] Muzaffar Ahmad, *S. A. Dange*, p. 16.

In the words of one centrist leader, the Right faction appeared bent on "being absorbed with the national bourgeoisie, perhaps even merging with the Congress," while the Left faction "seemed to be making every attempt to alienate the electoral base that we had so carefully built up." In order to avoid both of these extremes and perhaps preserve the unity of the Indian party, a number of prominent Communists attempted to mediate between the two major factions both at the state and at the national levels. The most prominent of these "centrists" were E. M. S. Namboodiripad, Jyoti Basu, and Bhupesh Gupta, all of whom had a personal stake in the future of parliamentary communism in India. The last two were prominent leaders of the electoral wing of the party in West Bengal.

Namboodiripad has been labeled by observers of Indian communism as belonging to the Right, Left, and centrist factions of the party at various times in his career, in large part because of his pragmatism and his ability to steer a rather individualistic course through the ideological and organizational debates that have plagued the party over the years. His strength in all of the major areas of party activity has made this achievement possible: he is the only Indian Communist leader who has a strong base in a state organizational apparatus and a state parliamentary party and is a leading party theoretician as well. Moreover, his position as Chief Minister in Kerala has given him added prestige throughout India, which has on occasion made it difficult for members of his own party to criticize him too severely. Namboodiripad's closest associates in the party argue that he is also the only original Communist thinker that the Indian party has produced, and they point to his large collection of writings on organizational and ideological questions as the source of a truly Indian solution to the vexing problems that have plagued Indian communism.

In his writings Namboodiripad has always differed both with the Right and with the Left factions in the party. As early as 1952 he argued that

. . . the struggle in India today is not between capitalism and Socialism, but between imperialism and feudalism on the one hand and the mass of our people on the other; further, . . . in this struggle capitalist economy, the capitalist class, has a role to play and . . . the mass of the people led by the working class can make use of it, provided they take all precautions that the capitalist elements are not allowed to drag the people into the arms of imperialism and feudalism. . . .[54]

[54] E. M. S. Namboodiripad, *On the Agrarian Question in India* (Bombay: People's Publishing House, 1952), p. 45, quoted in Marshall Windmiller, "Constitutional Communism in India," *Pacific Affairs* 31 (March 1958): 25.

As Marshall Windmiller has pointed out, Namboodiripad has always differed significantly from the Left faction of the party in his willingness to promote capitalism, particularly in the agricultural sector, in order to build a "rich peasant economy" while making "a deal with the capitalist class to create the industry needed to support . . . surplus agricultural labor."[55] At the same time Namboodiripad has always differed with the Right faction in his insistence on building a non-Congress coalition government in Kerala by means of mass struggle and has never hesitated to criticize the policies of Nehru, or even Gandhi.[56] In February 1963 Namboodiripad in fact established himself as the principal theoretician of the anti-Right when he submitted his thesis entitled *Revisionism and Dogmatism in the CPI* to a meeting of the National Council in New Delhi; he resigned from his position as general secretary of the national party when the thesis proved unacceptable to Dange. After his resignation, Namboodiripad moved closer to the Left faction by arguing that the Dange group had become "ultra-nationalistic and chauvinistic," that the CPI had failed to gain ground in India because it had tried to "tail behind the bourgeois nationalists," and that the Right faction had lost its claim to leadership by "handing over a large number of Communist workers and leaders to the police."[57]

Once Namboodiripad had resigned as general secretary, he did not immediately join the Left faction or even ally with it against the Right but instead tried to secure the support of Moscow in a final attempt to bring about a rapprochement between the two factions. In the March 1963 issue of the Soviet-controlled *World Marxist Review*, Namboodiripad (identified only as "a member of the CPI Central Secretariat") published a review article—presumably with the endorsement of the CPSU—in which he reiterated his basic thesis (which had by now also come to square with the Soviet thesis) that the Indian bourgeoisie had "not exhausted its progressive role" but that the Nehru government had to be severely criticized on a number of issues.[58] The major portion of Namboodiripad's article was devoted to criticism of "some

---

[55] Ibid., p. 26.

[56] Namboodiripad's writings on Kerala include two short volumes: *Twenty-eight Months in Kerala: A Retrospect* (New Delhi: People's Publishing House, 1959) and *Kerala: Yesterday, Today, and Tomorrow* (Calcutta: National Book Agency, 1967).

[57] *The Statesman*, February 15, 1963. After "EMS" resigned, his closest associate in Calcutta, Jolly Kaul, left to take up residence in New Delhi. (Kaul eventually quit the CPI and is now employed as a public relations officer in a private firm in Calcutta.) For Kaul's version of the events leading up to the split in 1964, see "The Split in the CPI," *India Quarterly* 20 (October–December 1964): 372–390.

[58] Gelman, "The Communist Party of India," p. 140.

comrades" for believing it possible to "walk in step with the government." Evidently armed with some support from Moscow, Namboodiripad began to make a variety of overtures to CPI leaders throughout India in an attempt to rally them behind his "centrist" position. In West Bengal he was most concerned with the possibility of securing support from Jyoti Basu and Bhupesh Gupta.

Basu then occupied a position in the state party similar in many respects to that held nationally by Namboodiripad. He was the unquestioned leader of the legislative wing of the state party and on the basis of his legislative leadership had always been able to maintain some support within the regular party organization. Moreover, Basu's knowledge of parliamentary politics was a great asset to the state party, and his prestige within West Bengal was in many ways comparable to that of Namboodiripad in Kerala. It is significant, however, that Basu never attempted to become a leading theoretician in the party, largely because he had never been able to gain a position of sufficient organizational strength to propagate his own views on theoretical questions. Basu's strength in the state party depended on his ability to secure support from both the regular party organization and the electoral organizations, and his involvement in theoretical debates would certainly have strained his relations with one or the other.

Because of his dependence on the regular party organization, Basu has always subjected himself to the discipline of the party and has engaged in public "self-criticism" on a number of occasions at the state party's behest. In 1959 he even took part in Indo-Chinese solidarity meetings and acted as the state party's principal spokesman for its China position, both in public and at central party meetings. But Basu was always distrusted by the Left faction of the state party and was occasionally subject to merciless attacks by the leaders of the regular organization for having deviated from Left Communist tenets. In January 1961, at a meeting of the state parliamentary party, he was accused by Pramode Das Gupta of having made a "deal" with Chief Minister B. C. Roy to settle the Berubari issue without the prior knowledge of the state party organization, and at the Burdwan conference in 1961 he was accused of an attempt to promote the electoral organizations of the party in Calcutta for his own personal or factional aggrandizement at the expense of the rural areas and the well-being of the state party organization.[59] When Basu negotiated a loan with a wealthy landowner in South Calcutta to purchase a printing press for the publication of party materials, he was accused

[59] *The Statesman*, January 24, 1961.

by Das Gupta of "individualism" (implying that he was attempting to promote his personal interests in the party), and his success in securing the nomination of Indrajit Gupta in a Calcutta by-election in 1960, despite the opposition of the regular party organization, was countered by the expulsion of Gupta from the State Secretariat.[60]

Despite the tense relations with the regular party organization, Basu continued to speak for the Left-dominated West Bengal organization at party meetings and in public throughout the years preceding the split and even declined an offer by the Soviet Union to spend two weeks in Moscow in July 1961, when the state party refused him permission to go unaccompanied by leaders of the Left faction.[61] After the Chinese attacks in late 1962, however, he became conspicuous by his absence from several crucial national party meetings at which ideological questions were discussed, and he reportedly welcomed the opportunity to resign from the Central Secretariat after the November 1 resolution, since his resignation enabled him to gain some distance from the ideological debate. In response to the resolution, Basu publicly called on all Communist MLAs to contribute to the Indian Defence Fund and was instrumental in pushing through the State Council a resolution in which the West Bengal CPI agreed to implement the November 1 resolutions of the National Council "in a united and disciplined manner," despite disagreements.[62] Nevertheless, Basu became the public symbol of the Left faction and of the pro-China stance of the CPI in West Bengal: in November 1962 he was burned in effigy in many parts of Calcutta, he was condemned by the Congress and Marxist Left parties in the Legislative Assembly as "a coward" and "a shameless opportunist,"[63] and he was among the first members of the CPI in West Bengal to be arrested by the government of India in November 1962 under the Defence of India Rules.

Inside the jails in 1963, a considerable section of the Left faction began openly to advocate a split, and many of the discussions inside the jails were concerned only with how to make the staging of the split serve the interests of the Left faction. Some of the leftists wanted to declare themselves a separate party inside the jails, but others argued that the leftists should allow the Dangeites to oust them from the party and leave Dange with the blame. In this atmosphere Jyoti Basu argued for party unity, and in October 1963 he collected twenty signatures among those in jail for a statement condemning the Left faction as

[60] Ibid., April 2, 1960.
[61] Ibid., July 20, 1961.
[62] Ibid., November 2, 1962, November 5, 1962, and November 11, 1962.
[63] *West Bengal Legislative Assembly Debates*, November 17, 1962.

"diehard dogmatists" who are "to be fought as ruthlessly as revisionists."[64] The signatories to this statement formed the core of a faction within the state that came to be branded as centrists; it was nominally led by Basu and sought alliances with other centrist factions in other states upon Basu's release from prison in late 1963. Three weeks after his release, Basu himself traveled to New Delhi, where he conferred with E. M. S. Namboodiripad about the possibility of a "third force" in the CPI.[65] It was at this point that Basu and Namboodiripad agreed to ally themselves at least temporarily with the Left faction in order to depose the Right leadership, which had ensconced itself in party committees during the period when the Left faction was in jail, but both Basu and Namboodiripad issued inner-party draft documents at the time that clearly established their centrist positions.[66]

Within West Bengal Basu refused to side with either the Right or Left faction at the meetings of the State Council in February 1964 at which the PCZ and POC clashed over the question of the conditions being laid down for the State Council by the CEC. A month later Basu and the centrist leadership in the state party combined with the Right faction at a party election committee meeting to defeat the Left faction by a vote of 12 to 11 in nominating Bhupesh Gupta for a seat in the Rajya Sabha (the upper house in the Indian Parliament).[67] When the issue of the Dange letters came to the fore, Basu wrote a personal letter to Dange asking him to consent to the establishment of a six-member party commission to determine the authenticity of the letters,[68] and the day before the walkout Basu, Namboodiripad, and Bhupesh Gupta made a last-ditch attempt to bring leaders from the two major factions together for private, informal talks that might settle differences at least temporarily.[69] On April eleventh, both Namboodiripad and Basu walked out with the Left faction, having

[64] *The Statesman*, October 5, 1963.

[65] Ibid., December 27, 1963.

[66] For Basu's statement, see Jyoti Basu, Niranjan Sen, et al., *On Some Questions Concerning the Ideological Controversy within the International Communist Movement* (New Delhi: 4 Windsor Place, 1964). The position of EMS is stated in E. M. S. Namboodiripad, *Note for the Programme of the CPI* (New Delhi: 4 Windsor Place, 1964), and criticism both of the Basu and of the Namboodiribad positions is found in P. Sundarayya et al., *A Contribution to Ideological Debate* (New Delhi: 4 Windsor Place, 1964) and M. Basavapunniah, *Our Views on E. M. S. Namboodiripad's Critique of Draft Programme* (New Dehli: n.p., 1964).

[67] *The Statesman*, March 10, 1964. Pramode Das Gupta's version of the election of Bhupesh Gupta is to be found in "An Aspect of Left Opportunism in West Bengal," *Desh Hitaishi*, October 21, 1967, pp. 1, 5.

[68] *The Statesman*, April 6, 1964.

[69] Ibid., April 11, 1964.

little alternative in light of their dependence on it for organizational support in electoral politics. But Gupta remained behind, moving an unsuccessful adjournment motion designed to bring the thirty-two members of the council back to the meetings.

After this event, since Basu was convinced that the split was complete, he tried to make peace with the Left faction within the confines of the new party, but Gupta continued to persist in his attempts to bring the two factions (now parties) back together, while other centrist leaders in West Bengal attempted to organize a third party that might eventually be able to reconcile them. In late May, Gupta succeeded in bringing Namboodiripad and Dange together in New Delhi for a series of talks, and a month later he and John Gollan (general secretary of the CPGB) tried to bring Basu, Pramode Das Gupta, and Dange together in a final effort to reconcile the Left, Right, and centrist factions.[70] The large Calcutta unit of the state party also attempted to reconcile the two major factions in May and June 1964, suggesting a series of compromise measures that ultimately proved unacceptable to the Left, while another group of 250 centrists (including 15 members of the State Council and 6 MLAs) held their own convention in Calcutta in August in a futile attempt to set up a third party that could incorporate both the Left and the Right.[71] By the end of the summer, however, it was clear that the split was irrevocable; both parties had already launched independent agitational movements and were holding meetings in preparation for separate party conferences.

The Consequences of the Split

If the split between the CPI and the CPM had involved only two major factions, the events of April 1964 might have at least reduced the need for accommodation within any one political party. If there had been only two factions in the communist movement in India, some sense of finality might have accompanied the split. But because three major factions were now divided between only two parties, factionalism continued to persist after the split in much the same manner as it had since Independence within the "united" CPI. One might even argue that factionalism within each of the Communist parties became much more intense after 1964 than it had been previously, particularly in West Bengal.

[70] A transcribed report of a portion of the talks in July is published in "Report on Unity Talks," in *Resolutions of the Tenali Convention of the Communist Party of India* [Marxist] (New Delhi: CPI [Marxist], 1964), pp. 29–35.
[71] *Link*, May 10, 1964, p. 19, and August 9, 1964, p. 15.

There are a number of reasons for the growth of factionalism after 1964. To begin with, both of the extreme factions (Right and Left) found it necessary to launch massive drives for recruitment of new members to support their positions, and both of them sought much greater control of their respective party organizations. But the centrists (some of whom were now in each of the parties) were also more determined than ever to fight against "revisionism" on the Right and "sectarianism" on the Left, with the result that they also redoubled their efforts to prevent either faction from gaining unquestioned control of either party. Moreover, the centrists were aided by two new factors that began to assume prominence after 1964: (1) the considerable support for the ideological position of the centrists that began to emanate from Moscow; and (2) the electoral victories of the Communist-dominated United Front alliances in Kerala (in 1965 and 1967) and in West Bengal (in 1967 and 1969). To the great distress of all Communists, each of these factors served to intensify conflict, but none of them was significant enough to bring about the triumph of any one faction or to produce great factional losses. As a result, the conflicts that the split in 1964 did not resolve have continued to characterize the history both of the CPI and of the CPM, and the cleavages within the united CPI have now been all but duplicated (but in two Communist parties instead of one). The creation of a third Communist party (the Communist party of India–Marxist-Leninist, or CPML), which was formed in April 1969, has brought only more of the same: it has produced more heated ideological debates in the CPI and the CPM, yet it has failed to unite the Communists to whom its appeal was directed.

In all of this maneuvering the CPM has thus far gained more than either the CPI or CPML. Not only has it demonstrated its superior organizational strength, both in terms of membership and in terms of its leadership of various political movements, it has also dominated the electoral fronts in both Kerala and West Bengal. At the same time, the CPM has been unable to make gains outside of Kerala and West Bengal, and it has suffered from more internal factionalism than either the CPI or CPML, mainly because its leadership has had to accommodate larger portions of the Left and centrist factions than either of the other two parties.

The CPI was clearly faced with the greatest task of reconstruction in West Bengal. Ten days after the walkout of April 10, the Central Executive Committee of the CPI had to disband the eight-man State Secretariat, since five of the eight had been among those who had

walked out at the National Council meetings. The extent to which the
CPI had to completely rebuild its party organization in West Bengal
was indicated by the fact that the new State Secretariat announced in
July contained none of the members of the previous Secretariat (seven
of the eight had joined with the CPM and the eighth had led the
opposition to Dange within the regular CPI). Moreover, the CPI could
secure the support of only 23 of the 102 members of the previous State
Council. The new CPI State Secretariat had to give up the previous
headquarters of the state party, which remained with the CPM under
threat of force, and the state CPI was therefore symbolically relocated
in a small, dark room on the ground floor of an old office building in
a congested, narrow lane in central Calcutta. For four months the
new state party headquarters of the CPI had no telephone, no type-
writer, and no signboard, and its leadership was preoccupied with the
establishment of a new vernacular newspaper (*Kalantar*) and hesitant
to choose a State Executive Committee because it wanted to lure
centrists into the party with offices. When the committee was finally
chosen, it immediately issued a circular to state party leaders in which
it declared that "even though the newly appointed Secretariat is
staffed by known Rightists it would not be difficult to make adjustments and accommodate the Centrists if they desired to be represented."[72] Eventually a number of centrists did drift back into the
regular CPI, but not in sufficient numbers to present a challenge to the
CPM. When the state Legislative Assembly reconvened in late July
1964, the CPI state legislative party was reconstituted under the
leadership of Somnath Lahiri, but it could muster only 12 of Bengal's
51 Communist MLAs.

Most of the MLAs in West Bengal followed Jyoti Basu into the
CPM, where they allied with Pramode Das Gupta and the regular
party organization and began to rebuild the state unit under a new
banner. That this was truly an alliance between two factions was
indicated at the first meeting of the "new" CPM,[73] at which both Basu
and Das Gupta were allowed to present their own factional reports
on the meetings of the National Council and the walkout, and each
was followed by a critical report by a member of the speaker's rival
faction, then by a sharp termination of the "discussion." After this
meeting both the Left and centrist factions began the job of screening
the 17,000 members of the state party for supporters, in preparation
for a conference to choose a new State Council. By the time the

[72] *The Statesman*, July 13, 1964.
[73] Ibid., April 25, 1964.

state conference of the CPM took place (in late October 1964), its Central Executive Committee had decided to revert back to the two-tier system of organization that had governed the party before the Amritsar conference in 1958, and the state conference in October was therefore asked to choose only a thirty-nine-member State Committee (the larger State Council having been abolished). The degree of control still exercised by the Left faction after the split was indicated by the fact that Jyoti Basu was able to secure the election only of himself and three of his followers (Niranjan Sen, Saroj Mukherjee, and Amritendu Mukherjee) to the State Committee, while the remaining thirty-five members were generally regarded as leftists or as organization men loyal to Pramode Das Gupta.[74]

In the words of one member of the State Secretariat of the CPI in an interview conducted in 1969, "After the split everything had changed, and yet things seemed to remain pretty much the same as before." In the regular CPI the Right faction now controlled the state unit of the party, but the leadership of that faction soon became opposed to the continuance of Dange as leader of the national party, and since 1964 a number of Bengali CPI leaders (Bhupesh Gupta, Somnath Lahiri, and Ranen Sen) have been prominent in a movement to "broaden the base of national CPI leadership." Within the state unit of the CPI the Right faction faced severe criticism from the centrists, who argued that the rightists had been somewhat arrogant and unrealistic in their exercise of power during their period of tenure in the POC, and in response to opposition both from national and from state leaders the Right faction has adopted much the same strategy as the Left faction had adopted in the united CPI. Since the split, Right faction leaders have opposed the national leadership of the CPI on a number of occasions, and the national leadership has usually settled for compromise solutions that were acceptable to the state leadership. At the state level the Right faction has used party discipline and an occasional compromise measure to bring about at least a semblance of unity, while it has concentrated on strengthening its control of the organization. Similarly, in the CPM the national party committees were quickly captured by a combination of Left and centrist faction leaders after the split, and CPM programs have since necessitated a series of compromise measures palatable to both factions. Moreover, the state leadership of the CPM has also reverted to its previous pattern of relations with the national leadership, with the centrists replacing the rightists as the main protagonists of the Left faction within the state.

[74] Ibid., October 27, 1964.

5

ELECTORAL POLITICS AND POLITICAL POWER

The factional problems that have plagued the Communists in West Bengal have also been present in other Indian political movements. Since 1947 more than fifty political parties have contested the elections for the Legislative Assembly in West Bengal, and a good many of them have won seats from time to time. In light of the fascination of Bengalis for Marxism-Leninism, it is not surprising that a number of these parties have been dominated by Marxist Left and Communist politicians. In fact, the questions that dominated discussions of politics in West Bengal before the 1967 elections were not those that sought to explain the growth of leftism in Bengal. Instead, they sought explanations for the remarkable (if tenuous) political stability of one of India's most problem-ridden states, a stability usually attributed to twenty years of uninterrupted Congress rule.

The elections of 1967 and 1969 have changed this focus of inquiry. With the defeat of the Congress party in West Bengal and the subsequent formation of a government generally regarded as Communist-dominated, a number of new questions have arisen. How can one account for the defeat of the Congress in 1967 and 1969? To what extent do these electoral defeats reflect the growth of leftism, or can they be accounted for by other factors? What has been the effect of the United Front governments on leftist unity and leftist strength? In short, have the events set in motion by the elections of 1967 and 1969 created greater opportunities for revolutionary forces in West Bengal, or have they served to impede them? The following chapter is an attempt to answer the first two of these questions; the last two are taken up in subsequent chapters.

Party Clusters

At first sight organizational politics in West Bengal seems like a hopeless maze of confusion. Of the more than fifty political parties that have contested elections to the state Legislative Assembly since 1947, many represent mere factions that have broken with the older parties, many are splinter groups from the various factions, and some of the splinter groups have in turn split two or three times themselves. In this atmosphere it may be reassuring to remind ourselves that the universe of Bengali organizational life is limited, at least in some respects. Only twenty of the fifty parties have ever won seats in the Legislative Assembly (see Table 3).[1] Moreover, there are some affinities between these twenty parties despite the fact that they are organizationally separate. In terms of their programs, they can be divided into five major clusters:

1.   The most successful vote-getting party in all five of the elections to the state Legislative Assembly has been the Indian National Congress, which in Bengal (as elsewhere in India) is an aggregative party committed to a democratic socialism that is constantly in need of redefinition.[2] The Congress in Bengal was free of severe factionalism until 1966, though a major split did occur in 1950, when Prafulla Chandra Ghosh resigned from the Congress, formed the Krishak Praja Mazdoor party (Peasants', People's, and Workers' party), and eventually combined with the Socialist party at the national level to form the Praja Socialist party (PSP).[3] But the Praja Socialists have since contested every election in West Bengal with little success and have been seriously affected by further factional splits. The most serious division in the PSP came in 1964, when the majority of its leadership withdrew to form the Samyukta Socialist party (SSP), and in both the 1967 and 1969 elections the Samyukta Socialists managed to outpoll the PSP by a small margin.[4]

The second split in the Congress, involving the defection of a large number of Congressmen into the Bangla Congress in 1966, has had a much greater impact on the politics of the state than the split in 1950. The Bangla Congress was instrumental in the formation of the United Front (UF) government in 1967, after defeating the Congress in enough constituencies to deprive it of a majority in the state

[1] The figures listed in the tables, and other election figures given in the text of this chapter, are drawn from the reports on the elections published by the Election Commission for the 1952, 1957, 1962, and 1967 elections. Since the report of the Election Commission for the 1969 elections was not available at the time of writing, figures for 1969 were drawn from the unofficial reports of each constituency published in *The Statesman* (Calcutta daily). Figures for the Praja Socialist party in 1952 include votes and seats obtained by the Socialists and the KMPP, since these two parties eventually merged with the PSP in the four elections that followed.

[2] Congress socialism is explored in Stanley Kochanek, *The Congress Party of India: The Dynamics of One-Party Democracy* (Princeton: Princeton University Press, 1968), pp. 188–210.

[3] See *The Statesman*, November 14, 1950, for a report on the split in 1950.

[4] The split between the SSP and PSP in West Bengal is analyzed in ibid., December 1, 1966.

TABLE 3

PERCENTAGE OF VOTES POLLED BY POLITICAL PARTIES
IN WEST BENGAL LEGISLATIVE ASSEMBLY ELECTIONS (1952–1969)

Political Party		1952	1957	1962	1967	1969
Congress		38.93	46.14	47.29	41.13	40.42
Bangla Congress		(founded in 1966)			10.44	8.00
PSP		11.87	9.85	4.99	1.88	1.25
SSP		(founded in 1964)			2.13	1.82
INDF		(founded in 1968)				0.82
	Subtotal	50.80	56.00	52.28	55.58	52.31
CPI		10.76	17.82	24.96	6.53	6.78
CPM		(founded in 1964)			18.11	19.55
	Subtotal	10.76	17.82	24.96	24.64	26.33
FB		5.29	3.84	4.61	3.87	5.40
FBM		—	0.85	0.32	0.21	0.19
FBR		1.51	(merged with PSP after 1952 elections)			
SUC		—	0.75	0.73	0.72	1.48
RSP		0.86	1.24	2.56	2.14	2.75
RCPI		0.43	0.42	0.42	0.31	0.37
WPI		—	—	0.28	0.34	0.35
	Subtotal	8.09	7.10	8.91	7.59	10.58
Jan Sangh		5.61	0.98	0.45	1.33	0.83
Hindu Mahasabha		2.37	2.04	0.80	—	0.13
Swatantra party		(founded in 1959)		0.57	0.81	0.07
	Subtotal	7.98	3.02	1.82	2.14	1.03
LSS (Purulia)		—	0.82	0.72	0.68	0.73
GL (Darjeeling)		0.46	0.43	0.40	0.45	0.52
PML		(founded in 1968)				1.50
	Subtotal	0.46	1.25	1.12	1.13	2.75
Unsuccessful parties and independents		21.91	14.81	10.88	8.92	7.00
	Total	100.00	100.00	100.00	100.00	100.00

Legislative Assembly for the first time since Independence. While both the Congress and the Bangla Congress have had some organizational defections since 1967, only one of the resulting splinter parties (the Indian National Democratic Front, or INDF) was able to win a seat in the Legislative Assembly in 1969. The universe of political parties that have split off from the Congress and won seats in the West Bengal Legislative Assembly is therefore limited to four: the PSP and SSP, the Bangla Congress, and the INDF. Their programs link these four parties to the Congress, since they all attempt to be aggregative, and since they all speak of a commitment to democratic socialism. Until 1967, this group of parties dominated the electoral politics of West Bengal (see Table 4).

2. A second group of political parties consists of those that have close ties with foreign Communist parties. These are the parties that are the subject of this book. As has already been pointed out, the CPI was the second largest party in the Legislative Assembly until 1964, when it relinquished this position to the CPM. In the 1967 and 1969 elections the CPM managed to outpoll the parent CPI by a considerable number of votes (Table 3), and the CPM is now the largest party in terms of seats, having surpassed the Congress in 1969 (Table 4). While the Communist parties are still in a minority in West Bengal (their combined vote in 1969 was only 26.33 percent, the highest it has ever been, and their combined number of seats was only 110 in an assembly of 280), they have grown very rapidly since Independence, and they occupied the most influential ministries in the coalition that governed the state in 1969–1970.

3. The most distinctively Bengali political parties are the large number of small Marxist Left groups that dot the political landscape. They stem from the small nationalist and terrorist societies that grew up in Bengal in the early part of the twentieth century and whose members were converted to Marxism in the jails in the 1930s. The largest of the Marxist Left parties is the Forward Bloc, which was created by Subhas Bose in 1940 in an attempt at left-wing unity. The Forward Bloc has also split a number of times since Independence, the two largest splinter groups being the Forward Bloc–Ruikar, which broke with the Forward Bloc in 1948 and merged with the PSP after the 1952 elections, and the Forward Bloc–Marxist, which split off from its parent in 1954. The other Marxist Left parties that have contested and won elections are the Revolutionary Communist party of India, or RCPI (founded by Saumyendranath Tagore, the grandnephew of the great poet, in 1934), the Revolutionary Socialist party, or RSP (founded in 1938), and two factions that split off from the RSP prior to the

TABLE 4

NUMBER OF SEATS WON BY POLITICAL PARTIES
IN WEST BENGAL LEGISLATIVE ASSEMBLY ELECTIONS (1952–1969)

Political Party		1952	1957	1962	1967	1969
Congress		150	152	157	127	55
Bangla Congress		(founded in 1966)			34	33
PSP		15	21	5	7	5
SSP		(founded in 1964)			7	9
INDF			(founded in 1968)			1
	Subtotal	165	173	162	175	103
CPI		28	46	50	16	30
CPM		(founded in 1964)			43	80
	Subtotal	28	46	50	59	110
FB		11	8	13	13	21
FBM		—	2	—	1	1
FBR		2	(merged with PSP after 1952 elections)			
SUC		—	2	—	4	7
RSP		—	3	9	6	12
RCPI		—	—	—	—	2
WPI		—	—	—	2	2
	Subtotal	13	15	22	26	45
Jan Sangh		9	—	—	1	—
Hindu Mahasabha		4	—	—	—	—
Swatantra party		(founded in 1959)		—	1	—
	Subtotal	13	—	—	2	—
LSS (Purulia)		—	7	4	5	4
GL (Darjeeling)		3	—	2	2	4
PML		(founded in 1968)				3
	Subtotal	3	7	6	7	11
Unsuccessful parties and independents		16	11	11	11	11
	Total seats	238	252	252	280	280

1952 elections, the Socialist Unity Centre (SUC) and the Worker's party of India (WPI).

The Marxist Left parties of Bengal differ from the Congress and its factions because they all claim to be revolutionary socialist parties: they advocate nationalization of industry, confiscation of land without compensation, and confiscation of foreign capital. Without exception they do not accept Gandhi's principle of nonviolence, they loathe "liberals" of any stripe, and they are convinced that the Congress "socialist pattern of society" is mere sham. They have a positive attraction to, almost a fascination for, militancy and violence, and many of them have traditionally argued that they are contesting elections only as a means for bringing about a revolutionary change in the constitution. At the same time they have fundamental differences with foreign Communist parties, and they are frequently hard pressed to determine whether their greater enemies are the Congress and rightist parties of Bengal or the Communist and other Marxist Left parties.[5] During World War II none of these parties supported the Soviet Union's "People's War" strategy, and during the Chinese invasion all but the SUC became militantly opposed both to the Chinese and to the Indian Communists. While these parties do not necessarily measure their success in terms of votes or the seats they gain in the Legislative Assembly, they have nevertheless been able to attain an important position in the electoral politics of the state. In the 1969 elections they garnered more than one-seventh of the seats in the Legislative Assembly (42 out of 280) and 10.58 percent of the vote. As a result of this success, 11 of the 30 Cabinet ministers in West Bengal in 1969–1970 were members of the Marxist Left parties.

4.   Little need be said about the other groupings that have won seats in West Bengal, since none of them has been very successful in the elections. The least successful of these groupings consists of the parties that are usually considered "rightist," parties that emphasize the preservation of traditional Indian values and that are rabidly anti-communist and anti-Marxist. In the five general elections since 1947, three such parties have won seats at one time or another in West Bengal, but the total number of seats won by all three—the Jan Sangh, Hindu Mahasabha, and Swatantra—has only been 15 in five elections. In 1967 Swatantra and Jan Sangh won one seat each (the Mahasabha none), and in 1969 all of the candidates of all three parties were soundly defeated.

[5] For a description and analysis of some of the ideological and factional splits among the Marxist Left parties of West Bengal, see Myron Weiner, *Party Politics in India* (Princeton: Princeton University Press, 1957), pp. 117–163.

5. Finally, there are three other parties that have contested and won elections in West Bengal at some point during the last five elections, each of which is based on local or communal attachments. The Lok Sevak Sangh is a Gandhian socialist party confined to Purulia District and is primarily pledged to furthering the interests of Purulia (Purulia is the area of Bihar that was added to West Bengal after the States Reorganization of 1956). Similarly, the Gurkha League represents the interests of the hill people of Darjeeling, and the Progressive Muslim League, which was founded only in 1968, seeks openly to represent the interests of Muslims. While these local and communal parties are of great importance in some few constituencies in one or two districts, thus far they have had virtually no impact in the wider arena of state politics.

When Bengal's numerous political parties are arranged into these five groupings, it becomes clear that there has been a fairly consistent pattern in the statewide voting results over the past five elections. In each one, the democratic socialist cluster of parties (the Congress and its offshoots) has obtained more than 50 percent of the vote, the percentage varying between 50.80 percent in 1952 and 56.0 percent in 1957 (see Table 3). The Congress party has always secured the largest percentage of the vote. Its portion has ranged from a low of 38.93 percent in 1952 to 47.29 percent in 1962. The Communist party secured a relatively small number of votes in the 1952 elections (10.76 percent) but steadily increased its electoral position until 1962, when it finally leveled off at around 25 percent; in both the 1967 and 1969 elections the Communists secured nearly the same portion of the vote as they had in 1962 (24.64 percent in 1967 and 26.33 percent in 1969). The percentage of the Marxist Left parties' vote has shown a very small increase. The gap between the lowest percentage they have obtained (7.10 percent in 1957) and the highest (10.58 percent in 1969) is slightly more than 3 percent. The rightists and the communal and local parties have never secured enough votes to be a significant force in the politics of the state.

Despite this fairly consistent pattern of statewide voting throughout the five elections, there has been a significant shift in the number of seats acquired by the various parties in recent years. Until 1967 the Congress had always been able to parlay its minority of votes into a legislative majority, gaining 150 seats with 38.93 percent of the vote in 1952, 152 seats with 46.14 percent of the vote in 1957, and 157 seats with 47.29 percent of the vote in 1962. In the 1967 and 1969 elections, however, the Congress continued to gain more than 40 percent of the votes, but its seats in the Legislative Assembly declined disproportionately, from a high of 157 in 1962 to 127 in 1967, then to a disastrous 55 in 1969. The failure of the Congress party to secure a majority of the seats in the last two elections is not owing to a loss of votes, but to their redistribution among opposition parties that have worked together in electoral alliances with increasing skill.

Over the course of the five elections there have been only two significant shifts in statewide voting patterns, one involving a decline in the number of unsuccessful parties and independents (from 22.37 percent of the vote in 1952 to a little more than 10 percent in 1962, and to only 7 percent in 1969), the second being the corresponding increase in the percentage of the vote secured by the Communist parties. This last shift not only indicates the success of the Communist parties in wooing independent voters and supporters of small and unsuccessful groups during the first three elections, it also reaffirms the point made earlier, that the statewide distribution of votes among various political parties has attained a remarkable degree of consistency, especially since 1962. The increase in the number of seats attained by the Communist and leftist parties in 1967 and 1969 must therefore be explained by an analysis of non-Congress electoral alliances, which have been designed to make the Communists and leftists more efficient in their effort to gain more and more seats from a relatively fixed percentage of votes.

Electoral Alliances

From the very first election in 1952 the Communist and Marxist Left parties in West Bengal were conscious of the need to promote leftist unity in order to outvote the Congress at the polls, and in every election they have been increasingly successful in devising electoral coalitions.[6] In 1952 there were two attempts at leftist electoral alliances, the United Socialist Organization of India (usoi) and the People's United Socialist Front (pusf). The usoi was originally conceived as an alliance of all Left parties, but it broke down over questions of ideology and strategy and finally amounted to an alliance between the cpi, the Socialist Republicans (a small and unsuccessful leftist party that was founded in 1947), and the Forward Bloc. The pusf was the rump of the usoi. It consisted of the parties that were unable to reach an agreement with the Communists: the Socialist party, the rcpi, and the Forward Bloc–Ruikar. In the context of the 1952

[6] In addition to newspaper reports and interviews, from which most of the information on party alliances was gathered, I have also consulted Subimal Pal, "The Leftist Alliance in West Bengal," *Indian Political Science Review* 1 (April–October 1967): 169–190.

elections the USOI was a great success. Largely because of electoral alliances in which the parties in the front agreed not to work against one another, the Communists secured 28 seats in the Legislative Assembly, the Forward Bloc 11, and the Socialist Republicans (running as independent candidates) 4. The USOI therefore obtained a total of 43 seats in the new Legislative Assembly and was easily the largest non-Congress bloc (Congress secured 152 seats out of 238). The PUSF, on the other hand, secured only 2 seats, with the result that two of the constituent parties in the PUSF (the Socialist party and the RCPI) eventually formed electoral fronts with other leftist parties, while the third, the Forward Bloc–Ruikar, went out of existence.

As a result of the relative success of the first electoral front in 1952, almost all the minor political parties of Bengal attempted to organize or to join electoral fronts in 1957. The largest of the three 1957 alliances (the United Left Election Committee, or ULEC) was again led by the CPI and consisted of the five major leftist parties at that time: the CPI, PSP, RSP, Forward Bloc, and Forward Bloc–Marxist. Once again the Communist-led electoral front gained the largest bloc of non-Congress seats (80 in an assembly of 252) and dwarfed both of the other electoral fronts. While the CPI-led ULEC was able to garner 80 seats in 1957, the noncommunist United Left Front (consisting of the SUC, Bolshevik, Democratic Vanguard, and Republican parties) was able to gain only 2 seats, and the United Democratic People's Front (made up of the RCPI, the Jan Sangh, Hindu Mahasabha, and a few independent Congressmen) failed to secure even one seat. As was the case in 1952, the parties in the noncommunist Left front were seriously affected by their failure to present a challenge to the Communists: both the SUC and the Bolshevik parties went into succeeding Communist-led electoral fronts, the Democratic Vanguard merged with the Workers' party of India, which in turn went into a Communist-led electoral front, and the Republican party became inactive.

By 1962 the pattern of leftist electoral fronts had therefore become quite predictable. It was clear, for example, that the largest leftist parties (the CPI, the Forward Bloc, and the RSP) could work together in electoral alliances and that they could either force smaller leftist parties out of the electoral arena or render them ineffective in terms of electoral politics. This point was driven home in the 1962 elections, when the Communist-led alliance of that year, the United Left Front (the name of the noncommunist Left front in the 1957 elections, adopted by the CPI in 1962 for tactical reasons), consisted of the CPI, Forward Bloc, Forward Bloc–Marxist, RSP, Bolshevik party, and RCPI. While the number of seats gained by the Communist-led electoral alliance diminished in the 1962 elections (from 80 in 1957 to 72 in 1962), both the Socialist Unity Centre and the Praja Socialist party, the two major Left parties that did not join leftist electoral fronts, suffered badly in terms of seats (the PSP declined from 21 seats in 1957 to 5 seats in 1962, and the SUC declined from 2 seats to none). By the time of the 1967 elections the SUC was therefore ready to join the Communists, while the PSP (which has continued to stay out of electoral alliances) has never been able to recover the position it held in the first two General Elections.

The reasons for the success of the CPI in forging electoral fronts in the first three elections involve the use of party funds for electoral purposes (the CPI has always been the wealthiest of the leftist parties) and the greater unity and strength that it gained from its attachment to an all-India party and an international movement. These organizational aspects of leftist politics have been dealt with elsewhere in some detail, but at this point it is important to note that the predominance of the CPI in leftist electoral fronts had unquestionably been established by 1962 (see Figure 1). By the 1967 elections it was still necessary for the various leftist and democratic socialist parties of West Bengal to engage in a great deal of negotiating in order to determine the kinds of electoral alliances they would join, but in the final analysis it was agreed that both of the electoral alliances to be created would be led by Communist parties. As a result of the split in the CPI in 1964, there were two electoral fronts in 1967: the People's United Left Front (PULF), led by the regular CPI, and the United Left Front (ULF), led by the CPM. As Figure 1 shows, these two electoral fronts were able to secure the cooperation of all of the significant Marxist Left parties of West Bengal, and of the Bangla Congress and SSP as well. The only democratic socialist party other than Congress that stood outside the two electoral fronts (the PSP) was severely beaten at the polls.

The 1967 Elections

The 1967 elections in West Bengal differed significantly from previous elections in at least two respects: (1) for the first time in the history of the state a non-Congress democratic socialist party (the Bangla Congress) emerged as an important factor in the elections; and (2) this party chose to ally itself with one of the Communist-dominated electoral fronts, thus making it possible for the non-Congress opposition to come to power. The impact of the Bangla Congress on the 1967 elections can be seen in Table 5, which traces the gains (in terms of votes) made by each of the major parties in the high-turnout elections

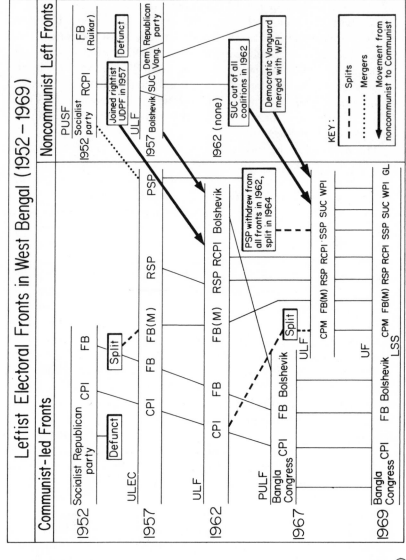

FIGURE 1
LEFTIST ELECTORAL
FRONTS IN WEST
BENGAL (1952–1969)

TABLE 5

DIFFERENCES IN VOTES POLLED BY MAJOR PARTIES IN WEST BENGAL
LEGISLATIVE ASSEMBLY ELECTIONS (1962 AND 1967)

Political Party	1962 Votes Polled	% Votes	1967 Votes Polled	% Votes	Difference (Votes Polled)
Congress	4,522,476	47.29	5,198,743	41.13	+676,267
CPI	2,386,834	24.96	933,407	6.53⎤	+801,802
CPM	(founded in 1964)		2,255,229	18.11⎦	
Bangla Congress	(founded in 1966)		1,325,013	10.44	+1,325,013
FB	441,098	4.61	491,704	3.87	+50,606
PSP	477,254	4.99	221,181	1.88⎤	+71,815
SSP	(founded in 1964)		327,888	2.13⎦	
Others and independents	1,735,739	18.15	1,925,409	15.91	+189,670
Total	9,563,391	100.00	12,688,574	100.00	+3,125,183

of 1967. Almost all of the parties in West Bengal gained more votes in 1967 than they had in 1962, but the Bangla Congress totals represented by far the largest increase. Congress was able to capture only 676,267 additional votes and the two Communist parties a total of 801,802, but the Bangla Congress secured a whopping total of 1,325,013, almost 42 percent of the additional votes cast in the 1967 elections. This alone would indicate that the Congress loss of 6.32 percent of the vote was picked up not by the Communist parties (for their percentage of the vote remained almost identical to what it was in the 1962 elections), but rather by the Bangla Congress, the dissident faction that had withdrawn from the Congress party only in 1966. Moreover, while the Bangla Congress cut into the Congress totals, it also made gains at the expense of other parties, amounting to another 4.12 percent.

The impact of the Bangla Congress can be seen in another way, by looking at the numbers and percentages of seats won in West Bengal in 1967 (see Table 6). If the increased size of the state assembly in 1967 is taken into account (there were 280 seats in 1967, compared to 252 in 1962), the Congress party would have had to gain 176 seats in the new assembly to maintain the same percentage of seats that it had won in 1962, but in fact it gained only 127 seats, 49 less than it needed. A comparison with the figures for the other parties shows that the bulk of the seats lost by the Congress party were picked up by the Bangla Congress, which won 34 seats. The two

TABLE 6

DIFFERENCES IN NUMBER OF SEATS WON IN WEST BENGAL
LEGISLATIVE ASSEMBLY ELECTIONS (1962 AND 1967)

Party	1962 Seats Won	1962 % Seats	1967 Seats Won	1967 % Seats	Actual Difference in Seats (1962–1967)	Seats Needed to Maintain 1962 Percentage	Adjusted Difference in Seats (1962–1967)
Congress	157	62.3	127	45.4	−30	176	−49
CPI	50	19.9	16	5.7⎫	+10	56	+3
CPM	—	—	43	15.3⎭			
Bangla Congress	—	—	34	12.2	+34	unknown	+34
FB	13	5.1	13	4.6	—	15	−2
PSP	5	2.5	7	2.5	+2	6	+1
Others and independents	27	10.2	39	14.3	+12	26	+14
Total	252	100.0	280	100.0	+28	280	—

Communist parties combined gained 3 seats more than the number needed to maintain their previous positions in the assembly, and the small Marxist Left parties and the independents gained an additional 14 seats. The overall picture is one of a narrow Congress defeat, partly because of the inability of the Congress to convert its minority of votes into a majority of seats, but primarily because of the emergence of the Bangla Congress.

In most party systems the Congress party might have attempted to form a coalition government after the 1967 elections, since it clearly had the largest number of seats in the new assembly (127 out of 280, the next largest party being the CPM with 43 seats), and since it was conceivable that some of the smaller parties and independents might have welcomed a Congress-led coalition. Indeed, the leader of the state Congress party, Atulya Ghosh, was rumored to have said shortly after the results were in that " . . . if the Prime Minister wanted, the Congress would even form a coalition with the Marxist Communists."[7] But in the final analysis the Congress received no encouragement from Mrs. Gandhi to enter into a coalition, and former Congress Chief Minister P. C. Sen stated flatly that he "would prefer the President's Rule to forming a Government with the help of any other party."[8] In addition, the leaders of the non-Congress opposition were so jubilant over the failure of the Congress to secure a

[7] *The Statesman*, February 25, 1967.
[8] Ibid.

majority that they quickly expressed their willingness to enter into a coalition government. The United Front government of 1967 was therefore formed by a coalition of fourteen parties and an independent, including all of the parties in the two Communist-led electoral fronts, plus the Gurkha League, the Lok Sevak Sangh, and the PSP. Since the two electoral fronts had a combined total of only 126 seats (1 less than the Congress and 15 short of a majority), the votes of all three of the non–electoral front parties plus the vote of one independent were necessary to maintain the United Front government in power.

Under such circumstances it is not surprising that the United Front government of 1967 fell apart in less than nine months, but the impact of its experience in 1967 on the elections of 1969 can be seen from the fact that all but one of the parties that took part in the United Front government of 1967 were able to coalesce against the Congress in the 1969 elections. The elections of 1969 therefore represent the culmination of attempts at unity on the part of the non-Congress parties of West Bengal, as is shown dramatically in Figure 1.

The 1969 Elections

The 1969 elections in West Bengal resulted in a decisive victory for the United Front, but they were much more competitive than the wide gap in the number of seats would indicate. The front secured almost four times as many seats as the Congress (214 to 55 for the Congress, with the remaining 11 seats split between non-Congress, nonfront parties and independents), but the difference in the percentage of votes secured by the front and the Congress was less than 10 percent (Congress gained 40.42 percent of the vote, compared to the 49.7 percent of the vote gained by the United Front parties and independents). In almost a quarter of the contests in which the Congress and the front were pitted against one another (65 of 270 constituencies) the margin between the two was less than 5 percent, and in almost half of them (another 117 of 270 constituencies) the gap between them was less than 10 percent. This is not to minimize the decisiveness of the United Front's victory, for it won more than 90 of its seats by a margin of 10 percent or more, but the voting figures put the extent of its victory in greater perspective.

What the election results did indicate was how much the electorate in West Bengal had become polarized between the Congress party and the Communist-dominated front of leftists by the 1969 elections. Before the elections there was a feeling among some observers, and among many politicians, that the voters of the state were looking for a third alternative, or a "third force," which could draw votes both from the Congress party and from the United Front. Unlike previous election years, therefore, there were a number of new parties that came into being in the year or so before the elections, and five of them opposed both the Congress and the United Front in a number of constituencies. Two of them, the Progressive Muslim League and the National Party of Bengal, directed their appeals primarily at Muslims, one (the Proutist party) fought the elections largely over regional and language issues, while the other two (Lok Dal and INDF) were essentially liberal socialist parties attempting to join a wide variety of interests. The extent to which these parties were rejected by the electorate can be seen from the fact that of the 372 candidates running with the five parties, only 4 (1 member of the INDF and 3 from the Progressive Muslim League) were ultimately victorious. The total vote polled by the five new parties was 242,651, or slightly more than 2 percent of the vote. More than 90 percent of the candidates forfeited their deposits.

That the voters of the state have come to conceive of the party system as the opposition of the Congress and the Communist-leftist front is also indicated by other data. The number of independents contesting in 1969 was only 90, compared to 602 in 1952, 346 in 1957, 324 in 1962, and 327 in 1967. The number of voters who voted for parties or independents other than the Congress or the Communist-dominated Left front was reduced to 10 percent (compared to 45.02 percent in 1952, 31.35 percent in 1957, 29.84 percent in 1962, and 14.17 percent in 1967). For the first time since Independence, therefore, a coalition of leftist parties was able to face the Congress in virtually every constituency in the state (270 of the 280 constituencies), in every one of which it ran unopposed by other *leftist* parties. On the other hand, the two leftist electoral fronts that ran in the 1967 elections had opposed one another in 126 constituencies, each damaging the electoral efficiency of the other to a considerable extent.

Rebuilding Party Support

In light of the severity of the Communist split in 1964 and the public censure of both the CPI and the CPM following the Chinese attacks in 1962, two facets of the electoral position of the Communists in the 1967 and 1969 elections are particularly striking: (1) the ability of the two Communist parties (and particularly the CPM) to maintain their previous level of electoral support; and (2) the willingness of the other opposition parties in West Bengal to continue to form coalitions with the Communists in elections.

The period immediately following the split in the CPI is remembered by most Bengali Communists as a time of great disappointment, uncertainty, and frustration. From the time of the Chinese invasion until the split in April 1964, most party members had been preoccupied with the events surrounding the intense factional conflicts within the united CPI, but the months following the split were consumed by an even more intense factionalism within the two parties, which confronted each other in a struggle for survival. A number of respected party comrades (including Shanti Sinha Roy, Khalil Syed, and Jolly Kaul) had already renounced the communist movement by 1964, while old allies like the Forward Bloc had begun to search for non-communist political partners.[9] A Communist-led attempt to stage a *hartal* in Calcutta in May 1964 failed for the first time since Independence to paralyze the city. The food demonstrations staged by the CPI and CPM in August and September were made up almost entirely of party regulars and generated far less popular support than the party had usually been able to mobilize on the food issue. Not only had party membership decreased, but the support of peasants, workers, and especially the urban middle class had declined considerably. All of this was accompanied by a noticeable demoralization in party ranks.

The most important factors in reversing this deterioration of the state communist movement, making it possible for the Communists to maintain their statewide support, revive their electoral alliances, and eventually come to power in the state ministries, were two events that had their origins beyond the borders of West Bengal. The first of these was a series of arrests of members of the Left faction within the CPM, carried out by the central government in late December 1964 and early January 1965; the second was the reimposition of President's Rule in Kerala in March 1965. Both the arrests of CPM members and the proclamation of President's Rule in Kerala were defended by central government leaders as in "the national interest." But both were widely resented in West Bengal.

The decision to arrest more than 900 members of the CPM throughout India, beginning with a wave of arrests on the night of December 30, 1964, was publicly attributed to the Indian Home Minister, G. L. Nanda, although it was certainly carried out with the approval of the Cabinet. Nanda argued that he was fully aware of the possibility that the Indian government might be bestowing "a halo of martyrdom" on the CPM, but in his words "[it was] setting up clandestine apparatus for subversive activities at such a speed that to smash it two or three months hence would have been a more painful operation than the current crackdown."[10] Nanda stated in Parliament and in radio

---

[9] In December 1964, the West Bengal unit of the Forward Bloc actually voted to merge with the SSP, but this action was subsequently vetoed by a margin of 68 to 52 at an all-India meeting of the Forward Bloc. See *The Statesman*, December 21, 1964.

[10] Quoted from a prepared statement by Nanda announcing the arrests, published in ibid., January 1, 1965.

broadcasts and press conferences that the Indian government had evidence of the reestablishment of "tech cells" within the CPM, that ". . . the leaders of the party have been preparing the rank and file for an armed revolution and guerrilla warfare," and that the CPM was attempting to establish "an overland link with China" by organizing a network of party cadres in the border areas (including the "Siliguri corridor" connecting northern and southern Bengal and the centrally administered territories of Tripura and Nagaland). "The object of the party," according to Nanda, was "to promote an internal revolution to synchronize with a fresh Chinese attack, destroying the democratic government of India through a kind of pincer movement which . . . was hoped for but could not materialize in 1962."[11]

Nanda's actions immediately met with severe criticism throughout West Bengal and other parts of India. Jyoti Basu, who had not been arrested despite his prominent position in the CPM, immediately met with President Radhakrishnan and challenged the Indian government to produce a white paper explaining the actions of the Home Ministry, thus dramatizing the lack of substantive evidence provided by Nanda in defense of the arrests. Basu stated publicly on a number of occasions that he would resign from the party if the Home Minister could provide convincing evidence that the CPM was engaged in subversive activities. In reaction to this challenge the Home Ministry did prepare a document, which was placed before the Indian Parliament, but its accusations against the CPM turned out to be much more moderate than Nanda's previous statements and noticeably lacking in evidence of "subversive activities."[12] The document quoted a great deal of the rhetoric of the Left faction after the Chinese invasion, in addition to detailed Chinese statements of support for the CPM, but it failed to reveal anything that was not known or could not be surmised about CPM activities. Even the anticommunist *Statesman* was surprised at "the lack of anything concrete" in the statement of the Home Ministry,[13] and Nanda's only attempt to come to his own defense was a bland assertion to the effect that he had held a great deal back "in the interests of security."[14] Even the state government was reportedly

[11] Quotations from Nanda's broadcast to the nation on All-India Radio, the full text of which appears in ibid., January 3, 1965.

[12] For the full text of the forty-five-page statement, which was also published and widely circulated throughout India by the Home Ministry, see Government of India, Ministry of Home Affairs, *Anti-National Activities of Pro-Peking Communists and Their Preparations for Subversion and Violence* (New Delhi, 1965).

[13] February 19, 1965.

[14] For Nanda's defense in Parliament, see *Lok Sabha Debates*, March 12, 1965. In June 1969, after the CPM came to power in West Bengal, Nanda argued that his decision to arrest the CPM in 1964–1965 had been based on "faulty intelligence"; see the *Hindusthan Standard* (Calcutta daily), June 18, 1969.

surprised at this series of sudden arrests of Communists long after the Chinese threat to India had subsided in the public mind, and the Chief Minister of West Bengal (P. C. Sen) was reported to have said to Jyoti Basu that he could provide no explanation beyond the thought that "there must have been some reason."

In this atmosphere the Indian press began to speculate that the Congress government at the national level had been motivated by internal political considerations. Two theories about the arrests were (and still are) widely current in India. One of these is that Nanda had sought to influence internal factionalism within the CPM by placing members of the Left faction in prison, in this way allowing CPM centrists to gain control of party committees in much the same manner as the Right faction had seized control of the CPI machinery in 1962–1963. This theory was all the more plausible because Nanda had not arrested prominent centrist leaders (such as E. M. S. Namboodiripad and Jyoti Basu), and it was given even greater credence by members of the Left Communist faction who blamed Basu and Namboodiripad for their arrests, in much the same manner as they had previously blamed Dange.[15] The second theory revolved around the electoral position of the CPM in Kerala, where elections for the state Legislative Assembly were scheduled for March 1965. The CPM and its electoral allies in Kerala were particularly effective in arguing that Nanda had staged the arrests to cripple the CPM in the Kerala election campaign, and the CPM ultimately made considerable gains in the elections as a result of this issue.[16] In the 1965 elections in Kerala the CPM emerged as the largest single state party (winning 40 of 126 seats), despite the fact that 27 of the successful CPM candidates ran while still under detention.

The electoral success of the CPM in Kerala in 1965 was not great enough to allow the Communists to readily form a second coalition ministry at that time, but it was clear that the CPM had outpolled the Congress and had seriously damaged the regular CPI in Kerala, which won only two seats. Perhaps more important, both the Indian opposition parties and Indian journalists were convinced that Nanda's arrests of CPM leaders before the election had been responsible for CPM gains. When Nanda refused to release even the detainees who had won in the state elections in order that they might participate in attempts to form a ministry, there was a rather farcical debate in the Indian

---

[15] See *Basu Joins the Revisionists* (Calcutta: n.p., 1965), a cyclostyled pamphlet circulated by some of the more extremist members of the Left faction. See also *The Statesman*, February 5, 1965.

[16] The CPM position on the arrests—both as regards the central government statements and the role of the CPI—is detailed in E. M. S. Namboodiripad, *What Really Happened in Kerala: The Story of the Disruptive Game Played by Right-wing Communists* (Calcutta: National Book Agency, 1966); see especially pp. 7–11, 55–59.

Lok Sabha in which opposition MPs argued about whether Nanda had "run amok" or had "gone mad."[17] And when President's Rule was subsequently proclaimed again in Kerala, only three weeks after the elections and before the release of the CPM detainees, a number of opposition party leaders walked out of the Lok Sabha in protest against what they called "the death of the Indian Constitution."[18]

The reaction of the opposition parties in West Bengal to the CPM arrests and the proclamation of President's Rule in Kerala in 1965 was perhaps even more severe than it was in the rest of India, and in many ways it was reminiscent of the response of state political leaders to the West Bengal Security Bill in 1948. Not only had Bengalis tired of constant references to the "Chinese threat" by state and central Congress leaders (whose programs had been seriously affected by the invasion); they were also concerned with the possibility that such measures as the Defence of India Rules, preventive detention, and President's Rule might be used against Marxist Left parties as well as against Communists. In the words of Kanai Bhattacharya of the Forward Bloc, his party had favored arrests of the CPI during the time when the Chinese were "active aggressors," but "in the absence of an immediate threat it would only have been fair for the Government to have placed the Communists on trial rather than using emergency powers that were no longer needed."[19] In the West Bengal Leglisative Assembly, not one member of the Marxist Left or Communist opposition parties would defend the actions of the Home Minister, and most opposition leaders were vociferous in their condemnation of the arrests and the handling of the Kerala events. In the months following the arrests, the Marxist Left and Communist parties of West Bengal began to cooperate in planning a series of demonstrations, which took place in late July 1965 and linked state economic issues with protests against the Defence of India Rules, preventive detention, and President's Rule. Most of the leftist leaders of Bengal who had remained outside the jails since the Chinese invasion now began to court arrest in a series of protest movements and violent activities. Within a year of the arrests and the events in Kerala, it was clear that Communist alliances with the Marxist Left parties of Bengal had been completely restored and party organizations rebuilt, largely on the basis of these demonstrations.

The "return" of the leftists as a powerful force in state politics was dramatically demonstrated in the Bengal *bundh* (a movement for complete stoppage of normal activities) of March 1966, which

[17] *Lok Sabha Debates*, March 10, 1965.
[18] Ibid., March 24, 1965.
[19] *West Bengal Legislative Assembly Debates*, May 7, 1965.

was the culmination of almost three months of agitational activities on the part of the leftist parties, indisputably led by the cadre of the CPM.[20] In preparation for the *bundh*, mass agitation was encouraged on a host of issues—food shortages, price increases, release of political detainees, redress of teacher and student grievances, and protest against the Defence of India Rules and President's Rule in Kerala, among others—frequently joined to enhance the size and militancy of a given demonstration. The movement started in January 1966 with frequent rallies and demonstrations held by leftist parties to create the necessary tempo and tension for a massive onslaught on the administration. Every possible grievance of the state population was discussed in bitter, angry tones until feelings had been worked up to a high pitch among a number of the major segments of the state population (students, teachers, peasants, clerks, bank employees). Only after considerable support had already been generated did the CPM begin to escalate the level of violence and militancy in mid-February. On February 16, 1966, 6 men were injured in a police firing at Basirhat, a Communist stronghold in 24-Parganas, and violence immediately broke out all over 24-Parganas. When a student was killed by the police the following day at Swarupnagar, another urban stronghold of the CPM in 24-Parganas, people began raiding markets to get food and kerosine (both of which had been severely rationed), and the "vanguard" of the raiders then became young college students, agitated over the death of the student at Swarupnagar. On February 19 students began to attack colleges with the intention of closing them down until the police explained the shooting, and by this time the regular CPM cadre had also initiated a series of attacks on police stations and the offices of block development officers in rural areas of 24-Parganas.

On February 22 all educational institutions in West Bengal were closed, while students throughout the state held "Martyrs' Day" ceremonies. When an attempt was made to reopen the schools on March 2, the result was again massive rioting. Another student was shot by the police at Krishnagar (in Nadia District), and all schools were again closed on March 5. After this second death, mob rule prevailed in Nadia for almost a week: two policemen were killed, the Krishnagar morgue was broken into, the body of the dead student was taken out in procession, and numerous buildings in Krishnagar

---

[20] This account of the Bengal *bundh* is drawn largely from newspaper reports, articles, and interviews but is heavily dependent on the excellent analysis (in four parts) by Kedar Ghosh, Amalendu Das Gupta, and Prasanta Sarkar, "The Bengal *Bundh*: An Analaysis," *The Statesman*, March 28–31, 1965. All figures and quotations not otherwise noted are taken from this series of articles.

were set on fire (including the railway station, all banks, 22 government buildings, and the home of a Congress minister.) On March 10 people converged on Calcutta from all over West Bengal, forming a procession of protest two miles long and completely paralyzing the city and much of the state for the next three days. These three days had been planned by the leftists as the culmination of the *bundh*, but the people's response surprised even the most optimistic of the leftist leaders.

During this month of almost constant violence the West Bengal Legislative Assembly was in chaos most of the time: the legislative highlights of the month included incidents where opposition leaders snatched the budget speech from the hands of the state Finance Minister, riots in the Legislative Assembly that resulted in the forcible ouster of 16 MLAs, and the arrest of 30 members of the state assembly under the Defence of India Rules. Damage to railways and trains in West Bengal during this period was estimated at more than 6 million rupees, damage to central government property alone was estimated at more than a crore (10 million rupees), and losses in terms of national income merely for the three days of the *bundh* in Calcutta were estimated by *The Statesman* at 6.5 crores (65 million rupees). The most conservative estimates placed the death toll for the demonstrations at 39 with 5500 arrests, figures that would have been much greater had auxiliary police not been called in periodically from other states and the Indian army not been present in West Bengal for almost a month. Most embarrassing for the Congress party were the serious disagreements that developed between state and central leaders as to how to cope with the movement, with Chief Minister P. C. Sen attempting to prevent either Mrs. Gandhi or Home Minister Nanda from appearing in Calcutta, on the assumption (which proved correct) that their appearance would only work to the advantage of the leftists. The Chief Minister and several of his colleagues threatened to resign at several points because of disagreements with the central government about procedures for dealing with the riots, and in consequence the state administration was frequently leaderless and confused, which in turn forced it to rely all the more on the army and the police.[21]

[21] Indicative of the confusion that prevailed among state and central leaders was an incident involving Mr. Samar Guha, secretary of the state PSP and a Member of Parliament. Guha had made an appointment to meet Mrs. Gandhi at Dum Dum Airport to offer his good offices, during her stopover in Calcutta on her return from Assam in March. But an hour before his appointment, Guha was arrested and detained by the state government, even though his party had never participated in the Bengal *bundh*. See Subimal Pal, "The Leftist Alliance in West Bengal," p. 173.

The Context of Electoral Alliances:
Party Factionalism and Food Policy

After its success in leading the Bengal *bundh*, which encouraged both of the strong factions within the party, the CPM in West Bengal became even more seriously divided than it had been previously over questions of electoral versus more revolutionary strategies. The centrists pointed to the *bundh* as proof that the CPM could immediately lead an alliance of leftist parties to positions of state political power in the February 1967 General Elections by capitalizing on the discontent that had been generated. But the Left faction saw the *bundh* as further evidence of a bottomless wellspring of discontent whose exploitation demanded a more revolutionary strategy. In the final analysis the CPM split again (in 1969) on this issue, with a portion of the Left faction going into the CPML, while the bulk of the party continued to pursue an electoral strategy. But in the summer of 1966 both factions were still in the CPM, and the party was faced with the need to unite behind a political strategy that would provide a solution to the vexing problem of electoral alliances.

The problem of devising a CPM electoral strategy for 1967 was further complicated by the rapid changes in the political environment that followed the Chinese and Pakistani war skirmishes of 1962 and 1965. Within less than a year after the Indo-Pakistani conflict of 1965, West Bengal had witnessed the first Bengal *bundh*, a major split in the state Congress party, and the formation of the Bangla Congress, all of which impinged on the electoral strategies of the Left parties. Moreover, these domestic political events were intimately related to the food crisis that had begun to develop in West Bengal in 1964 and had reached serious proportions in 1966, an effect of the recession that had hit India in the wake of two major land battles.

During the decade 1951–1961 the population of West Bengal (excluding Purulia, which was added in 1956) increased by 32.2 percent, compared with an all-India average increase of 21.6 percent. This increase was largely the result of the influx into West Bengal of more than four million Hindu refugees from East Pakistan in the period following partition. A high rate of population growth alone would have been enough to produce serious food shortages in West Bengal, but partition had created other food problems as well. After 1947 West Bengal was forced to shift a considerable portion of its arable land (11.4 percent by 1964–1965) from food crops to cash crops— principally jute and mesta—in an attempt to restore sources of industrial supply that had been cut off by the creation of an international boundary between the two Bengals.[22] Since Independence, therefore, the population of West Bengal has been increasing at a faster rate than the population in the rest of India, while more and more of its land has been diverted from the growing of food. Already deficient in food at the time of partition, West Bengal has grown more and more dependent on other areas of India to supply it, while the erratic fluctuations in crop production that have characterized all of India since Independence have been even more pronounced in West Bengal than they have been elsewhere. Complicating the political aspects of food policy in this environment is the specter of the Bengal famine of 1943, one of the worst in the history of India, and the emotions surrounding the partition of 1947, which is almost universally blamed for West Bengal's food shortages.[23]

In the mid-1960s, the unqualified opposition of Bengal's leftist politicians to the laissez-faire attitude of the state Congress party on the food issue added to the highly charged atmosphere. After Independence the West Bengal government had pursued a food policy remarkably free of government interference, even in the operation of the food-grain market. Rationing had been introduced in Bengal in 1944 by the Muslim League ministry headed by H. S. Suhrawaddy, but Suhrawaddy's rationing schemes had been so discredited (his men ran the ration shops) that the West Bengal government had encountered little difficulty in abolishing them. Moreover, leftist opposition groups tended to center on food policy issues because they directly involved the most powerful Congress leaders in the state government: Chief Minister P. C. Sen held the Food portfolio in the Cabinet from 1948, shortly after Independence, right up until the Congress government fell in 1967. Indeed, the Congress had based its electoral organizations in West Bengal on a number of groups that were especially significant in the state food production and distribution network: large and small landholders, millowners, the transport industry, and a host of shopkeepers and merchants. Because of the severity of the state's food problems, the political efficacy of the state Congress food policy had been tested by a number of food crises in the 1950s, but in spite of the vigilance of the opposition on this issue, the ability of the Congress to weather the crises had never been questioned.

[22] The effects of partition on West Bengal have never been fully traced, but for an introductory (and partisan) statement see Bidhan Chandra Roy, *Towards a Prosperous India* (Calcutta: Pulinbehari Sen, 1964), pp. 297–310.

[23] For the emotions surrounding famine and partition, see Tushar Kanti Ghosh, *The Bengal Tragedy*, 1st ed. (Lahore: Hero Publications, 1944) and *Recurrent Exodus of Minorities from East Pakistan and Disturbances in India: A Report* (New Delhi: Indian Commission of Jurists, 1965), pp. 1–20, 283–308.

In 1964, however, food prices began to rise rapidly throughout India, and scarcity was felt not only by consumers but also by wholesalers, millers, and retailers, despite bumper crops in rice and other food grains.[24] The reasons for this series of events have continued to be widely debated throughout India, but the West Bengal government was one of the first to offer the official explanation that this was "artificial scarcity in the midst of plenty."[25] In mid-May 1964, Food Minister P. C. Sen (who had also been Chief Minister since the death of B. C. Roy in July 1962) stated that there was "no reason why rice should be scarce" and argued that "a ring was operating to sabotage the state's food policy."[26] While the Chief Minister could not identify the speculators who engaged in such "sabotage," he was convinced that the food crisis had been brought about by "an unholy combination of a section of *jotedars* [large landholders] and rice millowners" who were attempting "to hoard food now, in the expectation of greater profits later on."[27] Chief Minister Sen could also give no reason for such an attempt at "conspiracy" in 1964, after seventeen years of relatively free trading in food grains, but at times indicated that he was "mystified" at the sharp increase in food prices and the sharp decline in food supply that characterized all of India in a year of excellent harvests.[28]

In response to the food crisis of 1964–1965, Sen began to introduce a series of rationing and price-control schemes, which eventually led to a system of cordoning in 1965 by means of which the state government hoped to control the distribution and the price of food grains (principally rice and wheat) in the large conurbation around Calcutta. The initial scheme called for a double cordon around Calcutta, involving 1000 men at 130 checkpoints on the streets leading in and out of the city and 15 traveling units checking railway cars and

[24] The nature of the 1964–1965 all-India food crisis is summarized in Michael Brecher, *Nehru's Mantle: The Politics of Succession in India* (New York: Praeger, 1966), pp. 138–150. Brecher also outlines the major positions in the debate over the origins of the crisis.

[25] Quoted from a statement by the state Food Ministry in *The Statesman*, May 12, 1964.

[26] Quoted in ibid., May 16, 1964.

[27] P. C. Sen, *New Dimensions: A Selection (1964–65) of Speeches and Statements of the Chief Minister of West Bengal* (Calcutta: Government of West Bengal, 1966), p. 181.

[28] One of Sen's political supporters and advisors, an economist educated in London, argued in a private interview that Sen had manifested "temporary insanity on the food issue," since all of his political and economic advisors had tried to dissuade him from his rationing and cordoning scheme in 1965–1966. Sen himself admitted privately after the 1967 elections that his food policy during these years was "certainly a political mistake, probably an economic one too."

passengers.[29] The area that was cordoned off was as much as 90 miles around (30 to 40 miles long and 2 to 5 miles wide) and contained some of the densest urban conglomerations in all of Asia. The object of the cordon was to restrict the movement of food grains into the city of Calcutta to those who were licensed by the state government to transport and sell them, and anyone who entered Calcutta with 6 ounces or more of rice or wheat was to be arrested by the police as a "hoarder" or a "black marketeer." Inside the city of Calcutta a series of fair-price shops was established by the state government on a break-even basis, and wholesalers who intended to sell food grains in Calcutta were required to sell them to the government at established prices. Outside the city food grains were procured by the state government from millers at fixed prices. In 1965 this policy was a relative success, largely because the market price of rice was lower than it was in Calcutta and the machinery for the elaborate procurement and rationing operations was run through millers who were Congress supporters in the rural areas and who gained from the policy at the expense of the mills inside Calcutta.[30] While the policy did alienate some of the millowners in the city and its suburban areas, since they had difficulty getting paddy (unprocessed rice) to their mills, it was extremely popular with most of the residents, who were now being provided with food grains at constant prices below the market level.

As a result of the success of the Calcutta scheme, Chief Minister Sen attempted to expand it in 1966 to a number of other areas throughout the state, but at this point he ran into a series of difficulties. The 1966 scheme called for monopoly procurement by the government of West Bengal or its agents (*panchayats* and cooperatives) of the marketable surplus of paddy for the entire year, from all rice-producing areas. No private trader was to be allowed to buy paddy, and a 100 percent levy was to be imposed on all rice mills.[31] All the producers of paddy throughout West Bengal were asked to surrender their marketable surplus of paddy to the government at fixed prices; this surplus was to be determined by a fairly complex system based on a table that had been worked out by an advisory committee of the state Food Ministry

[29] The Calcutta cordoning scheme is outlined in *The Statesman*, December 23, 1964, and December 24, 1964. See also Sen, *New Dimensions,* pp. 177–180.

[30] Evaluations of the Calcutta cordoning scheme appeared in *The Statesman* on June 24, 1965, and July 26, 1965. See also K. Rangachari, "Food Crisis Goes but Danger Remains," ibid., April 24, 1965.

[31] The 1966 state food policy is outlined in P. C. Sen, *From Here to New Horizons: A Selection (1965–66) of Speeches and Statements by the Chief Minister of West Bengal* (Calcutta: Publicity Advisor to the Chief Minister, Government of West Bengal, 1967), pp. 174–181.

(see Table 7). Those with the poorest (nonirrigated) and smallest plots of land were to be allowed to retain most of their harvested paddy for their own personal use, while those with the best (irrigated) and largest plots of land would be required to sell their marketable surplus to the state government at fixed rates. For rationing purposes the state government divided the population into five categories, providing rations throughout the year to those who owned no paddy land and for shorter periods of time as the size of holdings increased.[32] Anyone who owned more than four acres of nonirrigated land or more than three acres of irrigated land was to receive no rice rations.

TABLE 7

WEST BENGAL MARKETABLE SURPLUS TABLE,
PADDY PROCUREMENT ORDER, DECEMBER 1966

Land Owned (Nonirrigated)	Land Owned (Irrigated)	Levy (Marketable Surplus)
2 acres or less	1½ acres or less	none
2–3 acres	—	1½ quintals* per acre
3–5 acres	1½–2 acres	2 quintals per acre
5–10 acres	—	3 quintals per acre
—	2–3 acres	3½ quintals per acre
10–25 acres	—	4 quintals per acre
—	3–5 acres	4½ quintals per acre
—	5–7 acres	6 quintals per acre
—	7–10 acres	8 quintals per acre
—	10–25 acres	9 quintals per acre

* 1 quintal = 220.46 pounds
Source: The Statesman (Calcutta daily), November 18, 1965.

When this scheme was drafted, it was expected by the Food Ministry that the state government would be able to procure 1.5 million tons of paddy: 800,000 tons from rice mills, 150,000 tons from rural credit cooperatives, and 550,000 tons from other agencies (panchayats and husking mills).[33] The Paddy Levy Order that went into effect on December 1, 1965, therefore directed all producers to turn over to the government the amount of their levy (based on the table) by March 31, 1966. The producer was to sell his paddy either to a rice miller, a

---

[32] Rationing procedures are outlined in ibid., pp. 178–179.
[33] See Chief Minister Sen's statement in the West Bengal Legislative Assembly Debates, November 29, 1965.

rural credit cooperative, a *panchayat*, or a husking mill, and the state government would in turn procure the paddy from these four sources. In an attempt to benefit the rural poor, the state government did permit the purchase of paddy by cooperatives and *panchayats* from those who owned small plots of land but still chose to sell their produce to the government. In this way, the state government argued, rural poor who had often been forced to sell or give away their paddy at deflated prices (in order to meet rural debts) could benefit.[34]

It would be difficult to summarize all the difficulties that confronted the state government in its attempt to implement this elaborate scheme of rationing and procurement. On the day it was to go into effect, a *Statesman* editorial said

> . . . almost every section of the State's agricultural community appears to be confused and alarmed on the eve of the paddy procurement drive. Both the district administration and the Congress workers have failed during all these weeks to offer a clear picture of the Government's policy to the farmers. As a result, a sort of contagious fear has gripped the farmers, and to evade procurement in many districts they have already started the process of harvesting much before schedule.[35]

One of the problems of the state government stemmed from the discrepancy between the prices it offered producers—15 to 17 rupees per *maund* (82.28 pounds), depending on quality—and those they could secure on the open market, which were 35 rupees per *maund* and up.[36] Because of this discrepancy, most large landholders either tried to harvest their crops early, before the procurement drive started, or else tried to smuggle paddy through state cordons to Bihar, where there were famine conditions, or even to Pakistan. District administrators were overwhelmed with the enormousness of the task placed before them, and evasion was so great that by late January more than half of the West Bengal police force (30,000 out of 55,000 men) had been assigned full time to the cordoning operation.[37]

When arrests failed to stem the tide of evasion, Chief Minister Sen began to make concessions to some groups. Small landholders (owning up to five acres of irrigated land or seven acres of nonirrigated land) were exempted from the procurement levy on December 13,[38] and a

---

[34] Sen, *From Here to New Horizons*, p. 177.
[35] December 1, 1965.
[36] Ajit Roy, "Procurement Problems in West Bengal," ibid., December 10, 1965.
[37] *The Statesman*, January 23, 1966.
[38] Ibid., December 14, 1965.

week later district magistrates were permitted to reduce the amount of levy for any landholder at their own discretion "if they were satisfied that on a particular holding the yield was lower than the average."[39] In late December rice millers were allowed to purchase certain amounts of paddy on the open market; in mid-January 1966 procurement prices were raised across the board; and at the end of March, after the massive Bengal *bundh*, the Chief Minister lifted the cordon from the entire district of 24-Parganas and from several cities in the urban belt.[40] Instead of the 1.5 million tons that the state government had hoped to procure by March 31, it was able to procure only 500,000 tons, with the result that ration shops were almost always without adequate supplies and the black market in food grains flourished at even higher prices than the market level.[41] To complicate the situation still further, rainfall in West Bengal in 1966 was lower than in any year since 1922,[42] creating a drought that virtually eliminated the entire winter crop in some districts, and in the midst of the drought the central government devalued the rupee and set in motion a small inflation in the cities.[43] In this atmosphere it is not surprising that the leftist parties were able to carry out the Bengal *bundh* in March 1966 or that they were able to stage two more successful *hartals* (in April and September) in protest against food policy. Nor is it surprising that a factional dispute that had earlier developed within the Congress party led to a split at this moment.

The Alliance with the Bangla Congress

Prior to the summer of 1966 the Congress party in West Bengal was one of the most cohesive state Congress units in India. Although it had experienced a split in 1950 and a major factional dispute in the mid-1950s, for the most part the various interests within the party had managed to accommodate themselves to each other with a minimum of public quarreling. Indeed, shortly after the Communist party split in

[39] Ibid., December 22, 1965.
[40] Ibid., January 18, 1966, and April 2, 1966.
[41] Ibid., April 22, 1966, p. 1.
[42] Ibid., May 21, 1966.
[43] When the rupee was devalued in June 1966, *The Statesman* reported: "Seldom has a Government measure since Independence caused so much general concern in Calcutta as devaluation of the rupee, effective from Monday. There was almost general agreement that the measure would create fresh problems. Commodity market watchers, businessmen, industrialists, exporters and economists held that general commodity prices were bound to rise. . . ." (June 7, 1966.) For a Communist interpretation of devaluation see B. T. Ranadive, *The Devaluation Surrender* (Calcutta: National Book Agency, 1966).

1964, the political correspondent for *The Statesman* underscored the degree of unity that had been achieved by the Congress in West Bengal:

When most Congress parties in other states are riven by factional quarrels and plagued by the corroding distrust between leaderships . . . West Bengal has been an oasis of cooperation and mutual tolerance. . . . The state PCC is now a more closely knit organization than ever and in consequence the leadership enjoys a unique position on the all-India scene.[44]

Within a year a factional dispute did erupt, which was eventually to give birth to the Bangla Congress, but it is important to note that the Bangla Congress was not formed until the breakdown of P. C. Sen's food policies provided it with massive potential support.

The dispute that arose within the state Congress in July 1965 centered around the procedure that was to be used for enrolling Congress members in Midnapore District, with the Midnaporians charging the leadership of the state party with an attempt to pad the district's rolls with members loyal to Atulya Ghosh. The principal protagonists in the dispute were Ghosh and Ajoy Mukherjee of Midnapore, old friends who had fought together since the 1920s as Gandhians and Congress nationalists. Mukherjee was the unquestioned leader of the district Congress unit, and the leadership of the state party had always been well aware of the crucial position that he held, since Midnapore was the second largest district in West Bengal. Mukherjee had been given the Irrigation portfolio in every Congress Cabinet since Independence and in mid-1964 had been unanimously elected president of the state Congress party.

But in mid-1965 a number of Congress party members from Midnapore began to protest against the procedures for enrollment of party recruits, and Mukherjee agreed to take up their cause with the state party. At his urging, the Executive Committee of the West Bengal Pradesh Congress Committee (PCC) set up a high-powered commission to "inquire into" the affairs of the Midnapore District Congress, and Mukherjee initially concurred with this procedure, even though the committee was obviously stacked in favor of Atulya Ghosh.[45] Pressed by the Midnapore unit for stronger action, Mukherjee later dismissed the PCC general secretary, Nirmalendu De, one of the principal lieutenants of Atulya Ghosh, on the charge that De had been

[44] Kedar Ghosh, "West Bengal Congress: An Oasis of Harmony," *The Statesman*, July 29, 1964.
[45] The commission consisted of Atulya Ghosh himself, P. C. Sen, and R. L. Sinha, both then allied with the Ghosh faction. Ibid., August 4, 1965.

"persistently defying me and acting in contravention of my instructions and advice."[46] In response to this unexpected action, Atulya Ghosh decided to demonstrate his control of the organization and immediately pushed through resolutions censuring Mukherjee at meetings of the State Executive Committee and the regular pcc.[47]

From Mukherjee's point of view, he had been forced to support the leadership in Midnapore in order to maintain his own position in the district Congress, and he was extremely offended when Ghosh, his lifelong friend, chose to censure his actions.[48] Ghosh's position, on the other hand, was based on his concern to keep control of the party, and he now argues that he had no choice but to censure him once Mukherjee had decided to "remove" Nirmalendu De. Ghosh's associates contend that Ghosh had considered the factional dispute in Midnapore a minor party matter until Mukherjee himself became emotionally involved and aggressively anti-Ghosh. At that point (late August 1965) Ghosh, thinking that Mukherjee might have to be replaced, began to lend his support to the anti-Mukherjee faction in Midnapore.

Once Mukherjee was censured by the Congress Executive, the Communist and Marxist Left parties of West Bengal began to encourage him to form a Congress splinter group, but he initially refused to consider such a possibility. Instead, he sought to fight the censure resolution in the courts, arguing that the meeting at which the resolution had been passed had been called by De, whom he had technically dismissed. Even after he had been censured, Mukherjee refused to step down as state Congress president and tried to use his position in the party to secure the intervention of central party leaders. Finally, on January 20, 1966, the state Congress passed a no-confidence motion against Mukherjee (by a vote of 296 to 40), and he was forced to resign as party president. Mukherjee then began to tour the districts in order to sniff out the extent of Congress dissatisfaction with P. C. Sen's food policy, although he still argued publicly that he had "complete faith in the Congress High Command [at the Union level]" and that he was confident that Congress party leaders in New Delhi

---

[46] Ibid., September 2, 1965.

[47] The resolution of the State Executive Committee was passed by a margin of 28 to 2, and in the pcc as a whole by a margin of 310 to 1. See ibid., September 8, 1965, and September 12, 1965.

[48] Mukherjee's intense emotional involvement in the factional dispute in Midnapore, especially his conviction that Ghosh had attempted to work behind his back, is indicated in his description of the events surrounding the factional feud. See Ajoy Mukherjee, *Undemocratic Ways of West Bengal Congress* (Calcutta: Shri Rabi Chowdhury, 1965).

would intervene on his behalf in the affairs of the state Congress unit.[49] As this hope faded in the following month, Mukherjee became more and more critical of the Congress party, and he eventually supported the Bengal *bundh* against the food policy of the Congress government in late February and early March. Because of his public criticism of Congress and his support for the *bundh*, Mukherjee was expelled from the party for "indiscipline" on June 18.

The Bangla Congress, which was formed by Mukherjee shortly after his expulsion from the Congress, advocated essentially the same programs as the Congress, but with some differences in emphasis and a good many promises to improve on implementation. The first action of the new party was a "day of struggle" (August 15, 1966) against Congress food policy, and the major planks in the Bangla Congress campaign platform in 1967 emphasized "increased food production with a view to bringing down prices."[50] That the Bangla Congress quickly became a political party appealing to food-grain growers and millowners who had been alienated from the Congress can be seen from the fact that in 1967 it won all but 2 of its seats in rural constituencies where food-grain cultivation was the most crucial part of the economy. In Midnapore District, where it won 11 of its 34 seats, the average number of food-grain mills per constituency won by the Bangla Congress was 127.8, while the average number of mills in constituencies won by the Congress was only 69.5.[51] Similarly, in 24-Parganas the average number of food-grain mills per constituency won by the Bangla Congress was 123.6, while the average number in those won by the Congress was 77.8. In 1962 the Congress party had won 25 of the 32 constituencies in 24-Parganas and Midnapore with more than 100 food-grain mills, but in 1967 more than three-quarters of these (19 of the 25 constituencies) deserted the Congress for other parties (12 for the Bangla Congress).

While the Bangla Congress appealed primarily to disenchanted landowners and millowners, its leadership quickly realized that it would need other non-Congress allies if it was to survive in the

[49] For Mukherjee's activities after the vote of censure, see *The Statesman*, February 2, 1966; February 6, 1966; May 6, 1966; May 18, 1966; June 19, 1966; and July 8, 1966.

[50] *Election Platform of the Bangla Congress* (Calcutta: Bangla Congress, 1966), p. 3.

[51] Figures on food-grain mills in constituencies were compiled by comparing the figures given in the *District Census Handbooks* for Midnapore (pp. 403–421) and 24-Parganas (pp. 578–594) with the constituency results in the official report of the Election Commission for the Fourth General Elections. Since the figures in the *District Census Handbooks* are listed by police stations, which do not always correspond to the constituencies, figures could be compiled only for the constituencies whose boundaries could be determined using police stations. For this reason, only the constituencies in 24-Parganas and Midnapore could be analyzed.

segmented political system of West Bengal. Moreover, since there was no effective opposition to the Congress other than the Communist and Marxist Left parties, the Bangla Congress was forced to search for its allies among the leftists. Both Ajoy Mukherjee and Sushil Dhara (the general secretary of the new party) had been known as ardent anticommunists throughout the first two decades of Indian independence, but now both began to negotiate with the Communists in an effort to maximize the influence of their new party in the elections.[52] In mid-July 1966, for example, General Secretary Dhara met with Jyoti Basu and issued the following statement at the conclusion of these meetings:

> Our talks convinced me that the Bangla Congress must re-assess its attitude toward the Left Communists and explain to the ranks why such reassessment is necessary. . . . Still, the intensity of the feelings in the ranks against the Left Communists is so deep that it will take time to overcome it completely.[53]

While the overtures of the Bangla Congress to the Left Communists were eventually rejected by the CPM, the new party was able to ally with the regular CPI and the Forward Bloc in the successful PULF coalition of 1967. As was indicated previously, it was the success of this alliance that led to the Congress's failure to secure a majority in the state legislature for the first time since Independence.

Among the Communists, the decision by the regular CPI to ally with the Bangla Congress in the 1967 elections was to be expected. The CPI had in fact broken with the CPM at least in part because of its belief that alliance with "progressive Congress forces" would lead to revolutionary change throughout India. While the Bangla Congress was clearly a party of landholders and millowners much like the Congress, it was not difficult for the CPI to describe its members as "progressive elements," if only because the Bangla Congress leaders had had the courage to break with the Congress. The Bangla Congress also tried to encourage this image of itself by emphasizing the fact that Mukherjee had differed with state Congress party leaders on the issue of "corruption," and Mukherjee himself emphasized his commitments to Congress socialist ideals in numerous speeches in late 1966.

---

[52] Before the 1962 elections, for example, *The Statesman* reported that "Ajoy Mukherjee is said to have emerged as the Congress Party's best anti-Communist speaker in the districts because of his intimate way of talking." (January 23, 1962.) In November 1962, after the Chinese invasion, Sushil Dhara stated in the Legislative Assembly that "Communists at home are our enemy number one and the Chinese are enemy number two." See *West Bengal Legislative Assembly Debates,* November 17, 1962.

[53] *The Statesman,* July 17, 1966.

The CPI therefore labeled the willingness of the Bangla Congress to ally with Communists as an "upsurge for unity of all Left and democratic parties," and the PULF quickly devised an electoral strategy designed to cut into Congress strongholds in the countryside.[54]

The CPM's unwillingness to ally with the Bangla Congress stemmed from the electoral strategy that was devised by the Left Communist faction in late October 1966, which called for the total defeat of the regular CPI. Factionalism within the CPM, which had been raging since the split in 1964, initially resulted in a tentative decision (taken at Tenali in June 1966) to explore alliances with all non-Congress parties in West Bengal other than the "reactionaries" (Jan Sangh and Swatantra). But this decision had been roundly condemned by the Chinese (who were still supporting the CPM at that time) through circulars sent to the CPM both by the Albanian party of Labor and by the New Zealand Communist party. The famous "five flags" circular of the Albanians openly urged the CPM "to give up the path of expediency" as "treacherous," while the New Zealanders argued that elections could only lead to further Communist party splits. As a result of this encouragement from China, the Left faction in the CPM launched a new offensive against the parliamentary-minded centrists and pushed through a 1967 electoral strategy that was more in keeping with the views of Peking. At a meeting of the National Council of the CPM in Jullundhur in late October 1966, the CPM agreed that it would negotiate only with selected Left parties and that it would limit its electoral alliances to cases where it was allowed the largest single bloc of seats, and then only on the condition that it was guaranteed a majority of the seats in the alliance. The CPM also agreed to contest a number of seats where it had no chance of winning (such as those in North Bengal) in order that it might strengthen its organization for revolutionary rather than for electoral purposes.[55]

Although the centrist faction within the CPM was opposed to the electoral strategy that was adopted by the National Council in late October 1966, the centrists were faced with the choice of accepting it or risking another party split. The centrists in West Bengal, moreover, were in an even more difficult position, since the principal architect of the strategy, Pramode Das Gupta, controlled the state organizational

---

[54] For a CPI description of the "upsurge for unity of all Left and democratic parties" in West Bengal, see *Election Manifesto of the Communist Party of India* (Calcutta: CPI, 1967), pp. 15 ff. For an analysis of the electoral strategy of the PULF, see Dilip Mukherjee, "False Promises to Rural Voters," *The Statesman*, December 12, 1966.

[55] The 1967 election strategy of the CPM is analyzed in Kedar Ghosh, "How the Left Communists Wrecked the ULF," *The Statesman*, November 25, 1966.

apparatus that provided the bulk of party workers in the elections. For these reasons they agreed to implement the strategy, but their performance in the elections indicated that many of them did so rather halfheartedly: most of the energies of the CPM electoral leaders in West Bengal in 1967 were applied to constituencies where the CPM had an opportunity to defeat the Congress, while the constituencies where the CPM was fighting the CPI for second place were for the most part neglected. The efforts of electoral leaders in North Bengal, where the party had little chance of besting the Congress, were almost nil.

Conclusions

The period between the split in the Communist party in 1964 and the assumption of political power by a Communist-led coalition government in West Bengal in 1967 was characterized by rapid change in state political alignments. The split in the party did little to mitigate the factionalism within the communist movement, nor did it lead to greater organizational effectiveness on the part of either Communist party. The ability of the Communists to lead the food demonstrations in early 1966 was owing more to the failure of Congress food policy than to increased party effectiveness, although the failure of the food policy also produced the unexpected boon for the leftists of a split in the Congress itself. Ironically enough, the split in the Congress resulted in the formation of a new political party that was based on support from "vested interests" (landholders and millowners) who had been alienated from the Congress because of an attempt on the part of P. C. Sen to implement the party's socialist ideals, and yet it was the leftist parties of West Bengal that gained from the failure of the socialist experiment. In the final analysis, it was the unity of the leftist coalitions in 1967 and 1969 and the willingness of the leftists to form a coalition with the Bangla Congress that placed the Communist parties in positions of governmental power in 1967–1968 and 1969–1970.

If there were not so much factionalism among Communists in West Bengal, one might argue that Bengali communism has been fairly successful in pursuing Communist united front tactics since 1952. The Communists have led all of the electoral alliances in the state that have successfully opposed the Congress, and they have been able to reduce the influence of uncooperative political parties, in some cases to destroy the effectiveness of such parties entirely. But the Bengali Communists are seriously divided among themselves, and political power has only intensified the factionalism within the movement. It is the factionalism of the communist movement in the state that raises doubts about its ability to extend its present small gains to wider spheres of influence. From the point of view of the Communists, they are now confronted with a massive challenge, since the very logic of their position compels them to continue their efforts to reduce the influence of the non-Congress parties in the state coalition while struggling against the Congress at both the state and central levels.

6

POLITICAL POWER AND
THE REVOLT OF THE MAOISTS

The entry into the ministries of a Communist-led coalition government in West Bengal in 1967, and its return with an even larger legislative majority in 1969, posed innumerable difficulties for the parties involved. Most Communist parties that have come to power have gained control of the entire apparatus of a nation-state, and if they have used political alliances to capture office, they have at least had open to them the possibility of reducing the effectiveness of their allies through party control of the government. In every part of Asia but India, communism has come to power through war and violence rather than through parliamentary means. But the Communists in West Bengal entered the ministries in 1967 and 1969 as part of an electoral coalition, in alliance with thirteen other political parties whose members cover the ideological spectrum, with each Communist party in a minority position in both coalitions, and with the coalitions in control of only one of seventeen Indian states. By the time the coalition did gain control of the governmental machinery of West Bengal, the parliamentary system in India was already highly institutionalized, the Communists had failed to make significant gains outside of the two states of Kerala and West Bengal, and the Congress party was still in power in the Union government. In adjusting to their positions of partial power in tenuous state coalition governments, and in confronting the responsibilities of power in a constitutional system (and with the complexities of Indian federalism), the Communists in West Bengal have been seriously divided about the strategies they should pursue.

Political power has also changed the factional alignments within the state communist movement in a number of respects, enhancing the position of the electoralists while splitting the Left faction. It is still possible, however, to identify three major approaches to the organization of society among the leadership of the movement. One of them stems from the policies advocated by Moscow and the CPGB; a second is an independent, "modified Right" strategy being pursued by the centrists and the older Left faction leaders in the CPM; the third is a Maoist strategy advocated by the younger leaders of the Left faction.

The Left Faction and Political Power

Even before the decision was made to enter the ministries, there was serious disagreement among the Communists, particularly within the CPM, about the wisdom of joining a coalition government. The leadership of the CPM state party organization, heavily supported by the party's Left faction, had broken with the CPI in 1964 because of conflicts about electoral strategy. While the CPM had accepted a considerable portion of the centrist faction of the united CPI into its ranks after the split in 1964, the legislative-minded centrists had always been in a minority position in the higher councils of the state party. Indeed, the CPM fought the 1967 elections on the basis of an electoral strategy that was devised by Pramode Das Gupta, whose sole objective was the Left faction's wish to reduce the "revisionist" CPI to obscurity, even though the party expected that this would mean the continuation of Congress rule in West Bengal. When the Congress failed to obtain a majority, the Left faction was therefore caught off guard, and party factionalism immediately resurfaced.

The nature of the election results in 1967 presented the CPM with three alternatives: (1) the party could enter into a coalition in opposition to the Congress if it were willing to ally with the "revisionist" CPI and the "vested interests" in the Bangla Congress; (2) it could enter into a coalition against the CPI and the Bangla Congress only if it were willing to ally with the "reactionary" Congress party; (3) it could go into opposition against all political parties in the state by refusing to join a coalition, but in this case it would have remained out of power entirely. For the centrists in the CPM the first alternative was clearly the least of three evils. The centrists had always been opposed to a nonelectoral strategy in West Bengal but had been willing to ally with the Left faction in the state in order to gain the benefits of the superior organizational apparatus controlled by Pramode Das Gupta. Moreover, many of the centrists had been advocating a rapprochement with the CPI since the split in 1964, and cooperation in the ministries was seen as an excellent starting point.[1] Finally, the centrists would undoubtedly gain most of the ministerial appointments as well as the patronage that accompanied entry into the state

---

[1] In addition to the sources outlining the position of the centrist faction in Chapter 4, see Jyoti Basu, "The Need for Unity," *Link* (New Delhi weekly), January 26, 1968, pp. 21–22.

ministries; this was appealing to them not only because of the personal gains involved but also because of the leverage that it would give them within the CPM.

For many of the same reasons, the vast majority of the leadership of the Left faction in West Bengal was initially opposed to the entry of the CPM into the state ministries. But the leadership of the Left faction was also divided and confused on this issue, since it was conceivable that the state party could use the ministries to enhance the militancy of its cadre. The leadership of the regular party organization, led by Pramode Das Gupta, was clearly faced with the cruelest dilemma. A decision to join in the ministries would alienate a large portion of Das Gupta's own Left faction, on which his regular party organization depended for support, but a decision to remain out of the ministries would either leave the centrist faction in control of the Communist ministries (if the central leadership of the party supported Jyoti Basu) or, more likely, would split the party for a second time. In the final analysis Das Gupta himself voted against the decision to enter the ministries, but enough Left faction leaders deserted him in the State Secretariat (and in the Central Committee) to push through the resolution announcing the entry of the CPM into the United Front government.[2]

Once the CPM decided to enter the ministries, Das Gupta agreed to obey party discipline and rally his organization behind the electoralists in a united front strategy. But the result of Das Gupta's acquiescence was a revolt within the regular party organization in West Bengal. As soon as the decision was made to enter the ministries, a number of Left faction groups in West Bengal began to accuse the CPM leadership of "neo-revisionism" for its decision to participate in the ministerial coalition. Factionalism within the party became so intense during the first few months of the 1967 United Front government that five underground party journals appeared—*Commune, Chhatra Fauj* [Student's Army], *Dakshin Desh* [The South Country], *Bidroha* [Struggle], and *Santrash* [Terror]—each attacking the decision of the party, and each focusing its attack on Pramode Das Gupta.[3] By early May the dissidents had organized themselves on an ad hoc basis

[2] For the full text of the statement of the State Secretariat of the CPM announcing its willingness to participate in the state ministries, see *People's Democracy* (party organ of the CPM), March 5, 1967, p. 5. For a description of the inner-party maneuvering that took place during the drafting of the statement, see *Link*, February 26, 1967, p. 15, and March 5, 1967, p. 12.

[3] The activities of the dissidents in the CPM immediately after the assumption of power by the United Front are traced in *The Statesman* (Calcutta daily), May 31, 1967. See also *Link*, May 7, 1967, p. 16, and July 2, 1967, p. 16.

in the Antar Party Sodhanbad Birodhi Sangram Committee [Committee to Resist Revisionism within the Party], and by late May they had found an issue that they could all rally around.

The issue was the Naxalbari peasant agitation of the summer of 1967, which started in the Naxalbari subdivision of Darjeeling District (in the northern portion of West Bengal) and eventually spread to three contiguous subdivisions in the same district (Phansideoa, Kharibari, and Siliguri). The administrative area in which the disturbances occurred, which for purposes of brevity I shall call the Naxalbari area, comprises approximately 100 square miles of strategically located territory (bordered on the west by Nepal, on the east by Pakistan, and lying 30 to 50 miles from Sikkim, Tibetan China, and Bhutan to the north). This area is located at precisely the point where India's narrowest corridor, 13 to 14 miles wide, connects the main portions of India with its northeastern states and territories (Assam, NEFA, Nagaland, Manipur, and Tripura). If only for this reason, it is little wonder that the whole of India became particularly concerned when it learned of Communist-led peasant bands operating illegally in the area, with the support of the People's Republic of China, and with a coalition of Communist and Marxist Left parties in the state capital governing the area.

Because of the strategic location of the Naxalbari area, and because the Naxalbari agitation had immediate consequences for the United Front ministries in 1967, it has become infused with a great deal of emotion for both politicians and observers. The actions of the central and state governments in dealing with the agitation have been widely debated, comparisons have been made to the Telengana movement in Andhra in the late 1940s, and there have even been allegations that the movement in Naxalbari marked the early stages of an attempt by the Chinese to launch a Vietnam-like conflict in the subcontinent.[4]

The Naxalbari Movement

The Naxalbari area is distinguished from other rural sectors in West Bengal by its unusual patterns of cultivation, which in turn are a result of the numerous tea plantations in the area and the large proportion of tribal population.[5] Tea cultivation differs from that

---

[4] Most of the rumors and speculation are contained in *Naxalbari Agitation: Some Facts and Consequences (Reports Submitted to Bharatiya Jana Sangh Working Committee at Its Meeting at Simla on June 30 and July 1 and 2, 1967, by Bengal Pradesh Secretary)* (Delhi: Bharatiya Jana Sangh, 1967): see especially pp. 17–19.

[5] According to the *District Census Handbook* for Darjeeling (pp. 65–67), based on the 1961 census, scheduled castes constitute 22.03 percent of the Naxalbari area and scheduled tribes constitute 58.59 percent. These figures are much higher than the

found elsewhere in Bengal because it has developed along the lines of a
plantation economy, with substantial plots of land, widespread use of
migratory and day-wage labor, and foreign investment in the land.
Tribal cultivation differs from that found elsewhere in Bengal because
it is traditionally carried out by nomadic or seminomadic peoples who
prefer to engage in a shifting pattern of cultivation, moving from plot
to plot as weather conditions and the fertility of the soil dictate. The
combination of a tea-plantation economy and a large proportion of
tribal cultivators (Santhals, Rajbansis, Oraons, Mundas, and a small
number of Terai Gurkhas) has made for a long history of land disputes
in North Bengal, centered mainly on the issues of land grabbing,
squatting, and eviction. Owners of the plantations have traditionally
had only a third of their total lands under tea cultivation, with the
rest either allowed to lie fallow for technical reasons or else distributed
as *bakshish-khet* (for the private use of the workers on the plantation
in reward for services). Landless peasants in the area of the tea estates,
and particularly the nomadic or seminomadic tribals, have long
coveted the uncultivated lands of the plantations and have frequently
staked out their claims and fought to retain them in the courts.

In this atmosphere it is not surprising that the Naxalbari area has
had a history of peasant discontent and agitation. Indeed, unlike most
other areas of West Bengal, where peasant movements are led almost
solely by middle-class leadership from Calcutta, Naxalbari has
spawned an indigenous agrarian reform leadership led by the lower
classes. During the 1950s, for example, the Naxalbari area witnessed a
series of uprisings led by a sharecropper named Jangal—not to be
confused with Jangal Santhal, a prominent extremist in the 1967
agitation—who toured the area on horseback organizing sharecroppers
against landlords. In addition, the Naxalbari area has shared in the
problems common to most rural areas in Bengal: overcrowding on the
land, the existence of moneylenders and land speculators who thrive on
conditions of overcrowding, and factional disputes between political
parties led by Communist and Marxist Left politicians promising
various versions of a millenium.

The land reform legislation that was enacted in the 1950s has
complicated the land problem in Naxalbari still further. The West

averages for all of West Bengal (6.0 percent and 19.7 percent, respectively). One of the
few detailed surveys of the patterns of cultivation in the Naxalbari area that seeks
to relate the socioeconomic environment to the political situation is found in Maitreye
Bose, "Naxalbari: A Survey of the Problem," *Times of India* (New Delhi), July 17,
1967. The following account also leans heavily on my own observations and interviews during a trip to the Naxalbari area in April 1969.

Bengal Estates Acquisition Act of 1954 (which limited holdings to 25 acres or less and provided for redistribution of land to the landless) necessarily excluded the tea estates, since tea cultivation is not economically feasible on 25 acres or less. This has heightened the feelings of the landless and tribal cultivators that the Congress government is on the side of the landlords at the same time that it has created incomparable legal difficulties which are still being resolved. Not only has the tribal custom of itinerant cultivation, which involves a constant process of claiming and reclaiming land, made land reform legislation far more difficult to implement in the Naxalbari area than in other parts of the state, but the transfer of portions of Bihar to West Bengal (as a result of the States Reorganization of 1956) has made it necessary to adapt the land reform laws of two states, with all of the administrative difficulties that this entails.[6] The agitation in 1967 was directed against land reform measures that had been enacted after 1956, but these in turn could be traced back to the West Bengal Estates Acquisition Act of 1954. In 1954 the Congress had attempted to mitigate the effects of the exclusion of tea estates by providing for state acquisition of some paddy lands (lands under the cultivation of rice) from tea-garden management. But the management of the tea estates opposed this aspect of Congress reforms throughout the 1950s and in 1964 were successful in reversing the legislation on the basis of recommendations of the Tea Advisory Board. The peasant agitation in Naxalbari in 1967 sought to reverse the 1964 government order and to prevent *benami* transactions (transfer of land to relatives to escape the 25-acre ceiling).[7]

The 1967 agitation was led by Left faction members of the local CPM Krishak Samiti (Peasants' Organization), which had gained a considerable following after the failure of the region's previous large-scale peasant agitation in the 1950s. The members of the organization

[6] A senior officer of the West Bengal government, with more than thirty years of experience in land revenue work, stated in mid-1967 that he admitted to a knowledge and understanding of only 10 percent of the land legislation prevailing in West Bengal in the 1960s, but he was still considered the most knowledgable of the officers in the Naxalbari area. See Prasanta Sarkar, "Reasons for Uprising in Naxalbari," *The Statesman*, June 6, 1967.

[7] The deputy commissioner of Siliguri subdivision stated in an interview with a correspondent of *The Statesman* that about thirty individuals in the Naxalbari area had holdings in excess of the legal 25 acres, in one case as much as 6000 acres of paddy land. (Ibid.) For three perceptive analyses of the land problem in Naxalbari, from three radically different points of view, see Flibbertigibbet [Niranjan Majumdar], "Trouble up North," *Economic and Political Weekly* (Bombay), June 3, 1967, pp. 993–994; John Slee, "Police Action in Naxalbari," *Weekend Review* (New Delhi), July 22, 1967, pp. 15–18; and Indrajit Gupta, "Glimpses of Naxalbari," *New Age* (CPI weekly), July 30, 1967, pp. 15–16.

were for the most part young (the oldest of the twelve principal leaders identified by the police was 50 in 1967), but with considerable experience in the peasant movements of the area. To a greater extent than most peasant organizations in West Bengal, the leadership of the Krishak Samiti came from tribal, low-caste, and Muslim backgrounds. Its principal organizer was Kanu Sanyal, who was 35 years old in 1967, and who is usually depicted as a romantic figure. Sanyal is the son of a respectable and fairly wealthy family (his cousin is a famous Bengali film actress) who attended the well-known Kurseong English School in Darjeeling as a youth. Sanyal argues that he was inspired by the ideas of Subhas Bose during his early schooling and, on the basis of this inspiration, decided to relinquish his claim to the family's landholdings and to "integrate himself" with the tribals, poor peasants, and agricultural workers. As a result of the exceptional dedication with which he pursued this goal, Sanyal gained a fairly large following in the Naxalbari area and a reputation described by *Link* in the following terms:

The leader who commands extraordinary respect among the peasants, workers and the mass of the people is Kanu Sanyal. He does not own any land. . . . He has great contempt for the smug middle class. . . . He has been a dreamer since his boyhood and has always taken extreme positions. His revolutionary spirit took him to the Communist Party . . . but even policemen seem to have a soft corner for Kanu, the misguided dreamer.[8]

Clustered around Sanyal in the Krishak Samiti were a diverse group of young and frustrated peasant leaders who came from a variety of backgrounds. Jangal Santhal, the "field commander" of the Samiti's operations against landlords, was a professional "tribal revolutionary leader" who had twice been defeated in his bid for a seat in the Legislative Assembly (in 1962 he ran as a member of the CPI and in 1967 as a member of the CPM). Khokan Majumdar (alias Abdul Hamid, alias Abdul Halim) was the son of a Muslim peasant who had migrated from Barisal District in East Bengal to Darjeeling District prior to Independence. In his early boyhood he had worked as a ward boy in the Lake Medical Hospital in Darjeeling, but he was dismissed in 1948 because of his leftist political affiliations. He then worked as a "compounder" in several medical establishments until 1952, when he joined Kanu Sanyal in peasant organizational activities. Kamakshya Banerjee originally belonged to the PSP but was expelled from the party in the 1960s, only to join the SSP and be expelled again. When he joined

---

[8] *Link*, August 15, 1967. p. 85.

the CPI in 1965, he quickly gravitated to the Left Communist faction. Mujibar Rahman had originally joined the CPI in 1946 but was expelled from the party in 1957 in the aftermath of a factional dispute. He acquired a considerable amount of property in the Naxalbari area through marriage[9] and even worked for the Congress candidate in the 1962 elections. After the Indo-Pakistani conflict in 1965, he for some reason "established relations" with the Left Communists, was subsequently arrested for peasant agitational activities, and ended up working for Jangal Santhal in the 1967 elections.

The Krishak Samiti was a fairly loose-knit organization, directed by the "triumvirate" of Kanu Sanyal, Jangal Santhal, and Khokan Majumdar. All three members of the "triumvirate" had a long record of peasant agitation despite their youth. All of them had been arrested for their activities in the past, all were known as "professional revolutionaries" by the people in the Naxalbari area, and all of them were well known by the police. None of the leaders of the Krishak Samiti had ever risen very high in the CPM, but they were nevertheless key men in the organizational apparatus who had previously acted as brokers between the state leadership and the peasants. Aside from the "triumvirate," the Samiti was not at all of one mind, and it therefore depended for unity on the warm personal feelings that had developed between Kanu Sanyal and the other leaders in the group and (before the Naxalbari agitation) on the direction of the state party leadership. Among the "outer core" of its leadership[10] there were serious disagreements about goals, ideology, tactics, and strategy, and there were numerous inner-group tensions. The only source of agreement, aside from the attraction of Kanu Sanyal, was the feeling that the Congress party in the area had favored the landlords and tea interests to the detriment of the landless peasants and tribals and that the area's greatest need was to work politically for the creation of strong peasant organizations. How to go about this task effectively was a hotly debated issue among the leadership.

[9] Moni Lal Singh, another member of the leadership group of the Krishak Samiti, was one of the most prosperous farmers in the Naxalbari area in 1967. It was openly acknowledged by people in the district (and admitted by Moni Lal Singh) that he owned more land than the legal ceiling permitted, because of the *benami* transactions he had engaged in.

[10] Leadership of the Krishak Samiti was reported to have rested first with the "inner core" or "triumvirate" and then with an "outer core" of twelve leaders. The "outer core" included the following: Charu Mazumdar, Kamakshya Banerjee, Phani Das (alias Phani Master), Bansia Singh, Pralhad Singh, Moni Lal Singh, Shib Sharan Paharia, Kadaum Malik, Mujibar Rahman, and the three members of the triumvirate. Information on the Krishak Samiti was gathered from newspaper reports and interviews.

While the Krishak Samiti had originally been affiliated with the CPM, its leadership had become disenchanted with the factional struggles that followed the split in 1964 and had therefore begun to strike out on its own. As a result of organizational successes in the Naxalbari area, it was able to gain a great deal of autonomy in its relations with other CPM organs and front groups in northern Bengal. Officially, the CPM Darjeeling District Committee was in charge of the Krishak Samiti after 1964 (at least as far as the state CPM leadership was concerned), but the Krishak Samiti had also maintained close contacts with a group of dissident CPM leaders who had established a parallel District Committee in Darjeeling. The dissident CPM leadership had branded the regular CPM District Committee as "revisionist" and had been meeting separately since 1965.[11]

Confronted with severe factionalism at the local level, the state leadership of the CPM decided to intervene in the local dispute in 1965, and in doing so it concentrated its attention on the best-organized peasant association in the Naxalbari area, the Krishak Samiti of Kanu Sanyal. In the latter months of 1965 and throughout 1966 and early 1967, several leaders of the CPM (including Pramode Das Gupta, Hare Krishna Konar, and Ganesh Ghosh) made frequent trips to the area to discuss party matters with the Naxalbari faction. During the course of these meetings, the CPM leadership, and the leadership of the Krishak Samiti as well, had assumed that Congress would be returned to power in 1967, but with a somewhat depleted majority. According to the Krishak Samiti leadership, the state CPM had therefore agreed to assist it in fomenting a massive peasant agitation in the northern districts, to take place immediately after the elections.[12] In the words of a Samiti leader, the agitation was planned as a "handy tool to harass the new government." When the CPM ended up as part of the new government after the 1967 elections, however, a great deal of tension developed between the state party leadership and the local Krishak Samiti over the issue of the proposed agitation.

Once the CPM entered the ministries, it was unable to support the planned agitation, owing both to the factionalism within the state unit and to the position of the party in the new United Front coalition

---

[11] Internal factionalism in the Naxalbari area is decribed in the report of the recognized CPM unit in Siliguri to the state CPM; see "Situation in Naxalbari Area: Siliguri Local Committee Report," a nineteen-page document printed in *On Left Deviation* (Calcutta: CPM, 1967), pp. 25–44.

[12] Links between the Krishak Samiti and the CPM are analyzed in an article by a *Times of India* correspondent based on police reports; see "Impact of Naxalbari," *Times of India*, September 5, 1967. See also C. N. Chitta Ranjan, "Left CP and the Adventurists," *Mainstream* (New Delhi weekly), July 1, 1967, pp. 10–12.

government. At the same time, however, these factors made it impossible for the state unit to take action to prevent the Krishak Samiti from launching the agitation on its own. Relations between the Samiti and the state leadership had already been strained by the entry of the CPM into the United Front (a significant section of the Samiti did not want the CPM to enter the coalition), and they finally broke down entirely because of the ambivalent position of the state party unit on the question of the Naxalbari agitation. The decision to proceed with the agitation was therefore made at a Kisan [Peasant] Convention sponsored by the Samiti in March 1967, at which the state unit of the CPM was not represented. A description of the convention, related by "a 42-year-old delegate who has spent 14 years of his life in jail," appeared in *Link* magazine:

There were 500 delegates at the conference and some observers. Many came with bows and arrows. A discussion began on the tactics of the movement and its objectives. In the course of the discussion it was revealed that among those whose lands had been forcibly occupied were some workers of the Bijanagar tea estate. According to evidence collected by Left Communist leaders, 25 workers of the Mary View tea gardens had also fallen victims to forcible occupation of land. Some 20 of them were Left Communists.

The discussion at the Kisan Conference was very lively. One of the leaders— Kamakshya Banerjee—said that land could never belong to anyone who was not a peasant. This was hotly contested. A delegate—Jatin Singh—said that Marxism taught there must be worker-peasant unity. A delegate brushed aside the idea: "We must go ahead with peasant revolution. We must organise an armed uprising and set up a free zone in the area." Jatin challenged this understanding and said that revolution could not be achieved in a handful of villages of the Siliguri sub-division. "We must take into consideration the objective situation obtaining in the whole of West Bengal and the country." Delegates Thomas, Sarkar, Mujibar Rahman, and some others took a similar line.

But the discussion was abruptly concluded by Kanu Sanyal. He said: "Everything will depend upon our committee. It will decide to whom to give and to whom not to give land. We shall not give the smallest piece of land to those who are not with us." His eloquent summing up in the pithy local dialect settled the issue. Secretary of the Siliguri *Kisan Sabha* Malik said, "The decision has been taken, we must all go to implement it." Jangal Santhal, who presided over the conference, did not speak.[13]

This description of the Kisan Convention of March 1967, which is corroborated by a number of other sources, tells a great deal about the organization that launched the Naxalbari agitation. Like so many other movements in Bengal in this century, it appears that the Naxalbari

[13] "The Naxalbari Story," *Link*, August 15, 1967, p. 84.

movement was dependent on a very small group of people, clustered around a dedicated and respected leader who could sway those who were inclined to follow him at the precise moment when it was necessary to pull the divergent strands of the potential movement together. As is the case with so many of the small revolutionary organizations in Bengal that follow this pattern, the Samiti was not well organized and it was subject to disputes that ran the gamut of leftist politics in Bengal, but it was determined to act alone. While it had been associated with the CPM before the agitation, and while it picked up support from a variety of sources after the agitation had been launched in the summer of 1967, it is clear that its initial decision to proceed was almost entirely a result of the will of its only effective leader, Kanu Sanyal.

On the basis of existing reports of the Kisan Convention, it is clear that the Krishak Samiti had no concrete plans for the activities that it hoped to sponsor in the Naxalbari area. As Secretary Kadaum Malik stated, "The decision has been taken, we must all go to implement it." But the decision that had been made was simply to launch a widespread movement, while the matter of implementation had been left to the organizing committee of Kanu Sanyal. Sanyal himself had offered no battle plan, but simply the slogan that "everything will depend on our committee." Acting on this broad and ambiguous directive, the committee proceeded on a very pragmatic basis, reacting to events as they presented themselves, with a distinct lack of organizational control over the membership.

The Krishak Samiti was still convinced at this point that while the CPM would not assist in the planned agitation, the United Front government (of which the CPM was the principal member) could be counted on to restrain the activities of the police. The Samiti leadership therefore issued pleas for a massive campaign to occupy lands "illegally occupied by vested interests" and distributed vast amounts of literature asking support and threatening those who refused it. At the same time, the leadership began to organize bands of tribal followers (usually 200 to 500 each) in order to take "direct action" on the side of tribal and peasant cultivators who had felt themselves wronged in land disputes.

In the early stages of the movement (early March until May 23, 1967), the Naxalbari agitation was similar to many of the peasant movements that have been launched in West Bengal in the past two decades. Traveling in small groups, members of the Samiti would demonstrate before the home of a landlord who had engaged in *benami* transactions or who had offended members of the movement by evicting a peasant cultivator or hoarding large amounts of rice or grain. Occasionally such demonstrations would lead to the seizure of stored foods, and a scuffle between the demonstrators and the landlord (or the police or representatives of the state administration) would usually result in some minor injuries. In some cases the members of the Samiti forced their way onto the uncultivated lands of the tea estates, where they sought to "take possession of the land," either by ploughing or weeding it or by felling one or two trees, or simply by sticking a red flag into the ground.

But the Naxalbari agitation began to differ from the peasant movements common to Bengal in two respects, which became evident in late May and early June after the murder of a Gurkha policeman named Soman Wangdi on May 23. The initial reaction of the police to the Naxalbari agitation had been one of cautious support of the landholders in the area until clarification of the position of the new government in Calcutta should be received. The United Front ministry had pledged in its eighteen-point program "to recognize the rights of workers and peasants to voice their just demands and grievances" and also "not to suppress the democratic and legitimate struggles of the people," clauses that were interpreted in most circles as constituting a break with previous Congress policy. Under the previous Congress governments the police had always taken determined action against forcible occupation of land, but in light of the new policy statements of the United Front, and pending an answer to the question of the legality of various forms of protest in the eyes of the new government, the police in the area decided to move cautiously. However, when the policeman Wangdi was killed in a skirmish with tribals on May 23 (he was found with two arrows in his back, and the events surrounding his death are disputed), the local police in the area reacted by firing on a crowd of demonstrators the next day, and the leadership around Kanu Sanyal immediately responded with violence.

In the jargon of the United Front parties, the Samiti became both "sectarian" and "adventurist" after the police firing in late May. The movement became "sectarian" in the sense that its members began to attack anyone who refused to lend support (including sharecroppers and landless cultivators as well as small and large landholders), while it left unmolested anyone who supported the agitation.[14] The Samiti

[14] Peasant associations opposed to the Krishak Samiti in the Naxalbari area pointed out that it had forcibly taken away the land of Jangal, the sharecropper who had led the 1959 agitation, because of his refusal to support the movement. At the same time the Samiti had as one of its principal leaders Moni Lal Singh, a man who readily admitted that he controlled *benami* holdings. See ibid., June 25, 1967, p. 12.

became "adventurist" because it began to organize small bands that
roamed the Naxalbari area with bows, arrows, *tangis*, and other tribal
weapons, threatening a campaign of terrorism against all who
refused to support the movement. The leadership of the Samiti now
promised an all-out assault on the United Front ministry, Samiti
bands confronted police parties with arms, and its members started
seizing guns from people in the area who had licensed weapons.
Numerous instances of murder and arson were attributed to the
Samiti during June, July, and August 1967, and the literature of the
organization began to speak in glowing terms about the murder of
landlords, while it increasingly denounced the United Front.[15]

None of the available evidence indicates that these "sectarian" and
"adventurist" activities had been planned in the initial stages of the
agitation. The leaders of the movement had made no provision for
securing firearms and ammunition with which to fight the police, they
had not established any channels for underground communications,
and they had not planned for "escape routes" to neighboring Nepal or
Tibet. Instead, the existing evidence indicates that after the murder of
the policeman (for which they were held responsible), the leadership
of the Samiti became increasingly isolated from their previous bases
of support, so that they were driven to a "sectarian" and "adventurist"
stand. The United Front government took a strong position opposing
their activities, the state leadership of the CPM deserted them almost
entirely, and the police began to take effective measures to prevent
their activities and movement within the area. At this point they were
forced to go into hiding, and they quickly tried to establish a network
of communications (based on tribal drums and couriers) between the
"five pockets" into which the police had driven them.[16] Their hurried
attempts to collect weapons from private citizens who possessed licensed
pistols and rifles quickly proved futile, and they were eventually forced
to retreat to the swamps and wooded areas that dot the landscape in
northern Bengal.[17] After two investigations by ministerial teams
dispatched by the United Front government in Calcutta, and after

---

[15] In mid-June the Samiti issued a handbill that concluded as follows: "Friends,
in the fight between poor peasants and land-owners, the Cabinet is not impartial.
They have taken their side and the side is that of the owning class. This Cabinet has
refused to grant the right to the poor toiling people to revolt against injustice and
exploitation. That is why the responsibility to give support to the struggle of the
peasants has fallen on all democratic toiling and fighting people. That is why there
must be murder and arson. That is why our appeal to every patriot is to stand by the
peasants to make the struggle a success." Quoted in Biswanath Mukherjee, "Two
Faces of Naxalbari," ibid., August 20, 1967, p. 27.

[16] *Times of India*, June 29, 1967.

[17] Ibid., September 5, 1967.

considerable debate among the fourteen parties in the UF coalition, the state government finally agreed in mid-July to take determined action against the Naxalbari rebels. With the assent of the CPM ministers in the government, more than 1500 policemen were dispatched to the Naxalbari area to quell the disturbance, and in a matter of three weeks most of the leaders of the movement were in jail.

On the basis of this kind of evidence it would be difficult to argue that the Naxalbari agitation was a conspiracy against the government of West Bengal, launched either from the inside or from without. If it was, it was certainly ill planned and poorly coordinated. The only evidence that has come to light of foreign "intervention" in the agitation consists of a few volumes of the works of Mao Tse-tung translated into Bengali (but these are readily available in every city and town in West Bengal), some indication that the Samiti had tried (unsuccessfully) to contact the Communist party of Nepal for support, and a few statements in the Chinese press supporting the agitation. The Samiti leadership itself had as its declared goal only "the preparation of fighting cadres to make people aware of the need for a final showdown with vested interests. . . ."[18] Moreover, while it is clear that the "inner core" of Samiti leaders looked less to the immediate consequences of the agitation than to its long-run effects (their literature dwelt on the results that would be achieved in five, ten, or fifteen years), the "outer core" of the leadership certainly did not agree on goals or tactics.[19] The "triumvirate" of the Samiti may have seen their efforts as a struggle for power in the widest sense, involving the determination of who is to hold power and in the interests of whom, but the bulk of the membership envisaged the movement in narrow, local terms, thinking of it only as an outlet for accumulated frustrations.

This is not to argue that the movement can be dismissed as politically inconsequential, for it did occupy the attention of the first United Front government throughout the summer of 1967, and it has continued to furnish substance for political debate in many parts of India ever since. Moreover, for the communist movement in India and West Bengal, Naxalbari is somewhat of a watershed, for it furnished the rallying cry for a Maoist revolt that eventually led to the formation of India's third Communist party.

[18] *The Statesman*, May 31, 1967.
[19] As late as August 1967, some of the leaders of the Samiti were still hoping for negotiations with the UF government in Calcutta. Biswanath Mukherjee, who was a member of the UF Cabinet at this time, stated that some leaders in the Samiti had in fact wanted to accept the compromise solution offered by a Cabinet mission that went to Naxalbari in July 1967 but that "the counsel of the short-sighted and adventurist section prevailed." See "Two Faces of Naxalbari," p. 27.

Naxalbari and the Naxalites

Despite its numerous shortcomings and its ignominious failure, the Naxalbari agitation of the summer of 1967 evoked the support of a large number of people in West Bengal. It appealed primarily to young people and to urban intellectuals, but it struck responsive chords in most other segments of Bengali society as well. Ever since, Kanu Sanyal has been widely depicted in the Bengali press as a heroic revolutionary leader in the mold of Bengal's nationalist heroes.[20] His willingness to surrender his landed wealth in order to "integrate himself" with peasants has been emphasized in a manner reminiscent of the freedom fighters who fought for the independence of the country. His personal background and the publicity that his movement has received throughout India and the world have invited comparisons with Gandhi, Subhas Bose, C. R. Das, and a host of terrorist heroes from the Bengali past.[21] In the eyes of many Bengalis, Sanyal is the only modern political leader who has remained a "genuine revolutionary," seeking the support of "the masses" in order to do away with the electoral system, while the Communist and Marxist Left parties have compromised their revolutionary fervor by allying with the Bangla Congress and joining the ministries. In this romantic atmosphere, Sanyal and the Naxalbari agitators have frequently been viewed as the vanguard of a new wave of revolutionaries in Bengal, deserving the support of those who are not yet willing to succumb to the dictates of the Indian political system.

These romantic images of the Naxalbari phenomenon are generally regarded by those in positions of authority in India as the visions of incurable idealists. In much the same manner as many American college presidents have described the protest of American students,

[20] For an analysis of Bengali attitudes toward Sanyal and the Naxalites, see Amitava Das Gupta, "Chavan's Wrong Tackling of Naxalite Communists," *Hindusthan Standard* (Calcutta daily), May 13, 1969; see also *Ananda Bazaar Patrika* (Calcutta daily), May 2, 1969; Sumanta Banerjee, "Naxalbari: Between Yesterday and Tomorrow," *Frontier* (Calcutta weekly), May 17, 1969, pp. 8–10, and May 24, 1969, pp. 10–11; and the three-part biography of the Naxalite Hena Ganguly in the *Hindusthan Standard*, October 5–7, 1969.

[21] Even a number of Gandhians, in West Bengal and elsewhere, expressed support for the Naxalbari movement. The most articulare of them was Jayaprakash Narayan, a Gandhian of great conviction, who stated in June 1969 that his sympathy for the Naxalbari movement and its supporters stemmed from his desire to "do something for sharecroppers." Narayan explained that he "hoped to persuade the Naxalites to give up violent means," but he doubted "whether by democratic means the social revolution could be achieved." His support of the Naxalites, Narayan argued, stemmed from his willingness to "take to violence . . . if I am convinced that there is no deliverance of the people except through violence." See "Gandhians and Naxalites," *Thought* (New Delhi weekly), June 21, 1969, p. 5.

Indian political and social leaders have explained the Naxalites (supporters of Naxalbari) by referring to their sense of alienation and to the influence of writers like Marcuse and Sartre which has seemingly dominated the minds of young people throughout the world in the 1960s.[22] Evidence of this aspect of Naxalite support can be found in a host of small literary journals in Calcutta which have expressed their support for the Naxalbari movement in the manner of the editors of *Rupambara*; a journal of poetry.

Religion failed us. Politics failed us. Nations failed us. Isms failed us. We are lost. That is why Digambara Kavalu say they have nothing to do with all these Religions and Isms. Man should not be a pawn in a political game.[23]

Those Bengalis who believe that man should not be "a pawn in a political game" but who nevertheless have had to live in the highly politicized society of West Bengal since Independence have had few alternatives other than withdrawal on the one hand and protest on the other. And while most Bengali intellectuals have perhaps opted for the first alternative, others have continued to support the revolutionary and protest activities of men like Kanu Sanyal.

But the adoption of revolutionary and protest strategies in West Bengal is much too deeply rooted in the realities of Indian political life to be explained by a mere sense of romantic attachment or individual alienation on the part of young people and intellectuals. The introduction of the adult franchise after Independence brought about a shift of political power in Bengal from the urban middle classes to other groups and communities scattered throughout the state.[24] Because they are outnumbered, because numbers count in an electoral system, and because they have either been unwilling or unable to join in the electoral system, large portions of the urban middle class of West Bengal have secured fewer benefits than almost any other comparable group in India, particularly in light of the historic image that the Bengali *bhadralok* have of themselves. Political power within the state

[22] See S. K. Ghose, *Student Challenge round the World* (Calcutta: Eastern Law House, 1969), pp. 56 ff. Ghose is a former chief of police.

[23] *Rupambara* 1 (November–December 1968): 4. Support for the Naxalbari movement and the Naxalites was indicated by the editorial staff in interviews.

[24] The adoption of revolutionary and protest strategies in West Bengal is explored in greater detail in Marcus F. Franda, "The Politics of West Bengal," in *State Politics in India*, ed. Myron Weiner (Princeton: Princeton University Press, 1968), pp. 289 ff. Attitudes supporting revolutionary and protest strategies are explored in "Perceived Images of Political Authority among College Graduates in Calcutta," in ibid., pp. 87–116.

has passed to rural politicians and urban businessmen, who can appeal to caste and communal ties during election campaigns, and who use the patronage provided by office to maintain electoral alliances. Within India, political power in this century has passed to New Delhi and to non-Bengalis. While the Communist and Marxist Left parties secured the support of a large portion of the Bengali urban middle class throughout the 1950s and 1960s precisely because they could rally those who were protesting against the declining position of the Bengali urban middle class, in 1967 the same parties lost many of their previous supporters because they were willing to enter the ministries in alliance with political parties dominated by rural elites and urban businessmen.

The decision to enter the ministries in alliance with "vested interests" has alienated many of the supporters of the Communist and Marxist Left parties who believe that only a total revolution can restore their influence in society. In the eyes of these people, the electoral system and the Indian Constitution are structured in such a way that only those with wealth and rural influence can dominate governmental activities, both at the state and at the national level, a situation that works to the detriment of urban middle-class values. Because of the very nature of the electoral system, the Naxalites argue, both state and central governments (Congress or non-Congress) can only be representative of a less cultured, less refined group of people than the one that governed Bengal before Independence, and certainly than the one that ideally should govern. The efforts of politicans to attract votes, to appeal to caste and communal ties during election campaigns, and to use patronage as a political weapon do not conform to their ideas of how a democracy should operate or how it actually operates in some Western countries. The electoral process is therefore viewed as a sign of the "decadence and backwardness" of the people in power.

While the Communist and Marxist Left parties have argued that their entry into the ministries is simply a temporary tactical device, intended only to build bases for future revolutionary change, the Naxalites have viewed such arguments as mere rhetoric and revolutionary jargon. Moreover, as the United Front has increasingly found it necessary to compromise with business interests and rural landholders since 1967, the Naxalites have become more and more critical of the leftist politicians who chose to enter the ministries. Even before 1967, and especially after the split in the communist movement in 1964, many Bengali Marxists had become impatient with the ideological disputes and factions within the Communist and Marxist Left parties. At the same time, the fact that the recession and the food crisis of the mid-1960s are continuing into the 1970s in West Bengal (but not in other parts of India) has deepened the feeling among the Bengali urban middle class that West Bengal has been disadvantaged by its adherence to electoral democracy. Since the defeat of the Congress in eight states in 1967, there has been renewed hope in Bengali intellectual circles that a revolutionary situation might be developing in India, and the Naxalites have therefore argued for the organization of a series of peasant guerrilla bands like those contemplated by Kanu Sanyal in the latter stages of his Naxalbari movement.

Naxalbari and the CPM

There is considerable evidence to indicate that Sanyal and his supporters were taken by surprise when their small peasant movement evoked such widespread support in West Bengal.[25] The Naxalbari agitation stemmed from an internal factional dispute within the CPM, and it was not originally intended as a challenge to the entire communist movement in India. In its initial stages the agitation was designed to embarrass the Congress government; in its later stages it became a source of embarrassment for the United Front. It did present a number of dilemmas for the CPM, and particularly for Pramode Das Gupta, but it was not organized or planned well enough to topple either the state government or the leadership of any Communist party.

Yet the wave of support that has been manifest in the wake of the Naxalbari agitation has greatly encouraged Kanu Sanyal and the CPM members of the Left faction who had initially opposed the decision to enter the ministries. The younger members of the Left faction had for a long time been seeking new outlets for political expression, particularly in light of the unpopular dominance of Pramode Das Gupta within the communist movement. During their imprisonment in 1965, a number of younger party members had decided to make a bid for leadership of the faction, and upon their release they had been working for the establishment of a "Marx-Engels Institute" for political instruction, in an effort to challenge both Das Gupta and the centrists in the party. In addition, some members of the Left faction had also begun to publish pamphlets, newssheets, and leaflets challenging the party program, even before the 1967 elections. The leading figures in this movement—Sushital Roy Chowdhury,

---

[25] Pannalal Das Gupta, "What is the Naxalbari Path?" *Mainstream*, July 8, 1967, pp. 9–11

Parimal Das Gupta, Niranjan Bose, Saroj Dutta, Amulya Sen, and others—were younger intellectuals in the CPM, none of whom had yet risen above the district leadership level, and all of whom were under 40. While some of them had worked in the countryside on occasion, they were all based in Calcutta and its suburbs. When the Naxalbari agitation began to make headlines throughout India in the summer of 1967, they seized on the movement as a way of embarrassing the party leadership in the ministries, and a number of new Left faction journals began to circulate.

By the time of the police firing in Naxalbari in late May 1967, the dissent within the party had become so severe that 19 of the 39 members of the CPM State Committee were rumored to be "maintaining their channels with the dissidents" in the event of a failure of the ministries.[26] By the time of the police roundup in late July, the extremists claimed the support of 8000 of the 20,000 members of the state CPM.[27] The CPM state party leadership itself admitted that at least 4000 party members were supporting the Naxalite faction in August 1967, and it was for this reason that the party insisted that the United Front perform so many machinations before agreeing to police action in Naxalbari.[28] Pramode Das Gupta has since attempted to prevent the widespread defection of Naxalites from his party by working for the release of those arrested in 1967 (his efforts were successful in early 1969) and by consistently advocating Left faction programs at Central Committee meetings. But as long as the Central and State committees of the party are controlled by the centrist faction, Das Gupta can satisfy the wishes of the Naxalites only by withdrawing from the CPM, which he has been unwilling to do. Rather than split the party for a second time, Das Gupta has preferred to work from within to counter the influence of the centrist faction and to maintain his control of the organizational apparatus that is largely his creation.

Das Gupta and the older members of the Left faction leadership have therefore attempted to persuade the younger members of the Left faction in the state that it is possible for the CPM to remain in the state ministries while preserving its revolutionary goals. In a *maidan* speech shortly after the 1969 electoral victory, for example, Das Gupta told his followers,

We have adopted democracy in order to strengthen the democratic struggle, but we firmly believe that we would not be able to reach our goal through Parliamentary democracy. Our goal is socialism and for that is required the

[26] *Link*, June 4, 1967, p. 17.
[27] Ibid., July 30, 1967, p. 21.
[28] Ibid.

bloody revolution. We want to reach the state of clash between the Centre and the State through the path of Parliamentary democracy to such a level that it would spark off the bloody revolution.[29]

Within the party he at first attempted to stem the tide of the Left faction's revolt by proposing a campaign against "such bourgeois parties as the Bangla Congress," but this proposal was voted down by the CPM Central Committee.[30] After the police firing, he began to argue that unless the CPM pulled out of the ministries, the party would be split for a second time, but this too failed to impress the Central Committee.[31] When the CPM gained a larger share of the state ministries in the second United Front government, Das Gupta undertook to woo prominent Naxalites back into the party in an effort to influence the others through personal persuasion.[32] In the final analysis, Das Gupta has not been entirely without influence, either in the State Councils of the party or with the Naxalites, but his previous position of unquestioned dominance has been severely undermined since 1967.

The irony of Das Gupta's position since 1967 is that it is now he who must prevent a stampede to the left. Of particular concern to him is the attempt on the part of some centrists to enforce party discipline, which would result in the expulsion of all the party members who have actively supported the "Left deviationist" Naxalites, estimated at 4000 to 8000 members. Das Gupta has agreed to the expulsion of some of the principal leaders of the Naxalite faction, but any action on the part of the state CPM to expel the majority of those siding with the Naxalites would virtually wipe out his factional support. He has thus far succeeded in slowing the rate of withdrawals from the party, but only by relaxing the rules of party discipline to the point where inner-party debates are carried out in public and party members in the state regularly attack one another in the press.

The Formation of the CPML

To complicate matters for Das Gupta and the CPM, the dissident Left faction has now formed a new party, the Communist party of

---

[29] *Hindusthan Standard,* February 17, 1969. Das Gupta later retracted this statement under pressure from the central government and the CPM Central Executive Committee.

[30] *Link,* April 23, 1967, p. 9.

[31] Ibid., June 4, 1967, p. 17.

[32] In June 1969, for example, the state party proudly announced that one of the leading Naxalbari figures (Kamakshya Banerjee) was now working with the regular CPM. See *People's Democracy* (organ of the CPM), June 22, 1969, p. 3. But in December 1969 Banerjee was found dead, tied to a bamboo pole lying next to the railway tracks a mile and a half outside of Naxalbari. Presumably assassinated by Naxalites, Banerjee "bore a gaping wound on his throat and was completely disembowelled." *The Statesman,* December 4, 1969.

India–Marxist-Leninist (CPML), which is attempting to lure members of the CPM's Left faction into its ranks. The CPML was conceived in the summer of 1967 when the Naxalbari agitation began to attract attention throughout India, gaining support within the communist movement from dissident Left factions in a number of Indian states. In an attempt to promote some kind of all-India factional unity among the various supporters of the Naxalbari movement, younger Left faction members agreed to form an All-India Coordination Committee of Communist Revolutionaries (AICCCR), which met throughout 1967 and 1968 to discuss strategy and tactics.[33] Despite the almost identical programs adopted by the various Left faction groups in each of the states, the leadership of the AICCCR could not agree on the structure of the proposed third Communist party. Personality differences between the leadership around Tarimela Nagireddy in Andhra and the leadership of the AICCCR in West Bengal surfaced on a number of occasions, while juggling for leadership positions was reported to have disrupted several AICCCR meetings.[34] In the final analysis the West Bengal Naxalites could agree on a leadership clustered around Kanu Sanyal, but Sanyal and his colleagues were unacceptable to the Naxalites in Andhra, Kerala, and Madras. In early 1969, therefore, the Naxalites in West Bengal decided to launch a third Communist party on their own.

The CPML was formally inaugurated on the ninety-ninth birthday of Lenin (April 22, 1969), but it was announced at a May Day rally on the Calcutta *maidan*. The new party has attracted an all-India membership estimated at 20,000 or 30,000 and has been active in a number of Indian states, but its largest base of operations by far is in West Bengal.[35] In West Bengal it has attracted an active following usually estimated at between 4000 and 6000, and its support is drawn from a number of diverse sources. The leadership of the party derives from the younger members of the Left faction of the CPM (Kanu Sanyal is party chairman), and it has recruited a number of former members of the CPM and the CPI. Moreover, since the CPM has relaxed party discipline considerably in order to prevent defections to the CPML, some of its members have been collaborating with the CMPL but maintaining their membership in the CPM at the same time.[36] In

---

[33] An excellent summary of the Naxalite AICCCR phase is contained in O. P. Sangal, "Alphabet of Mao: AICCCR," *Citizen and Weekend Review* (New Delhi fortnightly), May 10, 1969, pp. 21–23.

[34] The position of the Andhra Naxalites is stated in Tarimela Nagireddy et al., *An Open Letter to Party Members* (Hyderabad: n.p., 1968), pp. 1–26.

[35] *Link*, May 25, 1969, p. 11.

[36] Satindranath Chakravarti, "A Party Is Born," *Now* (Calcutta weekly), June 13, 1969, pp. 9–11, and June 6, 1969, pp. 8–10.

addition, the CPML has attracted a number of new political participants, primarily among college students and the disenchanted urban middle class. While the party has had some appeal to the lower classes and disadvantaged, its most ardent supporters are college graduates, many of them from graduate schools in America or Europe. Indeed, the number of students returned from America supporting the CPML is so large that Pramode Das Gupta has effectively charged the CPML with CIA collaboration,[37] while less partisan observers have viewed the Naxalites as a cultural elite opposed to mass culture (much like the radicals in Weimar Germany or the New Left in the United States).

Because of the secrecy that has pervaded CPML affairs since its formation, data on the inner leadership of the party are difficult to obtain. The leadership of the CPML has argued that it is going to pursue a Jugantar strategy rather than the Anushilan strategy of the regular CPM and CPI, a reference to the two old terrorist federations of Bengal's nationalist era. Unlike the Anushilan Samity, which was organized in much the same manner as the two older Communist parties in West Bengal (with front groups, mass organizations, and so forth), the Jugantar revolutionaries were a highly secretive organization that surfaced only to carry out dramatic terrorist acts (such as the Chittagong Armoury Raid).[38] Openly acknowledging their adherence to a Jugantar style of revolutionary organization, the CPML leadership has agreed to meet secretly, to guard against public awareness of party activities, to shift headquarters frequently, and to surface only when revolutionary activities demand it. An organization of this type obviously requires far more discipline than either the CPI or the CPM has thus far been able to impose on its members and must necessarily be even more elitist. Just as the Jugantar group was always highly dependent on one or two leaders who controlled the operation of the entire organization, the CPML promises to represent the political will of Kanu Sanyal and perhaps a few of his closest associates.

International support for the CPML has come from the Chinese Communist party and its associates in the international movement, a turn of events owing mainly to the decision of the CPM to enter the West Bengal ministries and to quash the Naxalbari movement. Throughout the 1960s China pursued an extremely active foreign policy in South Asia, presumably designed to increase instability on

[37] See "The Growth of Adventurism in West Bengal: Central Committee Information Document," in *On Left Deviation*, p. 24.

[38] For a comparison of Anushilan and Jugantar strategies, see Gobinda Lall Banerjee, *Dynamics of Revolutionary Movement in India* (Calcutta: Sudhir Kumar Ghosh, 1965), pp. 18–20.

the subcontinent and to involve New Delhi and Rawalpindi in an armaments race that would detract from economic development in both nations.[39] Peking has effected a rapprochement with the Pakistani government while simultaneously lending support to internal Communist political leaders;[40] in India, diplomatic relations have been severely strained by the lingering Sino-Indian border dispute. Chinese attempts to prevent both America and the Soviet Union from promoting their objectives in South Asia have so far failed, and the Chinese have therefore maintained their hostile stance toward the present Indian regime. On the one hand this has involved a continuing confrontation of troops on the Sino-Indian border; on the other China is supporting and training rebels in the Naga Hills and in other parts of India where potential guerrilla movements exist.[41] From China's point of view the CPML is a potential guerrilla force that can be used to disrupt the orderly functioning of the Indian political system.

The first indication of Chinese support for the Naxalites within the CPM came in the form of a broadcast over Radio Peking on June 28, 1967, during the period when the United Front was in the process of evolving a policy for police action against the Naxalbari agitators. In what was described as "a talk on the revolutionary armed struggle of the Indian people," Radio Peking described the Naxalbari agitation as follows:

A phase of peasants' armed struggle led by the revolutionaries of the Indian Communist Party has been set up in the countryside in Darjeeling District of West Bengal State in India. This is the front paw of the revolutionary armed struggle launched by the Indian people under the guidance of Mao Tse-tung's teachings. This represents the general orientation of the Indian revolution at the present time. The people of India, China and the rest of the world hail the emergence of this revolutionary armed struggle.[42]

[39] China's foreign policy in South Asia is described in Russell Brines, *The Indo-Pakistani Conflict* (London: Pall Mall Press, 1968), pp. 160–213.

[40] For an excellent series of articles on Pakistan, see Dilip Mukherjee, "Pakistan," *The Statesman*, September 30–October 3, 1968. For an analysis of the internal politics of East Pakistan (with a brief treatment of the role of the Communists), see Jayanta Kumar Ray, *Democracy and Nationalism on Trial: A Study of East Pakistan* (Simla: Indian Institute of Advanced Study, 1968), pp. 370 ff.

[41] In December 1968 the Union Minister of State for External Affairs, Mr. B. R. Bhagat, confirmed reports that at least 1000 Naga rebels had been trained in China for purposes of guerrilla warfare and were attempting to infiltrate back into India. See *Amrita Bazaar Patrika*, December 24, 1968. For Peking's links with both the Naxalites and the Naga hostiles, see the *Hindusthan Standard*, September 21, 1969. On Peking's attitudes toward Indian communism, see Hemen Ray, "Peking and the Indian CP," *Problems of Communism* 15 (November 1966): 87–92.

[42] The complete text of the June 28 and June 30 broadcasts on the Naxalbari agitation are reprinted in *Mainstream*, July 8, 1967, pp. 14–16. Quotations in the text are taken from this published version.

In the same broadcast, and in subsequent pronouncements from Peking, the United Front governments and the two older Communist parties in India have been described by China as "tools of the Indian reactionaries to deceive the people and benumb their revolutionary militancy," while the decision to enter the ministries has been described as "reactionary counter-revolutionary double-dealing." The CPML has meanwhile been recognized by the CCP as "the only Communist Party in India," but thus far the Indian Home Ministry has argued that support for the CPML has been entirely verbal.[43] The Home Ministry of the Union government has stated on a number of occasions that "we are not silent spectators" with regard to the events surrounding the formation of the CPML and its ties with the Chinese, but thus far the government has had little reason for taking determined action against the Naxalites. Of particular concern to the Home Ministry, of course, is the possibility that central government action against the Naxalites might either make "martyrs" of the CPML leaders or alternatively might evoke a center-state conflict in the areas where the Communists have attained partial political power.

The Program of the CPML

There can be little question, however, that the CPML is making a determined effort to maintain the support of China and to emulate the Chinese example of a communist revolution based on peasant uprisings. Following the pronouncements of the CCP, the political program of the CPML starts from the assumption that the Indian nationalist movement was led by "the comprador-bureaucrat big bourgeoisie of India," whose "principal political mouth-piece was the Indian National Congress."[44] After Independence, the program argues, the Congress "betrayed the national freedom struggle to serve [its] own narrow reactionary class interests" by becoming imperialism's agent for ruling the country:

> British imperialist exploitation has not only continued uninterrupted, but even increased. Moreover, other imperialists, and especially U.S. imperialism, the No. 1 enemy of the world's people, and Soviet social-imperialism, the No. 1 accomplice of U.S. imperialism, who are jointly working for world domination and for re-dividing the world among themselves, have penetrated into India at an increasingly rapid rate.

[43] See, for example, *Amrita Bazaar Patrika*, December 10, 1968.

[44] The program of the CPML is contained in two documents drafted in early 1969: "Political Resolution of the Communist Party of India (Marxist-Leninist)," in *Liberation* 2 (May 1969): 4–16, and "Draft Political Programme for the Revolutionary Student and Youth Movement," ibid., April 1969, pp. 57–67. All quotations that are not otherwise noted are taken from these two documents.

In the thinking of the CPML, "the only way to achieve liberation from the existing reactionary system . . . is resolutely to overthrow by armed force the four enemies—U.S. imperialism, Soviet social-imperialism and their lackeys in this country, the comprador-bureaucrat big bourgeoisie and the feudal landlords. . . ." But thus far "the so-called communists and the other political parties in India have refused to undertake this revolutionary task." According to the CPML, the older Indian Communist and Marxist Left parties "pay only lip service to Marxism-Leninism but, in practice, have never cared to educate the workers, peasants, youth, students and the broad masses in Marxism-Leninism nor directed their struggles along the Marxist-Leninist line. On the contrary, they have kept the movement strictly within the bounds of laws which are based on exploitation and dragged them down into the mire of economism, reformism and parliamentarism."

Unlike the CPM and CPI, both of which now envisage a two-stage revolution in India, and both of which are participating in parliaments, the CPML is convinced that Indian Communists must "reject the hoax of parliamentarism" in order to bring out an "immediate revolution . . . through revolutionary people's war":

Today the basic task is to liberate the rural areas through revolutionary armed agrarian revolution and encircle the cities and, finally, to liberate the cities and thus complete the revolution throughout the country.

Relying heavily on analogies to Cuba and Vietnam, the CPML program argues that India presents an "excellent revolutionary situation: . . . the U.S. imperialists and their chief accomplice, the Soviet revisionists, are facing increasing difficulty in their dirty efforts to redivide and enslave the whole world . . . [and] the reactionary ruling classes are facing insoluble contradictions at home." On the other hand, the program argues, "Socialist China is performing miracles of socialist construction. The great proletarian cultural revolution has consolidated the dictatorship of the proletariat in every sphere of life and created conditions for the socialist man." In his May Day speech announcing the formation of the CPML, Kanu Sanyal emphasized the declaration of the CCP to the effect that ". . . by the year 2000, that is, only 31 years from now, the people of the whole world will be liberated from all kinds of exploitation of man by man and will celebrate the worldwide victory of Marxism, Leninism, and Mao Tse-tung's thought." In the words of Sanyal, "This is no mere declaration, it is an historic directive. Through this the great Communist Party of China points out to the communists of the whole world how excellent the world situation is for making revolution, and, at the same time, directs all of them to march forward boldly . . . the historic responsibility of carrying forward the Indian revolution has fallen on our shoulders."

In order to take advantage of the "excellent revolutionary situation" in India, the CPML has so far concentrated on two types of activities: (1) the organization and education of student groups on most Bengali college campuses; (2) party work in villages and towns among peasant cultivators and landless laborers. In these activities, the major thrust of CPML efforts is to bridge the gap that has always existed in Indian Communist parties between elite leaders and mass followers. In the words of the party program:

> . . . the advanced section [the urban youth and college students] will get isolated from the overwhelming majority . . . if it tries to advance into the struggle by itself without caring to inspire the backward sections in order to make them participate actively in the struggle. Taking the opportunity provided by the isolation of the advanced section, the reactionaries [such as Congress will] organise the broad sections of the backward masses and utilise them to serve the needs of counter-revolution.

To bridge the gap between elite leaders and mass followers, the CPML proposes to concentrate on the building of a new mass political organization of students and youth, fully integrated with peasants and workers. Through the building of a revolutionary mass organization the CPML hopes to create a political party where "the youth among the intelligentsia, the youth and student masses, [will] not only become an advanced section, an important detachment, in the anti-imperialist anti-feudal democratic revolution in our country, but [will] become one with workers and peasants." According to the leading party theoretician, Charu Mazumdar,

> . . . there can only be one criterion by which we should judge whether a youth or a student is a revolutionary. This criterion is whether or not he is willing to integrate himself with the broad masses of workers and peasants, does so in practice, and carries on mass work . . . those who cannot are at first non-revolutionaries and may in some cases join the counter-revolutionary camp afterwards. This is a lesson which we get not only from China but from every country in the world.[45]

While there is a great deal of Marxism and Mao in the program of the CPML, the views of the urban *bhadralok* living in and around Calcutta still predominate in party thinking. The principal charge against the "imperialists" is that they have "struck a deal with the Congress

[45] Charu Mazumdar, "To the Youth and the Students," *Deshabrati* (Naxalite publication), May 2, 1968, pp. 1, 4.

[and] partitioned the country";[46] the "treachery" of the regular CPI is due to its alliance with the Soviet Union in describing Nehru as "the representative of the progressive bourgeoisie";[47] the "most glaring example of comprador-bureaucrat double-dealing" is "the treatment meted out to the revolutionaries of Bengal in this century";[48] and the "people's urges" that "must be organised into powerful struggles on correct lines and directed to attain the revolutionary objective" are the middle-class "demands for education, employment, food, and *culture.*"[49] When Kanu Sanyal told a Bengali audience on May Day in 1969 that "the sparks from Naxalbari have spread to Bihar, Uttar Pradesh, Orissa and to Srikakulam district in Andhra," he evoked visions among the *bhadralok* of the days when Bengal held sway over the rest of India.[50] When he stated that "the utterly shameless manner in which Harekrishna Konar and company are serving the *jotedars* beats even the record of the notorious Congress ministers," he reminded his predominantly middle-class audience that they had lost political power in this century to rural elites. The constant references by the leaders of the CPML to the United Front as "the lackey of the comprador-bureaucrat Birlas and Tatas" merely voices the feelings of protest among the Bengali urban *bhadralok* in the face of continued control of industry in West Bengal by non-Bengalis, despite the election of a Communist-led coalition government in the state.

Because the CPML is still a party of urban *bhadralok* trying to obtain a mass base in order to overthrow a regime that is distasteful to it, the party's organizational focus must necessarily be on narrowing the gap between the leadership of the party and its potential followers. For this reason, the party has launched a two-pronged organizational offensive, first to educate students on the need to work in the villages, then to use students to educate the peasantry on the need for revolution. To further both of these objectives, the CPML has adopted "back to the village" slogans, and a number of party workers have been ordered to prepare reports on the climate for revolution in various parts of the state.[51] Following the party line, most of these reports by party workers

---

[46] *Liberation* 2 (May 1969): 10.

[47] Ibid., p. 12.

[48] *Chhatra Fauj* [Student's Army], February 28, 1969, p. 5.

[49] *Liberation* 2 (April 1969): 65. (Italics added.)

[50] Kanu Sanyal's May Day address is reprinted in full in ibid., May 1969, pp. 110–122. For a summary of Bengali reactions to the address, see *Basumati* (Bengali daily), May 2, 1969.

[51] In December 1968 the leadership of the CPML published an article by Charu Mazumdar, that called on all Naxalites to prepare "class analyses" of their villages.

have so far arrived at much the same conclusions as the following, by a "peasant organizer" from Murshidabad:

> From the very initial stages of organization they [the poor and middle peasants] show utmost eagerness and realise that for them there is no other alternative but to make revolution. They have great influence over the landless peasants, and fight in the front rank alongside the landless peasants.[52]

If the CPML were able to get poor and middle peasant cultivators to "fight in the front rank alongside the landless peasants," the party might be able to confront the state and central governments with a realistic challenge for political power in West Bengal. But the evidence thus far would indicate that the peasants' reception of the CPML has not been significantly different from their response to past organizational efforts by Bengali Communists. To take the most extreme case, in Phansideoa constituency (where Naxalbari is located), the vote of the Congress party actually *increased* after the Naxalbari agitation—from 45.36 percent in the 1967 assembly elections to 53.4 percent in 1969—primarily because of the voting behavior of poor and middle peasant cultivators.[53] This does not mean that the CPML has had no effect on state politics or that it lacks potential for future growth, but it does point up the limitations of its most concerted attempt so far to get widespread peasant support.

The Impact of the CPML

Despite its failures to initiate successful peasant uprisings, the CPML has been a significant force in state politics since 1967 and promises to play a larger role in the future. The CPML's appeal to college students, urban middle-class youth, and members of the Left faction in the CPM is based on its militant stance before the United Front government. Leaders of the CPML have been most vociferous in arguing

---

In Mazumdar's words, "Chairman Mao instructs us to make class analysis. . . . Chairman Mao teaches: 'We should rid our ranks of all impotent thinking; all views that overestimate the strength of the enemy and underestimate the strength of the people are wrong.'" See "To the Comrades Who Are Working in Villages," *Liberation* 2 (January 1969): 3–5.

[52] "An Investigation into the Nature and Forms of Exploitation: A Report of Class Analysis of a Murshidabad Village," ibid., June 1969, p. 90.

[53] See the analysis of the 1969 election results for Naxalbari in Amitava Das Gupta, "Why the Congress Lost in West Bengal," *Hindusthan Standard*, February 14, 1969. In Phansideoa constituency the Congress vote increased from 16,227 votes in 1967 to 20,974 in 1969, while CPM votes increased from 10,484 (29.4 percent) in 1967 to 11,228 (29.3 percent) in 1969. The remaining votes in both elections were scattered among independent candidates.

that the United Front governments pursued essentially the same policies as the Congress party: they allied themselves with big business interests and rural elites, they allowed foreign businessmen to continue to operate in West Bengal, they proposed no new measures for dealing with middle-class demands for food, education, employment, and "culture," they failed to secure benefits for West Bengal from the central government, and they met the demands of the middle class with the same kind of repressive measures and stalling devices used by previous Congress ministries. For these reasons, according to CPML literature:

. . . the policy of the UF is inviting all the enemies of the people into its folds. Far from being afraid of the UF, which is playing a counter-revolutionary role, the vested interests, criminals and CIA agents consider it to be their own organization. They know quite well that its role is to serve them while pretending to serve the people.[54]

Especially important for the maintenance of the CPML has been its success in confronting the United Front with these ideas. Using militant mass action, agitation, and propaganda—the same devices previously used by the CPI—the CPML was able to embarrass the United Front governments on a number of occasions, and in this way it established a leading position among the most militant urban middle classes.

Perhaps the most successful movement launched by the CPML thus far has been directed at the police force in West Bengal, which has long been a target of leftist criticism and was an especially vulnerable part of the UF government. In a series of incidents that began with the Naxalbari agitation, supporters of the CPML have attempted to provoke the police to take repressive action against political parties, and in those cases where policemen have acted against political agitators, the CPML has quickly set out to mobilize antipolice sentiment. Until now, the most successful action has been the statewide movement launched by the CPML following a confrontation between students and police at Durgapur (on the Bihar border) in June 1969, which has had widespread ramifications for the future of CPI and CPM involvement in state government.

Durgapur is one of the many completely new cities that have grown up in India since Independence. A small village in 1947, Durgapur has been developed with funds from the central and state governments, from private business, and from foreign assistance, to the point where

---

[54] "The Real Face of the UF," *Liberation* 2 (June 1969): 10.

it is now a leading industrial city in West Bengal (in 1969 its population was estimated at more than 200,000). Since industry in Durgapur, like that in other parts of the state, is dominated by non-Bengali businessmen and central government administrators, the city's growth has been opposed from the very beginning by large portions of the Bengali middle class, and Communist influence has steadily increased. Leaning heavily on middle-class trade unions, teachers, and students, the leftist parties have increased their votes in Durgapur constituency and in 1967 were able to unite behind a CPM candidate to defeat the Congress (the CPM secured 49.6 percent of the vote in Durgapur in 1967 and 51.6 percent in 1969, narrowly defeating the Congress on both occasions). Since 1967, both trade unions and student groups in Durgapur, like those in other parts of the state, have been jockeying for position, which has intensified industrial and student unrest. The general manager of the Durgapur steel plant estimated that there were 66 cases of work stoppages in his plant alone during the first four months of the UF government in 1969, resulting in as many as 9800 man-hours lost in one month (this compares with an average of only 15 stoppages and 10,800 man-hours lost *per year* during the period 1963–1966, when the Congress held power in the state).[55] Since the assumption of power by the UF government in 1967, numerous incidents of sabotage in Durgapur industries have been attributed to extremist trade unionists, and on occasion police, industrial security forces, managers, engineers, and college and school administrators have been assaulted.[56]

Taking advantage of the almost anarchic conditions that have prevailed in Durgapur since 1967, the CPML has sought to build a strong cadre among students in the Durgapur colleges and to use student groups to provoke the police and the UF. While earlier efforts to "expose" the police and the UF government succeeded on a small scale and in local areas, the incidents of June 1969 resulted in clashes between the police and CPML supporters which had statewide consequences. The incidents began with a motor accident witnessed by a group of Naxalite students, who argued that the accident could have been prevented if a policeman had performed his duties. According to the police, the students concerned beat up a traffic constable and raided both the police station and the residence of the officer in charge at the police station, injuring him and 5 other policemen.

[55] *The Statesman*, June 8, 1969. See also *Amrita Bazaar Patrika*, June 13, 1969, and June 20, 1969.
[56] *The Statesman*, June 8, 1969. A *Statesman* survey indicated that more than 60 engineers had left Durgapur during the first six months of 1969 as a result of political disturbances.

When the state police were called into Durgapur, the students kidnapped the subinspector of police and confined him to the campus of the Durgapur Regional Engineering College. As a result of the numerous subsequent clashes that took place between students and police, 1 student was killed and 125 injured, the police opened fire and made a lathi charge against students despite orders to desist from doing so, and the entire city of Durgapur was disrupted for almost a week.

The Durgapur incidents pointed up in a very graphic way the ability of the CPML and its supporters to influence the UF and the Communist parties in the state. If the UF government took the side of the police against the CPML, it would alienate many of its own supporters, even many of its party members, who were already attracted to the program of the CPML. Police repression of leftist political groups, it was thought, would finally convince many of the front's wavering supporters that the UF was essentially the same as the previous Congress governments in the state. On the other hand, if the front continued to immobilize the police, it would eventually face a police revolt, with a consequent breakdown of state government. The beginnings of a police revolt became evident after the Durgapur incidents.

The superintendent of police in West Bengal stated in June 1969 that policemen had become so agitated over the Durgapur incidents that they "could not be kept under any senior officer's control." In the words of Home Minister Jyoti Basu, "I can't say it was a police revolt, but it is clear that a certain section of the police went out of control."[57] In order to deal with a potential police revolt, the state government immediately took disciplinary action against the leading police officials involved in the Durgapur incidents and eventually suspended the secretary of the West Bengal Police Association on the charge that he had left his duties in Calcutta to investigate the Durgapur incidents without getting the approval of his superiors. In protest against the state government and the state political parties, the WBPA voted to observe a one-day hunger strike on July 15, 1969, during which they would perform their normal duties but wear badges to indicate their support of the association. At the same time, the WBPA prepared a report on the Durgapur incidents which has been summarized as follows:

. . . policemen at Durgapur have been suffering from a sense of insecurity, particularly since the attack by students on the family quarters . . . . Recently the police have been subjected to assault and humiliation by riotous mobs as a result of which the morale of the force has been shattered. There have been many such incidents: at Kasba, Islampur, Kultali, Amdanga and Bally.

[57] "Policemen in West Bengal," *Citizen and Weekend Review*, June 14, 1969, p. 21.

Recently the police in West Bengal has not only been debarred from performing its minimum duties of maintaining law and order but its functioning is being interfered with by the local party bosses of CPI(M). Policemen do not even have the right to defend themselves and their families in the face of mob fury. The Durgapur incident has shown that the police force is no longer prepared to take this kind of thing lying down.[58]

Faced with a near revolt among the police after the Durgapur incidents, the UF sought to consolidate support within the police force: large numbers of policemen who had been suspended or fired by the Congress before 1967 were rehired, senior police officials were replaced with UF appointees, and the leftist parties in the state organized an association of nongazetted police employees (the West Bengal Non-Gazetted Police Employees Committee, or WBNGPEC) as a competitor of the WBPA.[59] Predictably, these measures split the police force between those siding with and those against the UF.

If West Bengal were a sovereign, independent nation, or if the Communist parties were strong throughout India, one might argue that it would be advantageous for the Bengali Communists to create an anarchic situation. Under the present circumstances, however, anarchy in West Bengal has resulted in President's Rule by the central government, which will work as long as New Delhi is able to govern. Moreover, in a segmented society like India's, the possibility of anarchy in one state spreading to other states is diminished considerably. The organizational growth of communism in West Bengal since Independence, for example, has not been accompanied by a parallel growth even in the states adjoining West Bengal, despite numerous efforts by Bengalis to organize them. The combined vote of the two major Communist parties in the 1967 elections was 7.12 percent of the total in Assam, 8.19 percent in Bihar, and 6.42 percent in Orissa, and none of these figures represents significant changes from 1957 and 1962. Indeed, the principal opposition parties in each of the three states bordering on West Bengal are ideologically anticommunist and non-Marxist. Even if the Congress party loses a significant portion of its electoral support in future elections in these states, Congress votes are likely to go to noncommunist opposition parties.

It is for these reasons that neither the CPM nor the CPI is willing to view the present political situation in India as "an excellent revolutionary situation." In the words of the theoreticians in the CPM, "It is

[58] Ibid.
[59] *The Statesman*, June 16, 1969.

amazing that our critics [the CPML] can exaggerate the political crisis to the point of equating it with a revolutionary crisis":[60]

> It is precisely because we have no such phenomenon of warlord regimes, incessant wars among them and on the other hand, have a *centralised and unified regime* in the form of the Indian Union, that it is incumbent upon us to study concretely the contradictions that form the basis for revolutionary crisis and the disintegration of the ruling classes, their parties and their centralised state apparatus. . . . Refusal to undertake this study, the tendency to pooh-pooh these conflicts [between members of the ruling classes] as of no consequence, the facile idea that by pointing them out the mass struggles get diverted, and at the same time indulge in the tall talk of revolutionary situation and armed struggle is symptomatic of infantile phrase-mongering, not of a serious Marxist-Leninist attitude to the study of contradictions.[61]

Because of their conviction that India is not passing through a period ripe for a one-stage revolution, the leaders of both the CPI and the CPM have argued that "any further weakening or disorganising of the Party from a sectarian and left-opportunist deviation, we are of opinion, would only result in greater harm to the cause of the Indian revolution, and would come as a boon to the reactionary ruling classes."[62]

Yet however much the CPM and CPI might condemn the CPML and the Naxalites, they have as yet been unwilling to discipline CPML members and supporters. The leadership of the CPM allowed the Naxalites to remain within the fold of the party in order to prevent a split, and the UF government refused to use the police to inhibit CPML activities. The CPML was therefore able to drive the UF parties more and more toward Left Communist positions and to threaten both the unity and the effectiveness of the Communist-led state governments. Moreover, the Congress party in the state has not hesitated to support the Naxalites at times when their activities have been a source of embarrassment to the UF, and the noncommunist parties in the front have occasionally used the Naxalites to embarrass the CPM. The resulting situation has produced an intricate web of feuds and alliances in which every party and faction is constantly wary of "conspiracies" that might be launched against its interests.

---

[60] *Ideological Debate Summed Up by Politbureau* (Calcutta: CPM, 1968), p. 164.
[61] Ibid., p. 168. (Italics in the original.)
[62] Ibid., p. 183.

7

THE CPM AND PARTIAL POLITICAL POWER

While the CPM has had to deal with severe inner-party factionalism since 1967, it has also been confronted with a highly factionalized state political environment in which the other state parties have been more and more willing to ally against it. In this atmosphere the principal concern of the CPM has been its minority position in the United Front coalition and the tenuous nature of the coalition itself. Of particular concern to CPM leaders is the danger that the other parties in the United Front might coalesce against the CPM, either in alliance with the Congress or under the tutelage of the CPI. In its review of the 1967 election results, for example, the CPM Central Committee issued the following warnings to party members:

> . . . the democratic movement [that is, the CPM] must be always conscious of the danger of backsliding by those representatives of the vested interests [UF allies], and of sabotage of the working of democratic measures in the interests of the people, and even of their hatching conspiracies to scuttle these governments and join hands with the Congress to set up reactionary governments both in the states and at the Centre.[1]
> . . . .
> The struggle against the Revisionists—the Right Communists—will be prolonged and it has to be continued more patiently and skilfully. It is our work among the people and the correctness of our path that would convince the general mass of the people to swing over to us. We have to combine our exposure of Right Communist ideology, policies and tactics while working with them in the new ministries, in mass organisations, in common people's struggles.
> We must know how to demarcate and develop our independent ideology, policies and mass base, while working along with them and other petty bourgeois or bourgeois parties![2]

In line with this position, in 1967 the CPM Central Committee developed a tactic of immediately strengthening party organizations and mass movements in the two states where the party was strong, in an attempt

---

[1] *Election Review and Party's Tasks, Adopted by the Central Committee of the CPI (M) at Its Session in Calcutta, April 10 to 16, 1967* (Calcutta: CPM, 1967), pp. 8–9.
[2] Ibid., pp. 30–31.

to solidify the hold of the party on the state ministries. Questions of national and international importance to Communists were not to be entirely neglected, but in general they were at least temporarily postponed in light of the necessity to consolidate two strong state party units. Essential to the adoption of this tactic was its acceptability to a large portion of the centrist and Left factions in the CPM, since strong state party organizations would be important both for electoral and for nonelectoral strategies in the future.

In the words of the CPM party program, the "core and the basis" of the party's efforts in West Bengal and Kerala after the assumption of power in 1967 was to consist of a "firm alliance of the working class and the peasantry," brought about by aggressive party work in trade unions and peasant organizations and directed against other political parties in the states concerned.[3] For this reason it was essential that the CPM control the portfolios of Land and Land Revenue, Labour, and Home (especially Police), since these three ministries would determine in large measure the nature of governmental policy on the peasant and trade union fronts. In the first UF ministry in West Bengal, the CPM was able to gain control of the Land and Land Revenue portfolio but found its position in the coalition (43 of 141 seats) too weak to be granted charge of the Home or Labour ministries. But when the CPM secured 80 of the 214 seats in the second state coalition government, its bargaining position was considerably enhanced, and it immediately waged a successful struggle to add Labour and Home (Police) to its list of governmental portfolios.[4]

In order to placate both factions within the party, as well as the other constituent parties in the United Front, it was also necessary for the CPM to adopt a more flexible policy with regard to the areas and classes that it was willing to organize once it assumed political power. On the peasant front, for example, the party now took the position that "different sections of the peasantry play different roles in the revolution," implying that all rural classes could be courted by the party. In the words of a report prepared by the Central Committee,

The agricultural labourers and poor peasants who constitute seventy per cent of the rural households and are subjected to ruthless exploitation by landlords, by their very class position in present-day society, will be basic allies of the working class. The middle peasantry, too, are the victims of the depredation of

[3] This tactical line is detailed in *New Situation and Party's Tasks* (Calcutta: CPM, 1967).
[4] The bargaining that took place with regard to the state Labour and Home ministries in 1969 is detailed in "CPI(M) Resents Denial of Due Place and Role," *Amrita Bazaar Patrika* (Calcutta daily), February 20, 1969.

usurious capital, of feudal and capitalist landlords in the countryside and of the capitalist market, and landlord domination in rural life so affects their social position in innumerable ways as to make them reliable allies in the democratic front.

The rich peasants are another influential section among the peasantry. The Congress agrarian reforms have undoubtedly benefited certain sections of them ... [but] ... heavy taxation, high prices for industrial goods and inflation constantly harass them so as to make their future uncertain. . . . . By and large, they can also, therefore, be brought into the democratic front and retained as allies in the People's Democratic Revolution.[5]

In organizing the rural areas, moreover, the CPM showed a new flexibility after assuming political power. The report on the Kisan Front, just quoted, therefore argued that it would be "incorrect" to "make a rigid pattern of organisation for . . . all states and regions." Depending on the circumstances, the report argued, "State and District Committees [must] take full account of all the factors and take proper decisions as to whether, where, and how the agricultural labourers are to be organized."[6]

The new flexibility of the CPM was designed to meet the threat of other parties' making inroads into the rural areas by using the patronage of political office. By allowing local units to determine the forms of organization to be used as well as the class interests to be courted, the party made it possible for each local unit to ensure maximum support. Thus the party organized some areas by bringing influential middle and rich peasants into the party and using them as brokers to dispatch state patronage, while in other areas it led movements against large landholders with the backing of the state ministries. Regardless of the strategy that the party pursued in any given area, however, it inevitably collided with all the other parties in the United Front. This was particularly true in the case of the land redistribution movement, which created a large number of clashes between political parties throughout the state in 1969–1970.

The Peasant Front

The movement for land redistribution in West Bengal stems from the Congress land reform program, as embodied in the West Bengal Estates Acquisition Act of 1954, which theoretically placed a ceiling of 25 acres on landholdings but also provided a number of legal means for exceeding the ceiling. Three of the principle methods by which

---

[5] *Tasks on the Kisan Front, Resolutions of the Central Committee* (Calcutta: CPM, 1967), p. 15.

[6] Ibid., pp. 23–24.

lands in excess of 25 acres have been controlled are (1) *benami* transfer, which involves transfer of land titles to relatives; (2) holding of agricultural land as fisheries, which are excluded from the 25-acre ceiling in the legislation; (3) holding of land in excess of 25 acres through private agreements between landholders and tenants, or between landholders and the government, with the title to the land legally in the name of the tenant or state government but the produce apportioned as though the title were in the name of the landlord.[7] Shortly after the United Front came to power in 1967, the state Land and Land Revenue Minister (Hare Krishna Konar), a leading member of the cpm, indicated that the new policy of the state government would be to "recover land involved in *benami* and other transactions with popular cooperation," while the police in the rural areas were instructed by the new uf government "not to suppress the democratic and legitimate struggles of the people."[8] Konar then initiated a series of investigations to trace *benami* and other holdings in excess of 25 acres, and a number of parties in the front began to organize units that could carry out transfers of land by force.

During the first uf government, in 1967, the front claimed that it redistributed 248,000 acres of land, largely land that had been earmarked for transfer by the Congress government but had not yet been redistributed because of court cases, bureaucratic delay, and political favoritism. In addition, Konar argued that by April 1969 he had traced 153,000 acres of *benami* holdings and that the government had started court cases to reclaim this land as well.[9] Since the total acreage under cultivation in West Bengal is estimated at 13,400,000, the land involved in the uf's redistribution programs has amounted to only 3 percent of the total arable land, but Land Revenue sources argue that there is much more to be discovered,[10] and the existing transfers have already had a considerable impact at least on the style of politics in the state.

Since most of the land belonging to large landholders is held legally by rural elites highly conscious of their rights and extremely

[7] For the development of a land reform policy for West Bengal during Congress rule, see Marcus F. Franda, *West Bengal and the Federalizing Process in India* (Princeton: Princeton University Press, 1968), pp. 129–178.

[8] *The Statesman* (Calcutta daily), March 7, 1967.

[9] *Link* (Delhi weekly), April 20, 1969, p. 19.

[10] In a speech in the West Bengal Legislative Assembly, Land Revenue Minister Konar estimated that another 400,000 acres of land in excess of the 25-acre limit were still held by former *zamindars* and *jotedars*. See *West Bengal Legislative Assembly Debates*, March 18, 1969.

skillful in protecting them, the UF government and the CPM decided to move cautiously in implementing land redistribution programs in 1967 and 1969–1970. At the governmental level the state Land and Land Revenue Ministry established a series of Land Advisory Committees during the first UF government, consisting of lawyers, local governmental and party leaders, and leaders from various peasant groups, to inquire into the maze of consequences that would flow from various land reform measures. Soon after the formation of the second UF government, however, these committees had to be disbanded, since their membership had been reshuffled during the period when the UF was temporarily out of power.[11] In place of these committees, Land Revenue Minister Konar told his own Land Reform officers in the districts in 1969 to consult with leaders of local government bodies and with "representatives of local peasants' organizations" to test out the feasibility of new legislation. Konar also announced that his ministry was hiring its own team of lawyers to cope with the legal complexities of land litigation and legislation. In an obvious reference to his party's policy on the land issue, he announced that he had instructed his officers "to give due consideration to the suggestions placed by representatives of the political parties."[12]

While comprehensive land legislation was contemplated in 1970 or 1971, owing to the legal complexities of preparing legislation in this area, Konar argued in 1969 that "much can be done to retrieve the position if the whole administrative machinery is geared up and if proper and timely measures are taken at all levels to implement the existing provisions."[13] Particularly important in Konar's calculations were the behavior and cooperation of the police, mass organizations, and political parties in rural areas, each of which became crucial to the immediate policies of the United Front Land Revenue Ministry. From the time that Konar assumed the ministry in 1967, he argued that the police in West Bengal were "in the habit of readily going into action on the complaints of big *jotedars* [landholders]," and he therefore instructed police officials (through the Minister of Police, Jyoti Basu) that policemen were "to consult officers of the Land Revenue Department before they decided to act on the basis of *jotedars'* complaints."[14] At the same time Konar stated that government would make every effort to enlist the cooperation of rural mass organizations

[11] *Amrita Bazaar Patrika,* March 1, 1969.
[12] Ibid., March 21, 1969.
[13] *The Statesman,* March 18, 1969.
[14] Ibid.

in order to ensure "prompt action, instead of allowing time to *jotedars* to go for court injunctions which delay distribution of vested land."[15]

As a result of this policy a large number of rural political leaders in West Bengal began to organize peasants to take possession of lands held by *jotedars* in excess of the 25-acre ceiling—particularly *benami* lands, fisheries, and land held in the names of tenants and the state government—and the CPM State Secretariat even issued a directive to party workers to "recover *benami* lands and distribute them among the landless peasants."[16] But the CPM organizations in the countryside were by no means able to act in a united manner in implementing the party's new tactic, and the other political parties in the United Front resisted the CPM's attempts to monopolize the peasants' organization in support of the new government policies. In general, the CPM state leadership defended forcible occupation of agricultural land and fisheries by local party units in cases where large landholders held land illegally, but at the same time the party was seriously concerned that rash action by some local units might involve the party in more litigation than it could afford to finance. Deputy Chief Minister Basu, for example, warned local CPM supporters who seized a number of private fisheries that "the Government would support all forms of legitimate struggle of the people, but could not uphold *unlawful* actions."[17]

During the United Front ministries the CPM was also faced with constant opposition from the other political parties in the UF, who sought to use the policy of the Land Revenue Ministry to their own advantage, either by expanding their peasant organizations by the adoption of strategies like the CPM's or by resisting the CPM in the hope of discrediting the new tactic. Land Revenue Minister Konar did issue a warning to the other parties in the front that they should be wary of "indiscriminate acts of seizure" if they had "no mass base and little idea about land records,"[18] but his warnings did not deter the larger UF partners (CPI, Forward Bloc, SUC, RSP, and Bangla Congress) from active participation in the land redistribution program. The result was a flurry of political activity in the West Bengal countryside, with units of at least five major parties in the United Front organizing peasants to seize lands and fisheries, with a larger and

---

[15] Ibid.

[16] *Hindusthan Standard* (Calcutta daily), March 27, 1969.

[17] Ibid., April 10, 1969. (Italics added.)

[18] *Amrita Bazaar Patrika*, April 14, 1969. For the reaction of the regular CPI to this challenge, see Ajoy Dasgupta, "West Bengal: Peasants' Initiative," *New Age* (CPI weekly), May 4, 1969, p. 4.

larger volume of court cases and countercases being filed back and forth by landholders, tenants, government, and political parties, and with the administrative and police services remaining generally inactive.

While the ramifications of the UF land redistribution program will not be fully known for a number of years, its broad outlines are already becoming evident. At the risk of oversimplification, the consequences of the movement can be said to fall into two major categories:

1. There were innumerable physical clashes between the major political parties in the United Front in 1969–1970 in which two or more parties attempted to seize the same plot of land or one party sought to prevent the other from seizing it. In the month of May 1969, for example, Calcutta newspapers listed thirteen political murders that had resulted from clashes between parties in the United Front, and most party politicians agreed that this was a gross underestimate.[19] In order to prevent such clashes, a number of people in the United Front suggested that local "people's committees" be established consisting of representatives of a number of UF parties, but the CPM at first resisted attempts to create such committees. Its leaders argued that People's Committees should "emerge from a mass movement . . . and not be imposed on the people by the United Front," and the CPM State Secretariat therefore instructed its local units to organize People's Committees consisting only of CPM members and supporters from CPM-dominated peasant organizations.[20] In reaction to the formation of CPM committees, other parties in the United Front created similar party committees, with the result that five party organizations (CPM, CPI, Forward Bloc, RSP, and Bangla Congress) now have rural volunteer forces designed to "assist" the government in implementing land programs. Because of the CPM's determination to use government policy to reinforce its position in peasant organizations, and in light of the growing willingness of the other parties in the United Front to resist the CPM, clashes between the various UF parties have continued to increase steadily since 1967, even during periods of President's Rule.

2. A second major consequence of the land redistribution movement has been the revitalization of small and local landlord and fishery-owner organizations and, more important, the exploration of a variety

---

[19] Based on interviews. The journalists' estimates were so low because they were not always able to identify the political parties involved and were naturally unwilling to publish concrete statements without sufficient evidence.

[20] For the position of the CPM on the question of People's Committees, see Prasanta Sarkar, "Differences in UF over People's Committees," *The Statesman*, May 6, 1967. See also ibid., May 9, 1969.

of methods by which landlords could protect their interests. Some of the landholders in the state have been able to restrain political groups through the use of injunctions and other legal devices, and most of those who have had lands forcibly seized by political organizations have taken their cases to the courts. In addition, some landlords have threatened tenants with the withdrawal of agricultural loans or have issued other warnings to tenants, drawing on their authority and status as landholders in a peasant economy.[21] But even more effective has been the strategy used by many landholders of penetrating into one or another of the various political parties in the United Front in order to secure the backing of one front party against another.[22] Because of the success of this strategy, tensions within the United Front were strained to the breaking point in early 1970, since UF parties were vying with one another for the support of landless laborers and landholders, with party positions determined strictly on the basis of local factors. Even within state political parties (including the CPM), some local units were supporting the landless at the same time as other local units in neighboring areas were supporting the landed.[23]

In this atmosphere the impact of the CPM's new tactic and the state government's new policies were not as significant in effecting radical agrarian reforms in the Bengal countryside as they were in creating a new mood among Bengali politicians. At the most, the movement could have affected only 6 to 10 percent of the total arable land in West Bengal, and not all of this land was expected to go to the landless. Indeed, in cases where there was actual transfer of land from one family to another, both of the families were frequently landholders for many generations (many of the "landless" who procured land were refugees from East Pakistan whose families had been traditional landholders but who had been dispossessed after partition). Where land did actually pass to traditional tenant cultivators, many observers expected that it would eventually end up with landed rural influentials backed by one of the United Front political parties. While in some cases land was transferred from large landholders to small and middle landholding peasants who could be expected to retain their new rights to it, in other instances the redistribution movement worked to the advantage of the large landholders.[24] Land redistribution policy in West Bengal during

---

[21] Based on interviews in 1969 with both landholders and landless laborers in Midnapore and 24-Parganas.

[22] *Now* (Calcutta weekly), May 30, 1969, pp. 3–4.

[23] See, for example, "UF Partners Aid Fishery Owners," *Hindusthan Standard*, May 3, 1969.

[24] *Now*, May 30, 1969, pp. 3–4.

the two United Front governments could therefore be understood as a political device for transferring land from landed Congress supporters (who had the backing of the previous state governments) to a new group of rural influential landholders who were able to gain the backing of the United Front parties. Even Land Revenue Minister Konar acknowledged that the land redistribution movement would have little effect on the status of West Bengal's landless laborers, and he attempted to reassure middle and small peasant proprietors again and again that "everything would be done to protect the farmers' interests."[25]

However, despite the inability of the UF to effect significant land reforms, a number of observers in the state viewed the land redistribution movement as revolutionary in terms of *political* change. The movement did lead to increased expectations among small landholders that land would be redistributed on a large scale, it eroded the previous pattern of Congress support, and it contributed to changes in the social structure that have yet to be fully assessed. Similarly, the effect of the movement on the various political parties' support is yet to be determined, but almost everyone would agree that the CPM gained more than any of the other parties in securing short-run support, even though it was unable to gain a monopoly over the patronage dispensed by the United Front in the rural areas. Support for the United Front in the rural areas was apparently quite high, sustained largely by those who had not been included in the Congress patronage network, by the heightened expectations of the landless and poor peasant cultivators, and by some previous Congress supporters who successfully switched their allegiance to one of the United Front parties after 1967.

The Trade Union Front

In the terminology of Communist analysts, the CPM in West Bengal has been pursuing a "modified Right" strategy and "united front from below" tactics since the assumption of political power in 1967.[26] Like the classical Right Communist strategy, the modified Right strategy calls for a two-stage revolution, with the Communists coming to complete power only in the second stage and only after preconditions have been established in the first stage. During the first stage the Communists seek to ally with the broadest strata of the population

---

[25] *Hindusthan Standard*, May 19, 1969.

[26] For an analysis of the "modified Right" Communist strategy and "united front from below" tactics, see Donald S. Zagoria, "Communist Policy and the Struggle for the Developing Countries," *Proceedings of the Academy of Political Science* 28 (April 1965): 69 ff.

(particularly peasants and workers, but also the petty bourgeoisie and the anti-imperialist sections of the bourgeoisie) by outbidding the nationalist and reformist parties (such as the Congress and the Bangla Congress) for their support. However, like the classical Left Communist strategy, the modified Right strategy insists on leadership of the alliance by the "true" Communist party and a power base that is separate from that of the nationalist parties and the other parties in the alliance. The last requirement stems from the need to exert constant pressure on the nationalist parties and to prevent parties allied with the "true" Communist party from "backsliding" on the way to the second stage of the revolution. In short, the insistence on CPM leadership of the United Front in West Bengal has stemmed from the need for a "united front from below." In the words of a resolution of the CPM Central Committee,

The main pillar of our tactics is united front from below. That is so because there is a powerful urge for unity in the masses and without giving expression to it, without strengthening and turning it into an active force, the reformist and revisionist leaders will not have joint action or unity of action. Without pressure from below, from the ranks and the masses in general, the reformists will continue to evade joint action and weaken and disrupt the struggle.[27]

As was seen in the case of the peasant front, this strategy has dictated an alliance of the CPM with a broad range of interests in the countryside, but at the same time it has called for the CPM's continued insistence on its own organizational growth and its independence of the range of political parties arrayed against it. On the trade union front the strategy and tactics of the CPM have been devised in a similar manner. In the words of the Central Committee, "The effort for united front from below includes constant appeals to all sections of workers. . . . It consists of joint actions at the base, in factories, *under our initiative.*"[28] The tactics of the CPM, according to the Central Committee, ". . . aim at organizing a disciplined working class with revolutionary socialist consciousness, drawing it nearer the Party, with its best elements joining the Party in hundreds, enabling the class as a whole to play its historic political role in the revolutionary struggle."[29]

However, the position of the CPM in the trade union movement in West Bengal differs significantly from its position in the peasant organizations. In contrast to the mass peasant organizations in West

[27] *Tasks on the Trade Union Front, Resolution of the Central Committee of the Communist Party of India–Marxist* (Calcutta: CPM, 1967), p. 33.
[28] Ibid. (Italics in the original.)
[29] Ibid., pp. 3–4.

Bengal, which have never been well established, trade unions have effectively engaged in mass agitational activities and have played an important role in the politics of the state since the 1920s. By 1967 the CPM was clearly on the defensive in the all-India trade union front despite its control of large numbers of trade unions in the state, and a number of the other parties in the UF government (and even the Congress) could boast of large membership figures for affiliated trade unions. This was in sharp contrast to the peasant front, where the CPM was the only party that had attempted to form mass organizations on a large scale. The position of the party in the trade union front was acknowledged by the CPM Central Committee in a 1967 report to party members:

> We must constantly bear in mind that . . . we ourselves form a far from dominating and leading force in the organised trade unions, the other sections being stronger than us in many industries and equal to us in some industries.[30]

Because of its minority position in the trade union movement in 1967, the CPM has pursued what the Central Committee has called "the real bolshevik method of mobilising the masses." This has consisted of militant and aggressive tactics toward employers and other trade unions but "supplemented by offers of united front from the top which at times is a pre-condition of united front from below."[31]

The environment in which the CPM has been pursuing this strategy and tactical line has been one of great ferment and upheaval. The increased activities of all the trade unions in West Bengal after the UF's assumption of political power in 1967 is indicated by a number of factors, some of which are listed in Table 8. The table makes it quite clear that the activities of the trade unions in 1967 were far greater than in any previous year, regardless of the index that is being used. While complete figures are not available for 1968 and 1969, those that have been published show that the activities of trade unions in the state have continued to increase at an extremely rapid rate. Figures published by the Labour Department during the period of President's Rule in 1968, for example, showed that the number of men involved in work stoppages in 1968 was "nearly double the number in the previous year," while man-days lost in 1968 "surpassed all previous records, not only of West Bengal but of any other State of India."[32]

---

[30] Ibid., p. 30.

[31] Ibid., p. 31.

[32] Manindra Bhattacharjee, "1968: A Bad Year for Labour," *Hindusthan Standard Weekly Supplement*, December 31, 1968, p. iv.

TABLE 8

INDICES OF TRADE UNION ACTIVITY IN WEST BENGAL

	1964	1965	1966	1967
Number of disputes raised during the year	6187	6444	6720	10,331
Number of work stoppages	215	228	244	447
Number of men involved in work stoppages	113,695	123,654	154,354	169,259
Number of man-days lost	1,556,185	1,362,568	2,754,447	6,118,816
Number of unions	269	257	274	897
Membership (claimed by unions)	42,469	42,990	33,274	128,794

Source: Labour in West Bengal, 1967, compiled by Government of West Bengal, Statistics, Research and Publication Branch of the Labour Directorate (Calcutta: West Bengal Director of Information, 1967), pp. 1, 2, 14.

The reasons for this growth in trade union activity obviously stem from the two UF governments' approach to labor. Immediately upon taking office, the first UF Labour Minister (Subodh Banerjee of the SUC), supported by all of the parties in the United Front, announced "a break with the past, with the anti-people and bureaucratic policies and approach of the Congress."[33] The essential feature of Banerjee's "new approach" was the attempt "to enlist the people's cooperation for the implementation of policies rather than depend on the administrative machinery." Through a series of devices the Labour Ministry sought to create machinery that would "solve industrial disputes as expeditiously as possible and prohibit police interference in normal trade union disputes": all committees and boards of the Labour Department were completely reorganized "on a more democratic basis," the police were instructed not to interfere in "the legitimate democratic trade union movement," and layoff or retrenchment without the sanction of the government was "discouraged." Especially important for the style of trade union politics in the state was the decision by the first UF Labour Ministry to legalize the tactic of *gherao*.

A *gherao* consists essentially of a blockade, imposed by a number of trade union workers on the office of a manager or group of managers for a considerable period of time. The employees who are "gheraoing" the manager usually squat around him, shout slogans, and sometimes

---

[33] The Labour policy of the first UF government is described in Ajoy Dasgupta, "Bengal: A New Approach to People's Problems," *New Age*, April 16, 1967, p. 4. The quotations that follow are taken from this article.

take turns abusing him. In many cases food or water is not allowed to reach the person, and electricity, telephones, and bathroom facilities are frequently rendered inaccessible. *Gheraos* have varied in length from a few hours to several days, and the goal of those who stage *gheraos* is usually the extraction of signatures on documents that would not be signed under normal circumstances. The tactic had been in use in West Bengal for at least a decade prior to the assumption of political power by the United Front, but it had always been considered illegal and improper by the Congress governments. When it was declared legal by the state Labour Ministry in 1967, the number of *gheraos* throughout the state mushroomed disconcertingly. According to the most authoritative estimates available, there were 1018 *gheraos* in 583 establishments in West Bengal during the six-month period March–August 1967,[34] and only one party in the United Front (the Bangla Congress) has ceased to support *gheraos* since they were declared illegal by the Calcutta High Court.[35] Because of massive support by the other UF parties, *gheraos* have become a regular feature of life in West Bengal since 1967, despite the ruling of the judiciary.

The new approach of the state Labour Ministry, which did not change appreciably when the ministry was assumed by the CPM in February 1969, has provided an impetus to the organization of trade unions in the state. During the period March–September 1967, for example, 591 new trade unions were registered in West Bengal, by far the largest short-run increase that had ever taken place.[36] Moreover, the vast majority of these unions were affiliated with political parties, and their origins were unquestionably a result of the feeling on the part of workers that trade union organizations might be more effective now than they had been under the Congress regime. In this scramble to increase the unionization of workers, the CPM and the CPI have been by far the largest gainers, with the CPM adding 170 new trade unions between March and September 1967 and the CPI 140 during the same period, a combined total that accounts for more than half of the new trade unions founded in this period. That both the CPM and the CPI used the tactic of *gherao* to gain support among trade union workers is shown by the fact that 397 of the 1018 cases of *gherao* in March–August 1967 were instigated by CPM or CPI trade unions. The success

[34] Nitish R. De and Suresh Srivastava, "Gheraos in West Bengal—I," *Economic and Political Weekly* (Bombay), November 18, 1967, p. 2015.

[35] Relevant rulings of the Calcutta High Court on cases of *gherao* are reprinted in Arjun P. Aggarwal, *Gheraos and Industrial Relations* (Bombay: N. M. Tripathi Private Limited, 1968), pp. 172–175.

[36] Nitish R. De and Suresh Srivastava, "Gheraos in West Bengal—III," *Economic and Political Weekly*, December 2, 1967, p. 2099.

of the CPM in expanding its trade union base was strikingly demonstrated by its increased support among labor unions in the Calcutta industrial belt in the 1969 election campaigns.[37]

In addition to their acquisition of new affiliates, both the CPM and the CPI have made concerted efforts to infiltrate and capture trade unions that are presently affiliated with minor parties. A survey carried out by the CPI in May 1969, for example, indicated that the CPM had been able to capture the registered trade unions of other parties in 10 establishments during the months of February, March, and April 1969, while in 60 other industrial concerns it was still waging protracted fights with trade unions controlled by noncommunist parties.[38] According to the same survey, the CPM was gaining considerable ground among jute and textile industry unions in West Bengal, though it was perhaps losing some of its affiliates in the engineering industry. Of particular concern to the CPI was the fact that the CPM had either formed new trade unions or captured existing organizations in more than 200 establishments where there were unions affiliated with the CPI. As a result of the aggressiveness of CPM trade union organizers, some minor parties repeatedly threatened to quit the United Front,[39] while others have fought back with arms and assassination. The most serious clashes between parties thus far have all involved the CPM, with the RSP, SUC, SSP, Forward Bloc, and CPI in turn providing the opposition.[40]

Because the CPM is clearly the most aggressive of the state parties in seeking to enlarge its trade union affiliates, the other parties in the United Front (including the CPI) have been increasingly willing to unite against it. Of particular concern to the smaller parties in 1969–1970 was the policy that was proposed by state Labor Minister Krishnapada Ghosh (a brother-in-law of Pramode Das Gupta and representative of the CPM) when the CPM first assumed the state Labour Ministry, which limited trade union activities to one union in each establishment, to be elected by secret ballot.[41] Such a policy obviously

[37] This is pointed out in Ashok Mitra, "West Bengal for Communism," *Citizen and Weekend Review* (New Delhi fortnightly), March 22, 1969, p. 23.

[38] The results of the survey are detailed in *Amrita Bazaar Patrika*, May 14, 1969.

[39] In late May 1969, for example, the Gurkha League (GL) warned the CPM that it did not believe in violence but that it was "competent enough for a showdown if unwarranted trade union aggression by the CPI(M) continued." N. L. Gurung, Gurkha League MLA, told newsmen that the GL was "being forced to consider whether it should remain in the UF." See *The Statesman*, May 26, 1969.

[40] For an analysis of trade union feuds between rival parties in the UF, see Amitava Das Gupta, "Inter-Party Rivalries: A Real Danger to the United Front," *Hindusthan Standard*, May 27, 1969.

[41] The "one union in each establishment" formula is described in *Amrita Bazaar Patrika*, June 4, 1969.

benefited the larger parties in the front and might have contradicted either the Indian Constitution or the Trade Union Act of the central government. Moreover, since the CPM state Labour Minister controlled the trade union election machinery in the second UF government, and since the CPM had the most militant cadre of all of the UF parties, it obviously had a distinct advantage under the "one union in each establishment" formula. In spite of this, the CPM was able to push through state legislation embodying provisions that would make such a policy possible, largely because it received considerable support for the proposal from management groups, who in most factories had been harassed with the demands of a host of unions.[42] On the basis of management backing, the CPM was able to convince the Bangla Congress to support the measure, and since parties with strong trade union organizations stood to gain under the legislation, the CPI was also a advocate of the proposal.

The CPM and the State Coalition

The CPM is not the only party in the West Bengal government that has sought to establish a more direct relationship between the state government and the mass of the electorate. Aside from their activities in land redistribution and labor agitation, all of the political parties in the United Front agreed to the enactment of legislation in 1969–1970 raising the salaries and allowances of most state employees, schoolteachers, and policemen.[43] Moreover, legislation enacted with the support of all the UF parties now protects the rights of tenants against landlords and labor against management to a degree unknown during Congress rule. Ministers from all the UF parties used the powers of the state government to assist the jute, tea, engineering, and textile workers of the state in their successful campaign to gain significant salary and fringe-benefit concessions from industry. As a result of UF-sponsored legislation, all tenants in West Bengal have been given permanent rights to their homestead lands (based on minimal residence requirements), even in cases where tenants have no such rights to the fields they cultivate; more than 8 million cultivators who own less than 3 acres of land have been exempted from payment of all land revenue; and a series of minor administrative irritants enacted by the previous Congress government have been removed. Muslims, for example, no longer require citizenship certificates when selling their

---

[42] See ibid., September 11, 1969, and *The Statesman*, September 11, 1969, pp. 1, 12.

[43] For a survey of the legislation enacted by the United Front during the monsoon session of the state Legislative Assembly in 1969, see the *Hindusthan Standard*, October 8, 1969, and October 19, 1969.

property, the procedure for obtaining loans from cooperative societies has been streamlined to eliminate delays that worked to the advantage of rural influentials, and workers suspended by private firms are now entitled by state law to 50 percent of their wages during the first 90 days of their suspension and 75 percent of their wages after 90 days.

The effect of this flurry of governmental activity has been continued support for the United Front government by a majority of the voters of West Bengal. In every by-election to the Lok Sabha and state Legislative Assembly since February 1969 the UF won handily, in each case increasing the margin of victory over the previous two elections.[44] Similar data could be compiled for local and municipal elections in 1969 and 1970. Moreover, there are indications that the United Front has been able to carry out an important change in the state's commonest form of electoral organization. While the success of the Congress organization in West Bengal in the period before the 1967 elections was always dependent on an alliance of rural and urban influentials who could in turn influence the mass of the voters to support the Congress because of their place in Congress patronage networks, the United Front parties have relied more heavily on party committees and party regulars drawn from a cross section of the population.

In this atmosphere the United Front parties were reluctant to advocate a breakup of the state coalition when it was in power, despite their mutual dissatisfaction with the aggressive organizational tactics of the CPM. The Bangla Congress leadership, which eventually broke with the UF and brought down the state government, originally took the position that the front should continue but that the lawlessness and violence associated with UF policies should be resisted. To emphasize public support for this position, the Bangla Congress organized a large rally of its peasant supporters in Bankura in November 1969, and when the resolutions of this rally were neglected by front partners, the Chief Minister himself launched a three-day *satyagraha* that featured

---

[44] In May 1969, for example, V. K. Krishna Menon was elected to the Midnapore Lok Sabha seat in West Bengal by a margin of 106,761 votes, running as an independent with the backing of all of the United Front parties. This seat had been won in 1967 by Sachindra Maity of the Bangla Congress by a margin of 43,283 votes; the 1969 by-election was necessitated by the death of Mr. Maity. In December 1969 CPM candidates won by-elections to the state Legislative Assembly in Tollygunge constituency (in South Calcutta) and in Raina constituency in Burdwan District; in each case they were elected to fill seats caused by the death of a CPM MLA, and in each case they were supported by the United Front. The margin of victory in Raina was 8549 votes (compared to a margin of 7037 in February 1969 and a CPM loss in 1967) and in Tollygunge 24,707 votes (compared to a margin of 15,883 in February 1969 and 4982 in 1967).

a mass fast by more than 50,000 statewide supporters. Chief Minister Mukherjee argued that the policies of the United Front had led to a "general awakening" in the rural areas and among the poorer sections of the state population, and for this reason he did not want the state government to "fall just now." At the same time, however, he argued that there was a "feeling of insecurity of life and property" in the state which threatened to diminish the commitment of the population to orderly progress. He placed the blame for this situation squarely on the CPM.[45]

While the other major partner in the United Front—the CPI—did not publicly oppose the Chief Minister's three-day fast, some CPI leaders did attempt to dissuade him from resorting to public *satyagraha*. Like the Bangla Congress, the CPI argued that the United Front had "achieved more for the working class and the peasantry than had ever been achieved before," but CPI opposition to the CPM did not stem from concern about violence. According to the leader of the West Bengal CPI unit, the principal danger to the United Front was the "hegemonism" of the CPM rather than the violence associated with UF policies:

... despite what has happened, the United Front has at least introduced that amount of democracy which makes the mighty strike struggles take place and even succeed. The arrogance of capitalist owners has been broken in many cases and thus industrial crisis resolved to a very great extent. The food situation is very much improved. Every department is yielding better results than before. . . . But much remains to be done and more could be done if the CPM were not determined to pursue a policy of exterminating the United Front in order to build up itself as the only alternative to the Congress.[46]

Consistent with this position, the CPI in West Bengal organized a massive demonstration of its supporters on the Calcutta *maidan* in November 1969, in order to demonstrate that the accomplishments of the United Front had resulted in greater strength for the CPI as well as for the CPM.[47] Leaders of the CPI subsequently took the position that they would defend their own party when attacked by the "hegemonist CPM" but that the CPI would not take the initiative in breaking the UF coalition.

[45] For an analysis of the Chief Minister's strategy in undertaking his December fast, see *The Statesman*, November 6, 1969, and November 30, 1969. See also the *Hindustan Times* (New Delhi), December 4, 1969.

[46] Bhowani Sen, *CPM's Fight against United Front in West Bengal* (Calcutta: CPI, 1969), p. 19.

[47] The CPI press labeled the November 1969 CPI demonstration "the biggest ever rally organised by any political party in Calcutta, and for that matter in India." See *New Age*, November 23, 1969, p. 8.

While all of the smaller parties in the United Front objected to the aggressive policies of the CPM, each of them adopted different strategies in dealing with the largest front partner. Unlike the other small parties, the RSP refused to blame the CPM alone for interparty clashes but instead took the position that "no UF constituent can be fully absolved of the charge of partisan use of its Ministries."[48] Rather than pursue a defensive strategy directed only against the CPM, the RSP attempted to organize aggressively in areas of the state where it had traditionally won votes, clashing with a number of UF partners who were also active in RSP strongholds. The Forward Bloc has pursued a similar strategy but has directed most of its organizational efforts against the CPM and has not hesitated to attack the CPM publicly. Like all of the other non-CPM parties in the front, the Forward Bloc has advocated a truly broad-based United Front, in which each partner would have responsibility for areas where it had previously shown organizational strength.[49]

The delicate nature of relations between the CPM and its UF partners is indicated by the varying positions that the CPM has taken in response to increasing opposition. On the one hand, the CPM has attempted to convince politicians (and the electorate) that its aggressive organizational policies have resulted in statewide strength, in order to promote the image of the CPM as a single-party alternative to the Congress. On the other hand, CPM leaders have argued that their UF partners would be "falling into a trap" if they chose to break the United Front, since this would inevitably lead to President's Rule and perhaps to the resurgence of the Congress in consequence of the disunity of the leftist parties.[50] While the CPM has refused to soften its aggressive stance in organizational matters, it has occasionally apologized for the excesses of some of its party members, and it did consent to periodic compromises within the state Cabinet, only to have local party units fail to obey them.[51] To a certain extent the inconsistency of the party has been the result of a lack of inner-party discipline, but such indiscipline has in turn stemmed from the party's interest in maintaining organizational flexibility while implementing its policy.

The strategies of all the parties within the United Front governments were designed to meet a number of exigencies. State political

---

[48] *The Statesman*, October 4, 1969. For a detailed analysis of RSP strategy toward the Kerala and West Bengal United Fronts, see "Disarray in the United Front in Kerala and West Bengal," *The Call* (organ of the RSP) 21 (November 1969): 9–11.
[49] *Hindusthan Standard*, November 22, 1969.
[50] *The Statesman*, November 16, 1969.
[51] *Link*, November 2, 1969, pp. 16–17, and November 9, 1969, p. 19.

leaders were well aware that the state government "[did] not have enough money to meet . . . commitments already made,"[52] with the result that it would have had to find new sources of financial support if it had remained in power beyond 1970. Toward the end of UF rule in 1970, the state government did promulgate an ordinance imposing a 2 percent sales tax on fertilizers, tractors, and agricultural equipment and supplies, but the revenue from this tax was not even expected to approach the increased financial burdens it had assumed. The state government also secured an additional Rs. 20 crores from the Central Pool as a result of the Fifth Finance Commission recommendations, but even with this increase in the amount of funds allotted to it by the central government (and even when coupled with the increased revenue from the new sales tax), West Bengal expected to face a deficit of Rs. 25 crores during the fiscal year 1969–70.[53]

While other taxes have been proposed (on landholders owning more than 3 acres and on industrial firms), the likelihood of the state government's finding new tax revenue sufficient to meet budgetary deficits is considered quite remote. Some UF parties are already arguing that the new sales tax has adversely affected the cultivation of high-yielding varieties of paddy and wheat in a state that has never been able to achieve major increases in food output. Increased trade union activity and instability in the countryside have also damaged the reputation of West Bengal as a favorable climate for industrial investment, with the result that applications for licenses have declined in relation to other parts of India during recent years.[54] Most state political leaders therefore argued that imposition of new taxes on agricultural and industrial influentials by the United Front would break the tenuous mutual support that existed between many agricultural and industrial leaders and the United Front, creating

[52] These are the words of West Bengal Chief Minister (and Finance Minister) Ajoy Mukherjee in a report to the state Cabinet, as quoted in *The Statesman*, November 21, 1969. In the words of Deputy Chief Minister Jyoti Basu, "[The UF cannot continue] to please all sections of the people—the *jotedars*, blackmarketeers, hoarders and the like, and also the workers and the peasantry, at the same time. We do not know how to do it." *Hindustan Times*, December 4, 1969.

[53] *Hindusthan Standard*, November 18, 1969. A deficit of Rs. 25 crores for one year compares with a permanent state debt of Rs. 66 crores accumulated by the Congress state governments as of March 31, 1966. See K. Venketaraman, *States' Finances in India* (London: Allen & Unwin, 1968), p. 168.

[54] In response to a question in the Rajya Sabha in December 1969, Mr. Fakhruddin Ali Ahmed, Union Minister for Industrial Development, stated that West Bengal's share of applications for industrial licenses had declined from 15 percent of the total applications for all of India in 1964 to 11 percent of the total in 1969. *Times of India* (New Delhi), December 2, 1969.

further instability.[55] In this atmosphere most of the political leaders of West Bengal felt that the UF was living on borrowed time in 1969–1970, riding the wave of a temporary popularity that could not be maintained for very long. While none of the parties was anxious to desert the United Front, since this would leave them open to charges that they were responsible for bringing about the downfall of a popular government, all party leaders found it necessary to calculate the timing of their withdrawal.

The CPM and National Politics

The parties' timing of their withdrawal from the West Bengal United Front was heavily dependent on the assessment each had made of the fast-changing national political environment. Of particular concern to state party leaders were the events surrounding the split in the Congress party at the national level in late 1969, the fall of the United Front ministry in Kerala in October 1969, and the subsequent replacement of the Kerala ministry with a new state coalition headed by the CPI. Attempts by the pro-Indira Congress to woo Ajoy Mukherjee back into the fold in late 1969 resulted in a spate of rumors that the ruling Congress at the center would seek to create a new United Front coalition in West Bengal, while simultaneous events in Kerala encouraged speculation that the CPI might also try to form a new West Bengal coalition against the CPM.

In reaction to the highly factionalized state political environment and the rapid changes in national political alignments, the CPM persisted in the policy developed by its theoreticians in 1967. Its essential feature was the emphasis on a united front from below, in which the CPM maintained an independent base for itself while selectively cooperating with its friends to isolate its enemies. During the period 1967–1970, CPM theoreticians became much more specific about how the party would deal with the range of alternative political situations that could conceivably develop in the 1970s and even identified the CPM's planned response to a number of them.

The greatest danger to the CPM in the eyes of its theoreticians at both the central and state levels is the possibility that the Congress

---

[55] Cooperation between the United Front and Calcutta industrialists was established on the basis of a formula that was reiterated on a number of occasions by UF leaders. The essence of this formula was stated most bluntly by Deputy Chief Minister Jyoti Basu: "If the industrialists cooperate with the UF, the UF in turn will try to come to their assistance in securing raw materials, orders, licenses, finance, and so forth." *Amrita Bazaar Patrika*, October 5, 1969.

faction opposed to Prime Minister Indira Gandhi (which CPM members delight in calling the "Syndicate") might capture control of the Union or state governments. In this event, CPM theoreticians are convinced, "the Syndicate . . . would not hesitate to ban the CPI(M) and combine with the Swatantra and Jana Sangh."[56] In the eyes of CPM leaders, a victory by the Syndicate would therefore not only "arrest the process of mass radicalisation and the new mass polarisation" that the CPM has identified as the most significant aspect of India's changing political environment, it would also force the CPM to go underground once more and to relinquish its newly won organizational gains in some areas.[57] It is for this reason that the Naxalites and the CPML are considered such a great threat to the CPM, since their insistence on an insurrectionist strategy (which the CPM can quash only at the risk of a party split) encourages those who are inclined to use repression against all Communists.

Because of the great danger posed by the Syndicate, the CPM has extended selective support to Indira Gandhi during the course of the Congress split. During the presidential election campaign in August 1969, when Indira Gandhi reportedly supported V. V. Giri against Syndicate candidate N. Sanjiva Reddy, the CPM unanimously supported Giri, arguing that his election would be "a political victory for the popular and democratic forces against the forces of extreme reaction in the country."[58] For similar reasons the CPM has voted with the Indira Gandhi government since the split in the Lok Sabha in November 1969. But unlike the CPI, the CPM does not conceive of its support for Indira Gandhi as the prelude to a Congress-Communist coalition, since such a coalition would place it in a position of reliance on the Congress, which would threaten its independent base. In the words of P. Sundarayya, general secretary of the national CPM,

. . . we will support Mrs. Gandhi, but oppose her in all the steps that go against the people. . . . We doubt whether the Indira Gandhi groups, representing the same classes, the landlords and the big bourgeoisie—though differing from the Syndicate in the immediate tactics to be pursued to maintain their class regime—is capable of taking those steps that must be taken. . . .
The present task [of the CPM] is to develop the independent democratic movement to force her Government to take these measures.[59]

[56] The words are those of state CPM secretary Pramode Das Gupta, quoted in the *Hindusthan Standard*, November 10, 1969.
[57] *People's Democracy* (organ of the CPM), November 9, 1969.
[58] Ibid., August 31, 1969, p. 1.
[59] Quoted in the *Hindusthan Standard*, November 17, 1969.

While seeking to pressure the Indira Gandhi government into the adoption of a "clear-cut democratic programme and political line," the CPM has also warned party members that Indira Gandhi might be "led . . . into the dangerous illusion that she can fight single-handed both the Syndicate and the United Front of democratic forces led by the CPI(M) simultaneously."[60] Indeed, state leaders of the CPM in West Bengal argued after the Congress split that "a victory for the Syndicate ultimately means a ban on the CPM, and a victory for Indira Gandhi means either President's Rule or a CPI-Congress coalition for West Bengal."[61]

Either President's Rule or a Congress-CPI coalition in West Bengal was considered inevitable by the CPM, but neither of these alternatives was considered to be as disastrous as the possibility of a Syndicate victory and a ban on the party. During a period of President's Rule, or in the event of a Congress-CPI coalition, the CPM would most likely be allowed the freedom to organize, and this would enable party leaders to consolidate gains made during the period when the CPM held the ministries, to woo some of the Naxalites who were opposed to participation in the ministries, and to launch militant movements in opposition to a government in which the party was not a participant. Since a United Front government would almost certainly fail to meet the heightened expectations of the numerous groups supporting it, the United Front was necessarily considered a temporary alignment of forces to radicalize the state population and to strengthen the organization of the party.[62]

In the long run, CPM theoreticians conceive of their two strong state units (in Kerala and West Bengal) as "rallying points for the fighting masses all over India."[63] During periods when the party is in power at the state level, the Central Committee has argued that party leaders should

. . . undertake to expand the democratic rights of the people, undertake legislation for recognition of trade unions, settle outstanding wage disputes in

[60] Quoted from a CPM Politbureau statement, as reported in *The Statesman*, November 5, 1969.

[61] A near slogan quoted in a number of interviews conducted in November–December 1969.

[62] These were the conclusions reached by the Central Committee of the CPM after a special four-day session in Calcutta in late October 1969. See the report of the session in *The Statesman*, October 30, 1969, p. 1.

[63] These are the words used in a resolution of the Central Committee of the CPM, published shortly after its postelection meetings in Calcutta in April 1969. See *People's Democracy*, April 20, 1969, p. 11.

industries, take measures to provide employment or unemployment relief to the workers and educated youth; pass immediate radical agrarian legislation for land distribution and stopping of eviction, and grant homestead land, fair wages, and gratuitous relief during lean seasons to the agricultural labourers.[64]

When the party is out of power, state party leaders have been instructed to launch militant campaigns against state ministries that fail to undertake these measures and to work for "more viable United Fronts" committed to CPM programs.[65] The adoption of such measures at the state level at times when the CPM has held partial political power has reaffirmed the conviction of the leadership of the party that a mass political base can be built on the strength of this limited program. Moreover, it is considered especially significant by CPM leaders that such a program has engaged the cooperation of the electoral and the organizational factions within the party, thereby promoting the interests of both factions. The program has not only led to organizational gains for the cadre but has also resulted in greater electoral strength in Kerala and West Bengal.

At the national level, the CPM has proposed "a radical and immediate change in Centre-State relations," to be accomplished by a number of constitutional and policy changes. According to a resolution of the CPM Central Committee drafted in April 1969, the party has called for the following reforms:

1. All Concurrent List subjects should be transferred to the State List. All the Bills passed by the States in favour of the people in the present State and Concurrent Lists should be given assent by the President.

2. States should have more constitutional power to augment their resources pending which 75 per cent of Central revenues are to be transferred to the States.

3. All the Centrally-managed agricultural, industrial and educational, social and welfare departments and enterprises, with all the financial resources for them are to be handed over to the States to be managed.

4. Industrial Security Forces, the CRP [Central Reserve Police], and Border Security Forces are all to be handed over to the States, and it is for the States to keep law and order in the whole of the State and in all sectors and enterprises in the State.

5. The present IAS, ICS and other all-India services are to be handed over to the States and be under effective control of the States. Their recruitment, service conditions and disciplinary proceedings should all be under the State jurisdiction.[66]

[64] Ibid.
[65] *The Statesman*, November 1, 1969.
[66] *People's Democracy*, April 20, 1969, p. 11.

Advocacy by the CPM of radical changes in center-state relations is designed to articulate the interests of the party both at the central and at the state levels. As a number of observers have pointed out, most of the Indian states have been complaining since Independence of a lack of financial, rather than political, resources.[67] The first three reforms mentioned by the Central Committee in its April 1969 resolution are therefore extremely popular measures with state leaders in a number of political parties in many states. By advocating specific measures with regard to center-state issues, some CPM leaders hope to lay the basis for a future United Front coalition in New Delhi, which could perhaps be welded together most easily on the basis of a common program designed to increase state financial resources. At the same time, however, the CPM has linked decentralization of financial resources with a decentralization of bureaucratic and police power, in order to protect itself in West Bengal and Kerala in the event of a failure to gain participation in an all-India ministry. The five reforms advocated by the CPM Central Committee therefore lay the basis for a future confrontation between state ministries led by the CPM and Union governments led by the enemies of the CPM, at the same time that they hold out the promise of CPM cooperation with other state-based parties interested in greater financial allocations to the states.

While at first glance the advocacy of these five measures would indicate that the CPM is in favor of a decentralized Indian Union, this is not necessarily the goal of all of the members of the Central Committee. According to M. Basavapunniah, a leading CPM theoretician, the Central Committee, in advocating a new pattern of center-state relations, is merely "emphasizing . . . issues facing the democratic forces, which could pave the way for a united front on an all-India scale." In Basavapunniah's words, "The CPI(M) [favors] a strong Center, but not by a denial of democracy. . . ."[68] As a member of the CPM Central Committee stated even more clearly in a private interview,

The first three reforms [calling for greater financial resources for the states] are "carrots" that the CPM holds out to potential allies. The last two reforms [calling for control of the police and IAS by the states] are "sticks," or the price that our allies must pay if they want us to support them. In the final analysis we may want a centralized or a decentralized India—we may even go back to the nationality thesis—but in any case we must have control of the police and the administration in those states where we are [or have been] in power.[69]

[67] See, for example, Asok Chanda, "States' Discontent Increased by New Financial Awards," *The Statesman*, September 3, 1969.

[68] Quoted in the *Hindusthan Standard*, April 18, 1969.

[69] Quoted from a January 1970 interview with the author in New Delhi.

The ambiguous position that Central Committee leaders have taken on matters of center-state relations points up the dilemmas that have confronted the communist movement in India since Independence. If India were not a highly segmented and pluralist nation, one might argue that the CPM units in Kerala and West Bengal would have an interest in creating revolutionary situations in these two highly volatile areas. Feeding on radical movements in Kerala and West Bengal, the Communists could conceivably revolutionize more and more of the population in the two states—or at least convince significant numbers that electoral democracy is inadequate for India's needs—and this feeling might then spread to other parts of India. But as Myron Weiner has pointed out, India is more segmented socially and politically than any other major nation in the world:

> To a remarkable degree those political developments which occur in one segment do not affect developments in another . . .; one consequence of segmentation is that discontent is localized and instabilities are often quarantined. This feature of the Indian system may help us understand why it is that at any one time many of the Indian states are unstable, but the national government is unaffected and unperturbed. Were all the states unstable simultaneously, the national Congress organization and the national government could hardly remain stable. But typically only four or five states at any one time are seriously disturbed. . . .
>
> An analogy might be made to a large twelve-wheel truck with four tires on each of three axles. A flat on one tire does not create a flat on another, and it is possible for the vehicle to keep moving even if one or two tires are not functioning. In any event, the driver carries enough spares to keep the vehicle working so long as he does not have a large number of flats simultaneously.[70]

It is precisely the segmentation of Indian political and social life that has plagued the communist movement since Independence. For while the Communists have increased their strength in Kerala and West Bengal rather steadily, the movement has declined in two other states (Andhra and Punjab) and has remained relatively unimportant in the rest of India. The obvious danger for the two older Communist parties in the present context is that ineffective governments in Kerala and West Bengal may diminish their electoral support even in these two states, without affecting the rest of India.

The current tactical line of the CPM is designed to deal with the segmentation of Indian political and social life in a manner that has not previously been advocated by Indian Communists. Rather than pursue a strictly Left Communist strategy, which was attempted by the

[70] "Political Development in the Indian States," in *State Politics in India*, ed. Myron Weiner (Princeton: Princeton University Press, 1968), p. 53.

CPI in the period 1948–1951, the CPM has attempted to work within the ministries to bring about a "first-stage revolution." But unlike the united CPI after 1951, and unlike the present CPI, the CPM does not see the present Congress party as forming even a part of the government that will bring about a first-stage revolution, and some CPM leaders are not even certain that a national Indian government would be capable of carrying out such a revolution throughout the country. Some CPM leaders, particularly in the electoral organizations of the party, see a future national United Front composed of non-Congress and non-CPI parties, in which the CPM would gain partial control over national governmental institutions. But other CPM leaders, especially those who have strong support within the cadre, often speak of the future in words like those of Hare Krishna Konar (addressing a peasant conference in November 1969): ". . . the volunteer force of today will be the liberation army of tomorrow. Let us not be overwhelmed by conspirators, even if temporarily, as in Indonesia; let Vietnam be our guiding light."[71]

The value of the current tactical line of the CPM is that it has united both the electoral and organizational wings of the party, if only temporarily, behind militant mass movements that have been effective in strengthening state party organizations. By concentrating on limited programs designed to secure greater benefits for peasants and workers in two states, and by creating at least the preconditions for a confrontation with the Union government on center-state issues, the CPM hopes to be able to develop legislative and organizational experience in West Bengal and Kerala that can be applied in a variety of ways. On the basis of its experience so far, the central leadership of the party has found that it can afford to allow different factional interests within the party to move in different directions with minimal coordination. Electoralists within the CPM can attempt to solidify the hold of the party on the electorate of West Bengal, perhaps while seeking to bring about a United Front government in New Delhi. At the same time, the party cadre can attempt to gain new organizational bases in other Indian states as it seeks to radicalize the population in CPM strongholds. Building strong party organizations in other Indian states is a strategy that must necessarily be designed for the long run, but the experience of the CPM in two states has convinced most CPM leaders that the party has been able to identify the issues (primarily economic and center-state issues) that have made it possible for the

[71] Quoted in *The Statesman*, November 3, 1969. Konar's speech contrasts sharply with the speech of Jyoti Basu at the same conference, in which Basu spoke of capturing power in the whole country by electoral means. Ibid.

West Bengal and Kerala units to grow very rapidly over the course of a few decades.

The CPM and External Communist Parties

Whether or not the CPM is able to revolutionize the population in West Bengal, extend its organizational strength to other parts of India, or form a united front at the national level, it is clear that the party has gained a greater degree of organizational flexibility, independence, and effectiveness than is usually associated with Indian communism. This has largely been the result of the willingness of CPM leaders to concentrate on party organizational problems without constant reference to international Communist disputes. Following the split in the Indian communist movement in 1964, the CPM has sought selective support from external Communist parties but has refused to ally itself unequivocally with either the CPSU or the CCP. While the CPI has the unquestioned backing of the Soviets, and the CPML is now recognized by China as "the only Communist party in India," the CPM has attempted to establish itself as the *de facto* leader of the Indian communist movement on the basis of its independent party activities and the strengthening of its organizational base.

As I pointed out in Chapter 4, the leadership of the Left faction in the united CPI relied heavily on the Chinese position in the Communist ideological debate during the course of the events surrounding the split in the late 1950s and early 1960s, while centrist faction leaders sought the intervention of Moscow as a mediator in Indian Communist affairs. When significant sections of both the Left and centrist factions combined in the CPM after the 1964 split, party leaders could not immediately reconcile these diverse attachments to international ideological positions without risking further party disruption. The leadership of the party therefore took the position that "sharp differences in the world communist movement are not of recent origin"; that "our own inner-Party differences [are] explosive"; and that the "immediate need of the party" is "proper and thorough inner-Party discussions on all the ideological issues under dispute, so as to direct [the dispute] into some purposeful and constructive channels."[72] In order to bring about at least a temporary unity, the CPM

---

[72] *A Contribution to Ideological Debate*, by P. Sundarayya, M. Basavapunniah, N. Prasad Rao, A. K. Gopalan, Harkishan Singh Surjeet, Jagjit Sing Lyallpuri, P. Ramamurthi, M. R. Venkataraman, Jyoti Basu, Hare Krishna Konar, and Niranjan Sen (New Delhi: Des Raj Chadda, 1964), p. 1. This statement was authored by CPM leaders representing all factional viewpoints and who eventually made up the bulk of the Central Committee of the party.

leadership argued that factionalism within the Indian communist movement derived from the refusal of "the Dange group . . . to organize inner-party discussions," and the Calcutta conference of the CPM in October–November 1964 therefore directed the Central Committee of the party "to immediately organize inner-party discussions on the ideological questions . . . in a dispassionate manner."[73]

However, when many of the CPM leaders were arrested and detained by the government of India in late 1964 and early 1965 (before the Central Committee could meet), the proposed inner-party debate was necessarily postponed while the party concentrated on securing the release of its leadership and maintaining the efficiency of its organization. Even after the release of Central Committee members in mid-1966, the party leadership argued that it was "not desirable to open any discussion on the issues deferred," since the party was then "faced with serious and pressing problems of the people . . . and the fourth general elections." The Central Committee then directed the party press "to publish the authoritative pronouncements of [all] fraternal parties," in order that "comrades [could] familiarize themselves with all viewpoints." But in taking this action the committee made it clear that "our Party is not committed to any of them."[74]

Once the CPM made the decision to enter the state ministries after the 1967 elections, a defense of its position in terms of the international ideological debate could no longer be postponed, since the decision to enter the ministries had alienated China and given rise to speculation about a reunification of the CPM and the CPI. Less than six months later, the Central Committee of the party therefore explained in great detail the differences between the CPM and the Chinese positions in the ideological debate[75] and made arrangements to conduct the long-delayed inner-party discussion of ideological questions. In order to facilitate the discussion, the Central Committee drafted a fifty-four-page document describing a proposal by which disputed ideological questions could be resolved, which was circulated to all levels of the party.[76] Each party member was instructed "to express his or her views

[73] *Resolutions Adopted at the Seventh Congress, October 31 to November 7, 1964, Calcutta* (Calcutta: CPM, 1964), p. 19.

[74] *Resolutions of the Central Committee of the Communist Party of India* [Marxist], *Tenali, June 12–19, 1966* (Calcutta: CPM, 1966), pp. 26–27.

[75] *Divergent Views between Our Party and the CPC on Certain Fundamental Issues, Resolution Adopted by the Central Committee of the Communist Party of India (Marxist), Madurai, August 18–27, 1967* (Calcutta: CPM, 1967).

[76] *Central Committee's Draft for the Ideological Discussion, Adopted by the Central Committee of the Communist Party of India (Marxist), Madurai, August 18–27, 1967* (Calcutta: CPM, 1967). The procedure for conducting the inner-party discussion is detailed on pp. 1–2.

in his unit on the document frankly," and members of higher committees were forbidden to express their views in the lower committees. All units were instructed to send their opinions to the next higher unit in the party or to relay their criticisms directly to the Central Committee through their State Committees. This discussion, which was initially expected to last four months, was not completed until April 1968 (more than eight months later), and a central plenum of the CPM then passed a resolution embodying its results.[77]

Because of the revolt of the Left faction of the CPM in 1967, the party was unable to arrive at a resolution of the ideological debate that could be unanimously supported by all segments of the party. In the words of a CPM Politbureau statement:

> The inner-party discussions over the Central Committee's draft on ideological questions have clearly revealed that a section of our party members not only find themselves in fundamental disagreement with the ideological draft but also with the Party Programme and the Party's line on the current situation as enunciated in . . . resolutions of the Central Committee.
>
> . . . some comrades, contrary to the instructions of the Central Committee, thought it necessary to force the discussion on questions that were sought to be kept outside the discussion on the ideological draft.[78]

As has already been indicated, the response of the Politbureau and Central Committee of the CPM to the Left faction revolt in 1967 was to expunge the most extreme "Left deviationists" from the party and to seek to maintain the organizational backing of the bulk of the Left faction leaders. In ideological terms this meant that the party had to "fight against revisionism, while guarding against left-sectarian deviation," a stance that subjected the CPML and CPI to all of the strategic and tactical machinations that have been described earlier. In terms of the international ideological debate, the CPM found it necessary to depict "modern revisionism" as "*the main danger* in the international Communist movement at the present juncture," while merely warning party members "against slipping into left opportunism and sectarian errors."[79]

The decision of the CPM leaders to label Soviet revisionism as the "main danger" was partly a response to the severe factional quarrel between the CPM and the CPI and to the necessity for some CPM leaders to soften party criticism of the Left faction. At the same time, however, it stemmed from the widespread feeling among CPM members that

---

[77] *Ideological Resolution, Adopted by the Central Plenum, Burdwan, April 5-12, 1968* (Calcutta: CPM, 1968).

[78] *Ideological Debate Summed Up by Politbureau* (Calcutta: CPM, 1968), pp. 1-2.

[79] *Ideological Resolution*, p. 54. (Italics in original.)

communism in India had for too long been dominated by foreign Communist parties, with a consequent loss of dynamism in the Indian movement. The April 1968 resolution of the central plenum, for example, emphasized the need for "independence and equality among fraternal Communist Parties":

> A working class party can play the role of a revolutionary party only if it is firmly based on Marxism-Leninism and proletarian internationalism; only if it can, as correctly put by the CPC, "use its brains to think for itself" . . . [rather than] parrot the words of others, copy foreign experience without analysis, [and] run hither and thither in response to the baton of certain persons abroad. . . .[80]

In the eyes of CPM leaders, "this sound proletarian internationalist principle" was frequently "violated by big Parties," the "glaring example" of such violations being the actions of "the CPSU after its 20th Congress," although "the CPC . . . [was] also sometimes found to disregard this principle."[81] In order to stake out a more independent role for itself within India, the CPM found it necessary to criticize both the CPSU and the CCP for such violations.

Since April 1968 the CPM has maintained its independent position in the ideological debate, identifying most closely with Castro's Cuba, North Vietnam, North Korea, student protest groups in the United States, and the liberation movements in Africa, while calling on both the CPSU and the CCP to correct their "revisionist" and "sectarian" errors.[82] Party leaders and documents still praise the Chinese revolution of 1949 as "one of the biggest triumphs of the world working class and the imperishable doctrine of Marxism-Leninism" and emphasize Chinese achievements in industry, agriculture, science, technology, and education. According to CPM literature, China has far outstripped India in economic and technological development, has more ably prepared itself for defense against American "imperialism" by developing nuclear weapons, and has performed a great service to socialism in this century by "initiating the fight against modern revisionism." At the same time, the CCP is criticized for "its erroneous outlook," which "liquidates the existence of the socialist camp" and "rejects the necessity for united action of the socialist camp."[83] In a similar manner, the Soviet Union is praised for carrying out the first significant

[80] Ibid., pp. 50–52.

[81] Ibid., p. 53.

[82] Based on a content analysis of articles appearing in *People's Democracy* and *Desh Hitaishi* (CPM daily) in 1968–1970, and on interviews conducted in 1969–1970.

[83] *People's Democracy*, September 28, 1969, p. 1. For other CPM statements on China and the CCP, see ibid., August 4, 1968, pp. 1, 12; December 22, 1968, pp. 1, 12; December 29, 1968, p. 1; and February 23, 1969, pp. 4, 10.

socialist revolution and for supporting world revolution during the first four decades of Soviet rule. However, the CPSU is criticized for its present "lop-sided emphasis on the peace struggle," for "underplaying the importance of all-sided direct struggle against imperialism," and for "minimising in particular the significant role of the worldwide national liberation struggles at the present stage."[84] The CPM's affinity with Cuba, North Korea, North Vietnam, Indonesia, and the African liberation movements is in fact based on a common sentiment that the Soviet Union has failed to give adequate support to liberation movements in these areas.[85]

For many party members this ideological stance provides enough satisfaction to maintain a high level of party involvement. As one observer has pointed out,

> To the revolutionaries outside the socialist countries . . ., and even to many communists of Asia, Africa and Latin America, the obsessive desire of the Soviet Union to establish a working relationship with the U.S.A. and the frenzied efforts by China to instigate armed struggle in every nook and corner of the world [seem] equally futile. The impression [among many Asian Communists is] that both the socialist giants—rival claimants to the leadership of world revolution—[are] acting more and more as national states, as cynically opportunist Big Powers, and not as the trusted vanguard of a worldwide revolutionary process.
>
> Communism, of both the Soviet and Chinese varieties, [appears] to be turning into an Establishment, with hardly any message for . . . the socialist revolutionaries of the Third World.[86]

Among party *leaders* in the CPM, however, the ideological stance of the party is more closely tied to their own factional interests and their own contacts in the international communist movement. The centrists in the CPM, led by Jyoti Basu and E. M. S. Namboodiripad, are still critical of the party's unwillingness to seek the mediation of Moscow in Indian Communist disputes, but they have so far been reluctant to impose their views on the party. Basu and Namboodiripad did express a desire to be present at the meetings of world Communist parties in 1967 (on the occasion of the fiftieth anniversary of the Russian Revolution), but the Central Committee of the CPM refused their request to travel to Moscow for fear that "the dazzling atmosphere

[84] *CPI(M) Central Committee Statement on Moscow Conference* (Calcutta: CPM, 1969), p. 5.

[85] Ibid., pp. 2, 10.

[86] O. P. Sangal, "Moscow Meet Saw a Fractured Globe," *Citizen and Weekend Review*, June 28, 1969, p. 23.

of Moscow [might] lure them back to the pro-Soviet CPI."[87] Therefore, none of the meetings called by Moscow in 1967, 1968, and 1969 has been attended by CPM delegates,[88] and the CPM has kept itself informed of the meetings only by means of visits by Left and centrist faction leaders to Rumania and Great Britain,[89] both countries whose parties have cooled toward, but not broken with, Moscow.

While the centrists in the CPM have not been willing to press for closer relations with Moscow, they have insisted that pictures of Mao Tse-tung not be displayed at party conferences, that both China and the Soviet Union be equally blamed for Sino-Soviet border clashes, and that China be "corrected" for its open condemnation of the Soviet invasion of Czechoslovakia.[90] Moreover, centrist faction leaders have been able to include themselves in delegations selected by the CPM to travel to Europe and Vietnam and have been responsible for strong party statements criticizing Chinese support of Indian Naxalites.[91] Factional struggles over control of the domestic stance of the CPM therefore find parallels in the approach of various party leaders to international ideological disputes, leaving open the possibility that either international or domestic events might at some point in the future disrupt the balance that has been achieved in recent years.

Thus the new independence and flexibility of the CPM in matters of state and national politics must be viewed as the consequence of a precarious balance of competing forces within the party rather than as a consensus based on the firm commitment of major factional interests. Each of the resolutions adopted by the CPM since February 1967, whether on ideological or tactical issues, has created great strains and tensions among factions, and each has been passed only after inner-party accommodation on a host of amendments and alterations. Both Left and centrist faction leaders have differed publicly with the party on a number of occasions, both have been disciplined by the Central Committee, and both factions have resorted

[87] Ibid., November 4, 1967, p. 14.

[88] For greater detail on Indian participation in the Moscow meetings, see the *Times of India*, March 27, 1968, and *Thought* (New Delhi weekly), June 28, 1969, pp. 4–5.

[89] The links between Rumania and the CPM are analyzed in *People's Democracy*, August 17, 1969, pp. 2, 6–8, and October 12, 1969, pp. 3, 9–11. CPM members in Great Britain have formed their own "Association of Indian Communists of Great Britain" within the CPGB, composed of British and Indian CP members loyal to the CPM. See ibid., February 25, 1968, pp. 5, 8.

[90] See the *Hindusthan Standard*, December 24, 1968; *Amrita Bazaar Patrika*, March 17, 1969; and *People's Democracy*, August 25, 1968, pp. 1, 2, 7.

[91] *Amrita Bazaar Patrika*, December 8, 1968.

to threats and cajolery.[92] The success of CPM leaders in reconciling diverse factional interests both on political and on ideological matters since 1967 suggests that continued unity depends on organizational and electoral success, while the persistence of long-standing factional interests points to the fragile nature of party unity, which might shatter in the event of reverses.

[92] As, for example, when M. Basavapunniah warned the Left faction that "a single mistake will cost us a generation." Quoted in *The Statesman*, December 27, 1968.

8

THE CPI AND NATIONAL COALITION BUILDING

Although the CPML and the CPM maintain some ties to foreign Communist parties, both of them are primarily concerned with the regional political environment in West Bengal. The CPML, for example, aspires to a nationwide revolution, but its immediate goal is to create a revolutionary situation in Bengal in the hope that later it will spread to neighboring areas. Similarly, the CPM is attempting to consolidate its position in the two states (Kerala and West Bengal) where it can conceivably dominate state ministries in the near future. In contrast to these regional strategies, the CPI has focused its attention on New Delhi and allied itself unequivocally with the CPSU and the foreign policy of the Soviet Union. By the late 1960s the CPML had been recognized by China and its socialist allies as "the only Communist Party in India," while CPM leaders were attempting to establish closer fraternal relations with Rumania, the CPGB, and a few other Communist parties that remained nominally tied to the Soviet Union. But the CPI was still unquestionably the largest recipient of aid from Moscow. Since the split in 1964, the chairman of the national CPI has been known in Moscow as "the loyal Dange," the CPI has been favored with all of the visits and invitations to and from Moscow, and negotiations between Moscow and the CPM have been carried out through the via media of the CPI. For these reasons, one of the most useful ways of understanding the relationship between the Bengali communist movement and India's national and international political position is to focus on the strategy and goals of the CPI.

For at least a decade, the Soviet Union has been pursuing a number of interests in South Asia. On the one hand, Moscow is attempting to increase its influence in India while maintaining friendly relations with Pakistan; on the other hand, it is seeking to prevent either China or the United States from gaining leverage in South Asia by manipulating the Indo-Pakistani conflict "so that together [India and Pakistan] might devote their energies to containing China rather than to fighting each other."[1] To further these objectives, the Soviet Union and the

[1] William E. Griffith, *Sino-Soviet Relations, 1964–1965* (Cambridge: M.I.T. Press, 1967), p. 118.

CPSU have placed a great deal of emphasis on maintaining "politically correct and cooperative relations with India," yet they have sought to use the Indian communist movement as an instrument of "pressure and manipulation."[2] In what has now become a fairly common pattern in many countries, the Soviet Union has given considerable diplomatic support to New Delhi while seeking to bring about communist unity and influence through the auspices of the pro-Moscow CPI.

Regional Factionalism Since the Split

The short-term goal of the CPI and the CPSU is to gain influence in national coalition building. Indeed, at its first party congress after the April 1964 split, the CPI adopted a program that spoke of the need for a National Democratic Front (NDF) as the party's "central slogan of the period."[3] This reflected the desire of the leadership of the CPI and the CPSU to pursue "united front from above" tactics, "bringing together all the patriotic forces of the country, including the working class, the entire peasantry, the rich peasants and agricultural labourers, the intelligentsia and the non-monopolist bourgeoisie."[4] In the words of the party program, the National Democratic Front was conceived as "a transitional stage, in which power will be jointly exercised by all those classes which are interested in eradicating imperialist interests, routing the semi-feudal elements and breaking the power of the monopolies. . . . [While] the exclusive leadership of the working class would not yet be established [under] a National Democratic Front, the exclusive leadership of the bourgeoisie would no longer exist."[5]

The CPI's "united front from above" tactics differ significantly from the "united front from below" tactics of the CPM. Rather than concentrate on building a mass base in particular regions where the party is strong, the CPI has chosen to increase its strength by making "top alliances" with other leadership groups in India, in this way hoping to gain more influence in the present national government and eventually to absorb many of the supporters of its allies. This was essentially the strategy of the united CPI in the late 1930s, when the party witnessed its greatest period of growth through the absorption of much of the leadership of the Congress Socialists and the nationalist terrorist groups, a leadership that in turn brought many of its followers into

[2] Russell Brines, *The Indo-Pakistani Conflict* (London: Pall Mall Press, 1968), pp. 157–158.

[3] *The Programme of the Communist Party of India, As Adopted by the Seventh Congress of the Communist Party of India, Bombay, 13–23 December, 1964* (New Delhi: CPI, 1965), p. 43.

[4] Ibid., p. 39.

[5] Ibid., p. 41.

the party fold. While the present strategy of the CPM does not exclude such alliances with other parties, it insists on an independent and superior political base for itself in any of the alliances it enters into. Constant prodding of the noncommunist interests with which the CPM has allied itself is felt to be necessary among the leadership, mainly because of the threat that CPM members inclined toward the Naxalites might abandon the party in the event of a more moderate stand. Since the CPI has a much smaller Naxalite faction within its ranks, its leadership has been able to exercise a greater degree of flexibility in making alliances.

Moreover, united front from above tactics on the part of the CPI have been useful to the foreign policy interests of the Soviet Union, since they call for some degree of collaboration and cooperation between the CPI and the present Indian government. In the words of the party program,

The formation of the National Democratic Front does not [necessarily] mean progressive parties merging with the Congress or entering into a formal alliance with the Congress. Nevertheless, no National Democratic Front would be real unless the vast mass following of the Congress and the progressive sections of the Congress at various levels take their place in it. It is the task of the Communist Party to make ceaseless efforts to forge unity with the progressive forces within the Congress, directly and through common mass movements, to bring about a leftward shift in the policies of the government, to fight for the realisation of the demands of the National Democratic Front.[6]

If the CPI were to adopt a political strategy that brought it into open conflict with all sections of the Congress, as is the case with the CPM's united front from below, it would be difficult for the CPSU to continue to support the CPI and yet maintain cordial diplomatic relations with a Congress government in New Delhi. In addition, of course, united front from above tactics open up a number of possibilities for a continuing Communist influence on Indian policy makers which might not otherwise exist.

This is not to argue, however, that the CPI has been entirely united in its pursuit of a National Democratic Front or that relationships between Moscow and the CPI have not created tensions within the party. When the CPI inherited the intellectual leadership of the united Communists, it also inherited factional and ideological conflicts that date back to the origins of the party in the 1920s and 1930s, conflicts that have divided Indian intellectuals during the intervening years and continue to divide them in the 1970s. Definitions of India's class structure, interpretations of directives from Moscow and London, conceptions of party membership, party organi-

[6] Ibid., p. 44.

zation, and leadership promotion, as well as relations between regional, national, and international organs of the communist movement, all of these have become issues that have divided the CPI on a number of occasions since the split. While it would be impossible to trace the background and development of all of these issues in the present context, it is necessary to outline the ones that have influenced the operation of the CPI in West Bengal since 1964. In general, such issues have been related to three important factors: party strategy, party organization, and relations with the international movement.

On questions of party strategy, a significant section of the West Bengal unit of the CPI has argued since 1964 for greater party militancy in West Bengal as a means to counter the appeal of the CPM to the most volatile segments of the state population. In an effort to convince the leadership that the party should pursue a more militant stance, a number of younger leaders from West Bengal proposed an amendment to the party's resolution on ideological questions at the 1964 party congress questioning the unqualified acceptance of a stance of "peaceful transition to socialism," and CPI leader Amiya Das Gupta of West Bengal even argued that the party should give greater prominence to "nonpeaceful possibilities of transition."[7] After prolonged discussion, however, the party congress chose to reject Das Gupta's amendment for essentially two reasons, according to the CPI's Commission on Ideological Controversies:

> We reject [the Das Gupta amendment] . . . because equating the two possibilities [peaceful and nonpeaceful transition] in practice paralyses mass initiatives for a peaceful transition and leads to passivity. Besides, we all know from experience that equating the two possibilities is one of the sly methods by which left-sectarians attempt to smuggle in their adventurist tactics in the mass movement.[8]

For similar reasons the CPI Commission on the Political Resolution of 1964 rejected amendments that would have labeled the Indian government as having "shifted to the right" in its handling of food policy and the jailing of the CPM. Such a resolution, the national CPI leadership argued, would have made it more difficult to pursue alliances with "progressive Congressmen and others" while at the same time leaving the CPI itself open to adventurist tactics.[9]

[7] *Proceedings of the Seventh Congress of the Communist Party of India, Bombay, December 13–23, 1964,* vol. 3, *Discussions* (New Delhi: CPI, 1965), p. 20.

[8] Ibid., p. 16.

[9] Based on interviews and ibid., p. 23. The persistence of this issue as the basis for factional differences in West Bengal is traced out in Shivadas Banerjee, "Discontent among CPI Members," *The Statesman* (Calcutta daily), May 1, 1965. See also ibid., January 6, 1966, and Shib Shankar Mitra, "How to Begin under Present Circumstances," *Kalantar* (Bengal weekly of the CPI), May 17, 1969, p. 8.

The existence of ideological differences within the CPI has had a number of consequences for the party since the split in 1964. Perhaps the most obvious of these has been the continuing need for compromises of the same sort that characterized the united CPI. While the central leadership of the party has spelled out in general terms the line that local and regional party units are to follow, it has frequently found it necessary to state party doctrine so ambiguously that no clear formula for political action emerges. This manner of proceeding was in fact outlined explicitly by the Commission on the Draft Programme of the 1964 party congress:

> Our programme can only indicate in general terms how the NDF is initiated, how it develops and leads to mass national upsurge of struggle against reactionary and rightwing forces. It cannot make a cut-and-dry scheme for this. The main strategic and class principles of this are indicated and in doing this, we must keep both class and the national aspect of the NDF in the concrete conditions of India firmly in view.[10]

Confronted with the ideologically compromised directives being issued by the CPI leadership from New Delhi, local and state units have often floundered in interpreting party strategy, and the agonizing self-criticisms that characterized united CPI documents have continued to be a feature of party organizational reports since 1964. At the 1964 party congress, for example, the CPI organizational report included admissions of failure with regard to the functioning of mass organizations, the role of the leadership in party education, "the serious evil of leakage," and "the incorrect methods of gossip, loose talk, [and] back biting which have developed in the wake of individual functioning."[11]

As was the case with the united CPI, internal party factionalism and compromise have resulted in a great deal of autonomy for local and regional units on some issues, but the national leadership of the party

[10] *Discussions*, p. 38.

[11] Ibid., p. 56. For later statements of self-criticism on the part of party leaders, see *The Statesman*, January 13, 1966, and the Organisational Report adopted at the Eighth Congress of the CPI at Patna in February 1968, which was summarized as follows: ". . . the main organisational tasks of the Organisational Report remain where they were. The party continues to suffer from all those defects and weaknesses which were analysed and nailed down at the last Party Congress. Tendencies of indiscipline, bourgeois habits and methods persist. Mass organisations continue to remain weak. The gap between mass influence and organisation of the party still continues. The all-India party centre remains weak and ineffective. No improvement in the style of work has come about. The financial position of the party continues to be deplorable. The circulation of party journals remains poor." See *Documents Adopted by Eighth Congress of the Communist Party of India, Karyanandnagar, Patna, February 7–15, 1968* (New Delhi: CPI, 1968), p. 148.

has been hesitant to formalize a decentralized party structure. At the 1964 party congress a number of amendments to the constitutional and organizational reports of the party were intended to bring about decentralization, but none of these was accepted by the national leadership, which led to their defeat. One such amendment would have prevented CEC members from holding office in state or district units, another suggested giving greater powers to state and local units, and several others sought to restrict the powers of the chairman, the general secretary, and other national office bearers.[12] Similarly, proposals to "reserve a certain number of party positions for members of the working class and peasantry" were rejected at the 1964 congress, along with suggestions for "changing a certain percentage of leadership at every Congress."[13] Ironically enough, each of these proposals came from the desire on the part of some party members to develop new leadership, while the Party Commission on Organization rejected the proposals precisely because of the "considerable paucity of cadre in our party at present."[14]

While dissatisfaction with national leadership, party strategy, and organizational control have created a great deal of tension within the CPI, none of the factional conflicts within the party has as yet threatened the same degree of disruption that has plagued the CPM. In West Bengal the most vociferous party opponents of the CPI's national leadership chose to join together in 1968–1969 in a party reform group that came to be known as the "Soviet Critics" and that was based on opposition to Dange's defense of the Soviet action against Czechoslovakia in the summer of 1968.[15] The Soviet Critics sought to cluster together many of the Bengali party members who had differed with national chairman Dange for one reason or another, but in the final analysis Dange took strong action against two non-Bengali CPI members

[12] *Discussions*, pp. 58–59.
[13] Ibid., pp. 57, 62.
[14] Ibid., p. 57.
[15] The Soviet intervention in Czechoslovakia prompted considerable discussion within the CPI, some of which was eventually published without the backing of the party leadership. The most detailed discussions are provided in *Reactions on the Events in Czechoslovakia*, ed. Anand Gupta (Delhi: New Literature, 1968) and *Whither Czechoslovakia: Essays and Documents on the Czechoslovak Crisis*, ed. P. K. Sundaram (New Delhi: Dawn Publishers, 1969). An official party collection of documents and eyewitness accounts favorable to the Soviets is contained in *Behind the Crisis in Czechoslovakia*, ed. M. B. Rao (Delhi: People's Publishing House, 1968). While most of the all-India leaders of the CPI supported the Soviets from the beginning, the first supportive party resolution was passed only after the February 1969 elections, at meetings of the CPI National Council in April. For a summary of the crisis in the CPI by a veteran PSP leader, see Pradip Bose, *East European Turmoil and CPI* (Calcutta: Samajwadi Prakashani, 1968).

who had publicly criticized Soviet intervention in Czechoslovakia, and Bengal's Soviet Critics subsequently either were silenced or left the party.[16] During the course of this dispute the party lost some of its leading young intellectuals, but the threat to the party was not nearly so severe as the loss of cadre leaders produced by the factionalism within the CPM.

CPI Strategy in West Bengal

If the CPI has managed to escape the intense factional disruption that has pervaded the CPM, it has failed to use this advantage to gain superior organizational effectiveness in any single state. This is particularly relevant to an analysis of CPI strategy in West Bengal, since it is the superior organizational apparatus of the CPM there that has determined the approach of state CPI leaders to regional, national, and international issues. As has already been pointed out, both the CPI and the CPM secured essentially the same percentage of the national vote in the 1967 elections, but the distribution of the vote between states varied enormously, with corresponding differences in the subsequent orientations of the two parties. In the 1967 elections the CPI secured more than 5 percent of the vote in seven states (Kerala, West Bengal, Andhra Pradesh, Orissa, Punjab, Bihar, and Assam), but the largest percentage of the vote that it gained in any one state was 8.57 percent in Kerala (compared to 23.51 percent for the CPM). After the elections, the CPI agreed to support five state ministerial coalitions (in Kerala, West Bengal, Punjab, Bihar, and Uttar Pradesh), but it has since maintained its position in only two of these states (Kerala and West Bengal), and in both cases it has been confronted with the superior organization and the "anti-revisionist" hostility of the CPM. In West Bengal, where the CPI fared better than in any other state in the 1969 midterm elections, the CPI gained only 6.78 percent of the vote and 30 seats, compared to 19.55 percent of the vote and 80 seats for the CPM.

[16] The Soviet Critics have now banded together around a Bengali language journal with an English name (*Compass*), edited by an old revolutionary leader of Bengal, Pannalal Das Gupta. The Bengalis most frequently associated with *Compass* and the Soviet Critics are Subhas Mukherjee, Kalyan Dutta, Gautam Chatterjee, Boudhayan Chatterjee, Sushovan Sarkar, and Miss Sipra Sarkar. Their failure to lead a successful party reform group within the CPI in 1969 resulted largely from their inability to secure the backing of some of the older CPI leaders (such as Indrajit Gupta and Somnath Lahiri) who were opposed to the Soviet action in Czechoslovakia but unwilling to join with the young Soviet Critics in using this issue as the basis for a party reform movement. For an analysis of their failure, see *Amrita Bazaar Patrika* (Calcutta daily), May 15, 1969.

Even at the national level, the CPI advantage over the CPM is not substantial. In elections to the Lok Sabha in 1967, for example, the CPI outpolled the CPM by a little less than 1½ million votes (7.56 million to 6.14 million) and gained only 23 seats (compared to 19 for the CPM). While most of the CPI seats came from four states (5 each from Bihar, Uttar Pradesh, and West Bengal, and 3 from Kerala), the CPM Lok Sabha seats came almost exclusively from Kerala (9), West Bengal (5), and Madras (4). In both the assembly and Lok Sabha elections the two Communist parties were outvoted (on a national level) by a number of other parties: Congress, Jana Sangh, Swatantra, and SSP (see Table 9). Both the CPI and the CPM individually secured

TABLE 9

ELECTORAL POSITIONS OF MAJOR INDIAN PARTIES (1967)

Party	Legislative Assemblies		Lok Sabha	
	No. Votes	% Votes	No. Votes	% Votes
Congress	57,252,357	39.96	59,402,754	40.73
Jan Sangh	12,567,918	8.78	13,715,931	9.41
Swatantra	9,519,231	6.65	12,659,540	8.68
SSP	7,424,633	5.19	7,171,627	4.92
CPI	5,906,109	4.13	7,564,180	5.19
CPM	6,599,692	4.60	6,140,738	4.21

Source: Report on the Fourth General Elections in India, 1967 (New Delhi: Election Commission, 1967), pp. 21–22, 121–122.

approximately the same percentage of the national vote as the SSP, and together the two Communist parties would have challenged both Swatantra and Jana Sangh for the position of second largest party in India. But because of the split, each of the parties individually could rank no better than fifth among the national parties, with the CPI having a somewhat more legitimate claim to the title of a national party on the basis of its more even distribution of votes throughout India and its greater success in the Lok Sabha. In this connection it might also be mentioned that the CPI was more successful than the CPM in the prestige contests.

The 1967 and 1969 elections created a number of difficulties for the CPI, both at the national level and in West Bengal. In West Bengal the CPI has had to confront the aggressive political tactics of the CPM, if only to prevent the CPI cadre from being won over by the more militant CPM tactics. At the same time, however, most state CPI leaders have been convinced that it is the tactical line of the CPM that has prevented the leftist parties in West Bengal from making more dramatic electoral gains. Shortly after the 1967 elections, for example, the West Bengal State Council of the CPI met in Calcutta to analyze the election results and concluded that the failure of the CPM to cooperate in an electoral alliance was the principal factor preventing "a decisive shift in the balance of political forces to the left."[17] As an inner-party document pointed out,

Had a single united front, including both the Communist parties, been formed in West Bengal, instead of two rival fronts, the results might have been comparable to what was achieved in Kerala, the only state where both the parties were together in a common united front. The electorate saved the situation by inflicting a defeat on the Congress, but this does not obscure the negative effect of the quarrel between the Communist parties.[18]

CPI attempts to counter the aggressive organizational tactics initiated by the CPM have thus far been centered in areas of the state where the party has developed an electoral base of its own and in strongholds of the smaller Marxist Left parties where the CPI is either trying to gain an electoral base or trying to prevent the CPM from gaining one. While engaging in these activities, however, the bulk of the state leadership of the party has maintained its conviction that the CPI line of "top alliances" would be much more beneficial to the growth of leftism in the state, with the result that the state CPI has continued to issue appeals for leftist unity while attempting to cement relations with all the major state parties.

The position of the CPI in West Bengal is further complicated by the nature of the appeal that party leaders have committed themselves to. Because of the "united front from above" tactical line, the party is publicly seeking the support of all groups and classes in the state other than the "monopolist bourgeoisie." But owing to the history of the communist movement in the state and the highly politicized nature of most groups and classes, the CPI has found it difficult to make inroads into the established bases of other parties. Large landholders and middle peasants who have traditionally supported the Congress in West Bengal are reluctant to shift their support to a Communist party that has always evoked their distrust and disdain, while small landholders, landless laborers, and the disenchanted urban middle class have traditionally been attracted to parties that have pursued more militant

[17] *Link* (New Delhi weekly), March 5, 1967, p. 11.
[18] *Resolution on the Fourth General Elections, Draft for Discussion of the State Council* (Calcutta: CPI, 1967), p. 6.

protest strategies. Moreover, in many areas of the state the smaller Marxist Left parties have used their positions in the state ministries to provide patronage to local supporters in their electoral strongholds, thus fortifying their own party positions against the appeals both of the CPI and of the CPM. While the CPI has been able to retain its position in areas of previous electoral strength (in portions of Midnapore, 24-Parganas, and in small pockets elsewhere), it has thus far failed to make noticeable gains in other areas of the state.

In this atmosphere, the state leadership of the CPI has been forced to engage in a series of subtle maneuvers in its attempts to make the "united front from above" tactical line work, the most difficult aspect of which has been the ambiguous series of relationships it has had to accept in order to confront the challenge of the CPM. According to the CPI program, the CPM is one of the parties that must be courted for a future National Democratic Front, at the same time that a clear distinction must be established (in the eyes of all state party members and followers) between the party programs of the two Communist parties. For this reason, state CPI leaders were initially careful to moderate their criticisms of the CPM and to search for as many areas of agreement as possible. Throughout the period of the first United Front government in 1967, the CPI argued that the front was "truly united" and sought to minimize conflicts between its supporters and those of the CPM.[19] Once the front was ousted, the CPI immediately began to work for an electoral alliance of all of the parties in the front, and a number of concessions made by the CPI to the CPM were instrumental in bringing about the high degree of unity that characterized the electoral campaign of the front parties in late 1968 and early 1969. Shortly after the 1969 elections, CPI leaders even took the initiative in bringing about "unity talks" between prominent leaders of the two major Indian Communist parties.

The results of the talks indicate the great gulf that yawns between the present CPI and CPM strategies and the constraints that have inhibited close relations between the two parties since 1964.[20] The movement for the talks was initiated by the CPI National Council in April 1969, when the party leadership decided that "unity of the Communist forces" was "of decisive importance" and that the CPI would

[19] The attitude of the CPI toward the 1967 United Front in West Bengal is contained in the lengthy "Resolution on West Bengal" that appears in *Resolutions Adopted by Eighth Congress of the Communist Party of India, Karyanandnagar, Patna, 7–15 February, 1968* (New Delhi: CPI, 1968), pp. 9–13.

[20] Two excellent summaries of the Communist unity talks in June 1969 appear in *Link*, June 8, 1969, p. 11, and the *Citizen and Weekend Review*, June 14, 1969, p. 19. See also Diptendu Dey, "Why Namboodiripad Is So Afraid of Communist Unity," *Kalantar*, June 14, 1969, p. 6.

work for "joint blocs" of the two Communist parties (both in Parliament and in the state Legislative Assemblies) as well as for joint coordination committees at all party levels. When unity talks were proposed to the CPM, however, its leadership predictably divided between the centrist and Left Communist factions, with Jyoti Basu and E. M. S. Namboodiripad favoring the talks and Pramode Das Gupta opposing them. In this atmosphere the talks, which were held in early June 1969, produced little more than a statement that the leadership of the two parties would "meet again by mutual consent," and Pramode Das Gupta even refused to associate himself with this seemingly harmless statement. From Das Gupta's point of view, any agreement on the part of the CPM leadership to work in unity with the CPI could only constitute a victory for the CPI "revisionist" tactical line, forcing the CPM to make concessions on crucial issues despite its position of dominance in the Kerala and West Bengal electoral situations. Moreover, fearing there would be some Naxalite defections from the CPM even for engaging in the "unity talks," Das Gupta was all the more inclined to adopt a hostile stance.

Since the unity talks in mid-1969, relations between the two Communist parties have steadily deteriorated. As the CPM has become more aggressive on the peasant and trade union fronts, local units of the CPI in West Bengal have been increasingly forced to engage in confrontation (often violent) with CPM members. Moreover, once the Bangla Congress demonstrated its willingness to condemn the CPM publicly by engaging in a mass *satyagraha* against the violence associated with CPM activities, the state CPI was placed in a position of having to choose between its two major front partners. These conflicting pressures have further divided the state CPI leadership between those who would like to move toward a closer alliance with the CPM and those who would like to ally unequivocally with the Bangla Congress and the smaller Marxist Left parties, and this has in turn made additional compromises necessary. Moreover, relations between the two Communist parties in West Bengal have worsened enormously as a result of the events surrounding the October 1969 United Front split in Kerala.

The split in the Kerala United Front in October 1969 was brought about when the state CPI unit in Kerala twice joined the Congress in voting against the CPM in the state Legislative Assembly, the second vote being interpreted by CPM Chief Minister Namboodiripad as a vote of no confidence in his ministry.[21] When Namboodiripad resigned,

[21] The resignation of the Namboodiripad government in Kerala in October 1969 is analyzed in Ranajit Roy, "Kerala: The Morning After," *Hindusthan Standard* (Calcutta daily), October 29, 1969.

the CPI (on the initiative of its state unit in Kerala) hesitantly put together a tenuous "mini-front" of four parties (CPI, Muslim League, Kerala Congress, and the Indian Socialist party) to form a new ministry, with promises of support from a number of independents and the RSP.[22] From the point of view of the Kerala CPI, it was important that the new state government, headed by C. Achuta Menon, did not depend on the support of the Congress party, but the CPM in Kerala nevertheless accused the CPI of collaborating with the Congress to bring down the Namboodiripad government. In the words of a Kerala CPM resolution, "The CPI struck a clandestine deal with the Congress . . . to unseat the CP(M) from power and bring in a Congress-backed non-Marxist set-up."[23]

Immediately following these events, rumors spread throughout India that either the CPM or the CPI would move for a dissolution of the United Front in West Bengal. In order to deal with these rumors the CPI State Council held a special session in Calcutta in early November, after which CPI state secretary Ranen Sen issued a statement that the party had "no desire, plan, contemplation or design to topple the existing United Front Government in West Bengal," since "the situation in West Bengal is radically different from that in Kerala."[24] At the same time, however, the State Council passed a resolution at this two-day session which embodied the strongest condemnation of the CPM that had ever been made by the state CPI. Arguing that the CPM had become "sectarian," the state CPI resolution expressed its disapproval of the CPM's "super-bossism, misuse of administrative machinery in narrow partisan interest, and political gangsterism." Moreover, the state CPI for the first time passed a resolution publicly arguing that "the CPM is adopting the weapon of physical annihilation of the cadres of other parties of the UF," and State Secretary Sen issued both a plea for cooperation and a warning:

In spite of all this, the CPI draws the attention of the people to the supreme need for unity of all Leftist and democratic forces, including the CPI(M), because such unity is the surest guarantee of replacing Congress rule at the Centre. . . . But if we are attacked or chosen as prey of CPM killers we will have to take action for self-defense.[25]

---

[22] For an analysis of the CPI leadership of the "mini-front" government formed in Kerala in November 1969, see *Link*, November 9, 1969, pp. 14–17. See also *Amrita Bazaar Patrika*, November 2, 1969, and the *Hindusthan Standard*, October 28, 1969.

[23] *Link*, November 9, 1969, p. 14.

[24] *The Statesman*, November 5, 1969.

[25] Ibid. See also Bhowani Sen, *CPM's Fight against the United Front in West Bengal* (Calcutta: CPI, 1969).

The November 1969 resolution of the State Council of the CPI had immediate repercussions both on the peasant and on the trade union fronts in West Bengal. At a meeting of the state CPI's peasant front organization (the Paschimbanga Pradeshik Krishak Sabha), held shortly after the State Council meetings, CPI peasant leaders warned their followers against "Left adventurist and disruptive forces" and accused the Marxists of "creating disruption to further their own partisan aims at the cost of the peasant movement in the country."[26] Ananta Majhi, secretary of the CPI Krishak Sabha, even urged his organization to "recruit large armies of volunteers [in order to] wage war on two fronts—against jotedars, monopolists and vested interests and against disruptionist and adventurist forces." At the same time, the Krishak Sabha passed a series of resolutions affirming the party's conviction that the United Front had "strengthened the peasant movement in the state and intensified class struggle," emphasizing the CPI conviction that "the success of the United Front in the rural areas would have been much greater had the CPM agreed to work in unity with its partners."

In contrast to the CPM, the CPI tactical line envisages a much broader alliance of interests in the countryside, with an emphasis on rural harmony that is inimical to the CPM. Summarizing the November 1969 conference of the CPI Krishak Sabha, for example, Secretary Majhi called for "an alliance of agricultural labourers, sharecroppers and landless peasants with rich peasants to generate further momentum to the peasant movement in the state."[27] In Majhi's words, "agricultural labour and landless sharecroppers, being in a majority, are destined to become the vanguard of the movement . . . but, for their own interest they should rope in middle and rich peasants." In order to "rope in" rich and middle peasants, and to unify the efforts of front partners, the CPI Krishak Sabha emphasized the need for unity among all peasant cultivators, to be accomplished by a series of measures recommended at the November conference. To reassure rich and middle peasants, the Krishak Sabha sought to clarify the goals of the United Front in the countryside by advocating an agreed means of determining right of ownership, a rational formula for distribution of *benami* lands seized by members of UF parties, and by providing for machinery to arbitrate and mediate disputes between local party leaders and peasant

[26] A summary of the three-day Krishak Sabha meetings is contained in the *Hindusthan Standard*, November 9, 1969.

[27] Ibid. For other reports on the November 1969 conference, see *The Statesman*, October 29, 1969; the *Hindusthan Standard*, November 7, 1969, and November 10, 1969; and *Amrita Bazaar Patrika*, November 11, 1969.

followers. The Krishak Sabha then sought to consolidate these proposals by recommending that coordination committees (to be called "village councils") be established at the village level consisting of members of all of the UF parties active in a given village and that a UF committee be established at the Cabinet level to mediate disputes and conflicts originating in the "village councils."

Like similar recommendations made previously by UF partners, the November 1969 recommendations of the CPI Krishak Sabha were unacceptable to the CPM both on ideological and on political grounds. For ideological reasons, the CPM was determined to maintain its organizational independence and superiority within the front, a tactical goal that could be fulfilled much more readily by the organization of red-scarfed, red-helmeted CPM "volunteers" than by the establishment of UF "coordination committees." Moreover, the tactical line of the CPM, while it did not exclude cooperation with wealthy and middle peasants, emphasized confrontation between various rural interests and placed a higher priority on the recruitment of the poorer sections of the population. Even if ideological considerations could be disregarded, however, the CPM had little to gain by agreeing to the establishment of coordination committees in the countryside, since none of the UF parties could conceivably match the organizational strength of the CPM in the rural areas in the absence of such committees. In this atmosphere it is little wonder that the CPI suggestions for unity, harmony, and coordination were quickly rejected by the CPM Krishak Sabha meetings, which were held at approximately the same time.[28]

Similar conflicts between the CPI and CPM were evident on the trade union front in late 1969 and early 1970, despite the different ways in which Communist organization of the trade unions and the peasantry was conducted. Unlike the peasant front, where the united All-India Kisan Sabha divided into two factions shortly after the split in the CPI in 1964, the Communist-dominated All-India Trade Union Congress (AITUC) continued to act as a united-front organization for all Communists in India throughout the 1960s. In late 1969, however, a dispute broke out between the two Communist parties over the question of the location of the AITUC session for 1970. The CPM proposed that the session be held in its stronghold of Calcutta, since "the most significant gains of workers have been made over the past few months in West Bengal." In reply to this proposal, however, S. A. Dange condemned

---

[28] An analysis of the CPM meetings in November 1969 is contained in "Politicising Peasants?" *Frontier* (Calcutta weekly), November 8, 1969, p. 3.

"the way in which the CPI(M) is attacking CPI unions and their leaders and workers" and argued that a Calcutta session would not promote unity. In a written reply to CPM Politbureau leader P. Ramamurti, Dange bluntly stated that "your people will simply break up the session [if it is held in Calcutta] by sheer gangsterism."[29]

The dispute within the AITUC in late 1969 and early 1970 was complicated by variations in the regional strength of the two Communist parties within the organization and by the struggle to add new unions under the control of the two parties. At the all-India level of the AITUC, the CPM in late 1969 controlled only 44 of the 200 members of the AITUC General Council, a number representing the relative strength of the CPM in the organization. In West Bengal, Kerala, and Madras, however, the CPM was stronger among trade unions than the CPI, and in West Bengal it controlled the Bengal Provincial Trade Union Congress (BPTUC, the state congress of trade unions affiliated with the AITUC) in much the same manner as Dange and the CPI controlled the AITUC at the national level. During the course of the rapid unionization of workers that had taken place in West Bengal after the 1967 elections, most of the new trade unions that had been brought into being by the Communist parties in the state had been recognized by the BPTUC, but a number of the CPM unions had failed to gain such recognition from the AITUC. AITUC leaders argued that a number of new CPM unions could not be recognized by the AITUC because the new unions were established as rivals to already existing AITUC trade unions in the industries concerned, an obvious reference to the CPM policy of opposing the CPI by forming rival unions. According to the AITUC Secretariat in New Delhi in early 1970, the AITUC had received a total of 952 applications for membership in 1969, approximately 250 from CPM trade unions, 200 from unions controlled jointly by the CPI and the CPM, and more than 500 from unions dominated by the CPI. Of these 952 applications, 50 were rejected because they were found to be "rival unions," and 42 of the rejected unions were admittedly controlled by the CPM.[30]

Lacking a position of strength within the national AITUC from which to challenge CPI dominance, the CPM was not only concerned about the attitude of the AITUC toward its new unions; it was also very agitated by a proposed amendment to the AITUC constitution that would have made it possible for the CPI to oust CPM office bearers. This amendment,

---

[29] *The Statesman*, November 20, 1969.

[30] Figures for the AITUC and the BPTUC are based on interviews with trade union leaders in New Delhi and Calcutta in 1969–1970. For an analysis of the factionalism within the AITUC during these years, see *The Statesman*, January 9, 1970.

which provided for disciplinary action against all AITUC officers associated with the activities of "rival unions," was approved by the AITUC Secretariat in early November 1969, pending approval by a three-fourths vote of the delegates scheduled to attend the AITUC congress in Guntur (in Andhra Pradesh) in late January 1970.[31] Since the CPI controlled more than three-fourths of the voting delegates, it was clear that the amendment would be passed easily, despite objections and threatened demonstrations by the CPM. In the final analysis, however, the CPM refused to accept its position as junior partner within the AITUC, deciding instead to form a rival organization. At a late December meeting of the AITUC Working Committee, the CPM members of the committee walked out in protest, and in early January 1970 the CPM Politbureau issued a directive to its members to abstain from attendance at the Guntur session.[32] By the time the session was held, in late January 1970, a new CPM trade union front was already in the process of formation.

The growing polarization of the two Communist parties in West Bengal has had a number of consequences for all of the parties associated with the United Front and could conceivably affect state Congress politics as well. Almost all of the parties within the United Front have witnessed internal party factionalism, between segments of the party favoring a CPM strategy of continual confrontation and other segments inclined toward a CPI strategy of cooperation and harmony among front partners.[33] While both the SSP and the PSP have split publicly on this issue, all of the other parties in the front have found it necessary to debate the issue at great length, and the Bangla Congress has even expelled its vice-president for "conspiring with the CPM."[34] On most occasions the CPI has been supported by its allies in the 1967 PULF electoral alliance (the Bangla Congress, the Forward Bloc, and the Bolshevik party) and has picked up support from a section of the

[31] *Hindusthan Standard*, November 7, 1969.

[32] Ibid., January 6, 1970. See also *The Statesman*, January 9, 1970.

[33] The background of the ideological divisions within the smaller Marxist Left parties in West Bengal is told in Jiten Sen, "The Importance of Being a Small Left Party," *Hindusthan Standard*, November 23, 1968. For a more recent analysis of differences within Marxist Left parties, see "UF in Twilight in West Bengal," *Citizen and Weekend Review*, January 10, 1970, pp. 19–20. See also "Ideological Rift in Forward Bloc." *Amrita Bazaar Patrika*, January 1, 1970, and Sachchidanand Sinha, "SSP: Critical Decisions Ahead," ibid., January 3, 1970.

[34] Bangla Congress Vice-President Sukumar Roy was expelled by the party in December 1969, when a tape-recorded conversation between Roy and CPM leaders indicated that Roy had planned to split the Bangla Congress, taking a portion of the party into a new coalition with the CPM. See *Amrita Bazaar Patrika*, December 30, 1969, and January 1, 1970.

ssp, suc, and Gurkha League, as well as from a psp dissident faction. While the other uf parties have tried to avoid taking sides publicly in the dispute in order to preserve internal unity, party leaders from all of the uf partners have singled out the cpm on occasion for its aggressive and violent style of politics. Even party leaders who tend toward a politics of confrontation have resented the manner in which the cpm has attempted to move into constituencies previously dominated by the Marxist Left parties.

The smaller Marxist Left parties in West Bengal are in a much different position than either the Bangla Congress or the two Communist parties. Under no circumstances can the Marxist leftists expect to dominate a future United Front government, and none of the Marxist Left parties is unequivocally aligned with any of the three major front partners. For all of the United Front parties, the United Front experience has been rewarding, not only because of the patronage and psychological benefits that party leaders and members have derived from ousting the Congress, but also because of the opportunity they have had to strengthen their positions in their subregional strongholds. None of these parties has yet taken the Bangla Congress's position that the present United Front should be broken, although several have threatened to break with it if the cpm persists in its aggressive organizational tactics. If one of the smaller Marxist Left parties were to call for a breakup of the United Front, it would run the risk of alienating itself from a popular government, losing its position within the front (and thus its patronage) and, most likely, creating a split within its ranks. Without running these risks, each of the smaller Marxist Left parties has condemned the "hegemonism" of the cpm while preserving party options for future alliances if the present United Front should cease to exist.

At the same time, a number of the leaders of the smaller Marxist Left parties have sought to bring about the kind of United Front government they want by acting as mediators between the cpi, cpm, and Bangla Congress. Two of the most prominent people involved in such mediation efforts have been Makhan Paul of the rsp and Bibhuti Dasgupta of the Lok Sevak Sangh.[35] However, since their efforts have been directed at a number of institutional devices designed to produce greater unity within the front—a code of conduct for ministers and party leaders, consultative committees at various levels, and agreements to cancel polemics among uf partners—the mediators have demonstrated a bias toward the tactics of the cpi. For this reason

[35] Uf mediation efforts are analyzed in ibid., January 7, 1970.

the CPM has been the most difficult of the UF partners for the mediators to deal with, since it has often refused even to attend mediation sessions without preconditions or else has accepted mediation agreements only to break them in subsequent party activities.

The CPI and the Congress Split

Perhaps the most intractable problem for UF mediators has been the different attitudes of the two Communist parties toward the Congress split. As has already been pointed out, the attitudes of CPM and CPI leaders toward the Congress was one of the principal factors involved in the split in 1964, and the different Communist attitudes toward the Congress has been one of the distinguishing features of the two major Communist tactical lines throughout the 1960s. When tensions developed within the Congress party, leading to the split in late 1969, both of the Communist parties were forced at least to consider altering their stance toward the Congress, and CPI leaders were especially hopeful that the Congress split would bring about a reorientation of the CPM.

For at least some members of the Congress party, the split in 1969 was intimately related to the question of alliance with the Communists, and much of the public debate about the split revolved around the possibility that Indira Gandhi and her supporters might choose to ally informally with the CPI, if not formally. Indeed, for a group of "Young Turks" within the Congress, the question of a Congress alliance with the Communists was unquestionably the most significant aspect of the events surrounding the division within the party. In a major speech in May 1969, for example, Congress Young Turk leader Chandra Sekhar advocated "a [Congress] dialogue with all progressive forces, whatever their political affiliations, to bring them together in the struggle against concentration of economic power."[36] Elaborating on this speech in subsequent press conferences, Chandra Sekhar spoke of the possibility of forming a "united front [of] Congressmen, the PSP, the SSP and the CPI" in order to bring about "a confrontation with the defenders of monopolies" and urged the CPM to "join the struggle if it can work within the bounds of the Constitution." Similar proposals for unity between Congress and Communist forces have also been issued by Vasantrao Patil, president

[36] Chandra Sekhar's speech and subsequent press conferences are quoted extensively in *Link*, May 4, 1969, pp. 11–13, from which all quotations in this paragraph are taken. See also Jyoti Das Gupta, "A Political Review of the Inner-Party Conflict in the Congress," *Kalantar*, July 19, 1969, pp. 1, 11.

of the Maharashtra Congress, and by a number of other young Congress leaders.[37]

Before 1969 the Congress party had never seriously considered the possibility of coalescing with the Communists, despite occasional attempts by some members to move the party closer to the Communist position on a number of issues. Indeed, only after the 1967 elections did a number of prominent Congressmen begin to advocate selective alliances with either the CPI or the CPM, but most of these suggestions were devised to maintain the short-term political advantage of the Congress in various states. As has already been pointed out, Atulya Ghosh broached the possibility of a Congress-CPM alliance in West Bengal when the Congress failed to win a majority in the state Legislative Assembly in 1967, and similar proposals by prominent Congressmen have been made in other states as well. Just before the 1967 elections, Kamaraj Nadar proposed a limited electoral alliance with the CPI in Madras in an effort to confront more effectively a DMK united front that included the CPM, and Uttar Pradesh Congress president Kamlapati Tripathi suggested in a speech on the floor of the Uttar Pradesh state Legislative Assembly in 1968 that the CPI leave the non-Congress state coalition government—the Samyukta Vidhayak Dal (United Legislators' party), or SVD—to join a government with the Congress.[38] Chandra Sekhar's proposal in May 1969, however, called for much more than a short-term tactical alliance between the Congress and the CPI, since it contained a plea for "united action" with the Communists on the basis of a concrete ideological program.

Because of their concern for the ideological aspects of the split, the factional conflicts that took place within the Congress in 1969 acquired special significance for the Congress and CPI members who had sought a mutual alliance. Ideologically minded Congressmen, like their counterparts in the Communist parties, now trace the immediate origins of the split to a speech by Congress President S. Nijalingappa at the April 1969 Faridabad session of the Congress, in which he attacked the bad management and loss of profits that have characterized India's undertakings in the public sector and condemned Chandra Sekhar and the Young Turks for "crying hoarse against monopolistic tendencies."[39] In the eyes of many ideologues, it was the reaction of Mrs. Gandhi to this speech that led the Prime Minister to request the resignation of Finance Minister Morarji Desai and sub-

---

[37] *Kalantar*, July 19, 1969, pp. 1, 11. See also *Link*, July 6, 1969, p. 21.
[38] *Link*, May 4, 1969, p. 11 See also Kashyap, *The Politics of Defection*, p. 161.
[39] *Link*, May 4, 1969, p. 15.

sequently to nationalize India's fourteen largest banks, measures that had long been advocated both by the CPI and by Chandra Sekhar's followers in the Congress. The ideological aspects of the Congress split were also emphasized by many Congress Socialists and CPI leaders when Indira Gandhi supported the Communist-backed candidate for India's president in August 1969 against the nominee who had been selected by her own party, and when she maneuvered herself into a position where her government became dependent for its survival on Communist votes in the Lok Sabha. Moreover, a popular image of Indira Gandhi as a likely ally of the CPI was encouraged during the course of the split by the constant charges on the part of her Congress opponents that her government was becoming "subservient to Russia";[40] that she herself was a Communist;[41] that she had favored the CPI in conflicts between the United Front and the West Bengal Congress in 1967;[42] and that her government was passing through a phase of Communist collaboration like that attempted by Sukarno of Indonesia in the mid-1960s.[43]

Adding even greater weight to the possibility of a CPI-Congress coalition in India, at least in the eyes of many Indians, is the welter of evidence that CPI leaders have maintained their friendships (and even kinship relations) with Congress leaders since Independence to an extent that has not been true for the leadership of the CPM and other Marxist Left parties. Prominent Congress leaders like V. K. Krishna Menon, K. D. Malaviya, and K. D.'s nephew H. D. Malaviya, for example, have acted as high-level advisors both to the Congress and to the CPI, as a result of friendships that date back to the pre-Independence period, while other people associated with the Congress (such as Mrs. Kamala Ratnam and Mrs. Aruna Asaf Ali, both wives of Indian diplomats) have frequently appeared as speakers at Communist party rallies. Leaders of the CPI in West Bengal who are close relatives of prominent Congressmen include Mrs. Renu Chakravorty, a niece of Congress Chief Minister B. C. Roy; Biswanath Mukherjee, brother of Ajoy Mukherjee, the Bangla Congress leader who defected from the Congress in 1966; and Kalyan Roy, the son of Kiron Shankar Roy, West Bengal's first Congress Home Minister. An analysis of friend-

---

[40] This was the charge of Morarji Desai at the Organization Congress session in December 1969. See the *Hindusthan Standard*, December 22, 1969.

[41] Former Chief Minister P. C. Sen of West Bengal, reported in *Amrita Bazaar Patrika*, December 7, 1969.

[42] West Bengal PCC President Pratap Chunder in the *Hindusthan Standard*, January 5, 1970.

[43] Organization Congress President S. Nijalingappa at the annual session in December. See ibid., December 22, 1969.

ship and intermarriage patterns among political leaders in West Bengal would indicate that social intercourse between many intellectuals in the Congress and communist movements has been especially close since Independence, despite political party rivalry.[44]

In this atmosphere it was not difficult for CPI leaders to interpret the Congress split in 1969 as an indication of the wisdom of the party program and tactical line that they had been pursuing since 1964, and this has since become a position of almost unreserved support for Indira Gandhi's ruling Congress. In the words of West Bengal CPI leader Bhowani Sen,

The result of the Presidential Election [of August 1969] marks the beginning of a new period and a new correlation of forces in the country's political set-up. It was not an accident that the election of the President became linked up with the exit of Sri Morarji Desai from the Ministry and nationalisation of 14 big banks as an anti-monopoly measure.

This combination symbolised the confrontation between the combined forces of Right Reaction on the one side and the forces of the Centre and the Left on the other. Nationalisation of the banks followed by the victory of Sri V. V. Giri in the Presidential election signified a defeat of the ultra-reactionaries within the Congress, collectively known as the Syndicate, allied with the Jana Sangh and the Swatantra Party. It also signified the advance of national democratic forces composed of Communists and some other left groups outside the Congress as well as those within the Congress who are against Right Reaction. It is a big blow to the monopolies and their allies.[45]

Echoing his party's stance toward the Congress split, Bhowani Sen argued that "the CPI had detected the contradiction between the monopolies and the rest of the bourgeoisie" in its 1964 program and had then "predicted that the crisis of the capitalist path was bound to develop and produce a split in the ranks of the national bourgeoisie": "Such a split [was] bound to have its repercussions inside the Congress, so that a section of Congressmen would be forced to fight the Right, and thereby come close to the Communist and other Left forces outside the Congress."[46] Continuing to elaborate the party line, Sen argued that developments resulting from the Congress split would "ultimately give birth to a National Democratic Front against imperialism, remnants of feudalism and the Indian monopolies. Based on the contradiction between these forces and the whole people, the National

[44] For an analysis of friendship and kinship patterns between Congressmen and Communists in West Bengal, see my essay, *Marxism and the Bengali Elite* (Cambridge: M.I.T. Center for International Studies, forthcoming).

[45] Bhowani Sen, "Trend of National Political Development," *Mainstream* (New Delhi weekly), Annual Number, September 1969, p. 50.

[46] Ibid.

Democratic Revolution [is] visualised as an intermediate stage for the country's transition towards socialism, or as the precursor to the socialist revolution."[47]

On the basis of its identification of the Congress split as a phenomenon resulting from factors discussed in its party program, the CPI was quick to initiate a series of demonstrations in support of the Indira Gandhi faction of the Congress party. Before President Giri's election in August 1969, the CPI held a series of "mass gatherings" to explain the significance of the presidential election, in an effort to convince the presidential electors that the sentiment of India's masses was overwhelmingly with the Prime Minister's candidate. After the elections the CPI held a series of "victory celebrations" throughout India at which party leaders encouraged further division within the Congress, called on Indira Gandhi to institute more radical socialist programs, and proposed greater unity between progressive Congressmen, Communists, and Left forces. When the split within the Congress organization finally culminated in a division between the Ruling and Organization Congress parties in the Lok Sabha in November 1969, the CPI immediately pledged its support to the Ruling Congress.

But the CPI interpretation of the Congress split has by no means been shared by all leftist political parties and observers. The RSP in West Bengal, for example, argued that the split was merely "the outward expression of a deep schism inside the ruling party" and that there was little to gain by celebrating President Giri's victory. Similarly, the SUC has argued that "strengthening of the Indira Gandhi group represented a danger because it would spread illusions about social democracy," a position that has also been adopted by some factional leaders in the Forward Bloc and the RCPI.[48] As CPI leader Mohit Sen himself has pointed out, the CPM party assessment of the split was in fact much closer to the position taken by many Indian leftists than the CPI analysis, and perhaps closer to the usual interpretation of the factors behind the split:

It is interesting that the approach to the split in the Congress adopted by some quite radical and revolutionary commentators corresponds almost exactly to that taken by the editorial writers and correspondents of the monopoly press. Both sets of commentators are anxious to demonstrate that the split amounts to very little and that it is all the result of personal pique or at the very best of intense factional squabbling. It would not be unfair to point out that this is also the viewpoint of most of the leaders of the Syndicate Congress.[49]

[47] Ibid.

[48] The attitudes of West Bengal's Marxist Left parties toward the Congress split are detailed in *Link*, August 31, 1969, p. 15, and September 7, 1969, p. 21.

[49] Mohit Sen, "Congress Split and the Left," *Economic and Political Weekly* (Bombay), December 13, 1969, p. 1925.

Confronted with divergent interpretations among the leftist forces about the significance of the Congress split, the CPI has since launched a renewed campaign to mitigate some of the conflicts between India's leftists, in an effort to move them closer to a position of support for "left unity." At its first meeting after the Congress split, the National Council of the CPI could agree that "the unfolding national situation [was] something that the CPI had envisaged for some years"; that it represented "a successful political breakthrough"; and that it presented the party with "a new political situation" that was "full of promise and exhilarating challenge."[50] The National Council could also agree with the CPM that all sections of the Indira Gandhi Congress did not represent "the same ideological and political trends," since there were many "vacillating and even reactionary sections in her camp [who would] seek to obstruct radicalisation of the organization as well as progressive measures." Nevertheless, the National Council argued that "political initiative among the supporters of Indira Gandhi today rest with those who are for a fight against the extreme Right and who broadly stand for progressive policies and measures." In a resolution adopted by the National Council at its November 1969 meetings, the CPI leadership therefore argued that it was "in the national interest" to strengthen the "progressive forces . . . in their struggle for bringing about urgently-needed radical changes in Governmental policies."

Moreover, because a greater degree of party unity became evident as a result of the Congress split, at its November 1969 meetings the CPI National Council was able to formalize the two-pronged strategy that it had evolved in West Bengal and Kerala since its entry into the state ministries in 1967. On the one hand, the party decided to launch "united mass struggles" against "the Syndicate–Jana Sangh–Swatantra axis" as a means for mobilizing campaigns in common with "all progressive forces, including Congressmen," and for bringing about "further differentiation" within the Ruling Congress. But at the same time, the National Council decided to launch a series of new "mass movements" by agricultural workers and poor peasants in order to combat the aggressive organizational tactics of the CPM in the countryside. Explicit recognition of this two-pronged strategy on the part of the national leadership has had the advantage for the party of satisfying a number of different factional interests on the basis of concrete party policies. By providing for "united mass struggles" with all Left forces against "right reaction," the National Council resolution has affirmed central leadership support for political activities by

[50] The November 1969 meetings are extensively covered in *Link*, November 30, 1969, pp. 14–15. All quotations extracted from the resolutions passed at this meeting are taken from this published account.

party members who seek to pursue "top alliances" with other parties, while the call for "mass struggles" in the countryside enables members of the CPI cadre to confront the CPM and the Naxalites with greater assurance of national party backing. As a number of observers have pointed out, the CPI's two-pronged strategy is perhaps as close as the party could come to pursuing the tactics of the CPM, at least within the context of "united front from above."

Problems of Left Unity

Despite the greater degree of unity within the CPI during the last few years, the dilemmas that the party has encountered in applying its tactical line are in many respects more vexing than the ones that have confronted the CPM and the CPML. While the CPI has been successful in welding successful electoral fronts together in 1967 and 1969, it has failed to make noticeable gains in acquiring new sources of support, and the state coalitions that it has joined have been ineffective and unstable. In the process of applying its tactical line the CPI has constantly striven for unity among all Left forces, but its programs have repeatedly been rejected by competing Communist and Marxist Left parties. Moreover, although CPI theoreticians argue that they foresaw the split in the Congress in 1969, party leaders have thus far been unsuccessful in courting a Congress leadership reluctant to ally with Communists of any stripe. To an even greater extent than is true for the CPM, the CPI is facing threats from both the Naxalites on the left and the Congress on the right.

According to CPI theoreticians, the organizational activities of the Naxalites have posed two "dangers" for the Indian communist movement: first, the possibility that the "formation [of the CPML] will carry splittism and disruption a step further," and second, the danger that the activities of the Naxalites will "mean the dissipation of some revolutionary energy into wholly wrong and self-defeating channels."[51] Rather than launch insurrectionist movements in India's rural areas, the CPI has attempted to convince the Naxalites that they should work for "an electoral alliance of all left and democratic forces to defeat the Congress at the Center in 1972,"[52] a policy that stems in turn from the CPI assessment of the contemporary revolutionary situation in India. In the eyes of the CPI leadership,

There is not a ghost of a chance for that type of a long drawnout armed guerrilla warfare which went on in China for 22 years to succeed in India. Here

[51] *New Age* (CPI weekly), May 11, 1969, p. 2.
[52] *Review of Fourth General Elections, Adopted by the National Council of the CPI, Calcutta, 23–30 April, 1967* (New Delhi: CPI, 1967), p. 48.

and there some type of armed resistance might go on for some time. But it cannot take you to final victory as in China. In India any revolution can succeed only under the direct leadership of the proletariat, with cities as the leading center of revolution.[53]

Of particular concern to the CPI is the possibility that future suppression of the Naxalites might result in suppression of the entire communist movement in India, which could conceivably inflict more damage on the CPI than on either the CPM or the CPML. Sections of these two parties have in fact *sought* repression of the Indian communist movement on occasion, in an effort to build more militant cadres and ferret out the softer party elements that have joined the communist movement since 1967. If the CPI is to continue with a tactical line of Left unity, it can ill afford to be identified with guerrilla Communists who seek to exterminate the segments of the population that the CPI is courting. The general secretary of the CPI claims that the activities of the CPML and the Naxalites can only "help the reactionary forces, landlords and other blood-suckers of the people to confuse and divert the people's attention for fighting the communist movement and other progressive forces."[54] By splitting the communist movement further, CPI Chairman Dange has argued, the CPML will not only diminish the impact of the Communist and progressive forces but will also enable "the Home Minister and the Congress to suppress the left forces with greater violence."[55]

Like the CPM, the CPI has also been concerned with the way in which the CPML and the Naxalite groups have penetrated into student unions and youth groups in India at the expense of the two older Communist parties. In the words of one CPI theoretician,

It is but an open secret that large sections among the rank and file of the two Communist Parties . . . are silently in support of the extremist [Naxalite] terrorist activities. In private talk they hail the terrorists, though they are not sure whether the time is ripe for such activities. . . . Left-oriented students . . . are full of praise for the "heroic young leaders" of the Naxalite attacks.[56]

In order to deal with the disenchantment of the younger generation of Indian leftists, the CPI has attempted to lecture the Naxalites and to establish study circles in which the party program is explained in great

[53] C. Rajeswara Rao, "Naxalite Movement: Origin and Harmful Consequences," *New Age*, June 29, 1969, p. 9.
[54] Ibid.
[55] S. A. Dange, *Law and Order: Whose and for Whom?* (New Delhi: People's Publishing House, 1967), p. 14.
[56] C. Surendran, "Extremism and Left Movement," *Mainstream*, April 5, 1969, p. 28.

detail, and it has also expressed support for many of the movements launched by the CPML. The thrust of the teaching that CPI theoreticians have been engaged in has been summarized by CPI leader Mohit Sen as follows: "[The Naxalites] have cultivated a remarkable ability to simply expunge from their minds the summing up of four decades of revolutionary activity; they seem to be unaware of the basic tenet of successful Communists in this century, that the ideology does not commit . . . the revolutionaries in any country to only one form of revolution, any one type of struggle."[57] In addition to their attempts at party education, which have been focused on college and university students as well, the CPI has also acknowledged its past failures to organize the tribals and landless cultivators by intensifying party activities in these spheres. This stratagem serves the dual function of combating similar CPM organizational efforts while at the same time it creates a new party appeal to rural workers, who might otherwise be tempted to join the CPML. In the final analysis, however, the two older Communist parties can satisfy the Naxalites only by withdrawing from the state ministries and by adopting more extreme policies. This the older parties have been unwilling to do.

In a sense one might argue that the CPI's courting of the Ruling Congress has been much more successful than its attempts to bring about unity among Communists and Marxist Left politicans. The CPI has been successful in maneuvering itself into a position where the Ruling Congress in New Delhi is occasionally dependent on Communist votes in the Lok Sabha, and party channels to the upper echelons of the Ruling Congress are smoother than they have been in many years.[58] However, the dependence of the Congress on the CPI is still limited to a select number of issues, and it is conceivable that the Ruling Congress (both in New Delhi and in West Bengal) could simply use the CPI to strengthen its electoral base in the next elections, only to turn against it when the time came to form a government.[59] Because of the association of the CPI with Moscow and the CPSU, most political parties in India have an interest in isolating themselves from the Communists as much as possible, and for this reason a CPI alliance with the Ruling Congress would be secure only under circumstances where the support of the CPI was essential for the maintenance of a

---

[57] Mohit Sen, "What Is a Revolutionary?" ibid., April 19, 1969, p. 31.

[58] Amitava Das Gupta, "Leftists May Use Mr. Menon as a Lever to Curb Rightists," *Hindusthan Standard*, May 20, 1969.

[59] This possibility is explored in Ashis Barman, "The Congress Split and CPM Dilemma," *Amrita Bazaar Patrika*, December 5, 1969. See also C. Subramaniam, "The Task before the Congress," ibid., December 21, 1969.

governmental coalition. Barring either a significant shift in the orientation of the Ruling Congress toward Moscow or a considerable increase in the strength of the CPI, a Congress-CPI coalition is not likely to play a significant role in national coalition building.

9

COMMUNISM IN A BENGALI ENVIRONMENT

The communist movement in India has frequently been described as foreign in origin and overly servile toward the leaders of foreign Communist parties. The most recent authoritative analysis of Indian communism, for example, argues that "the communist movement in pre-Independence India was a colonial adjunct of the Communist Party of Great Britain, which in turn was suborned to Moscow,"[1] a statement frequently echoed by Indian Communist leaders when condemning their colleagues for what they see as post-Independence subservience to the Soviet Union, to China, or to a variety of other fraternal movements. Questions concerning the relations that should exist between fraternal parties in the international movement have plagued Indian communism since the time when M. N. Roy first established working agreements between India and Moscow, and foreign developments have always played a major role in determining the tactics and strategies of Indian Communist parties. Indeed, the dependence of the Indian movement on foreign Communists has been the major theme of almost every article and book that has been written about the CPI and its offshoots.

This emphasis on relations between Indian and foreign Communists is understandable, since most of the major decisions that have been made by India's Communist leaders have been the result of directives issued from abroad. But there is a circularity involved in the attempt to understand Indian communism solely in terms of its foreign relations. Most analysts who argue that Indian communism has slavishly followed the dictates of Moscow and Peking conclude that it has *for this reason* been plagued by constant failure and intense factionalism and that the Indian Communists' continual attempt to look to foreigners for leadership and direction can only perpetuate the malaise of the Indian movement. The circularity that is involved here results from the welter of evidence that Indian Communists have

[1] Mohan Ram, *Indian Communism: Split within a Split* (Delhi: Vikas Publications, 1969), p. 1.

sought the intervention of foreigners only because they felt they needed assistance in revolutionizing the domestic environment. This raises the possibility that the dependence of Indian Communists on foreigners is not the *cause* of the failures of the movement but rather an inevitable effect of the failure to devise an indigenous means for revolutionizing India. If the attachment of Indian communism to foreign sources is merely a *symptom* of the inability of party leaders to deal with the Indian environment, then the dynamics of the movement must be explained with reference to the indigenous environment.

In the preceding pages an attempt has been made to look at the indigenous sources of the communist movement in one of its Indian strongholds by focusing on the regional, national, and international factors that have determined party tactics and goals. In the process, it has become clear that the international movement has played a decisive role in determining the overall strategies and tactics of Bengali Communists, but it is at least equally clear that the national and international leaders of the communist movement have not found their Bengali comrades as subservient or as slavish as one is often led to believe. National and international communism have been used by Bengali Communists to mediate factional conflicts, to settle internal party disputes, and to provide leadership and direction when the resources of Bengal's own leadership were found wanting. But Bengalis have also at times attempted to give the lead to the national and international movement, although only when political activities in Bengal have been at issue. One can argue that the Bengali movement has not been creative enough, that it has not succeeded in revolutionizing Bengal and other parts of India, but admission of these facts (and they are admitted by most Communists in Bengal) does not necessarily imply that Bengalis have not tried to act on their own.

Indeed, on the basis of an isolated analysis of the Bengali movement, one would have to argue that the Communist failure in Bengal has not been a result of an overdependence on Moscow or Peking but has instead stemmed from the failure of all Communist leadership— regional, national, and international—yet to devise a means for bringing about a revolution in Bengal and in India. This failure is not a singular one, since no one else has been able to revolutionize Bengal or India either, but it becomes more significant for the Communists because of their constant attempts to bring about fundamental political change. It is the perseverence of Bengali Communists and the experience they have gained by constant failure that make them more important than the many other groups and leaders advocating change.

The communist movement in Bengal has not succeeded, but it always looks as if it may be on the verge of doing so. The Communists have constantly been disappointed, factionalism has become more and more intense, and party members have been forced more and more to compromise their understanding of Marxism-Leninism, but the movement continues to thrive and to attract new supporters.

In this sense the communist movement differs from other political movements in Bengal. The Communists have built a more effective and dedicated cadre than any of the other political parties and have also devised more regularized procedures for securing financial backing, imposing party discipline, and communicating between party units. These achievements unquestionably stem from the attachment of Bengali Communists to their national and international comrades, indicating the influence of foreign political ideas on the regional movement. It is precisely because they use foreign sources to secure financial backing and to inform their organizational life that Bengali Communists are frequently accused of being disloyal, or antinational, or foreign to Bengal. And yet the Bengali communist movement also shares many traits that are distinctively Indian and Bengali, and it cannot be understood without an appreciation of its regional and national environment.

The Regional Moorings of Bengali Communism

The most distinctive regional aspect of the Bengali movement is its continued recruitment of leadership from a regional elite, the *bhadralok* of Bengal. This is not to argue that all *bhadralok* are Communists, or that the *bhadralok* who are Communists conceive of themselves as a traditional elite group. The elitist aspects of the Bengali movement are simply a result of the recruitment of *bhadralok* to Marxist ideas and forms of political organization in this century, a recruitment made possible by the remarkable similarity of *bhadralok* and Marxist conceptions and goals. The universal conviction among Bengali Communists that India's other major political movements are responsible for a terrible decline in the quality of Indian life is a conviction that is widely shared by a *bhadralok* elite that has itself witnessed a more rapid decline in this century than any comparable group in India. Communist attacks on imperialists, reactionaries, feudal elements, and neocolonialists arouse familiar images among almost all Bengali *bhadralok* families: images of the hated British and the anglicized ruling and commercial groups that have controlled Calcutta and partitioned Bengal; images of traditional Hindu revivalists who seek to reclaim for the Brahmanic heartland of India a hegemony that Bengali elites have resisted for centuries; images of Indian democracy since 1947, which has worked to the advantage of a new class of *banyas* and merchants who have threatened *bhadralok* dominance; and, finally, images of an Indian government that is overly representative of the Hindi-speaking areas (as exemplified by the fact that all of India's Prime Ministers and the largest bloc of central government Cabinet Ministers have been drawn from the Hindi-speaking areas of Uttar Pradesh).

The leadership of the Bengali communist movement has played upon these images, emphasizing them in speeches and pamphlets and reinforcing them in slogans and campaigns.[2] In part this has been the result of the social origins of the Bengali Communist leadership, which is almost exclusively *bhadralok*, in part it has stemmed from the need to win elections in a relatively well established electoral democracy. For whatever reason, Bengali Communists have romanticized Bengal's terrorist tradition and have sought to project themselves as the successors to the Bengali nationalist tradition, despite the disdain of Marxist theorists for "mere terrorism." Bengali Communists have also elevated the intellectual pursuits of their members almost beyond criticism, despite the frequent conflicts between Marxist ideology and the academic conclusions reached by Bengali Communist intellectuals.[3] The fragile nature of the *bhadralok* attachment to Marxism and communism is shown by the constant recurrence of factional disputes emerging from the inner contradictions of the *bhadralok*-Marxist marriage.

In this sense factionalism among Bengali Communists is only partly a result of the basic ideological conflicts that have wracked the national and international communist movements. More often than not, Communist jargon is used by Bengalis to define and publicize a dispute that has its origins closer to home. Factionalism is rampant in Bengali society, not only among Communists but among all political

---

[2] See, for example, the 104-page pamphlet *West Bengal Accuses! Memorandum Containing Charges against the Congress Government in West Bengal Submitted to the President of the Indian Union by the West Bengal State Council of the Communist Party of India* (New Delhi: CPI, 1959), which could serve as a catalogue of all the demands made by the Communists in West Bengal over the past two decades.

[3] Examples include the collaboration of Utpal Dutta in the production of an American film (*The Guru*) against the wishes of some of his fellow CPM party members, or the similar participation of CPI leader Dilip Bose (an avid reader of the physical sciences and the proprietor of the CPI bookstore) in USIS programs related to space travel.

parties and groups, as well as in all Bengali institutions (including the schools, the family, and the bureaucracy). In fact, if the Bengali Communists were able to escape from intense factional conflict, one might be able to argue more effectively that they were somehow foreign to Bengal.

Bengali factionalism is a complex matter, sharing many of the attributes of a partisanship that seems endemic to Indian life. In Bengal, as elsewhere in India, one can identify the phenomenon that Harold Gould has labeled "ethnoconceptualization," ". . . a long-established, culturally patterned tendency to regard endogamous, ritually and functionally differentiated social units *as if* they were natural species."[4]

Whether they are called "factions"—as political scientists like Paul Brass and anthropologists like Oscar Lewis have preferred to do—or something else, I would hold that the relatively small, intensely personalistic structures which abound at every level of Indian political life, and which so rarely assimilate themselves to large structures, are social manifestations of a largely unconscious "jati model" which governs group formation. Because the overwhelming majority of Indians are dominated in so many aspects of their individual and collective lives by *consciously formulated* caste structures *in being*, they rather inevitably and understandably seek to reproduce the *essential properties* sociologically and psychologically inherent in these structures in contemporary social spheres like politics and bureaucracies. . . .[5]

As Gould has pointed out, Indian factions—if we can call them that—bear "many emotional and structural resemblances to a socioreligious *jati*: they tend to be intensely personalistic; they demand nearly total absorption of an individual's ego in their aims and activities; loyalty is primarily to persons and not ideas or issues; and subordination to leaders is modeled after the *guru-chela* relationship."[6]

Ethnoconceptualization in Bengali life is reinforced by a number of other factors that also tend to promote political factionalism. The Bengali region within India can be divided into a number of distinct subregions, each with its own history, cultural traditions, and economic patterns, which in turn demand the loyalty of their residents. The Gurkhas of Darjeeling District, for example, feeling threatened by the fact that they form such a minor part of the state of West Bengal and the Indian nation, have formed their own political party, the Gurkha League. A Gurkha youth who becomes interested in Marxism must

---

[4] Harold A. Gould, "Toward a 'Jati Model' for Indian Politics," *Economic and Political Weekly* (Bombay), February 1, 1969, p. 293. (Italics in original.)
[5] Ibid., p. 295. (Italics in original.)
[6] Ibid.

therefore choose between membership in a Communist party or the Gurkha League and, regardless of his choice, must be constantly aware of the fact that he is both a Gurkha and a Marxist. If he chooses to enter a Communist party, he must attempt to rally the members of his own community behind him, since other party leaders tend to rally their community and subregional supporters in order to support their factional interests. Because the Gurkha League is better established in Gurkha areas, Gurkha youth who become interested in Marxism are likely to join a Marxist faction within the Gurkha League rather than form a Gurkha faction within a Communist or Marxist Left party.[7]

Similar subregional attachments can be identified in most of Bengal's political parties: the Lok Sevak Sangh is composed exclusively of a leadership drawn from Purulia District, the portion of the state added after the States Reorganization controversy of the mid-1950s; the RSP (despite its aspirations for an all-India following) has won almost all of its electoral support in three North Bengal districts (Murshidabad, West Dinajpur, and Jalpaiguri); similarly, the Forward Bloc has been concentrated in the districts of Hooghly, How-rah, Birbhum, and Cooch-Behar.[8] Like the Gurkha youth of Darjeeling District, young Marxists who have ties to an LSS, RSP, or Forward Bloc stronghold tend to associate themselves with a faction within the smaller Marxist Left party, instead of joining a Communist party that is inadequately represented by leaders from their subregion. Factions within the Communist parties are themselves frequently associated with a particular subregion of the state, as well as with a particular leader: the large CPI faction in Midnapore, the Konar faction of the CPM in Burdwan, the CPML faction in Naxalbari, and the Jyoti Basu and Pramode Das Gupta factions centered in Calcutta.

Perhaps more important for an understanding of the intensity of Bengali factionalism are the kinds of human relationships that have developed in Bengali life as a result of the elitist nature of its traditional society. As Weiner has pointed out,

Bengal is characterized by the existence of hierarchical and generally authoritarian patterns within all institutions, from the family to schools, universities, administration and government, which serve to inhibit the

[7] For a review article on Gurkha League factionalism, see *The Statesman* (Calcutta daily), March 21, 1957; for more recent developments see the *Hindusthan Standard* (Calcutta daily), January 31, 1969.

[8] The subregional attachments of Bengali political parties are analyzed in detail in Marcus F. Franda, "Intra-Regional Factionalism and Coalition-Building in West Bengal," *Journal of Commonwealth Political Studies* 8 (November 1970): 187–205.

development of innovating individuals. Men in authority view innovations within their institutions as devices to threaten their positions; they also tend to view new ideas from underlings as intolerable threats to their status. As a result, men with ambition express fidelity and humility to authority. When they attack authority it is not one's personal superior, but rather impersonal institutions, such as government, and in impersonal ways, as in the street demonstrations.[9]

Hierarchical and authoritarian patterns also dominate party organizations, with the result that leadership groups within parties tend to become so well entrenched and so intolerant of threats to their status that factional organizations grow up around almost every aspirant for a high-level party post. Practically every party in West Bengal has had severe problems transferring power from the older nationalist generation to the post-Independence generation that is now coming of age, and almost every promising young party leader has achieved recognition on the basis of his ability to muster an inner-party factional following. In the Communist parties in West Bengal, where leaders can use the strict rules of discipline usually associated with Leninist organization, hierarchical and authoritarian behavior on the part of leadership sets has been responsible for a factionalism even more intense than is usual in Bengal.

To add to the factional problems that have historically been associated with the communist movement in West Bengal, the state is now becoming increasingly politicized in a period of economic decline, so that fewer and fewer resources are being distributed to more and more aspiring politicians. As has already been pointed out, this factor has become especially crucial for the development of factions within the Communist parties since their entry into the ministries. To a greater extent than in most other societies, the rewards in Bengali politics flow to political leaders, and to a much lesser extent to their supporters and followers. The leaders of political parties are asked to speak at a variety of social and political functions, with fees of upward of 100 rupees per appearance (in a society where the *average monthly* income is less than 100 rupees), and it is the leadership that has access to party funds and negotiations with other parties and the government. When an electoral party is out of power, its leadership will frequently be consulted by the government, and such things as "payoffs" and "deals" between opposition leaders and the state government are mentioned too often to be totally lacking in substance. When an electoral party gains power, it is the leadership

---

[9] Myron Weiner, "Notes on Political Development in West Bengal," in *Political Change in South Asia* (Calcutta: Firma K. L. Mukhopadhyay, 1963), pp. 255–256.

that enters the ministries and manages the patronage system. Taking all of these factors into consideration, it is little wonder that political leaders have a personal interest in *heading* separate parties or factions rather than *collaborating* at the secondary levels of aggregative political party organizations. But this leads in a vicious circle to an intensification of factional disputes, encouragement of party splits, and strains within political alliances.

The nature of political factionalism in Bengal has had a number of consequences for the Bengali communist movement, but it has been especially crucial in determining organizational matters and in its effects on Communist attempts to acquire a mass following. Within the party organizations that make up the movement, warm and friendly relations have developed among factional leaders on the basis of past recruitment patterns. The older intellectuals in the movement have worked together in enough campaigns to have learned to trust one another and have established lines of authority among themselves. At the same time, the older intellectuals in the movement have increasingly learned to distrust the older terrorist leadership, recruited from an entirely different segment of Bengali society, and both the older terrorists and the older intellectuals have at times opposed the electoral leadership that has been gaining ground within the movement since 1947. The younger Communist leadership, on the other hand has found that the three older Communist factions are so well entrenched and so jealous of their factional prerogatives that aspirations for leadership can be satisfied only by the creation of new factional groupings and parties. Ideally a Communist party should have a strong, united leadership and "iron rules of discipline," but because factional positions are so highly coveted in Bengali society, Communist unity has not been possible.

The Communist cadres that have approached the Bengali masses have therefore done so from elitist factional positions, which has lessened the impact of an ideology that would seem to have a natural appeal for the common people of Bengal. Almost every observer who has seen Bengal will agree that the Bengali "masses" live in a state of poverty, filth, and human degradation that would be difficult to equal anywhere, a condition that has been progressively deteriorating during this century. Moreover, as Francine Frankel has pointed out, the introduction of new farming methods under the Intensive Agricultural Development Programme (IADP) has only served to widen the gap between rich and poor:

> The majority of farmers [in Bengal]—probably as many as 75 percent to 80 percent in the rice belt—have experienced a relative decline in their economic position [since the introduction of the IADP]; and some proportion,

representing unprotected tenants cultivating under oral lease, have suffered an absolute deterioration in their living standard. . . .[10]

After witnessing the widening gap between rich and poor in Bengal, one can only agree with Frankel that the poor "are becoming more embittered and radicalized; and probably more convinced than ever of the Marxists' political propaganda that fundamental social change can only be accomplished by the complete overturn of the existing property system."[11]

The dilemma of the Communist parties in Bengal is that the increasing radicalization of the peasantry (and the proletariat in the cities as well) has not brought about unambiguous gains for the Communists. Since the mass of the Bengali peasantry and laboring classes is organized on the basis of elite leaders and mass followers tied together by traditional ethnoconceptual ideas and authoritarian behavior patterns, the strength of almost all the Communist and Marxist Left factions and parties has been growing during the past few years. This has produced a situation that the Communists describe as "a shift to the left forces," but it has also been accompanied by a more intense factionalism among the Communist and Marxist Left parties than has ever been witnessed in India. From the point of view of the peasants and laboring classes, the United Front governments have forced everyone in West Bengal to make a choice as to which party in the front can best serve individual and family interests, since it has been clear from the outset of the first UF government that the demands of all of the disadvantaged in West Bengal could not be met. In choosing between the various political parties in the United Front, Bengali peasants and laborers have therefore generally affiliated with parties with which they could most easily establish a community, subregional, or other factional relation, a strategem that has at least promised greater access to the limited amount of patronage that has accrued to the new government.[12] During the course of these developments, the CPM has unquestionably made the greatest gains, but no one would argue that it has yet even approached a position where it could gain a clear majority for itself in the state Legislative Assembly, nor has the

[10] Quoted from portions of a report prepared for the United States Agency for International Development; see Francine Frankel "Agricultural Modernization and Social Change," *Mainstream* (New Delhi weekly), December 13, 1969, p. 17.

[11] Ibid., p. 36.

[12] The report of a survey of peasant reactions to the United Front governments is contained in *The Hindu* (Madras), December 23, 1969. The results of this survey, which are stated above, are corroborated by other sources and by interviews.

CPM made any noticeable gains in bringing about a situation that could be seized upon to foment violent revolution.

In the absence of either a state government controlled by a single party or a violent revolution in Bengal and/or India, the present pattern of ineffective coalition government is likely to continue to be a feature of Bengali political life. The basic problem of coalition building in West Bengal is that there is very little of value that can be divided among partners in a coalition. Demands are too high, groups too numerous and politicized, and resources too scarce to make for a stable coalition that can continue to satisfy as many factions and subregions as are needed to build a majority. The Congress organization was able to overcome this difficulty during the first two decades of Independence by carefully staking out an appeal to 40 percent of the state population, depending for its electoral victories on the factionalism that existed among the remaining 60 percent. But a Communist party could only duplicate the Congress strategy if it could depend on the constant fragmentation of its opposition and if it was willing to become so aggregative as to surrender its claim to ideological rigor. In a sense, the CPM cadre has already risked the possibility of being captured by the party's aggregative electoral wing because of its heavy involvement in the patronage of the state ministries.

One possibility for breaking the present deadlock in West Bengal is a revived aggregative coalition like that of the Congress; another is a total transformation in the pattern of relations between party leaders and followers. If a given set of state leaders could convince a sufficient portion of the peasantry and the proletariat that it could produce gains for the majority of the people in the state—across caste, community, and subregional ties—then the level of political awareness in the state is high enough so that such an appeal could form the basis of a strong party alliance or coalition. To make such an appeal effective, however, a political party would have to find sufficient resources to satisfy the heightened expectations of a large number of different groups and individuals, a task that seems beyond the realm of possibility given the present state of economic development in West Bengal. For a variety of reasons, West Bengal has not shared in the "green revolution" as much as other parts of India,[13] and in late 1969 funds for family planning programs were not even being distributed in the state because of a factional dispute in the state Health

---

[13] S. Sengupta and M. G. Ghosh, "HYVP for Rice: Performance in a West Bengal District," *Economic and Political Weekly*, October 26, 1968, pp. A-26–28.

Ministry.[14] Thus, the rate of population growth in West Bengal continues to exceed that of almost every state in India, while the economic reverses that were set in motion by the partition of Bengal in 1947 have recently accelerated.[15]

The Search for a National Strategy

The increasing frustration that has been the lot of Bengali Communists attempting to revolutionize their regional environment has led many of them to search for national strategies that might contribute to revolution over a wider area. Especially since the formation of the first United Front ministry in West Bengal in 1967, many Bengali Communists have become convinced that continued Communist control of only one or two Indian states might lead to a diminution of Communist strength and party fervor. Not only does the possibility exist that ineffective Communist state governments might diminish electoral support without affecting other states in India, but there is also a possibility that a regional strategy within an electoral system might lead to the irreversible absorption of Communist party cadres into the network of electoral politics. If India were not a highly segmented and pluralist nation, the Communists in West Bengal might be able to speed up the process of revolutionizing the state population without having to worry about the possibility of repression by the rest of the Indian Union. It is the segmentation of Indian political and social life at the national level that makes it possible for Union governments to isolate and quarantine the bases in which the Communists have made some gains, thus lessening the national impact of regional communism and deepening the need for a national strategy.

In this atmosphere, the extremists within the Indian communist movement have been the most ardent proponents of a national strategy, with the Maoists on the left working for a "people's war" throughout the country and the pro-Soviets on the right attempting to assemble the diverse strands of Indian leftism in a national coalition. Instead of building up strong regional bases, as the CPM has attempted to do, both the Maoists and the pro-Soviets have emphasized the need for a Communist conception of the all-India aspects of the present political situation, and both extremes have tried to build party

[14] Based on interviews conducted in August and September 1969 with the Union Minister for Family Planning, Dr. S. Chandrasekhar, and Dr. A. M. O. Ghani, the leading figure in the CPM concerned with family planning policy.

[15] "Economic Growth in West Bengal Has Slowed Down," *Eastern Economist* (Bombay), July 26, 1968, pp. 242–251. See also the excellent series of articles on the West Bengal economy in the *Hindusthan Standard*, September 20, 1969 (*Weekly Supplement*); September 22, 1969; and September 24, 1969.

organizations that are more representative of India's diversity than the cadre of the CPM. Paradoxically, however, the principal shortcoming of both Left and Right Communist extremists is their continued inability to overcome the hurdles of Indian segmentation and the factionalism within their own ranks.

The factional problems that have plagued national strategies can be seen most clearly in the case of the Left Communists, almost all of whom can agree that the present "task" of Indian communism is "the establishment of guerrilla bases in rural areas, to encircle and liberate the cities and ultimately to emancipate the whole country."[16] All Maoist factions in India can agree that the older leadership of the Indian communist movement has failed to take advantage of rural discontent, primarily because it has sought to organize the rural areas along regional and subregional lines for electoral purposes. In the words of one Maoist leader from West Bengal, "There is little point in trying to encircle and liberate only one city, such as Calcutta, when the rest of the cities in India remain in a feudal and moribund condition. We can use the experience that we have gained in Calcutta, and in the areas around Calcutta, but our next step must be the *extension* of our base rather than the concentration of the organization in one area."[17] Despite basic agreement among Maoists on this proposition, India's Left Communists have now divided themselves along a whole range of factional positions, based both on regional and subregional divisions and on differing tactical lines.

From a national point of view, the principal Maoist factions in India have been those led by Tarimela Nagi Reddy in Andhra and the CPML group in West Bengal. But while struggles over regional leadership have obviously played a part in dividing these groups, it would be a mistake to assume that regional considerations were the only factors at work in separating the two, since a number of Andhra Maoists are in the CPML and a number of Bengalis are followers of Nagi Reddy. Moreover, while the leadership of the Andhra Maoists consists of men who entered politics during the Telengana campaigns that rocked South India from 1946 to 1951, they have by now changed their focus of attack considerably. They no longer support Telengana separatism but have instead decided to concentrate on the organization of the poorest (primarily tribal) sections of the population, in order to create revolutionary bases that are relevant to a large number of

[16] A detailed comparison of various Maoist strategies in India is provided in Mohan Ram, *Indian Communism*, pp. 210 ff.

[17] Based on an interview conducted in Hooghly District in West Bengal in September 1969.

Indian situations. Similarly, while the CPML leadership is centered around the heroes of the Naxalbari movement of 1967, the party is now active throughout India and is trying to build on its Naxalbari experience in such a way as to bring about revolutionary situations in a number of different Indian states.

As defined by Maoist factional theoreticians, the principal differences among India's Left Communists have to do with the answers to three tactical questions: (1) Is guerrilla warfare to be the only form of struggle pursued at the present stage of revolutionary development? (2) What is to be the role of Communist mass organizations in the struggle? (3) What kind of Communist organization can best bring about a "people's war" in India?[18] In answer to these three questions, the leadership of the CPML has opted for an exclusive emphasis on guerrilla warfare as the only form of struggle appropriate to the present stage, while the Nagi Reddy group is attempting to link both agrarian development programs and urban mass movements with guerrilla activites. The "Immediate Programme" of Nagi Reddy's Revolutionary Communist Committee, for example, calls for the establishment of "village committees" and "village soviets" in areas of Maoist activity, and these committees are viewed as vehicles to consolidate Communist gains and prepare for guerrilla war. Similarly, CPML theoreticians have constantly denigrated the work of Communist mass organizations in India, particularly trade unions, while the Andhra Maoists have attached considerable importance to work in mass organizations and in urban areas. Both of these differences are in turn related to the different conceptions of party organization that have been elaborated by the CPML and the Nagi Reddy groups: the former has emphasized a conspiratorial and secret style of organizational work, while the latter has sought to maintain both legal and illegal party cadres.

Regardless of the differences between party theoreticians over the tactical line to be pursued by Maoists, however, both the CPML and the Nagi Reddy groups have encountered considerable difficulty in making a "people's war" strategy work. As has already been pointed out, the CPML in West Bengal has met with some success when organizing urban college students for protest demonstrations against the United Front government of West Bengal but has thus far failed to capitalize on the fervor of its youthful urban cadres to create peasant bases in the countryside. Attempts by the Bengali Left Communist leadership to promote Maoist organizations in the rural areas of West Bengal

[18] Mohan Ram, *Indian Communism*, pp. 262–263.

have led to the same old dilemmas that the Bengali *bhadralok* have always encountered when attempting to revolutionize *abhadra* peasants, while the organizational efforts of Bengalis in non-Bengali areas have met with even greater resistance. In this atmosphere, CPML theoreticians have continued to espouse a party program that calls for organizational work that is relevant to a number of non-Bengali areas, and CPML leaders have relentlessly sought to extend their base outside of Bengal, but the major impact of the CPML is still confined to the consequences that it has for the Bengali unit of the CPM and for the West Bengal United Front.

The Andhra Maoists, who have perhaps made greater gains among the Girijan tribals of Srikakulam District than Maoist groups in any of India's other rural areas, have nevertheless encountered problems similar to those of the CPML. Not only have they failed to extend their gains in Srikakulam to other parts of Andhra and India, they have also suffered a considerable loss of high-level leadership because of the arrests carried out by the Indian government in late 1969 and early 1970. The Nagi Reddy group has placed little emphasis on conspiratorial organization, and since their leadership is concentrated in a state that is still controlled by the Congress, the leadership of the Andhra Maoists has been exposed to much severer governmental repression than the leadership of the CPML. By early 1970 more than thirty members of the elite Revolutionary Communist Committee (including Tarimela Nagi Reddy himself) were languishing in jail awaiting trial, while the leadership of the CPML had still evaded arrest. As one might expect, the result has been a decline both in the morale and in the activities of the Andhra Maoists.[19]

When the assessment of the Indian political situation by Left Communist theoreticians is set alongside the failure of Maoist practitioners in the field, the ideological position both of the CPML and of the Nagi Reddy group takes on an air of unreality that is reminiscent of India's experience with communism since the 1920s. In the eyes of CPI as well as CPM theoreticians, the possibility of a Communist revolution in India in the near future is much more remote than the Maoists would like to think. Even if the Congress movement should lose its electoral majority in New Delhi in the next few years, there is a strong possibility that Congress groups will be able to form stable coalition governments, either with the rightist parties (Swatantra and Jan Sangh) or with regional parties (such as the Dravida Munetra Kazagham of Madras or the Akali Dal in Punjab), all of which are

[19] Based on interviews with Andhra Maoists in April 1970.

better established in state political systems than the Communists. Should ministerial coalitions fail in New Delhi at some point in the future, the Communists would then have to face severe opposition from a highly institutionalized military, police, judicial, and bureaucratic network, which is unreservedly anticommunist and highly intent on maintaining the unity of the nation. In light of these factors, both CPM and CPI theoreticians have attempted to educate India's youthful Maoist extremists in the manner of the CPM Politbureau:

> They [the Maoists] are anxious to teach the "ignorant" CPM the elementary truth that the present Indian state is a bourgeois-landlord state led by the big bourgeoisie, and that state power essentially lies in the military, police, courts, judiciary and bureaucracy. Since the state power is not in any way broken or weakened due to the electoral defeats of the Congress party, it is "atrocious" on the part of the CPM to speak about "breaking the Congress monopoly of power!"
>
> . . . May we, first of all, tell our critics that they do not understand the difference between the *concept of breaking state power* and the *concept of breaking the monopoly of that power by one political party*, namely the Congress Party?
>
> The bourgeois-landlord state power can never be broken except through a people's democratic revolution or socialist revolution. But before that . . . breaking up the one-party monopoly of power is considered as an important step forward, and thus the slogan of breaking the Congress monopoly is advanced. If anyone is to understand it as a substitute to the people's democratic revolution which alone can break the bourgeois-landlord state power, he should blame his colossal political ignorance in the matter.[20]

Many of the Maoist leaders and theoreticians in India are fully conscious of the difference between the concepts of breaking state power and breaking the monopoly of the Congress—indeed, some of the Maoist factions have even divided along these lines—and yet all Maoists are still convinced that the focus of the Communists should be the former rather than the latter. These people look forward to a period of great chaos in India in the next few years, perhaps brought about by the complete downfall of the Congress in the next elections, perhaps as a result of Congress party factionalism and major splits in the Congress movement, or perhaps as a consequence of economic collapse. They look forward to a series of internecine wars between India's competing regional politicians and to Chinese assistance for their guerrilla activities, which are intended to take advantage of a state of anarchy. And yet, because of their rigid emphasis on historical models—Russia, China, Cuba, Vietnam—the Maoists still lack the

---

[20] *Ideological Debate Summed Up by Politbureau* (Calcutta: CPM, 1968), pp. 163–164. (Italics in original.)

creative impulse that would seem necessary to bring about a significant advance toward their revolutionary goals.

The other bloc of national strategists—the pro-Soviets within the CPI—have attempted to strengthen their own tactical position in precisely the areas where the Maoists are accused of weakness. If the Maoists have failed to take sufficient account of India's highly institutionalized military, police, judicial, and bureaucratic network, the pro-Soviets within the CPI have attached so much importance to this network that they have become bent on capturing it. While the Maoists have discounted the efficacy of electoral alliance building in the present Indian political situation, the pro-Soviets within the CPI have directed most of their energies toward the creation of a national coalition that includes the Communists. In these endeavors both the Left and Right Communist extremes in India can be accused of a lack of imagination, since both are pursuing rather time-worn strategies, and both have placed a heavy reliance on assistance from foreign communist movements.

As has already been pointed out, the ability of the CPI to play a significant role in national coalition building will depend on its ability to increase its electoral strength in the states and on a shift in the orientation of the Ruling Congress and other political parties toward Moscow. In its present position the CPI controls 23 of the 521 Lok Sabha seats and is a minority partner in two state coalition governments, a base that is too narrow to enable it to determine the makeup of a national coalition without considerable assistance. Of the non-Congress Left parties that could conceivably ally with the CPI in a national coalition, the SSP controls 23 Lok Sabha seats, the CPM 19, and the PSP 13, while perhaps another 20 seats are held by leftist independents and leftists in regional parties. This means that even if the CPI could bring about Left unity among all parties besides the Congress, it would still have a bloc of only 100 or so of the 521 seats in the present Lok Sabha. If only for this reason, the CPI must necessarily include the Ruling Congress with its 221 Lok Sabha seats among the parties to be courted with its slogan of Left unity.

These figures point up the extent to which the CPI is dependent on the Ruling Congress for the success of its strategy of building a national coalition of Left forces; in addition, they point to the difficulties confronting the party. While the non-Congress Left parties are divided on the question of allying with the Congress, the Ruling Congress is divided between well-entrenched regional factions that have taken a strong stand on the question of alliance with the Communists. In order to build a national Left unity coalition, the CPI must convince the non-Congress Left parties that it is in their interest to ally temporarily with the Congress as it simultaneously persuades the Ruling Congress that it should ally with the Communists. Because of the aggregative nature of the Ruling Congress, the very attempt to bring about a CPI-Congress coalition is likely to split the party into procommunist and anticommunist factions, forcing the leadership of the Ruling Congress either to split the party again or to seek noncommunist allies. It is because of these considerations that the leadership of the Ruling Congress has thus far argued that it would not consider the possibility of coalescing with the Communists but has instead sought to cement its relationships with regional parties (such as the DMK, the Akali Dal, and the Bangla Congress).

Two factors could conceivably break this stalemate. If the CPI could achieve considerable gains in future electoral contests, the party would have a stronger base from which to bargain with both the leftists and the Ruling Congress. Alternatively, if the pro-Moscow elements in the Ruling Congress, the CPM, and the Left parties could gain greater control over party machinery, the CPI and the CPSU might be able to combine their influence in national political affairs with a series of Soviet diplomatic initiatives to bring about a national coalition oriented toward Moscow. The first of these possibilities is unlikely so long as the CPM is sufficiently hostile toward the CPI to be willing to sacrifice its own marginal electoral gains to defeat CPI candidates, but Soviet (or CPGB or Rumanian) intervention could conceivably bring about a temporary truce between India's two major warring Communist parties. In short, the prospects for the CPI strategy depend almost entirely on relations between Moscow and a number of different party and governmental leaders in India.

International Politics and the Question of Pakistan

If the attitude of the Soviet Union toward South Asia during the next few years has a considerable impact on India's national political alignments, it will also influence the nature of regional political developments as well. Nowhere is this clearer than in Bengal, where the decline of the Bengali-speaking peoples of both India and Pakistan in this century has become intimately intertwined with the Bengali fascination for Marxism and communism. Taken together, the Bengalis in East Pakistan and West Bengal constitute the seventh-largest language group in the world, and yet they have been unable to translate their numbers into political power. At the time of partition they were unable to bring about a united Bengal, despite the desire and the willingness of the most prominent Hindu and Muslim Bengali leaders to do so,[21] and since partition the principal political dynamic both in West Bengal and in East Pakistan has been the feeling that Bengalis are being exploited by non-Bengalis. In the words of a *Statesman* editorial in June 1950, "They [the Bengalis] are constantly aware also of past glories and present potentialities. They do not forget either that Calcutta was long the country's capital or that Bengalis took the lead in the freedom movement. Once they swayed the destinies of India; now they cannot even determine their own."[22]

Many Bengalis, and especially the new generation of Bengali youth, have placed their hopes for the future in revolution, to be carried out in collaboration with the Soviet Union, China, or perhaps other Indian or Asian Communists. (One might compare this tendency to look for foreign allies against the Hindi and other South Asian *Staatsvolk* with wartime pro-German currents in Croatia and the pro-Soviet and later pro-Chinese policies of Albania, both directed against Serb hegemony.) Suspicious of the English-speaking peoples and the non-Bengali Indian and Pakistani communities that have been held responsible for the decline of Bengali greatness in this century, many Bengalis have turned to revolutionary and protest activities directed against those whom they have learned to distrust since childhood. This is not to argue that all Bengalis are regional chauvinists, for there are influential people on both sides of the border who would like to bring about an accommodation between Bengali and non-Bengali interests within the framework of the two nation-states. What is clear, however, is the manner in which Bengalis have adapted Marxism and communism to their urge for a regional identity and regional political power.

Nevertheless, in the eyes of foreign communist movements the activities of Bengali Communists would appear to count for much less at this point in time than many Bengali revolutionaries would like to

---

[21] Perhaps most Bengalis, including the Communists, were hopeful in the years preceding partition that something would come of the schemes put forth by Sarat Bose and H. S. Suhrawardy (Chief Minister of the United Bengal Provincial Government under the British) for a "united Bengal," independent of both India and Pakistan. These schemes are described in Sarat Chandra Bose, *I Warned My Countrymen* (Calcutta: Netaji Research Bureau, 1968), pp. 183–194. Included in this volume are letters both from Gandhi and from Jinnah entertaining the Bose proposals for a united Bengal; see pp. 254, 348–352. For the position of various sections of the Muslim community regarding the question of a united Bengal, see Hassan Suhrawaddy, "The Indian Crisis: Muslim Viewpoints," in *Hindustan or Pakistan?*, ed. S. L. Chopra (Lahore: Ilami Markaz, 1955), pp. 6–25, and Kamruddin Ahmad, *The Social History of East Pakistan* (Dacca: Pioneer Press, 1967), especially pp. 81–88.

[22] Quoted in John Broomfield, *Elite Conflict in a Plural Society: Twentieth-Century Bengal* (Berkeley: University of California Press, 1968), p. xviii.

think. Both the Soviet Union and China have pursued an activist foreign policy in South Asia during the last two decades, but in both cases the principal focus of their activities has been national and international rather than regional. In a sense one can argue that the two Communist giants have reacted more to each other's diplomatic initiatives, and to the United States, than they have to the changes that have taken place within India and Pakistan. Throughout the 1950s, for example, the Soviet Union adopted a hostile stance toward Pakistan, vetoing several Security Council resolutions designed to settle the Kashmir dispute through plebiscite or bilateral negotiations, in an effort to penalize Pakistan for allying itself with the United States. Then, in the 1960s, Russia increasingly adopted a more neutral attitude toward the Indo-Pakistani conflict as Pakistani relations with the United States cooled and Sino-Pakistani relations became more cordial.

The importance of China and Pakistan in the determination of Soviet policy toward India can be seen from the way in which Moscow has responded to changes in Sino-Pakistani relations. Throughout the 1950s China pursued relations with Pakistan that were "diplomatically correct" but cool: the Chinese were much less hostile toward Pakistan than the Soviets were in their condemnation of the Baghdad Pact; Peking refused to come out in favor of India on the Kashmir question; and Chou En-lai even attempted to mediate disputes between India, Pakistan, and the Soviet Union at the Bandung Conference in April 1955.[23] In the 1960s these relations have become increasingly friendly. Pakistan voted to seat China in the United Nations in 1961, a Sino-Pakistani border agreement was reached in 1963, air services were initiated between Canton, Shanghai, Dacca, and Karachi in 1964, and expressions of Chinese support for Pakistan were issued on a number of occasions during the 1965 Indo-Pakistani conflict. Since 1965 cordial relations between China and Pakistan have continued to grow, accompanied by trade agreements and cultural exchanges, and China now has considerable support among Pakistani political and military leaders.[24]

In the long run, Soviet interests in Pakistan will most likely center on the western wing, which is culturally and geographically linked to the Middle East, while China's principal interest is likely to focus on

[23] An excellent short summary of Pakistan's relations with China in the 1950s and early 1960s appears in Khalid B. Sayeed, *The Political System of Pakistan* (Boston: Houghton Mifflin, 1967), pp. 274 ff.

[24] See, for example, the report of Lieutenant General Hamid Khan, who led the Pakistani delegation to the twentieth anniversary celebrations of the People's Republic of China, in *Dawn* (Karachi daily), October 6, 1969.

the East Pakistani territories bordering on India and Burma. So long as Pakistan manages to maintain friendly relations with the Soviet Union and China, it is unlikely that either of the two Communist giants will overtly support internal Communist revolutionary groups in Pakistan (as China is presently doing in India, or as the Soviet Union supported the CPI in the late 1940s). However, both India and Pakistan have at times been concerned with the possibility that either Moscow or Peking may some day find it advantageous to support internal insurrectionist movements, particularly in the northeastern regions of India and in East Pakistan. In 1959, for example, when Chinese probings beyond the McMahon line were interpreted as a threat to East Pakistan, Field Marshal Ayub Khan stated in an interview with a British correspondent that "a Russian-Chinese drive to the Indian Ocean is a major aim in the Communist drive for World domination."[25] Again, in July 1960, President Ayub issued a series of statements from East Bengal in which he argued that pro-Peking Communists "operating out of Calcutta" were carrying on a campaign for "a weak federal structure, too many provinces, and an ineffective government for Pakistan," a conspiracy that was also reported (with slight alterations and additions) by the Indian Home Ministry in New Delhi in 1964.[26]

The difficulty of assessing the role of Pakistan in future Communist activities in South Asia stems from the lack of public information available on the Pakistan Communist party (PCP). It is fairly certain that the Communist party in East Pakistan was slightly larger than the CPI in West Bengal at the time of Independence, since most of the Bengali Communists who had been active in pre-Independence Bengal chose Pakistan after 1947.[27] However, it is also clear that the PCP has suffered a sharp decline in membership and effectiveness since partition, largely because of the predominance among its leadership of Hindu *bhadralok* in a nation that is overwhelmingly Muslim. Moreover, because neither the Soviet Union nor China has shown much interest in playing a part in the domestic communist movement in Pakistan, and because of the severe repression of the movement by the Pakistan government, the older Communist trade union and peasant bases in East Bengal have been considerably weakened. The most successful Communist members and fellow travelers still active on the trade

---

[25] *Pakistan Observer* (Dacca), November 19, 1959, quoted in Sayeed, *Political System of Pakistan*, p. 273.

[26] *The Statesman*, July 26, 1960.

[27] There is a more detailed account of developments in the East Pakistan communist movement since 1947 in Marcus F. Franda, "Communism and Regional Politics in East Pakistan," *Asian Survey* 10 (August 1970): 588–606.

union front in East Bengal have found it possible to continue their organizational work only by divesting themselves of their reputation as Communists, and some of them have even begun to organize along communal rather than class lines. Such activities have not only weakened the organizational base of the party, they have also intensified factional disputes among Pakistani leftists and have forced more and more of the leftist leadership in Pakistan to search for a theoretical position that would justify a commitment to communism.

The factions that have arisen in East Pakistan in the course of this search are roughly similar to those in India. One group of theoreticians has identified with the current Moscow line of collaborating with the bourgeoisie in a "top alliance," expecting that through personal influence (and with the support of Soviet foreign policy) the ruling groups in Pakistan could be expected to complete the first-stage (anti-imperialist and antifeudal) bourgeois-democratic revolution, later to be followed by a socialist revolution. This is essentially the strategy of the CPI in India. A second group of theoreticians is much closer to the CPM and favors a "modified Right" or "neo-Maoist" strategy. In the Pakistani context, however, both the classical Right and "modified Right" strategies have had little appeal for Communists and their potential supporters, since the Communists do not have the kind of influence in institutional life that would permit the creation of an effective top alliance. Some of the Communists are presently attempting to gain such influence by penetrating into the National Awami Party (NAP) of Maulana Bhashani, hoping eventually to capture a share of political power in the eastern wing and to use this power base to promote a first-stage revolution.[28] But alliance with Bhashani's NAP, or with any of Pakistan's other legal parties, creates a number of problems for Bengali Communists. Not only does a strategy of alliance with NAP assume that the possibility of coming to power is an extremely long-range one, it also carries with it the probability that the Communists will be used by NAP and other parties for their own purposes, without any benefit to the communist movement in Pakistan. Most importantly, it does not provide much of an opportunity for the creation of an independent base for the Communists, and it makes the

[28] Maulana Abdul Hamid Khan Bhashani, the 85-year-old leader of NAP, has described the program of his party as the attempt "to establish socialism which does not interfere with religion but stops exploitation of religion." At the present time NAP is among the most active political parties demanding an electoral framework for the pursuit of party programs. See *Morning News* (Dacca), October 6, 1969. For a discussion of NAP's internal factionalism and its relations with the more popular Awami League in East Pakistan, see *Holiday* (Dacca), October 5, 1969. See also Tapan Das, *Pakistan Politics* (Delhi: People's Publishing House, 1969), pp. 48–52.

communist movement dependent on the whims of noncommunist leaders for the foreseeable future.

For these reasons, the more militant Communist strategists in East Pakistan now argue that only a Maoist strategy can succeed in building a viable communist movement. Like the Naxalites in West Bengal, the proponents of a Maoist strategy in East Pakistan advocate an organization based on student activists, with direct appeals to workers, poor peasants, and the large number of clerks and other petty bourgeois who have become more and more disenchanted in recent years. Only through violent denunciations of the top leaders of all other political parties and of the imperialist nations, the Maoists argue, can the designs of the "vested interests" and "imperialists" be exposed and support won for the eventual revolution. Also according to this strategy, the Communist party in Pakistan must cooperate with others only in order to organize revolutionary and protest movements designed to expose the "imperialist United States," the "social-imperialist Soviet Union," and the "reactionary, feudal, and bourgeois" elements in Pakistan itself. While the Maoists view armed struggle as an eventual necessity, the present task of the PCP (in their view) is to raise the level of political consciousness among the masses in preparation for it.

While talk of revolutionary and protest movements in East Pakistan is frequently dismissed as the idle gossip of incurable romantics and naïve youth, the influence of such movements in the eastern wing has in the past had a considerable impact on the politics of Pakistan. Students and protest groups initiated the movement against the government of the Muslim League (the party that formulated and realized the demand for Pakistan) in the early 1950s, and these same groups provided the bulk of the workers for the opposition parties that defeated the Muslim League in the 1954 elections. During the Ayub Khan regime, when opposition political parties were rendered ineffective by severe governmental repression, protest groups (again led by students) organized massive political movements in 1963–1964, campaigned actively for Fatima Jinnah in the presidential election of January 1965, and eventually rallied opposition politicians, dissatisfied middle-class groups, government clerks, and labor unions behind a series of widespread protest demonstrations that lasted from November 1968 to March 1969 and ended by toppling the Ayub Khan government.[29]

[29] For an excellent analysis of Pakistani student politics, based on a questionnaire returned by 563 students in both wings, see Talukder Manirazzaman, "Perspectives and Political Orientations of University Students in Pakistan," unpublished manuscript available from the author, head of the Political Science Department, Rajshahi University, Rajshahi, East Pakistan.

Certainly the Communists did not play a large part in any of these demonstrations, but students with a leftist orientation did, and Pakistani Maoists simply argue that the possibility that protest movements will be won over to a revolutionary Communist strategy is much less remote than the possibility that Communists will gain influence through a top alliance with "vested interests" and "imperialists."

From the point of view of the Maoists in East Pakistan, the considerable discontent that exists is deeply rooted in the realities of Pakistani life and could conceivably be organized by a Maoist-type party in the future. Since Independence, Pakistan has been dominated by the bureaucracy and the military, both of which have in turn been dominated by non-Bengalis.[30] Moreover, East Pakistanis have effectively charged on a number of occasions that they are being exploited economically by West Pakistan while being discriminated against in terms of educational benefits, language policy, and a host of other important matters.[31] While some political party leaders in East

[30] The dominance of the military and bureaucracy in Pakistani politics is analyzed in M. Rashiduzzaman, *Pakistan: A Study of Government and Politics* (Dacca: Ideal Library, 1967); see especially pp. 261 ff. The extent to which the military and the bureaucracy have been dominated by non-Bengalis is indicated by the following figures (for 1955–1956), which have been adapted from Richard D. Lambert, "Factors in Bengali Regionalism in Pakistan," *Far Eastern Survey* 28 (April 1959): 54.

	From West Pakistan	From East Pakistan
Secretaries	19	0
Joint secretaries	38	3
Deputy secretaries	123	10
Undersecretaries	510	38
Lieutenant generals	3	0
Major generals	20	0
Brigadiers	34	1
Colonels	49	1
Lieutenant colonels	198	2
Majors	590	10
Air Force personnel	640	60
Naval officers	593	7
Total	2816	132

While there have been some attempts to correct this disparity since 1955–1956, recently available figures suggest that the gap is still as wide in 1969 as it was in the mid-fifties. In late 1969, for example, East Pakistan had one major general in the army and no representatives among the ten leading figures in the post-Ayub Martial Law Administration; see Mohammed Ayoob, "Hopes Belied in Pakistan," *Citizen and Weekend Review* (New Delhi fortnightly), April 12, 1969, pp. 32–33.

[31] For an analysis of the economic, cultural, and social grievances of East Bengalis, see Lambert, "Bengali Regionalism in Pakistan." A more recent statement is Mira Deb, "Pakistan: Neglected Grievances," *Citizen and Weekend Review*, May 10, 1969, pp. 28–29.

Pakistan are now hopeful that demands for the correction of disparities between the two wings will be met through the reinstallation of electoral democracy (the Bengalis constitute 54 percent of the total population of Pakistan), most observers agree that a parliamentary system, if it works at all in Pakistan, is not likely to put the regions on an equal footing for a long time to come.

In this atmosphere, Maoist theoreticians argue that the demands of the Awami League (AL) and the NAP for an electoral system that would enable Bengalis to outvote West Pakistan will eventually result in the disenchantment of East Pakistanis with electoral systems. Moreover, the arguments of the classical Right and modified Right Communist strategists that support for electoral demands is merely a temporary tactical device designed to build bases for future revolutionary change are viewed by the Maoists as mere rhetoric and revolutionary jargon. Because of their extreme disgust with the results of parliamentary democracy, the Maoists have refused to support even temporarily the demand for an electoral system and have instead sought to work out a nonelectoral strategy that could promote revolution in the eastern wing.

But the attempt to devise a nonelectoral strategy in Pakistan brings the Maoists face to face with the twin dilemmas that have confronted all South Asian Communists since they first began organizing in the 1920s. The first of them relates to the question of the stability of India and Pakistan as nation-states; the second is related to the possibilities for guerrilla warfare and insurrection. At some points in the past the Communists have decided that neither India nor Pakistan was viable as a national entity, with the result that regional separatist movements were supported by Communists on the basis of the "nationality thesis."[32] But support for regional movements has always hindered the communist movement in its attempts to influence national policy making, so that the "nationality thesis" has been increasingly underplayed or omitted from party considerations since the early 1950s. The second dilemma has arisen whenever the communist movement has viewed the Indian and Pakistani national governments as essentially unstable, raising the question of how best to take advantage of instability. There are a number of compelling reasons for adopting a guerrilla strategy in certain parts of the subcontinent—and the case for

[32] The history of the Indian Communist experience with the "nationality thesis" is recounted in Selig S. Harrison, "Communism in India: The Dilemma of the CPI," *Problems of Communism* 8 (March–April 1959): 27–35.

such a strategy is probably strongest in Bengal[33]—but each attempt to initiate guerrilla or other insurrectionist activities has resulted in ignominious failure.

The tragedy of the Bengali-speaking people in this century is intimately bound up with these twin dilemmas. Many Bengali leftists, both in India and in Pakistan, now argue that the only solution to the problem lies in the creation of a united Bengal,[34] brought about by guerrilla warfare and supported by the Chinese. But neither the Indian nor Pakistani strategists who advocate this solution have yet devised a means for initiating a guerrilla movement, and Chinese support is by no means assured. Moreover, there are considerable factional differences among Communist and Marxist Left strategists on the question of linking a Maoist strategy with the demand for a united Bengal, since the two do not necessarily need to be linked together.

Barring considerable change in the respective positions of Bengalis and non-Bengalis, however, support for millenarian movements is likely to grow on both sides of the international border that now separates West Bengal from East Pakistan. Therefore, to many observers, and to many politicians both in India and in Pakistan, the Maoists are a force that will have be to reckoned with in the next decade. But the activities of those who advocate a guerrilla movement and/or a united Bengal must be placed in the perspective of the domestic politics of India and Pakistan, as well as in the context of the international interests of the nations that are concerned with Bengal. A separatist movement based on the demand for a united Communist Bengal would run counter to the interests of most of the party politicians now active in India and Pakistan and would certainly be resisted both by the Indian and by the Pakistani military and bureaucracy. Moreover, at the present time it has little appeal for any of the three inter-

[33] Regarding the possibility of insurrectionist movements in the Bengali region, leftists on both sides of the border are fond of quoting Stalin's statement to three Bengalis in 1949 to the effect that "Telengana is far from the center of revolution," a statement that the Bengalis at that time interpreted as supporting the Communist insurrection in Bengal.

[34] Sentiments for a united Bengal are seldom expressed openly by leftists, since they so easily lead to conspiracy charges on both sides of the border. The last Marxist Left party in West Bengal to advocate a united Bengal in public was the Forward Bloc (Ruikar or Subhasist faction), which in the 1952 elections called for "a Bengali Union of Socialist Republics . . . a people's state unifying all shades of differences and autonomy in a federal government." See *The Statesman*, September 9, 1951. A recent discussion of the idea of a united Bengal is contained in Debendra Nath Banerjee, *East Pakistan: A Case-Study in Muslim Politics* (Delhi: Vikas Publications, 1969), pp. 169–178.

national powers with interests in the subcontinent, with the result that
Bengali guerrilla bands would have to win over the populace, collect
weapons, and secure fighting experience while at the same time
opposing the resistance of party politicians, two highly trained bureaucratic and intelligence networks, and two mobilized armies with
guerrilla training,[35] all supported by international power blocs.

In this atmosphere, the significance of the Maoist movement in
Bengal does not depend on the possibility that it will achieve its
long-range goals. For the immediate future the Maoists are of political
interest because of the influence that they are likely to have on the
course of Bengali regional politics and the future of the communist
movement in India and Pakistan. During the last few years the
Naxalites in West Bengal have been successful in securing the support
of a large portion of the politically active student groups in the state,
and these groups have had a significant impact on state politics. While
it is much more difficult to judge the sentiments of students in East
Bengal, since political activity is severely constrained by government,
both their rhetoric and their activities bear a striking resemblance to
those of the Naxalites across the border.[36] Bengali students in India
and Pakistan read the history of Bengal's past greatness, and yet the
vast majority of them are now unable to obtain jobs commensurate
with their status and education because of what they almost universally
believe to be discrimination against Bengal on the part of the non-
Bengali portions of India and Pakistan. Today's Bengali college
students have not witnessed the widespread communal killing that took
place before and after partition, and they have become increasingly
distrustful of traditional religious groups and traditional ideas. On
both sides of the border students are extremely active in politics and
attracted to the older Bengali terrorist leaders who in the past have

[35] The Indian army has received guerrilla training in actual combat with the
separatist Nagas and Mizos of the northeastern territories, while Pakistani training
has yet to be extensively tested. For a discussion of guerrilla warfare in South Asia,
and its relationship to possible Chinese interests, written by a leading member of the
Praja Socialist party of West Bengal, see Pradip Bose, *Sino-Pak Collusion and East
Pakistan* (Calcutta: Samajwadi Prakashani, 1966), pp. 9 ff.; see also Brines, *The
Indo-Pakistani Conflict*, pp. 415–416, 419, 427.

[36] Both in West Bengal and in East Pakistan the more militant student groups have
sought to (1) paralyze the educational system in an effort to create greater militancy
among Bengali students; (2) entice the military and police into open confrontation in
an effort to "expose" the repressive nature of government; (3) ally with peasant and
trade union groups on an ad hoc basis in an effort to induce such groups to resort to
violence; (4) introduce revolutionary slogans based on analogies to China and Vietnam. For evidence, cf. the analysis in Chapter 6 and the descriptions of the
East Pakistan student movement in the *Pakistan Observer*, October 1, 1969; *Eastern
Tribune* (Dacca), October 3, 1969; and *Holiday*, October 12, 1969.

refused to compromise with the electoral, bureaucratic, and military regimes of the post-Independence period. In short, the Bengali student atmosphere is one that thrives on revolutionary and protest strategies built around regional demands.

For Communist party members within Pakistan, the strategy of the Maoists is especially appealing, despite its millenarian character. The adoption of such a strategy lessens the dependence of the Communists on the established political parties and the "vested interests" allied with the government, while it simultaneously carries with it an appeal to the influential and potentially revolutionary student groups in East Pakistan. At the same time, a Maoist strategy could align Communists with the strong regional feelings and interests of Bengalis in a manner that does not run counter to (but does not depend on) attachment to Islam. In the changed conditions of international communism, and in light of the increasing political frustrations of Bengal, it is conceivable that the Naxalite communist movement could grow in East Pakistan in much the same manner as it has in West Bengal. While many of its followers wait for changes in the domestic politics of India and Pakistan to thrust Naxalites into positions of political influence, the leadership of the movement could be building a more substantial Communist following. Paradoxically, it is the present organizational weakness of the communist movement in Pakistan that makes a Maoist strategy more appealing to domestic Communists than any of its alternatives.

Conclusions

At the beginning of this book I put three broad and important sets of questions whose answers would, it was hoped, give direction to further study of the nature of communism in West Bengal and in India: (1) What are the sources of communism in West Bengal? Why have Bengalis been so active in the communist movement while other Indians have for the most part sought alternative outlets for political expression and participation? (2) What are Bengali Communists attempting to accomplish, and how do they go about it? (3) What has been the impact of the Bengali communist movement on state and on national politics, and on the Communists themselves? In response to the first question I have argued that the sources of Bengali communism are primarily regional, being intimately related to the decline of Bengal in this century and to the Bengali search for a new regional identity and regional political power. The ability of Bengali revolutionaries to adapt communism and Marxism to their own regional traditions and perceived political needs explains their high level of involvement with communist and Marxist ideas, despite the absence of such involvement in most parts of India. The second question, concerning the goals of Bengali Communists, has many answers. For reasons that have been explored in great detail, the Bengali communist movement has been continually wracked by intense factionalism, which has led it to try different political tactics and strategies, ranging from those of millenarian regionalists to those of the electoral politicians to those of international conspirators. In this atmosphere, the impact of the movement has been confined primarily to Bengal, even though events there have occasionally influenced the nature of Indian communism in a number of important ways. Not only have Bengali Communists been unable to affect the course of international communist movements, they are now heavily dependent on the Soviet Union and China for extending their gains.

These conclusions point to the need for research of a kind that might contribute to greater understanding of Bengali and Indian communism. Because this book has concentrated on a particular regional movement in its national and international environment, it has been possible to do no more than refer to the importance of subregional factional groupings and interests. Much more research is necessary before we can fully understand the effects of subregional factionalism in India on regional movements. I have hinted at the differences between the regional movement in Bengal and the one in the other Indian Communist stronghold in Kerala and have pointed to the ways in which the Bengal and Kerala regional movements have occasionally influenced one another, but regional studies of other Indian states, comparisons between communist movements in the various Indian regions, and analysis of the ways in which differing regional movements have interacted with one another are all topics that cry out for research. Finally, the lack of creativity among Bengali and Indian Communists and the dependence of the Indian movement on foreign Communist parties as a result of domestic failures must be explored in greater detail. At a time when international communism is becoming more and more variegated, we need to know more about the diversities within domestic communist movements.

POSTSCRIPT: 1970–1971

In late 1970 and early 1971, while this book was in press, a number of significant events took place in both West and East Bengal. While it is still too early to analyze these events in great detail, the reader should be aware of their occurrence, and some effort should be made to relate them to the analysis presented in the preceding pages.

On December 7, 1970, national and provincial elections were held throughout Pakistan (East and West) for the purpose of selecting a Constituent Assembly that could draft a new constitution and return the government to civilian rule. In East Bengal, the elections indicated overwhelming support for Sheikh Mujibur Rahman's East Pakistan Awami League (EPAL), as the following table shows:

TABLE 10

ELECTION RESULTS, EAST PAKISTAN, DECEMBER 1970

| | National Assembly | | Provincial Assembly | |
	No. Seats	% Vote	No. Seats	% Vote
EPAL	160	72.6	288	76.5
Pro-Moscow leftists	0	1.8	1	2.9
Pro-Peking NAP	0	0.3	0	0.8
Others	2	25.3	11	19.8
Totals	162	100.0	300	100.0

Source: Talukder Maniruzzaman, "The Leftist Movement in East Pakistan," to be included in a collection of essays on regional radicalism in South Asia edited by Paul R. Brass and Marcus F. Franda.

The overwhelming success of the East Pakistan Awami League can only be explained in terms of the great upsurge of Bengali regionalism that swept East Bengal in late 1970 and early 1971. Before the 1970 elections, Sheikh Mujibur Rahman, who had spent a number of years in jail under the Ayub Khan regime, had formulated a six-point program of autonomy for East Pakistan, and the EPAL program had attracted enormous popular support. Moreover, Sheikh Mujib—as he was known affectionately in East Bengal—had preempted the potential appeal of the pro-Moscow leftists in East Pakistan by promising nationalization of banks, insurance companies, and big industrial enterprises, shares of ownership to workers in small- and medium-scale industries, and exemption from land revenue for lower-class peasants in East Bengal.[1]

The Maoists in East Bengal were divided into too many factions to provide an alternative to the East Pakistan Awami League in 1971; many of them were in any case opposed to participation in electoral politics. Most of the Maoists therefore joined in an attempted boycott of the 1970 elections in East Bengal, but these efforts were generally acknowledged to be a failure (57.7 percent of the registered voters cast their ballots despite the "boycott"). As negotiations between West and East Pakistan dragged on for four months after the 1970 elections, the Awami League gained in popularity, while both the rightist and leftist parties became more and more factionalized.

Finally, in March 1971, the course of regional and national politics in Pakistan was permanently altered when federal troops (almost exclusively drawn from West Pakistan) moved brutally, swiftly, and decisively against the leadership of the EPAL. During the course of the next few months, Sheikh Mujib and most of his closest political friends and allies were either jailed or executed, and the ensuing riots in East Bengal were quickly quashed by the army, the police, and the air force, all controlled by West Pakistan. The West Pakistan government later claimed that Sheikh Mujib had clandestinely attempted to bring about a coup in East Bengal while negotiating with the West Pakistanis for a new Constituent Assembly.[2] According to this official government version, the EPAL had engaged in excessive brutality against some army officers who had refused to accede to EPAL plans for a coup, thus forcing the West Pakistan government to retaliate against EPAL leadership. Official statements by EPAL leaders deny plans for a coup and argue that the West Pakistan government apparently had no intention of granting any degree of autonomy to East Bengal.[3]

Regardless of the circumstances surrounding the events of the first and second weeks of March 1971, it is clear that a new guerrilla movement has now been launched in East Bengal under the leadership of EPAL leaders who were close to Sheikh Mujibur Rahman. The goal

[1] Manifesto of the East Pakistan Awami League (Dacca, 1970), pp. 1–13.

[2] *Christian Science Monitor*, April 7, 1971, and April 23, 1971.

[3] The position of the EPAL leadership regarding the events of March and April 1971 is detailed in S. N. Sen, *Bangladesh: The Truth* (Calcutta: Calcutta University Bangladesh Sahayak Samiti, 1971); see especially pp. 17 ff.

of this movement is the complete secession of East Bengal from Pakistan and the formation of a new nation to be known as Bangladesh (the country of Bengalis). At the time of writing (June 1971), guerrilla activities are still going on in East Bengal, but there is every indication that the West Pakistan government has restored at least temporary order to the chaotic situation that prevailed in March.[4]

While at first glance it would seem that the leftist parties would be able to capitalize on the renewal of revolutionary nationalism and regionalism among Bengalis, their tactical and strategic dilemmas remain unresolved. Since both Moscow and Peking are supporting the West Pakistan government against the Bengali secessionist movement, both pro-Moscow and pro-Peking leftists in East Bengal are now identified to varying degrees with Rawalpindi and the West Pakistan military. In order to rid themselves of this image, they would have to adopt a secessionist slogan, but this would mean a major break with the leading international Communist powers. On the other hand, so long as the Communists in East Bengal remain allied to Moscow or Peking and these major powers continue in turn to support West Pakistan, the ability of the Communists to take advantage of Bengali regional revolutionary fervor is seriously diminished. As one might expect, factional struggles among leftists in East Bengal continue to revolve around this dilemma, with no ideological solution yet in sight.[5]

Unlike West Bengal, where the CPM has emerged as a major regional political party relatively independent of Moscow and Peking, in East Bengal the regional aspirations of Bengalis have now been captured by a non-Marxist and noncommunist political party willing to engage in guerrilla warfare (the EPAL). Some reports emanating from Pakistan would indicate that the West Pakistan government is attempting to split the EPAL into two factions, with one faction willing to form a government under the tutelage of the Pakistan military and the other faction leading the guerrillas, but even if this should happen, the leadership of both factions would still be non-Marxist and non-communist. The result would still be—as I stated in the conclusion—

---

[4] For an account of the guerrilla strategy of the EPAL, see Hiranmay Karlekar, "War Without End: Military Prospects in Bangla Desh," *The Statesman* (Calcutta daily), April 24, 1971. On the counterinsurgency strategy of the West Pakistan government, see John Walker, "Will Military Glue Repair Pakistan?" *Christian Science Monitor*, March 30, 1971.

[5] For an account of factional struggles among leftist politicians in East Bengal immediately after the establishment of the Bangladesh movement, see Chandrasekhar Sarkar, "Mukti Fouj [Liberation Army] Prepares for Guerrilla War," *The Statesman*, April 13, 1971. See also ibid., April 17, 1971.

a relatively unstable governmental situation in East Bengal, coupled with a great deal of factionalism among the leftists and a growing millenarian urge among young political activists.

As one might expect, the secessionist movement in East Bengal has had repercussions on the political situation in West Bengal. But before assessing its impact, it is necessary to bring the reader up to date on the electoral alignments that resulted from the March 1971 elections to the West Bengal Legislative Assembly. The March 1971 elections were the result of a decision by Prime Minister Indira Gandhi to link the 1971 Indian national elections to the state elections in those Indian states where President's Rule had been in effect. For this reason, three state Legislative Assembly elections (in Orissa, Tamil Nadu, and West Bengal) were held concurrently with the national Lok Sabha elections in 1971.

In the West Bengal Legislative Assembly elections, the CPM was allied with four small Marxist Left parties and four independent candidates in an electoral coalition known as the United Left Front (ULF), which succeeded in capturing a total of 123 of 277 seats (see Table 11). Allied against the CPM was a four-party electoral coalition led by the CPI, known as the United Left Democratic Front (ULDF), as well as nine other parties that succeeded in capturing at least one seat each. While the ULDF could win only 25 seats in the state assembly, Indira Gandhi's New Congress garnered a total of 105 seats, and these two totals, when combined with the totals of other parties running independently of electoral coalitions, were enough to keep the CPM at least temporarily out of power. After the 1971 elections, a new state government was formed in West Bengal, with nine political parties tenuously allied with each other in the ministries, but this government fell within a month.[6]

Perhaps the most significant aspect of the 1971 elections in West Bengal was the establishment of the CPM as the leading political party in an electoral situation that was even more highly factionalized than it had been before. Because of their bitter experience with the CPM during the two United Front governments, in 1971 none of the major Marxist Left and democratic socialist parties of West Bengal was willing to ally

[6] Six of the nine parties in the 1971 state coalition government were represented in the ministries: the New Congress, Bangla Congress, Gurkha League, Muslim League, PSP, and SSP. Three of the nine parties supporting the ministry chose not to be represented in the ministries: the CPI, Forward Bloc, and the Old Congress. The combined number of seats for the nine parties in the coalition was 141, 1 more than a majority if all 280 members of the state Legislative Assembly had been elected and 2 more than a majority in a 277-member assembly.

TABLE 11

ELECTION RESULTS, WEST BENGAL LEGISLATIVE ASSEMBLY, MARCH 1971

Party	Number of Seats	% Votes
ULF		
CPM	111	32.4
RCPI	3	0.5
WPI	2	0.4
FBM	2	0.2
Biplabi Bangla Congress	1	0.1
Independents allied with CPM	4	0.8
ULDF		
CPI	13	8.7
FB	3	2.9
SUC	7	2.1
GL	2	0.3
Others		
New Congress (Indira Gandhi)	105	28.9
Old Congress (Nijalingappa)	2	5.8
Bangla Congress	5	5.4
PSP	3	0.6
SSP	1	0.5
RSP	3	2.2
Muslim League	7	2.3
Jharkhand party	2	0.7
Jan Sangh	1	0.3
Independent candidates and unsuccessful parties	0	4.9
Totals	277[a]	100.0

[a] Elections were not held in three constituencies because of the deaths of candidates during the period of polling.

Source: *The Statesman* (Calcutta daily), March 15–20, 1971.

with it in electoral coalitions, and yet the CPM was able to expand considerably. Abandoned by its former electoral allies, the CPM was forced to run candidates throughout the state, contesting in 236 of the 277 constituencies (85 percent), exactly two and a half times as many constituencies as the party contested in 1969 (97 of 280 constituencies, or 34 percent of the total). Despite this, the CPM not only expanded its percentage of the vote (from 19.6 percent in 1969 to 32.4 percent in 1971) and its percentage of the seats (from 29 percent to 40 percent), but it also established itself as the first or second party (in terms of votes received) in every district in the state except Midnapore and Purulia (see Table 12).

TABLE 12

LEADING ELECTORAL PARTIES IN WEST BENGAL BY DISTRICT, 1971
LEGISLATIVE ASSEMBLY ELECTIONS

District	New Congress	CPM	Largest Third-Party Vote	
Darjeeling	34.4%	30.0%	GL	22.7%
Jalpaiguri	32.2	23.2	RSP	10.8
Cooch-Behar	44.9	24.0	FB	20.5
West Dinajpur	41.2	21.7	RSP	11.0
Malda	29.6	24.4	Old Congress	12.3
Murshidabad	24.6	13.7	RSP	12.7
Nadia	26.4	37.9	Bangla Congress	6.6
24-Parganas	26.1	39.6	CPI	10.0
Calcutta	41.2	33.6	CPI	10.3
Howrah	27.2	46.0	FB	11.5
Hooghly	27.4	39.0	Old Congress	9.1
Midnapore	25.0	17.6	CPI	20.2
Purulia	41.6	13.1	LSS	15.2
Bankura	28.4	34.3	Bangla Congress	12.8
Burdwan	24.1	52.2	Old Congress	7.4
Birbhum	19.3	31.2	Bangla Congress	12.5

Source: *The Statesman* (Calcutta daily), March 10–15, 1971.

In contrast to the CPM, none of the other former UF partners made electoral gains in 1971. The three largest parties aligned with the CPM in the 1967 and 1969 UF governments all suffered serious setbacks, with the Bangla Congress losing 28 of the 33 seats it had won in 1969, the CPI losing 17 out of 30 seats, and the Forward Bloc 18 out of 21. Of the smaller Marxist Left and democratic socialist parties, only one (the SUC) managed to oppose the CPM and retain its previous electoral position, while the small parties that remained allied with the CPM either maintained or expanded their electoral positions.

The electoral gains of the CPM in 1971 are undoubtedly impressive, but they must be analyzed in the perspective of the factional situation that existed during the period of polling. Because of the inter- and intra-party feuding that had resulted from the two UF governments, none of the electoral alliances against the CPM was very effective, and the leading anti-CPM force in the state (the New Congress) refused to join electoral coalitions. The result was a series of four- or five-cornered contests in virtually every constituency in the state, with the CPM and New Congress opposed in almost every instance by two or three smaller Marxist Left or democratic socialist parties. In this atmosphere, the CPM could win 111 seats with an average vote per constituency of only 31 percent, while the New Congress could win 105 seats with an average constituency vote of 27.6 percent.[7] Had effective electoral alliances been made against the CPM, the party certainly would have suffered considerably in terms of seats won.

In short, while the CPM did maintain its position as one of the leading electoral forces in West Bengal, that position is by no means secure. The party was able to best its former UF partners in constituencies that had been marked by interparty feuding, but its showing in this respect was not conclusive. Moreover, while the CPM did depend to a greater extent than ever before on votes from rural areas, the vast majority of these rural gains were in constituencies adjacent to those the party had won in previous elections (Burdwan, Bankura, Howrah, Hooghly, Nadia, and 24-Parganas). The election results have therefore been subject to different interpretations, which have in turn kindled the ever-present factionalism within the CPM.

Since the formation of the 1971 state government (known as the Democratic Coalition), three major issues have occupied the attention of the political leadership of West Bengal: 1) the question of recognition of the Bangladesh government in East Bengal; 2) strategies for dealing with the massive influx of new refugees from East Bengal; and 3) policies proposed to restore an atmosphere of law and order in West Bengal. Since the resolution of each of these issues obviously requires the cooperation of the central government, and since issues related to the future status of Bangladesh involve questions of foreign policy, the new government in West Bengal found itself increasingly entangled in national and international political affairs. In the wake of these developments, the Communist and Marxist Left parties of West Bengal experienced new internal factionalism.

Recognition of Bangladesh
As was the case in the Nigerian civil war when Ibo leaders attempted to establish the new state of Biafra, the leaders of the Bangladesh movement consider international recognition to be of the utmost importance. As soon as the secessionist government was established in East Bengal in March 1971, appeals were sent to all the major powers and to several other countries for immediate recognition of Bangladesh. After each of these appeals was rejected—by the

---

[7] A detailed analysis of the 1971 elections to the West Bengal Legislative Assembly appears in John O. Field and Marcus F. Franda, *An Electoral Profile of the Communist Parties of West Bengal* (New Delhi: Manohar Book Publishers, forthcoming).

United States, by the Soviet Union, by the Chinese, and by every other country that was contacted—the Bangladesh leadership began to exert enormous pressure on India, on the grounds that recognition by India would set in motion a series of events that would lead to recognition by other countries.[8] Moreover, as guerrilla activities against the West Pakistan military began to spread, the Bangladesh leadership became increasingly aware of its dependence on India for arms, for refuge, and for food and other supplies in the event of a protracted conflict.

Faced with a situation that could potentially involve both civil and international war for India, the new Indian government acted quickly but calmly. The Indian Parliament passed a unanimous resolution expressing its sympathy and support for the people of East Bengal (but withholding recognition of Bangladesh), and the Indian Ministry of External Affairs made a number of overtures to the Secretary-General of the United Nations, calling for his personal intervention although refusing to take the matter up formally with the General Assembly. In addition, the Indira Gandhi government, and especially the Prime Minister herself, made every effort to range world opinion against the alleged barbarities of the West Pakistan government, at the same time making elaborate plans for the accommodation of as many as five million new refugees from East Bengal. At one point, shortly after the Bangladesh government was established, it was estimated that New Delhi was spending more than half a million rupees per day for the rehabilitation of new refugees.[9]

The actions of the Indira Gandhi government were immediately debated by radical politicians in both East and West Bengal and at least for the time being served to divide the opposition. Naxalite theoreticians generally argued that the ultimate goal of the Indira Gandhi government was the establishment of a bourgeois regime in East Pakistan led by Sheikh Mujibur Rahman and the EPAL, a prospect that the Naxalites viewed as "no alternative to Yahya Khan."[10] Both the CPM and CPI in West Bengal took more moderate public positions, simply arguing that Indira Gandhi was not as concerned with the situation as she might be, but both parties were too divided internally to provide a clear counterproposal. The Kerala unit of the CPI—less emotionally involved than the Bengalis—was able to stage a "Bangladesh Day" on May 15, 1971, the purpose of which was to persuade the Indian government to recognize Bangladesh

---

[8] See Kuldip Nayar, "New Delhi and Bangladesh," *The Statesman*, May 5, 1971.

[9] Kuldip Nayar, "The Unending Stream of Refugees from Bangladesh," ibid., May 12, 1971.

[10] Quoted in a letter to the author from a Naxalite theoretician, May 3, 1971.

at once and to provide "all material and moral support to the people who are struggling to free themselves from West Pakistan's subjugation."[11]

In the face of criticism and protest, Indira Gandhi herself maintained an aggressive posture, traveling to the border areas of West Bengal for a series of public meetings with refugees and freedom fighters. During these appearances, she argued that the question of refugees was of far more immediate importance than the question of recognition. In her words, "The main consideration [for Indian policy] should be the question of whether recognition by India will help the Bangladesh people. . . . I think it will not help them at this time . . . recognition should not be given at the wrong time."[12]

Surprisingly, the major opposition to Indira Gandhi's policy did not come from the radical and leftist parties of West Bengal but rather from the new state coalition government, led by the New Congress. In a Bengali New Year's Day message broadcast by All-India Radio from Calcutta, the Deputy Chief Minister of the new state government (Mr. Bijoy Singh Nahar, a leading member of the New Congress in West Bengal), called for stronger Indian measures in support of Bangladesh, and a few weeks later the Chief Minister of the new government (Ajoy Mukherjee) introduced a resolution in the state Legislative Assembly demanding the immediate recognition of the Bangladesh government by India.[13] By June 1971, therefore, both Indira Gandhi and the new state government had coopted the popular appeal of this issue from the Communist and Marxist Left parties, although the potential for massive opposition to the state and central governments was obviously enormous.

The influx of new refugees

Even more worrisome for the Indian government than the question of recognition is the continuing influx of new refugees from East Bengal. On this issue the Indira Gandhi government has taken the position that it will provide temporary assistance but that new refugees will have to return to East Bengal as soon as possible. Emphasizing that India is a poor country, the Prime Minister has warned the refugees that they should not expect to remain in India for long periods of time but should instead make plans for achieving "normality" in East Bengal.[14] At the same time,

---

[11] *The Statesman*, May 13, 1971.
[12] Ibid., May 18, 1971.
[13] An account of Nahar's address appears in ibid., April 18, 1971. Details of the West Bengal Assembly resolution are in ibid., May 8, 1971.
[14] *Christian Science Monitor*, April 29, 1971, and May 20, 1971.

the government has sought international assistance for the refugees and has expressed the hope that "international bodies might create conditions for the evacuees to return to their homeland."[15]

The current refugee problem in India is complicated by the fact that many of the refugees from East Bengal conceive of themselves as guerrilla fighters, with varying degrees of loyalty to India and West Bengal. Many of these people are in search of weapons and ammunition in India and are therefore willing to engage in a variety of activities that can only add to the already acute problem of civil disorder in West Bengal. Moreover, since the Pakistan army has an interest in stopping this flow of potential guerrillas back and forth between the two countries, Pakistani soldiers have frequently fired on people attempting to cross the border, with the result that a number of incidents between Pakistani and Indian soldiers have occurred. Both India and Pakistan have expressed the fear that such incidents might lead to war.[16]

The question of law and order

In an effort to cope with the problem of law and order in West Bengal, the central government has now promulgated a new ordinance permitting preventive detention, despite the traditional opposition to preventive detention on the part of many people in West Bengal. In the short time it was in power, the state government attempted to restructure and revive the intelligence wing of the state Home Ministry, which was seriously dislocated during the period of the two United Front governments, taking the position that "perhaps certain unconventional methods need to be adopted" to deal with the problem of law and order in the state.[17] As one might expect, these activities of the state and central governments have met with intense protest from the CPI, CPM, and Naxalites. As this book goes to press, the CPI is leading a movement in the Lok Sabha to defeat the preventive detention ordinance, the CPM is protesting the fourth declaration of President's Rule in the state, and the Naxalites are intensifying their efforts to kill police officers, party workers, and electoral candidates.

---

[15] *The Statesman*, May 18, 1971.

[16] On the disputes between India and Pakistan over the question of Bangladesh, see Denzil Peiris, "India Studies Armed Aid for East Pakistan," *Christian Science Monitor*, May 28, 1971; Qutubuddin Aziz, "Pakistanis Sift Foreign Reaction," ibid., April 19, 1971; and Denzil Peiris, "Pakistan and India Deescalate," ibid., May 3, 1971.

[17] *The Statesman*, May 15, 1971.

INDEX